The Princeton Review®

PSAT/ NMSQT®

PREP

with 2 Practice Tests,
2023–2024 Edition

The Staff of The Princeton Review

PrincetonReview.com

Penguin
Random
House

The Princeton Review
110 East 42nd Street, 7th Floor
New York, NY 10017

Published in the United States by Penguin Random House LLC, New York.

ISBN: 978-0-593-51658-4
eBook ISBN: 978-0-593-51659-1
ISSN: 2687-8755

PSAT/NMSQT is a registered trademark of the College Board and the National Merit Scholarship Corporation, which are not affiliated with, and do not endorse, this product.

The Princeton Review is not affiliated with Princeton University.

The material in this book is up-to-date at the time of publication. However, changes may have been instituted by the testing body in the test after this book was published. If there are any important late-breaking developments, changes, or corrections to the materials in this book, we will post that information online in the Student Tools. Register your book and check your Student Tools to see if there are any updates posted there.

Editor: Patricia Murphy
Production Editors: Emma Parker and Heidi Torres
Production Artist: Deborah Weber

Printed in the United States of America.

10 9 8 7 6 5 4

2023–2024 Edition

Editorial
Rob Franek, Editor-in-Chief
David Soto, Senior Director, Data Operations
Stephen Koch, Senior Manager, Data Operations
Deborah Weber, Director of Production
Jason Ullmeyer, Production Design Manager
Jennifer Chapman, Senior Production Artist
Selena Coppock, Director of Editorial
Orion McBean, Senior Editor
Aaron Riccio, Senior Editor
Meave Shelton, Senior Editor
Chris Chimera, Editor
Patricia Murphy, Editor
Laura Rose, Editor

Penguin Random House Publishing Team
Tom Russell, VP, Publisher
Alison Stoltzfus, Senior Director, Publishing
Brett Wright, Senior Editor
Emily Hoffman, Assistant Managing Editor
Ellen Reed, Production Manager
Suzanne Lee, Designer

Eugenia Lo, Publishing Assistant

For customer service, please contact **editorialsupport@review.com**, and be sure to include:

- full title of the book

- ISBN

- page number

Acknowledgments

Special thanks to Kenneth Brenner, Sara Kuperstein, Amy Minster, and Scott O'Neal for their contributions to this edition.

Thanks also to Anne Bader, Kevin Baldwin, Grace Cannon, Nicole Cosme, April Davis, Gina Donegan, Anne Goldberg-Baldwin, Brian Hong, Brad Kelly, Aaron Lindh, Jomil London, Dave MacKenzie, Jason Morgan, Amanda Nowotny, Danielle Perrini, Gabby Peterson, Xander Posner, Jess Thomas, Christina Torturo, and Jimmy Williams.

The Princeton Review would also like to thank Deborah Weber, Emma Parker, and Heidi Torres for their time and attention to each page.

Special thanks to Adam Robinson, who conceived of and perfected the Joe Bloggs approach to standardized tests, and many other techniques in this book.

Contents

Get More (Free) Content
at **PrincetonReview.com/prep**

As easy as 1·2·3

1 Go to PrincetonReview.com/prep or scan the **QR code** and enter the following ISBN for your book: **9780593516584**

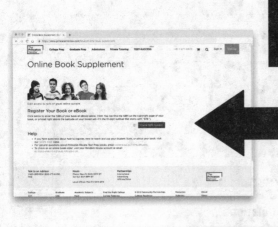

2 Answer a few simple questions to set up an exclusive Princeton Review account. *(If you already have one, you can just log in.)*

3 Enjoy access to your **FREE** content!

Once you've registered, you can...

- Access and print out one more full-length practice test as well as the corresponding answers and explanations

- Use our online tools to take your practice tests digitally or use our online proctor to time you while you take the test in the book, then enter your answers online.

- Enter your answers in our online bubble sheet to get an approximate scaled score with explanations

- Get valuable advice about the college application process

- If you're still choosing between colleges, use our searchable rankings of *The Best 389 Colleges* to find out more information about your dream school

- Access printable resources, including a study guide, a score conversion table, and more

- Check to see if there have been any corrections or updates to this edition

Need to report a potential **content** issue?

Contact **EditorialSupport@review.com** and include:

- full title of the book
- ISBN
- page number

Need to report a **technical** issue?

Contact **TPRStudentTech@review.com** and provide:

- your full name
- email address used to register the book
- full book title and ISBN
- Operating system (Mac/PC) and browser (Chrome, Firefox, Safari, etc.)

Look For These Icons Throughout The Book

 ONLINE PRACTICE TESTS

 ONLINE ARTICLES

 PROVEN TECHNIQUES

 APPLIED STRATEGIES

 STUDY BREAK

 MORE GREAT BOOKS

Part I
Orientation

Chapter 1
What Is the Digital PSAT/NMSQT?

The Digital PSAT/NMSQT—from now on, we'll just call it the PSAT—is a standardized test given primarily to high school juniors to give them a "preliminary" idea of how well they could do on SAT question types. The test is also used to determine which students are eligible for National Merit Scholar recognition. This chapter will give you a general overview of the test and how it is used, along with the basics to start your preparation. We'll also give you a glimpse at the other tests in College Board's Suite of Assessments: the PSAT 8/9 and the PSAT 10.

THE DIGITAL PSAT/NMSQT

College Board's "Suite of Assessments" ranges from the PSAT 8/9 to the SAT. If you are reading this book, you are likely most interested in the PSAT at this time, so we'll start there. Just like the other tests in the Suite, the PSAT contains a Reading and Writing section and a Math section, each divided into two modules. The content of all the tests in the Suite is similar, and the number of questions and time per module are identical.

This is what College Board says about the Reading and Writing section:

"The section focuses on key elements of comprehension, rhetoric, and language use that the best available evidence identifies as necessary for college readiness and success. In this section, students answer multiple-choice questions requiring them to read, comprehend, and use information and ideas in texts; analyze the craft and structure of texts; revise texts to improve the rhetorical expression of ideas; and edit texts to conform to core conventions of Standard English."

Here is the Princeton Review's take: Be prepared to justify your selected answer with evidence from the text and/or graph provided. This test is not about making up anything; it's about finding the correct answer based on the text.

College Board has this to say about the Math section:

"The digital SAT Suite Math section focuses on key elements of algebra, advanced math, problem solving and data analysis, and geometry and trigonometry (except for the PSAT 8/9 which does not test trigonometry) that evidence identifies as necessary for college and career readiness and success. Over the course of the Math section, students answer multiple choice and student-produced response (SPR) questions that measure their fluency with, understanding of, and ability to apply the math concepts, skills, and practices that are most essential for readiness for entry-level postsecondary work."

Here is the Princeton Review's take: Expect to see Algebra I and II, some Geometry, and questions that have charts, graphs, data tables, scatterplots, or other forms of data.

The Digital Suite of Assessments has a built-in Desmos calculator that can be used on all Math questions. In addition, students may bring their own approved calculators if they prefer. Even though this tool is always at hand, it is up to the test-taker to determine whether the calculator will help solve a question. According to the College Board, "students who make use of structure or their ability to reason will probably finish before students who use a calculator."

The bottom line: Write down your work and use the calculator for tedious calculations, but a calculator most likely will not be necessary to solve most of the questions.

All questions in the Reading and Writing section are multiple-choice. Most of the Math questions are multiple-choice, but about 25% of the questions are "student-produced responses," for which students enter their own answers. Each correct answer earns points, and there is no penalty for an incorrect response or a question left blank.

The bottom line: Don't leave anything blank!

> **Psst...**
> College Board makes the PSAT 8/9, the PSAT 10, and PSAT/NMSQT. But when we refer to just the plain old "PSAT" in this book, we're referring to the PSAT/NMSQT.

When Is the PSAT Given?

Prior to the switch to Digital, the PSAT was officially administered twice each year, typically on a Wednesday and Saturday of the same week in October. Now, the Digital PSAT will be administered in a testing window of several days. Your school will announce the exact dates at the beginning of the school year, and you can find out more about the testing windows at PrincetonReview.com or through College Board at CollegeBoard.org.

> **Keep on Schedule**
> You'll officially take the PSAT in the fall of your junior year. Plan to take the SAT anytime between the winter of your junior year and the fall of your senior year.

How Do I Sign Up for the PSAT?

You don't have to do anything to sign up for the PSAT; your school will do all the work for you. Test registration fees can vary from school to school, so be sure to check with your school counselor if you have questions about how much the PSAT will cost you.

What About Students with Special Needs?

If you have a diagnosed physical or learning disability, you will probably qualify for accommodations on the PSAT. However, it's important that you get the process started early. The first step is to speak to your school counselor who handles learning disabilities. Only your counselor can file the appropriate paperwork. You'll also need to gather some information (documentation of your condition) from a licensed practitioner and some other information from your school. Then your school counselor will file the application for you. You will need to apply for accommodations only once; with that single application you'll qualify for accommodations on the PSAT, SAT, and AP Exams. The one exception to this rule is that if you change school districts, you'll need to have a counselor at the new school refile your paperwork.

Does the PSAT Play a Role in College Admissions?

No! The PSAT plays no role in college admissions. It's really just a practice test for the SAT. The one exception is for that very small group of students, about 4 percent of all students nationwide, whose PSAT scores qualify them for National Merit recognition. (We'll tell you more than you ever wanted to know about that in the next chapter.) Recognition as a commended scholar, semifinalist, or finalist for National Merit is a fairly impressive addition to your college admissions portfolio and is something that you should certainly pursue if you are seriously in contention for it.

What Happens to the Score Report from the PSAT?

Only you, your high school, and the National Merit Scholarship Corporation (which co-sponsors the PSAT) will receive a copy of your score report. It won't be sent to colleges.

Do I need to prepare for the PSAT?

You might be thinking, *If colleges don't see my PSAT score, why do I need to bother doing well on this test? Do I even need to prep for it?* That's a very good question because the truth is that you don't necessarily need to prepare for or do well on the PSAT. If you don't think that with a little bit of preparation you could score in the top 4% of PSAT test-takers in your state, then there's virtually no benefit to scoring better-than-okay on the PSAT. That being said, if you plan to take the SAT, your PSAT preparation will transfer, so there's no harm in preparing for a slightly easier version of a test you will be taking soon enough. However, if you plan to take the ACT instead of the SAT, aren't aiming to qualify for National Merit, and don't have any other reason to do well on the PSAT, you have our permission to put this book down in favor of a more worthwhile activity.

WHAT DOES THE PSAT TEST?

As you begin your prep, it's useful to remember that the PSAT is not a test of how capable you are academically, how good of a person you are, or how successful you will be in life. The PSAT simply tests how well you take the PSAT. That's it. And performing well on the PSAT is a skill that can be learned like any other. The Princeton Review was founded over 40 years ago on this very simple idea, and—as our students' test scores show—our approach is the one that works. It can feel extremely daunting to hear that changes to tests could heavily influence your college admission outlook. However, remember that any standardized test is a coachable test. A beatable test.

> **The PSAT doesn't measure the stuff that matters.** It measures neither intelligence nor the depth and breadth of what you're learning in high school. It doesn't predict college grades as well as your high school grades do. Colleges know there is more to you as a student—and as a person—than how you do on a single test.

Who Writes the PSAT?

The PSAT is written and administered by the College Board and used for scholarships by National Merit Scholarship Corporation. You might think that the people at College Board are educators, professors of education, or teachers. They're not. They are people who just happen to make a living writing tests. In fact, they write hundreds of tests, for all kinds of organizations.

The folks at College Board aren't really paid to educate; they're paid to write and administer tests. And even though you'll be paying them to take the PSAT, you're not their customer. The actual customers College Board caters to are the colleges, which get the information they want at no cost. This means that you should take everything that College Board says with a grain of salt and realize that its testing "advice" isn't always the best advice. (Getting testing advice from College Board is a bit like getting baseball advice from the opposing team.)

Every test reflects the interests of the people who write it. If you know who writes the test, you will know a lot more about what kinds of answers will be considered "correct" answers on that test.

HOW IS THE PSAT STRUCTURED AND SCORED?

Category	PSAT/NMSQT
Time Overall	134 minutes plus break
Components	• Reading and Writing section • Math section
Number of Questions	• Reading and Writing: 54, including 4 experimental questions • Math: 44, including 4 experimental questions
Answer Choices	• Reading and Writing: all multiple-choice with 4 answers per question • Math: 75% multiple-choice with 4 answers per question, 25% student-produced responses
Time by Section	• Reading and Writing: 64 minutes in two 32-minute modules • Math: 70 minutes in two 35-minute modules
Relationship Between Modules	• Module 1 has a broad mix of levels of difficulty. • Performance on Module 1 determines the difficulty of Module 2. • Students who do well on Module 1 will get a Module 2 that is harder, on average. • Students who do less well on Module 1 will get a Module 2 that is easier, on average.
Scoring	• The score is based on the number of questions correct and the difficulty of the questions seen. • Students who do well on Module 1 are put into a higher bracket of possible scores. • Students who do less well on Module 1 are put into a lower bracket of possible scores. • Section scores range from 160 to 760. • Total score is the sum of the section scores and ranges from 320 to 1520.

With the move to a digital PSAT starting in fall of 2023, College Board took the opportunity to alter not just the delivery format but the content of the test from its previous version. All Reading and Writing questions are now attached to short texts, with one question per text. There will be a wide range of text complexities presented, and the passages will cover a variety of topics from history, science, and literature (even some poetry).

The Math content is fairly similar to the form it took on paper tests in 2022 and earlier. There is a strong focus on algebra, problem-solving, and analytical topics, and it includes some high-level content such as trigonometry. Some questions require student-produced responses, and these will be scattered throughout the Math modules. As previously stated, calculator use will be allowed on all math questions.

As you can see from the table above, both sections (Reading-Writing and Math) are divided into two modules. On the Digital PSAT, your performance on the first module in each section will determine the makeup of your second module. Do well on the first module, and you will see a harder (on average) mix of questions on the second module. Miss more questions in the first module, and you will get an easier (on average) difficulty for the second module. You always want to do as well as possible, of course, but it's worth keeping in mind that you will need to get the hard second module on each section in order to earn a top score.

To help you do your best, we recommend that you review the explanations for the questions in the drills and the practice tests, even if you answer a question correctly. You may discover techniques that help to shave seconds from your solutions. A large part of what's being tested is your ability to use the appropriate tools in a strategic fashion, and while there may be multiple ways to solve a given problem, you'll want to focus on the most efficient path to a solution.

Scoring on the PSAT

The PSAT is scored on a scale of 320–1520, which is the sum of the two section scores that range from 160–760. The two sections are the Reading and Writing section and the Math section. Wrong answers are not penalized, so you're advised never to leave a question blank—even if that means blindly picking a letter and clicking it for any uncompleted questions before time runs out.

So, how do the two modules work together to determine your score in a section? Well, if your raw score is high enough on the first module, you will automatically be bumped into a possible score range that is overall higher than you would be in if you had a lower raw score on the first module, though the two ranges may overlap some. Some questions within a module are also weighted, so doing better on those will increase your score more than doing well on easier, non-weighted questions. As such, your score is determined not only by how many questions you got right but also by how hard the questions were that you did. Although the scoring curve on each Digital PSAT may calculate your score slightly differently, you will always have two jobs: understanding which questions can maximize your score and building your stamina to stay sharp through both modules in each section. Throughout this book, we will show you how to do just that.

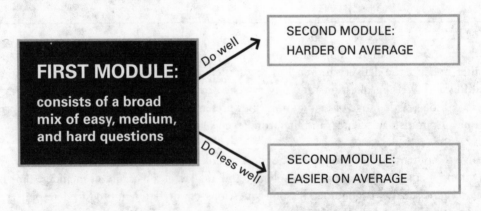

On the recent paper-and-pencil versions of the SAT Suite of Assessments, various subscores and cross-test scores were reported in addition to the section and overall scores. On the Digital Suite, only your section scores and total score will be reported.

What Does the PSAT Score Mean for My SAT Score?

The SAT is scored on a 1600 scale, whereas the PSAT is scored on a 1520 scale. However, because the PSAT and SAT are aligned by College Board to be scored on the same scale, your PSAT score indicates the approximate SAT score you would earn were you to have taken the SAT on that same day. Since the PSAT is slightly easier, you can't score quite as high on it as you can on the SAT.

PSAT 10

Now that we've covered some basics about the PSAT, let's discuss how it works with the other tests in the SAT Suite of assessments. Though there is a test called the PSAT 10, it is identical to the structure of the PSAT/NMSQT in terms of both number of questions and time limits per section. Just as with the SAT and the PSAT, the PSAT 10 includes a Reading and Writing section and a Math section. The major differences between the PSAT and the PSAT 10 are who takes the PSAT 10 and when: 10th-graders, sometime in the spring. Additionally, the PSAT 10 test does not qualify you for National Merit Scholarship consideration.

PSAT 8/9

The PSAT 8/9 is designed for eighth and ninth graders, as the name would imply. The Digital version of the test will also match the other tests in the Suite in terms of structure, timing, and number of questions. The content of each section is comparable to the content of the SAT and PSAT, but it is a little easier and is therefore scored on a somewhat lower scale.

WHAT'S WITH ALL THESE TESTS?!

So, if the PSAT 8/9, the PSAT 10, and the PSAT/NMSQT all have the same sections, number of modules, number of questions, and time to take them, what exactly ARE the differences between the tests? There are two main ones: the content covered on each test and the possible score ranges. See the chart below for a comparison of all the tests in the Digital SAT Suite of Assessments.

Test	PSAT 8/9	PSAT 10 and PSAT/NMSQT	SAT
Reading and Writing Content	Information and Ideas (≈26%) Craft and Structure (≈28%) Expression of Ideas (≈20%) Standard English Conventions (≈26%)	Information and Ideas (≈26%) Craft and Structure (≈28%) Expression of Ideas (≈20%) Standard English Conventions (≈26%)	Information and Ideas (≈26%) Craft and Structure (≈28%) Expression of Ideas (≈20%) Standard English Conventions (≈26%)
Text Complexity	Grades 6 through 11	Grades 6 through 14	Grades 6 through 14
Math Content	Algebra (≈42.5%) Advanced Math (≈20%) Problem-Solving and Data Analysis (≈25%) Geometry (≈12.5%)	Algebra (≈35%) Advanced Math (≈32.5%) Problem-Solving and Data Analysis (≈20%) Geometry and Trigonometry (≈12.5%)	Algebra (≈35%) Advanced Math (≈35%) Problem-Solving and Data Analysis (≈15%) Geometry and Trigonometry (≈15%)
Math Topics Excluded	Rational and Radical Equations, Trigonometry, Circles, Evaluating Statistical Claims and Making Inferences	Circles, Making Inferences from Statistical Samples	
Section Score Range	120 to 720	160 to 760	200 to 800
Total Score Range	240 to 1440	320 to 1520	400 to 1600

According to College Board, the SAT Suite of Assessments is designed to reflect how prepared you are for college and the working world. By creating a series of tests given over several years, College Board claims to measure a student's progress toward readiness for higher education and beyond. The tests in the Suite all use the same vertical scale, meaning that the score you get on a PSAT 8/9 should be the same score you'd get on the PSAT or SAT if you took those tests on the same day.

College Board maintains that the best way to prepare for the test is to do the following:

- Take challenging courses
- Do your homework
- Prepare for tests and quizzes
- Ask and answer lots of questions

We at the Princeton Review are dubious about these claims, especially in regard to college and career readiness. Moreover, we think the best way to prepare for an exam is to know the content and structure of that exam. By reading this book, you are already on your way to improving your test scores.

WHAT IS THE PRINCETON REVIEW?

The Princeton Review is the nation's leading test-preparation company. In just a few years from our founding in 1981, we became the nation's leader in SAT preparation, primarily because our techniques work. We offer courses and private tutoring for all of the major standardized tests, and we publish a series of books to help in your search for the right school. If you'd like more information about our programs or books, give us a call at 800-2-REVIEW, or check out our website at PrincetonReview.com.

> **Shortcuts**
> The Princeton Review's techniques are the closest thing there is to a shortcut to the PSAT. However, there is no shortcut to learning these techniques.

HOW TO USE THIS BOOK

This book is divided into five parts. The first three parts of the book contain Practice Test 1, general testing strategies, and question-specific problem-solving instruction. Use the first practice test as a diagnostic tool to see which sections of the test you need to work on when you read through the content chapters. The last part of the book contains drill answers and explanations. After working through the content chapters and checking your answers and the explanations to the chapter drills, take Practice Test 2 online and apply everything you've learned to improve your score. The "Session-by-Session Study Guide" starting on **page 13** will give you a plan of attack for these tests and the rest of the book. There is no single plan that will fit everyone, so be prepared to adapt the plan and use it according to your own needs.

Practice Test 1 will give you an idea of your strengths and weaknesses, both of which can be sources of improvement. If you're already good at something, additional practice can make you great at it; if you're not so good at something, what you should do about it depends on how important it is. If the concept is one that frequently appears on the test, you should spend a lot of time on it; if it comes up only once in a while, you should spend very little time working on it and remember that it's something you should either put off until you've completed easier things or skip it entirely.

Use our online tools to take your practice tests digitally or use our online proctor to time you while you take the test in the book, then enter your answers online. Either way, you'll see your results and a breakdown of the question categories. See page 30 for more info.

How do you know what's important? We'll tell you throughout this book, when we discuss techniques like Plugging In and so forth, but you can also get an idea of what to focus on simply by observing how this book is laid out. The Reading and Writing Introduction tells you how to jump to the questions you want to work on first. In the Math chapters, the most important concepts appear first. For example, if you're shaky on Reading, you know you'll need to devote some time to Reading questions because there is a total of 25–29 such questions on the test. And if you're not so confident when it comes to geometry, don't panic. Geometry questions appear only in the last math chapter, which tells you that this topic isn't as much of a priority as Plugging In or Math Basics.

One important note: In this book, the sample questions are in numerical order within a chapter. The question number does not indicate where you can expect to see a similar question on the test. As we'll show you later, what really matters is your *Personal* Order of Difficulty.

How Much Should I Prepare for the PSAT?

If you're in that very small percentage of students who are in contention for National Merit recognition, it may be worth your while to put in a good deal of time to prepare for this test. After all, your extra hard work may well put you in a better position for National Merit recognition. Otherwise, you should prepare enough so that you feel more in control of the test and have a better testing experience.

> **Study**
> If you were getting ready to take a biology test, you'd study biology. If you were preparing for a basketball game, you'd practice basketball. So, if you're preparing for the PSAT (and eventually the SAT), study the PSAT. The PSAT can't test *everything*, so concentrate on learning what it *does* test.

(Nothing feels quite as awful as being dragged through a testing experience feeling like you don't know what you're being tested on or what to expect—except perhaps dental surgery.) The other reason to prepare for the PSAT is that it will give you some testing skills that will help you begin to prepare for the test that actually counts: the SAT.

The bottom line is this: The best reason to prepare for the PSAT is that it will help you get an early start on your preparation for the SAT.

How Can I Be Prepared if the Test is So New?

If you've done any research on the Digital PSAT, you may have found that there isn't all that much information available. In fact, if you're preparing for the 2023 Digital PSAT, you'll be among the first students to take this new version of the test. This might seem nerve-wracking, especially if you took the PSAT 10 or started your SAT prep early and are now facing a somewhat different test.

The good news is that everyone else taking the Digital PSAT is in the same position as you. The National Merit cutoffs are based on percentiles, which means that you only need to do better than the other students who take the test, not hit an arbitrary score. Rest assured that by completing the practice in this book and applying our strategies, you will be much better prepared than the vast majority of students, even if some aspects of the test are a little mysterious.

Time Management

To manage your PSAT preparation, make use of the study guide on the following pages. This guide will break down the seemingly daunting task of PSAT prep into bite-sized pieces we call "sessions." We have mapped out tasks for each session to be sure you get the most out of this book. The tests will be the first and last sessions, so you should be sure to plan to have about two-and-a-half hours for these sessions. Most other sessions will last between an hour and two hours, so plan to take a short break in the middle, and if it looks like the session is going to exceed two hours, feel free to stop and pick up where you left off on the next day.

When You Take a Practice Test

You'll see when to take practice tests in the session outlines. Here are some guidelines for taking these tests:

- If possible, take your practice tests online. Although one test is printed in this book, taking it online instead of on paper will allow you to become more comfortable with the online environment.
- When taking an online test, make sure to practice using the online tools. Use the annotation tool to mark important text in the passages and questions. Use the Answer Eliminator to get rid of the wrong answers. Mark questions you want to return to.
- Take a practice test in one sitting, under conditions similar to those of a proctored test. Sit in a quiet place and remove distractions like phones from the area. You need to build up your endurance for the real test, and you also need an accurate picture of how you will do. However, do take a 10-minute break between the Reading and Writing section and the Math section. On the real test you will have a break, so it's important not to skip it on the practice tests.
- If you take your tests online, you will be able to use the on-screen timer to keep track of the time remaining in each module. If you take the first test in the book instead of online, you can time yourself or use the online proctor in your student portal. Just make sure you do not allow yourself to go over time for any module.
- Whether you take a test online or on paper, write down the things you need in order to answer the question. For the Digital PSAT, you will get three sheets of scratch paper. Make sure to write down calculations or make notes you need. Do not write on the questions or answers themselves on the paper test, as you will not be able to do so on the Digital PSAT.

For more information about how to take and score your practice tests, see page 30.

Session-by-Session Study Guide

Session Zero You're involved in this session right now. Finish reading the first chapter so you'll know what the test is about, how it is used, and what to expect from the rest of the book. This step probably won't take you long, so if you have about two-and-a-half hours after you complete Chapter 1, you can go on to Session One and take the first practice test.

Session One Take Practice Test 1 and score it. You'll use this result to get an idea of your strengths and weaknesses, and the parts of each section you should concentrate on. Note that our explanations refer to concepts discussed elsewhere in this book, so you may want to wait until after Session Four before reviewing this test.

Session Two Work through Chapters 2 and 3 of the Orientation and Chapter 6, Reading and Writing Introduction.

Session Three Read Chapter 7, Reading Comprehension.

Session Four Work through the Math Basics in Chapter 11 and the corresponding drills. Then do Chapter 8, Rules Questions: Punctuation.

Session Five Work through the Math Techniques section in Chapter 12 and associated drills. Take a look at Chapter 9, Rules: Grammar.

Session Six Review Advanced Math, Chapter 13. As you work through this chapter, be sure to apply techniques like Plugging In that you learned in Chapter 12. Since these techniques are central to doing well on the Math section, you can never practice them too much. If there's time, start Chapter 14.

Session Seven Work through Geometry and Trigonometry in Chapter 14. When you finish, read through Chapter 10, Rhetoric. This will complete your work in the content chapters.

Session Eight Take Practice Test 2, available online in your student portal. Use the techniques you've been practicing throughout the book. Score your test and go through the explanations, focusing on where you may have missed the opportunity to use a technique and your decisions about whether you should have attempted a question or not, given your pacing goals and Personal Order of Difficulty.

Some of the terminology in the study guide may be unfamiliar to you now, but don't worry, you'll get to know it soon. Also, you'll want to refer back to this study guide at each session to keep yourself on track.

So, what are you waiting for? Go ahead and dive into the Digital PSAT!

Chapter 2
All About the National Merit Scholarships

The NMSQT part of the name PSAT/NMSQT stands for National Merit Scholarship Qualifying Test. That means the PSAT serves as the test that will establish whether you are eligible for National Merit recognition. This chapter will help you figure out what that may mean for you and even other scholarships you may qualify for.

WHAT IS THE NATIONAL MERIT SCHOLARSHIP PROGRAM?

You might think that the PSAT is simply a warm-up for the SAT, but the National Merit Scholarship Program makes the PSAT an important test in its own right.

The mission of National Merit Scholarship Corporation (NMSC) is to recognize and honor the academically talented students of the United States. NMSC accomplishes this mission by conducting nationwide academic scholarship programs. The enduring goals of NMSC's scholarship programs are the following:

- to promote a wider and deeper respect for learning in general and for exceptionally talented individuals in particular
- to shine a spotlight on brilliant students and encourage the pursuit of academic excellence at all levels of education
- to stimulate increased support from organizations that wish to sponsor scholarships for outstanding scholastic talent

The National Merit Scholarship Program is an academic competition for recognition and scholarships that began in 1955. High school students enter the National Merit Program by taking the Preliminary SAT/National Merit Scholarship Qualifying Test (PSAT/NMSQT) and by meeting published program entry and participation requirements.

HOW DO I QUALIFY FOR NATIONAL MERIT?

To participate in the National Merit Scholarship Program, a student must:

1. take the PSAT/NMSQT in the specified year of the high school program and **no later than** the third year in grades 9 through 12, regardless of grade classification or educational pattern;
2. be enrolled as a high school student (traditional or homeschooled), progressing normally toward graduation or completion of high school, and planning to enroll full time in college no later than the fall following completion of high school; and
3. be a citizen of the United States or be a U.S. lawful permanent resident (or have applied for permanent residence, the application for which has not been denied) and intend to become a U.S. citizen at the earliest opportunity allowed by law.

The Index

How does your PSAT score qualify you for National Merit? The National Merit Scholarship Corporation uses a selection index. Prior to the release of the Digital PSAT in fall of 2023, the selection index was two times the sum of your Reading, Writing and Language, and Math Test scores. With the Digital PSAT, students will no longer get these test scores out of 38. At the time of this writing, the National Merit Scholarship Corporation had not released plans for the new method of calculating the selection index, but it will likely be based on percentiles. Qualifying scores are likely to continue to vary from state to state, so check with your school counselor as to what the cutoff score is for your school year in your state.

The Awards and the Process

In the fall of their senior year, about 50,000 students will receive one of two letters from NMSC (National Merit Scholarship Corporation): either a Letter of Commendation or a letter stating that they have qualified as semifinalists for National Merit.

Commended Students   Roughly two-thirds of these students (about 34,000 total students each year) will receive a Letter of Commendation by virtue of their high scores on the test. This looks great on your college application, so if you have a reasonable chance of getting one, it's definitely worth your time to prepare for the PSAT. Make no mistake, though, these letters are not easy to get. They are awarded to students who score between the 95th and the mid-99th percentiles—that means to the top four to five percent in the country.

If you receive this honorable mention from NMSC, you should be extremely proud of yourself. Even though you won't continue in the process for National Merit scholarships, this commendation does make you eligible for special scholarships sponsored by certain companies and organizations, which vary in their amounts and eligibility requirements.

Semifinalists   The other third of these students—those 16,000 students who score in the upper 99th percentile in their states—will be notified that they are National Merit semifinalists. If you qualify, you'll get a letter announcing your status as a semifinalist, along with information about the requirements for qualification as a finalist. These include maintaining high grades, performing well on your SAT, and getting an endorsement from your principal.

Becoming a National Merit semifinalist is quite impressive, and if you manage it, you should certainly mention it on your college applications.

What does "scoring in the upper 99th percentile in the state" mean? It means that you're essentially competing against the other people in your state for those semifinalist positions. Since some states have higher average scores than others, this means that if you're in states like New York, New Jersey, Maryland, Connecticut, or Massachusetts, you need a higher score to qualify than if you live in other states.

Finalists   The majority of semifinalists (more than 90 percent) go on to qualify as finalists. Students who meet all of the eligibility requirements will be notified in February of their senior year that they have qualified as finalists. This means that they are now eligible for scholarship money, though it doesn't necessarily mean that they'll get any. In fact, only about half of National Merit finalists actually win scholarships through NMSC. What determines whether a student gets money or not? There is a final screening process, based on criteria that NMSC doesn't release to the public, to determine who actually gets these scholarships. 2,500 finalists earn $2,500 one-time scholarships from NMSC, and approximately 1,000 more win corporate-sponsored merit scholarships, which are typically given to children of the sponsors' employees, residents of certain communities, and students who plan to study or work in specific fields. The monetary amount of corporate-sponsored scholarships can be anywhere from $500–$10,000, and some are one-time scholarships, while others are given for each year of study. Some students who meet the corporation's qualifications but aren't finalists will also earn Special Scholarships. Approximately an additional 4,000 students will be offered college-sponsored scholarships from the schools they plan to attend. These awards range from $500 to $2,000 and are renewable for four years.

If you're willing to forgo the name-brand recognition of an Ivy, a state school can be an excellent choice—and if it offers you a National Merit scholar- ship, the trade-off can be more than worth it. Check out *The Best 389 Colleges,* 2024 Edition, for well researched profiles of public and private schools.

Though the amounts of money may not be huge, every little bit helps. One other point to keep in mind is that while most of the scholarships through NMSC are relatively small, many universities seek out National Merit finalists because of their academic abilities and (who are we kidding?) because the universities like to brag about how many such students chose them. For this reason, a number of state schools and less elite universities offer significant scholarships to National Merit finalists and sometimes semifinalists as well. Some schools offer full tuition for National Merit finalists, including the University of Alabama, Fordham University, University of Tulsa, University of Mississippi, Washington State University, Texas Tech University, and quite a few others. Many more schools award incomplete but large scholarships to National Merit finalists and semifinalists.

Aside from the possibility of winning a scholarship, the award itself looks great in your portfolio. So, if you think you are in contention for National Merit recognition, practice diligently and smartly! If not, don't sweat it too much, but prepare for the PSAT anyway because it is good practice for the SAT.

But I'm Not a Junior in High School Yet…

If you are not yet a junior, and you're interested in National Merit, you will have to take the test again your junior year in order to qualify.

A certain number of schools give the PSAT to students in their sophomore year—and some- times even earlier. These schools hope that earlier exposure to these tests will help their stu- dents perform better in later years. If you're not yet in your junior year, the PSAT won't count for National Merit scholarship purposes, so it's really just a trial run for you. It's still a good idea to go into the test prepared in order to feel and perform your best. After all, there's noth- ing more unpleasant than a distressing testing experience, except maybe having a tooth drilled or watching the sad downward spiral of certain pop stars.

What if I'm in a Nonstandard Course of Study?

If you're going to spend only three years in secondary school, you have two options for when to take the PSAT for National Merit purposes: you can take it either in your next-to-last year or in your last year of secondary school. However, our advice is this: if you're in any program other than a usual four-year high school, be sure to talk to your school counselor, who will consult with NMSC and help ensure that you take the PSAT at the right time. This is important, because not taking the PSAT at the right time can disqualify you from National Merit recognition.

What If I Miss the PSAT Administration My Junior Year?

If you aren't concerned about National Merit scholarships, there's no reason to do anything in particular—except, perhaps, to obtain a few PSAT booklets to practice with, just to see what fun you missed.

However, if you want to be eligible for National Merit recognition, then swift action on your part is required. If an emergency arises that prevents you from taking the PSAT, you should write to the National Merit Scholarship Corporation *immediately* to request alternate testing dates. If your request is received soon enough, NMSC should be able to accommodate you. (NMSC says that this kind of request must absolutely be received by April 1 following the missed PSAT administration.) You'll also need a signature from a school official.

For More Information

If you have any questions or problems, the best person to consult is your school counselor, who can help make sure you're on the right track. If you need further help, contact your local Princeton Review office at 800-2-REVIEW or PrincetonReview.com, or you can contact National Merit directly:

National Merit Scholarship Corporation
1560 Sherman Avenue, Suite 200
Evanston, IL 60201-4897
(847) 866-5100
NationalMerit.org

WHAT OTHER SCHOLARSHIPS CAN I APPLY TO?

In addition to the National Merit Scholarships, you can also apply to College Board's new Opportunity Scholarships and their partner scholarships. If you opt in to the free Student Search Service® when you take the PSAT/NMSQT, the College Board will further connect you to scholarship partners who offer over $300 million annually in scholarships to qualifying students!

College Board BigFuture® Scholarships

Beginning with the 2020 class, the College Board began offering a scholarship program with $5 million in scholarships each year to qualifying high school juniors in the United States, Puerto Rico, and other U.S. territories. The program consists of six different tasks designed to help students divide the process of applying to college from start to finish. Completing each step gives students the opportunity to enter to win one of the $40,000 scholarships or one of hundreds of $500 scholarships awarded each month. The more tasks a student completes, the more chances that student has to win. The six tasks are as follows:

1. **Build Your College List**
2. **Practice for the SAT**
3. **Explore Scholarships**
4. **Strengthen Your College List**
5. **Complete the FAFSA**
6. **Apply to Colleges**

For information regarding the official rules on how to qualify for these drawings, visit College Board's BigFuture® website: bigfuture.collegeboard.org.

Other Partner Scholarships

Hispanic Scholarship Fund
When to apply: accepting applications from January 1st to March 15th of your junior year
www.hsf.net/scholarship

United Negro College Fund (UNCF)
When to apply: Anytime
www.uncf.org/

American Indian Graduate Center
When to apply: Anytime
www.nativehire.org/american-indian-graduate-center/

Asian Pacific Islander American Scholars
When to apply: September to January of your junior year
www.apiascholars.org/

Children of Fallen Patriots
When to apply: Anytime
www.fallenpatriots.org/

Chapter 3
General Strategies

The first step to cracking the PSAT is to know how best to approach the test. The PSAT is not like the tests you've taken in school, so you need to learn to look at it in a different way. This chapter will show test-taking strategies that immediately improve your score. Make sure you fully understand these concepts before moving on to the following chapters. Good luck!

BASIC PRINCIPLES OF CRACKING THE TEST

What the College Board Is Good At

The folks at the College Board have been writing standardized tests for nearly a century, and they write tests for all sorts of programs. They have administered the test so many times that they know exactly how you will approach it. They know how you'll attack certain questions, what sort of mistakes you'll probably make, and even what answer you'll be most likely to pick. Freaky, isn't it?

However, the College Board's strength is also a weakness. Because the test is standardized, the PSAT has to ask the same type of questions over and over again. Sure, the numbers or the words might change, but the basics don't. With enough practice, you can learn to think like the test-writers. But try to use your powers for good, okay?

The PSAT Isn't School

Our job isn't to teach you math or English—leave that to your supersmart schoolteachers. Instead, we're going to teach you what the PSAT is and how to crack the PSAT. You'll soon see that the PSAT involves a very different skill set from the one you use in school.

> **No Penalty for Incorrect Answers!**
> You will NOT be penalized on the PSAT for any wrong answers. This means you should always guess, even if this means choosing an answer at random.

Be warned that some of the approaches we're going to show you may seem counterintuitive or unnatural. Some of these strategies may be very different from the way you learned to approach similar questions in school but trust us! Try tackling the questions using our techniques and keep practicing until they become easier. You'll see a real improvement in your score.

Let's take a look at the questions.

Cracking Multiple-Choice Questions

What's the capital of Azerbaijan?

Give up?

Unless you spend your spare time studying an atlas or live in that part of the world, this may stump you. If this question came up on a test, you'd have to skip it, wouldn't you? Well, maybe not. Let's turn this question into a multiple-choice question—just like all the questions on the PSAT Reading and Writing section, and the majority of questions you'll find on the PSAT Math section—and see if you can figure out the answer anyway.

1 ⌖ Mark for Review

What is the capital of Azerbaijan?

Ⓐ Washington, D.C.

Ⓑ Paris

Ⓒ London

Ⓓ Baku

The question doesn't seem that hard anymore, does it? Of course, we made our example extremely easy. (By the way, there won't actually be any questions about geography on the PSAT that aren't answered by the accompanying text.) But you'd be surprised by how many people give up on PSAT questions that aren't much more difficult than this one just because they don't know the correct answer right off the top of their heads. "Capital of Azerbaijan? Oh, no! I've never heard of Azerbaijan!"

These students don't stop to think that they might be able to find the correct answer simply by eliminating all of the answer choices they know are wrong.

You Already Know Almost All of the Answers

Most of the questions on the PSAT are multiple-choice questions, and every multiple-choice question has four answer choices. One of those choices, and only one, will be the correct answer to the question. You don't have to come up with the answer from scratch. You just have to identify it.

How will you do that?

It's Not About Finding the Right Answer

The Digital PSAT tools will include an answer eliminator, so any wrong answers you find can be crossed off directly on the screen. If you need a more subtle system of rating the answers, write A, B, C, D on your scratch paper to mark them accordingly. Try using the following notations:

✔   Put a check mark next to an answer you like.

〜   Put a squiggle next to an answer you kind of like.

?   Put a question mark next to an answer you don't understand.

A̶   Cross out the letter of any answer choice you KNOW is wrong.

You can always come up with your own system. Just make sure you are consistent.

Look for the Wrong Answers Instead of the Right Ones

Why? Because wrong answers are usually easier to find than the right ones. After all, there are more of them! Remember the question about Azerbaijan? Even though you didn't know the answer off the top of your head, you easily figured it out by eliminating the three obviously incorrect choices. You looked for wrong answers first.

In other words, you used the Process of Elimination, which we'll call POE for short. This is an extremely important concept, one we'll come back to again and again. It's one of the keys to improving your PSAT score. When you finish reading this book, you will be able to use POE to answer many questions that you may not understand.

The great artist Michelangelo once said that when he looked at a block of marble, he could see a statue inside. All he had to do to make a sculpture was to chip away everything that wasn't part of it. You should approach difficult PSAT multiple-choice questions in the same way, by chipping away everything that's not correct. By first eliminating the most obviously incorrect choices on difficult questions, you will be able to focus your attention on the few choices that remain.

PROCESS OF ELIMINATION (POE)

There won't be many questions on the PSAT in which incorrect choices will be as easy to eliminate as they were on the Azerbaijan question. But if you read this book carefully, you'll learn how to eliminate at least one choice on almost any PSAT multiple-choice question, if not two or even three choices.

What good is it to eliminate just one or two choices on a four-choice PSAT question?

Plenty. In fact, for most students, it's an important key to earning higher scores. Here's another example:

---

2   🔖 Mark for Review

What is the capital of Qatar?

(A) Paris

(B) Dukhan

(C) Tokyo

(D) Doha

On this question you'll almost certainly be able to eliminate two of the four choices by using POE. That means you're still not sure of the answer. You know that the capital of Qatar has to be either Doha or Dukhan, but you don't know which.

Should you skip the question and go on? Or should you guess?

Close Your Eyes and Point

There is no guessing penalty on the PSAT, so you should enter an answer for every question. If you get down to two answers, just pick one of them. There's no harm in doing so.

You're going to hear a lot of mixed opinions about answer you should guess or whether you should guess at all. Let's clear up a few misconceptions about guessing.

FALSE: Don't answer a question unless you're absolutely sure of the answer.

> You will almost certainly have teachers and school counselors who tell you this. Don't listen to them! While the SAT used to penalize students for wrong answers prior to 2016, no tests in the current "Suite of Assessments" do this now. Put something down for every question: you might get a freebie.

FALSE: If you have to guess, guess (C).

> This is a weird misconception, and obviously it's not true. As a general rule, if someone says something really weird sounding about the PSAT, it's safest not to believe that person. (And we at The Princeton Review have gone through every PSAT and SAT and found that there isn't a "better" letter to guess, so just pick your favorite!)

FALSE: Always pick the [fill in the blank].

Be careful with directives that tell you that this or that answer, or type of answer is always right. It's much safer to learn the rules and to have a solid guessing strategy in place.

As far as guessing is concerned, we do have a small piece of advice. First and foremost, make sure of one thing:

> Answer every question on the PSAT. There's no penalty.

LETTER OF THE DAY (LOTD)

Sometimes you won't be able to eliminate any answers, and other times there will be questions that you won't have time to look at. For those, we have a simple solution. Pick a "Letter of the Day," or LOTD (from A to D), and use that letter for all the questions for which you weren't able to eliminate any choices.

This is a quick and easy way to make sure that you've entered an answer for every question. It also has some potential statistical advantages. If all the answers show up about one-fourth of the time and you guess the same answer every time you have to guess, you're likely to get a couple of freebies.

LOTD should absolutely be an afterthought; it's far more important and helpful to your score to eliminate answer choices. But for those questions you don't know at all, LOTD is better than full-on random guessing or no strategy at all.

Get Ready...
Check out *Stress-Free SAT: A Step-by-Step Beginner's Guide to SAT Preparation* for everything you need to know about the SAT exam.

PACE YOURSELF

LOTD should remind us about something very important: there's a very good chance that you won't answer every question on the test. Instead, work at a pace that lets you avoid careless mistakes, and don't stress about the questions you don't get to.

Think about it this way. In each given module, there will be questions that you can tackle quickly and accurately and others that will take you more time and effort. Why should you spend 4 or 5 minutes on one question when you may get two or three questions that are easier for you in the same amount of time?

Another tool you can use on the Digital PSAT to help pace yourself is the Mark for Review tool. If you see a question that looks like it might be time consuming or that you aren't sure how to solve, but you still want to come back to it if there is time, mark it. You can see the marked questions at a glance both at the end of the section or by opening the section overview at any time. This will allow you to quickly find the ones you want to work after you've done all the questions you know you can do quickly and accurately.

Unless you're currently scoring in the 650+ range on the two sections, you shouldn't be working all the questions.

> Slow down, score more. You're not scored on *how many questions you do*. You're scored on *how many questions you answer correctly*. Doing fewer questions can mean more correct answers overall!

EMBRACE YOUR POOD

Embrace your *what* now? POOD! It stands for "Personal Order of Difficulty." The Digital PSAT will put questions in a rough order of difficulty, by content domain on the Reading and Writing section and overall on the Math section. But this Order of Difficulty (OOD) is only what College Board thinks about the question levels, not how you will do on them. So, rather than doing the questions in order, you need to be particularly vigilant about applying your *Personal* Order of Difficulty (POOD).

Think about it this way. There's someone writing the words that you're reading right now. So, what happens if you are asked, *Who is the author of PSAT/NMSQT Prep?* Do you know the answer to that question? Maybe not. Do we know the answer to that question? Absolutely.

So, you can't exactly say that that question is "difficult," but you can say that certain people would have an easier time answering it. Pace yourself. Work carefully on questions you know how to do to make sure you get them right. Mark questions you want to come back to later.

As we've begun to suggest with our Pacing, POE, and Letter of the Day strategies, The Princeton Review's strategies are all about making the test your own, to whatever extent that is possible. We call this idea POOD because we believe it is essential that you identify the questions that you find easy or hard and that you work the test in a way most suitable to your goals and strengths.

As you familiarize yourself with the rest of our strategies, keep all of this in mind. You may be surprised to find out how you perform on particular question types and sections. This test may be standardized, but the biggest improvements are usually reserved for those who can treat the test in a personalized, nonstandardized way.

Summary

- When you don't know the right answer to a multiple-choice question, look for wrong answers instead. They're usually easier to find.

- When you find a wrong answer choice, eliminate it. In other words, use Process of Elimination, or POE.

- There's no penalty for wrong answers, so there's no reason NOT to guess.

- There will likely be at least a few questions you simply don't get to or where you're finding it difficult to eliminate even one answer choice. When this happens, use the LOTD (Letter of the Day) strategy.

- Pace yourself. Work carefully on questions you know how to do to make sure you get them right. Mark questions you want to come back to later. Use LOTD on any you know are not worth your time or effort or that you know you are unlikely to get right.

- Make the test your own. When you can work the test to suit your strengths (and use our strategies to overcome any weaknesses), you'll be on your way to a higher score.

Part II
Practice Test 1

HOW TO TAKE THE DIGITAL PSAT ON PAPER

The Digital PSAT will be administered online, so it is best if you take your practice tests in the online tools for this book. However, if you prefer to take this test on paper, you can do so by either indicating your answers as described in the directions for print tests included with each module or by entering your answers as you go onto the answer sheet on pages 93–94.

On the Digital PSAT, you will only get two modules in each section, and the second module you get in each section will be determined by your performance on the first module in that section. Therefore, for both RW and Math, the following test contains a standard first module and two options for the second module, one easier and one harder. You should take the appropriate second module based on your performance in the first module, as detailed below, but you can feel free to use the other module for extra practice later.

In order to navigate the practice test in this book instead of online, take the following steps.

- [ ] Take Reading and Writing Module 1, allowing yourself 32 minutes to complete it.

- [ ] Go to the answer key on page 96 and determine the number of questions you got correct in RW Module 1.

- [ ] If you get fewer than 15 questions correct, take RW Module 2—Easier, which starts on page 43. If you get 15 or more questions correct, take RW Module 2—Harder, which starts on page 54.

- [ ] Whichever RW Module 2 you take, start it immediately and allow yourself 32 minutes to complete it.

- [ ] Take a 10-minute break between RW Module 2 and Math Module 1.

- [ ] Take Math Module 1, allowing yourself 35 minutes to complete it.

- [ ] Go to the answer key on page 96 and determine the number of questions you got correct in Math Module 1.

- [ ] If you get fewer than 14 questions correct, take Math Module 2—Easier, which starts on page 74. If you get 14 or more questions correct, take Math Module 2—Harder, which starts on page 84.

- [ ] Whichever Math Module you take, start it immediately and allow yourself 35 minutes to complete it.

- [ ] After you finish the test, check your answers to RW Module 2 and Math Module 2.

- [ ] Only after you complete the entire test should you read the explanations for the questions, which start on page 97 and are also available online.

- [ ] Go to your online student tools to see the latest information about scoring and to get your estimated score.

Chapter 4
Practice Test 1

PSAT Prep Test 1—Reading and Writing
Module 1

Turn to Section 1 of your answer sheet to answer the questions in this section.

---

1 ☐ Mark for Review

Spanish neuroscientist Joaquin M. Fuster's work on memory and the prefrontal cortex has been widely acclaimed. Accordingly, he was _____ by the Fussen Foundation for his excellence in neuroscience research.

Which choice completes the text with the most logical and precise word or phrase?

(A) criticized

(B) surprised

(C) recognized

(D) worshiped

---

2 ☐ Mark for Review

Performer Nastio Mosquito is a multifaceted artist who explores the power of language through online videos, large-scale art installations, poetry, and song. Mosquito delivers _____ performances that blend art, politics, and entertainment while still remaining true to his main theme of African cultural inheritance.

Which choice completes the text with the most logical and precise word or phrase?

(A) diverse

(B) costly

(C) humorous

(D) brief

CONTINUE

3 ☐ Mark for Review

The following text is from Henry Guy Carleton's 1884 short story "The Thompson Street Poker Club."

When Mr. Tooter Williams entered the gilded halls of the Thompson Street Poker Club Saturday evening it was evident that fortune had smeared him with prosperity. He wore a straw hat with a blue ribbon, an expression of serene content, and a glass amethyst on his third finger whose effulgence irradiated the whole room and made the envious eyes of Mr. Cyanide Whiffles stand out like a crab's.

As used in the text, what does the word "smeared" most nearly mean?

Ⓐ Deceived

Ⓑ Gifted

Ⓒ Assaulted

Ⓓ Criticized

4 ☐ Mark for Review

As a member of the non-profit group Servas International, writer and poet Susan Deer Cloud regularly hosts travelers from abroad at her home in the Catskill Mountains. Through the group's mission of hospitality and through her own writings, Deer Cloud hopes to _____ a sense of peace and cross-cultural understanding in those she interacts with.

Which choice completes the text with the most logical and precise word or phrase?

Ⓐ demand

Ⓑ fabricate

Ⓒ instill

Ⓓ concede

5 ☐ Mark for Review

National metrication is an ongoing proposal by an array of diverse organizations within the United States to convert the country's measurement standards from customary to metric. Proponents of the proposal have criticized what they view as limited efforts initiated by the national government to educate the public regarding the benefits of the metric system, which they believe would _____ the competitiveness of American products and services in world markets.

Which choice completes the text with the most logical and precise word or phrase?

Ⓐ refute

Ⓑ dilute

Ⓒ uphold

Ⓓ buttress

CONTINUE

6 ☐ Mark for Review

The modern public is probably more familiar with the wives of Henry VIII than with any other queens in history—or at least with the respective pictures that history has painted of them. Anne Boleyn, Henry's admittedly ambitious second wife, was the self-promoting social climber, while his first wife, Catherine of Aragon, has all but been canonized as the pious innocent victim of Henry's tyranny. Third wife Jane Seymour is typically only considered in contrast to her predecessor: Anne was brazen while Jane was demure. Anne of Cleves was unattractive, Catherine Howard was a flighty teenager, and Catherine Parr was the sensible one who escaped Henry's wrath unscathed. If one looks beyond these reductive descriptions, one might be surprised to learn that Catherine of Aragon had been a ruthless military leader and Anne Boleyn fought nobly for charitable causes: quite contrary to their traditional depictions.

Which choices best states the main purpose of the text?

- (A) To draw attention to information not commonly known about Catherine of Aragon and Anne Boleyn

- (B) To deny that all of Henry VIII's wives possessed the character traits traditionally ascribed to them

- (C) To criticize the tendency to view each of Henry VIII's wives solely in terms of their usefulness to Henry himself

- (D) To discuss both the traditionally associated and uncommonly known character traits of Henry VIII's wives

7 ☐ Mark for Review

Text 1

What can contribute to climate change besides the already well-documented impact of human-caused, or anthropogenic, carbon dioxide production? Some scientists caution that, while long-term human impact on global temperatures cannot be understated, sudden environmental events in a specific region can have global implications that are no less critical to understand and thus must be as carefully monitored as anthropogenic events are.

Text 2

A team of researchers led by Lilly Damany-Pearce at the University of Exeter conducted a series of satellite and surface-based observations to determine the effect of a series of Australian wildfires on the temperature of Earth's lower stratosphere. By observing photos from the satellites and inputting atmospheric data in a cutting-edge climate model, Damany-Pearce and her team were able to establish a causal connection between the ignition of the wildfires and the subsequent rise in mean lower stratosphere temperature during the exact same period.

Based on the texts, how would Damany-Pearce and her team most likely describe the view of the scientists presented in Text 1?

- (A) It likely is only relevant to wildfires rather than other environmental events.

- (B) It has merit as a viewpoint due to the evidence collected by Damany-Pearce and her team.

- (C) It has dubious value even though Damany-Pearce and her team seem to have discovered corroborating evidence.

- (D) It may seem appealing, but it is contradictory to Damany-Pearce and her team's findings.

CONTINUE ➤

8 ☐ Mark for Review

The following text is adapted from Robert Louis Stevenson's 1886 novel *Kidnapped*. The narrator has just delivered a letter to his uncle, whom he describes in this excerpt.

As soon as the last chain was up, the man rejoined me. He was a mean, stooping, narrow-shouldered, clay-faced creature; and his age might have been anything between fifty and seventy. His nightcap was of flannel, and so was the nightgown that he wore, instead of coat and waistcoat, over his ragged shirt. He was long unshaved; but what most distressed and even daunted me, he would neither take his eyes away from me nor look me fairly in the face. What he was, whether by trade or birth, was more than I could fathom; but he seemed most like an old, unprofitable serving-man, who should have been left in charge of that big house upon board wages.

According to the text, what is true about the narrator's uncle?

(A) He reacts jovially and greets the narrator joyfully despite the late hour.

(B) He is surprised by the narrator's visit and is ill-prepared for it.

(C) He instills a sense of familial pride in the narrator.

(D) He presents himself in a manner the narrator finds unfavorable.

9 ☐ Mark for Review

Dolphin-assisted therapy, or DAT, utilizes the concept of swimming with dolphins to improve a patient's mental and physical well-being. A team of researchers has posited that, while the influence of DAT on neurodevelopmental disorders, such as autism, remains unknown, the therapy is likely beneficial for non-neurodevelopmental conditions, such as anxiety disorder, as the calming influence of water and positive dolphin responsiveness to distress in humans have both been well-documented.

Which finding, if true, would most support the researchers' hypothesis?

(A) Individuals diagnosed with anxiety disorder reported lower levels of anxiety at the end of DAT treatment.

(B) Individuals diagnosed with autism reported the same levels of anxiety at the start and end of DAT treatment.

(C) The anxiety levels of those diagnosed with anxiety disorder fluctuated with no general trend throughout DAT treatment.

(D) The anxiety levels of those diagnosed with anxiety disorder increased while the anxiety levels of those diagnosed with autism decreased throughout DAT treatment.

CONTINUE ➜

10 ☐ Mark for Review

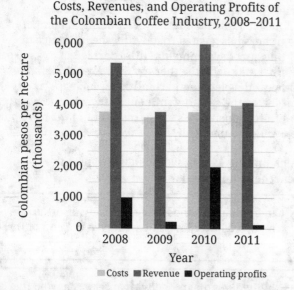

Costs, Revenues, and Operating Profits of the Colombian Coffee Industry, 2008–2011

Relative to other producers, coffee producers must often cope with a particularly volatile market, due to unforeseen gluts, climate change, and economic conditions in coffee-consuming countries. Researchers have tried to help growers and producers control their markets and decrease volatility by examining the growth and loss of costs, revenues, and operating profits in the long- and short-term. A group of economists examined coffee production in the nation of Colombia, a traditionally strong coffee producing country, from 2008 through 2011. It concluded that, even with the volatility in the market, so long as coffee producers could increase their revenues, their efforts would remain profitable.

Which choice best describes data from the graph that supports the study's conclusion?

- (A) Both costs and revenues increased every year from 2008 to 2011.

- (B) When revenues increased from 2009 to 2010, so did operating profits.

- (C) Costs remained relatively stable each year from 2008 to 2011.

- (D) When costs decreased from 2008 to 2009, so did operating profits.

11 ☐ Mark for Review

Born in 1877 in New York City, Rosalie Edge was an environmentalist who sought to improve conservation efforts towards many species, especially birds. During an interview regarding her 1962 book *Silent Spring*, scientist Rachel Carson claimed that Edge's work was instrumental in facilitating her own ornithological research, particularly concerning birds of prey such as hawks.

Which statement, if true, would most directly support Carson's claim?

- (A) Some of the birds that Carson studied had previously been studied by Edge and her fellow environmentalists.

- (B) Edge established Hawk Mountain Sanctuary, the world's first nature preserve for birds of prey, and Carson is recorded as having visited the preserve several times prior to 1962.

- (C) Edge's conservation work demonstrated an extremely proficient level of ornithological knowledge, as seen in her many detailed books on birds of prey.

- (D) During her career, Edge was widely acclaimed by her colleagues, as one colleague called her one of the only truly honest and selfish forces in conservation.

CONTINUE ➡

12 ☐ Mark for Review

"Marianne's Dream" is an 1817 poem by Percy Bryce Shelley. In the poem, a lady named Marianne experiences unpleasant sights and sounds while having a nightmare: _____

Which quotation from "Marianne's Dream" most effectively illustrates this claim?

- (A) "At first all deadly shapes were driven / Tumultuously across her sleep, / And o'er the vast cope of bending heaven / All ghastly-visaged clouds did sweep;"

- (B) "On two dread mountains, from whose crest, / Might seem, the eagle, for her brood, / Would ne'er have hung her dizzy nest, / Those tower-encircled cities stood."

- (C) "She looked, the flames were dim, the flood / Grew tranquil as a woodland river / Winding through hills in solitude; / Those marble shapes then seemed to quiver,"

- (D) "The Lady grew sick with a weight of fear / To see that Anchor ever hanging, / And veiled her eyes; she then did hear / The sound as of a dim low clanging,"

13 ☐ Mark for Review

The *door-in-the-face* technique involves initially making an outrageous or unappealing request or offer, which the other person is highly likely to refuse, then following up with a more reasonable one. The subject is more likely to look favorably upon this second request or offer because it seems acceptable compared to the initial proposition. So, if an employee wants the best raise in annual salary from her boss that she can get, she might succeed by asking for a _____

Which choice most logically completes the text?

- (A) 50% raise, then asking for a 5% raise.

- (B) 3% raise, then asking for a 2% raise.

- (C) 10% raise, then asking for a 50% raise.

- (D) 3% raise, then asking for a 3% raise again.

CONTINUE ➤

14 ▢ Mark for Review

There have been rumors of "sea serpents" in Scotland's Loch Ness for centuries, which some have theorized are actually aquatic animals that are "undiscovered" by science (at least in living form) that somehow survived their apparent extinctions millions of years ago. Many believe these elusive creatures are *plesiosaurs*—Mesozoic marine reptiles with extremely long necks. However, plesiosaurs are believed to have been cold-blooded, and a cold-blooded animal could never survive in the frigid waters of Loch Ness. So, _____

Which choice most logically completes the text?

Ⓐ unless plesiosaurs were warm-blooded, there are no undiscovered aquatic animals in Loch Ness.

Ⓑ unless plesiosaurs were cold-blooded, there are no undiscovered aquatic animals in Loch Ness.

Ⓒ if plesiosaurs are cold-blooded, there are no plesiosaurs in Loch Ness.

Ⓓ if there are no plesiosaurs in Loch Ness, there are no undiscovered aquatic animals in Loch Ness.

15 ▢ Mark for Review

According to research, people tend to attribute positive personality traits to those who are physically attractive. When people were rated as physically attractive by participants, _____ personalities were also rated as confident, intelligent, responsible, and sociable.

Which choice completes the text so that it conforms to the conventions of Standard English?

Ⓐ they're

Ⓑ their

Ⓒ it's

Ⓓ its

16 ▢ Mark for Review

A writer and performer famous for numerous spoken solo performances, Margo Kane highlights the lives of youth in Native American communities. Her theater company strives to provide opportunities for First Nations _____ to share their experiences and promote their traditions.

Which choice completes the text so that it conforms to the conventions of Standard English?

Ⓐ artists,

Ⓑ artists—

Ⓒ artists:

Ⓓ artists

CONTINUE ➡

17 ☐ Mark for Review

While focusing on number theory and cryptography, Shafi Goldwasser became a professor at multiple universities simultaneously and earned the Turing Award in 2012. By 2020, she _____ a leader of Project CETI, an initiative focused on sperm whale communication.

Which choice completes the text so that it conforms to the conventions of Standard English?

(A) will become

(B) becomes

(C) has become

(D) had become

18 ☐ Mark for Review

Charles Drew was a blood transfusion medical researcher and surgeon during World War _____ work developed the first blood banks and saved the lives of thousands of Allied soldiers.

Which choice completes the text so that it conforms to the conventions of Standard English?

(A) II his

(B) II and his

(C) II, his

(D) II. His

19 ☐ Mark for Review

Lab-grown diamonds are made up of the same compound as natural diamonds (pure carbon), and they exhibit similar properties. Modern researchers have improved upon the initial _____ to make the lab-growing process more efficient.

Which choice completes the text so that it conforms to the conventions of Standard English?

(A) method, developed by Percy Bridgman,

(B) method, developed by Percy Bridgman

(C) method developed by Percy Bridgman,

(D) method developed by Percy Bridgman

20 ☐ Mark for Review

Douglas Kearney is a poet and opera-writer from the US. *Crescent City*, one of his most famous operas, _____ extensive recognition, and he has since earned the Campbell Opera Librettist Prize.

Which choice completes the text so that it conforms to the conventions of Standard English?

(A) have received

(B) has received

(C) receive

(D) are receiving

CONTINUE

21 ☐ Mark for Review

Achromatopsia, a heritable genetic condition, causes photosensitivity and color blindness due to inactive cones in the eyes. Scientists used gene therapy on one eye of children with the condition to determine whether the inactive cones could be restored. In each patient, the treated eye was able to detect some colors, and _____ able to perform other cone-related tasks.

Which choice completes the text so that it conforms to the conventions of Standard English?

(A) one was

(B) it was

(C) they were

(D) we were

22 ☐ Mark for Review

Researchers in California have found that a lack of sleep reduces humans' natural drive to help other people. In states with Daylight Saving Time, donations to charities were reduced by 10% the week after the time change, when many people lose an hour of sleep; _____ this reduction was not seen in states that do not observe Daylight Saving Time.

Which choice completes the text with the most logical transition?

(A) in addition,

(B) however,

(C) initially,

(D) otherwise,

23 ☐ Mark for Review

Dominican artist Firelei Báez, known for creating complex pieces on old maps and documents, explores Western thought through the lens of non-Western media. She combines symbols and abstract images with figures from folklore, literature, and living plants to represent historical events and themes. _____ Báez created a sculpture in 2021 that reimagined Haitian ruins as if they had been discovered in East Boston in modern times.

Which choice completes the text with the most logical transition?

(A) For example,

(B) Additionally,

(C) Consequently,

(D) However,

24 ☐ Mark for Review

Borobudur, located in Indonesia, is the largest Buddhist temple in the world. The temple was likely built sometime in the 9th century, but the Hindu kingdoms declined in the 14th century when Islam became much more popular as a religion. _____ the temple was abandoned.

Which choice completes the text with the most logical transition?

(A) For instance,

(B) Besides that,

(C) Subsequently,

(D) Also,

CONTINUE ➡

25 ▢ Mark for Review

While researching a topic, a student has taken the following notes:

- Cirrus clouds are a type of high cloud.
- They form between 4,000 and 20,000 meters above sea level.
- They look wispy and delicate.
- Cumulus clouds are a type of low cloud.
- They form less than 2,000 meters above sea level.
- They look fluffy and cotton-like.

The student wants to highlight the differences between cirrus and cumulus clouds. Which choice most effectively uses relevant information from the notes to accomplish this goal?

- (A) Cirrus clouds look wispy and delicate.

- (B) Cirrus clouds are a type of high cloud and form between 4,000 and 20,000 meters above sea level, and cumulus clouds are a type of low cloud and form less than 2,000 meters above sea level.

- (C) Low clouds can form less than 2,000 meters above sea level, but high clouds can form between 4,000 and 20,000 meters above sea level.

- (D) Cumulus clouds, which appear fluffy and cotton-like, are a type of low cloud.

26 ▢ Mark for Review

While researching a topic, a student has taken the following notes:

- Weddell seals are extraordinary divers and can dive for twenty minutes and sometimes up to ninety minutes.
- Even Weddell seal pups can dive for long periods.
- To be able to dive for long periods, Weddell seal pups need high levels of iron to carry oxygen while they are underwater.
- Weddell seals have a longer lactation period, six to seven weeks, than that of other seals, which made researchers curious.
- When they analyzed Weddell seal mothers' milk, they found large amounts of iron.
- The longer lactation period allows seal mothers to give their pups large amounts of iron.

The student wants to emphasize how Weddell seal mothers provide a benefit to their seal pups. Which choice most effectively uses relevant information from the notes to accomplish this goal?

- (A) Weddell seal pups receive large amounts of iron from their mothers' milk, which enables them to dive for long periods.

- (B) Weddell seals need high levels of iron to dive for up to ninety minutes.

- (C) Weddell seal mothers have longer lactation periods for their pups than do other true seals.

- (D) Large amounts of iron are found in the milk of Weddell seal mothers.

CONTINUE ➡

‒ ‒

27 ☐ Mark for Review

While researching a topic, a student has taken the following notes:

- Lloma de Betxí was a Bronze Age settlement near Paterna.
- Paterna is in northeastern Spain, on the left bank of the Turia River near Valencia.
- Lloma de Betxí was used between 1800 and 1300 BCE.
- During this time, inhabitants grew grain crops and raised cattle.
- Inhabitants during this time used bronze tools in farming.

The student wants to introduce the timeframe of Lloma de Betxí to an audience unfamiliar with the location of Paterna. Which choice most effectively uses relevant information from the notes to accomplish this goal?

(A) In northeastern Spain, near Valencia, is Lloma de Betxí, a Bronze Age settlement inhabited between 1800 and 1300 BCE.

(B) Paterna is located on the left bank of the Turia River near Valencia, Spain.

(C) Between 1800 and 1300 BCE, inhabitants of Lloma de Betxí near Paterna grew grain crops and raised cattle.

(D) Lloma de Betxí is an example of the use of bronze tools in farming in northeastern Spain.

CONTINUE ➡

PSAT Prep Test 1—Reading and Writing
Module 2—Easier

Turn to Section 1 of your answer sheet to answer the questions in this section.

---

1 ☐ Mark for Review

The following text is from Jane Porter's 1809 novel *The Scottish Chiefs*. The excerpt describes Lady Wallace, a central character, describing her emotions towards her husband, Edward.

Wherever Lady Wallace moved,—whether looking out from her window on the accidental passenger, or taking her morning or moonlight walks through the glen, leaning on the arm of her husband,—she had the rapture of hearing his steps greeted and followed by the blessings of the poor destitute, and the prayers of them who were ready to perish.

As used in the text, what does the word "accidental" most nearly mean?

(A) Joyful

(B) Random

(C) Angry

(D) Jealous

---

2 ☐ Mark for Review

Photographer Deana Lawson is an American artist and photographer whose work has been praised for its ability to convey intimate details of the African American experience. As a young college student hoping to learn more about African American artists, she was _____ by the lack of available texts about artists, specifically photographers, of color in her university library. Lawson was motivated to fill this void herself by independently learning about these artists, such as photographer Lorna Simpson, whose work inspired Lawson to become a photographer herself.

Which choice completes the text with the most logical and precise word or phrase?

(A) excited

(B) unaffected

(C) encouraged

(D) surprised

CONTINUE ➡

--- --- --- --- --- --- --- --- --- --- --- --- --- --- --- --- --- --- --- ---

3 🔖 Mark for Review

In addition to John Mawurndjul's many accomplishments as an artist, he has also achieved great success as a _____. He has tutored his wife and daughter, both accomplished painters themselves, and founded his own school to teach the next generation of Aboriginal artists.

Which choice completes the text with the most logical and precise word or phrase?

- Ⓐ mentor
- Ⓑ muralist
- Ⓒ technician
- Ⓓ painter

4 🔖 Mark for Review

Poet William Ernest Henley often described the resilience of the human spirit in the face of adversity. In his 1975 poem "Invictus," he describes the _____ of a character who perseveres even in the face of certain death.

Which choice completes the text with the most logical and precise word or phrase?

- Ⓐ tenacity
- Ⓑ cheerfulness
- Ⓒ artistry
- Ⓓ sorrow

5 🔖 Mark for Review

Intrauterine adhesion is _____ by the appearance of fibrosis in the uterine cavity. While routine examinations may reveal the presence of fibrosis in patients, undetected and untreated intrauterine adhesion can cause immense difficulty for reproductive health.

Which choice completes the text with the most logical and precise word or phrase?

- Ⓐ diminished
- Ⓑ nullified
- Ⓒ altered
- Ⓓ typified

CONTINUE ➡️

6 ☐ Mark for Review

Wind turbines generate electricity in remote locations but can be hazardous to birds, which get caught in their turbines. Researchers identified six pairs of adjacent wind turbines and painted one turbine in each pair black, leaving the other white, trying to determine whether distinct colors might deter birds and prevent casualties. They tallied the number of birds killed in each of the turbines for 5 years and compared the data to a prior 5-year period, finding that fatalities for the painted turbines were down 72%. Noting that collisions with unpainted turbines actually increased, they posited that perhaps the birds were avoiding the painted turbines but moving toward the unpainted turbines.

Which choice best describes the function of the fourth sentence of the text?

(A) It clarifies how the findings of the study differed from those of earlier studies.

(B) It explains how the central hypothesis was fundamentally flawed.

(C) It presents an adjustment to the researchers' theory based on an unexpected outcome.

(D) It describes an initial challenge that the researchers eventually overcame.

7 ☐ Mark for Review

The following text is from Victor Cherbuliez's 1863 novel *Count Kostia*. This excerpt describes the events which set the rest of the novel into motion.

At the beginning of the summer of 1850, a Russian nobleman, Count Kostia Petrovitch Leminof, had the misfortune to lose his wife suddenly, and in the flower of her beauty. She was his junior by twelve years. This cruel loss, for which he was totally unprepared, threw him into a state of profound melancholy; and some months later, seeking to mitigate his grief by the distractions of travel, he left his domains near Moscow, never intending to return. Accompanied by his twin children, ten years of age, a priest who had served them as tutor, and a serf named Ivan, he repaired to Odessa, and then took passage on a merchant ship for Martinique. Disembarking at St. Pierre, he took lodgings in a remote part of the suburbs.

Which choice best states the main purpose of the text?

(A) To discuss an emotional event and its consequences for a family

(B) To highlight the popular travel destinations of Russian nobility

(C) To explain the cultural enrichment that one can experience through overseas travel

(D) To criticize Count Kostia for moving on from the death of his wife too quickly

CONTINUE →

8 ☐ Mark for Review

The following text is adapted from Sir Arthur Conan Doyle's 1902 short story "The Leather Funnel." The narrator is approaching the home of an old friend who lives in Paris, France.

My friend, Lionel Dacre, lived in the Avenue de Wagram, Paris. His house was that small one, with the iron railings and grass plot in front of it, on the left-hand side as you pass down from the Arc de Triomphe. I fancy that it had been there long before the avenue was constructed, for the grey tiles were stained with lichens, and the walls were mildewed and discoloured with age. It looked a small house from the street, five windows in front, if I remember right, but it deepened into a single long chamber at the back.

According to the text, what is true about the house of Lionel Dacre?

Ⓐ It is one of the oldest houses in Paris.

Ⓑ It is larger than it appears from the street.

Ⓒ It has a front yard and a back yard.

Ⓓ It is overgrown with lichens and other plants.

9 ☐ Mark for Review

Andy Goldsworthy is an environmental artist who has used objects formed by nature as a point of inspiration to create large-scale sculptures. His piece *Cairn* features rock balancing, a method by which one selects small rocks and looks for points in which they 'lock' into each other to create a larger unique form. The act of balancing rocks is often found to be relaxing and meditative, qualities which Goldsworthy has cited in his own artistic process. He has even compared his style of work to picking potatoes, believing that the repetition and rhythm are integral to his final product.

What choice states the main idea of the text?

Ⓐ Rock balancing is a new art form that places natural elements into large outdoor settings.

Ⓑ Goldsworthy appreciates certain qualities of rock balancing in composing some of his work.

Ⓒ Goldsworthy's *Cairn* is unlike any other piece of environmental art because it uses balancing rocks.

Ⓓ Repeating actions such as picking vegetables often influences the work of environmental artists.

CONTINUE ➤

10 🔖 Mark for Review

A Lady of Quality is an 1896 novel by Frances Hodgson Burnett. Mistress Clorinda Wildairs, the main character, has settled on a spouse, an elderly Earl. During a disagreement with her sister, Anne, Mistress Clorinda defends her feelings towards her chosen partner, declaring, _____

Which quotation from *A Lady of Quality* most effectively illustrates this claim?

- (A) "From this night all men must bend so—all men on whom I deign to cast my eyes."

- (B) "I love my Lord of Dunstanwolde as well as any other man, and better than some, for I do not hate him."

- (C) "*I* am a woman and I do not suffer—for I *will* not, that I swear!"

- (D) "Do not be a fool, Anne, and carry yourself too humbly before the world."

11 🔖 Mark for Review

Weight, BMI, and Serum Homocysteine Levels of Patients Suffering from NAFLD

	Weight (kg)	BMI (kg/m²)	Serum homocysteine levels
B12 Group initial	87.25	31.42	15.1
B12 Group final	85.7	30.74	11.5
Placebo group initial	92.7	30.67	14.5
Placebo group final	91.61	32.31	14.1

A group of scientists conducted a study to determine whether vitamin B12 could reduce serum homocysteine levels in patients suffering from non-alcoholic fatty liver disease (NAFLD). Forty patients were split into two equal groups: an experimental group was given a daily dose of 1000 mg of vitamin B12 for 12 weeks, and the control group was given only a placebo. After measuring these levels for 12 weeks, researchers noted a reduction in serum homocysteine levels, weight, and BMI (Body Mass Index) for the vitamin B12 group only. This led the researchers to conclude that vitamin B12 may be effective in helping patients with NAFLD.

Which choice best describes data from the table that supports the researchers' conclusion?

- (A) The serum homocysteine levels in the placebo group decreased from 14.5 to 14.1 during the study.

- (B) The weight levels and BMI decreased for the placebo group during the study.

- (C) The serum homocysteine levels in the B12 group decreased from 15.1 to 11.5 during the study.

- (D) The weight levels increased for the B12 group but decreased for the placebo group during the study.

CONTINUE ➡

12 ☐ Mark for Review

"A Piece of Bread" is an 1887 short story by Francois Coppee. In the story, a soldier named Jean-Victor, who experienced a difficult upbringing at an asylum, or orphanage, shares one of his only positive memories from his childhood with his comrade: _____

Which quotation from "A Piece of Bread" most effectively illustrates this claim?

(A) "Fortunately for me; at these times I have always remembered the good Sister at the Asylum, who so often told me to be honest, and I seemed to feel her warm little hand upon my forehead."

(B) "The master and mistress, two old Limousins— afterwards murdered, were terrible misers, and the bread, cut in tiny pieces for each meal, was kept under lock and key the rest of the time."

(C) "But the managers could not know everything, and had no suspicion that the children were abused."

(D) "I am used to that for I have picked up enough of it; and crusts from the dust, and when they were too hard and dry, I would soak them all night in my basin."

13 ☐ Mark for Review

Nutritional Content in One Standard Serving of Four Common Breakfast Foods

Food	Serving size (g)	Total sugars (g)	Calories
Plain bagel	105	5.3	271
Corn flake cereal	28	2.9	100
Frosted cake doughnut	67	21.4	296
Blueberry muffin	113	16.7	470

Excess sugar consumption is often derided by health professionals for several reasons, among which are increased risk of high blood pressure and increased risk of diabetes. Some foods with high sugar content are popular American breakfast foods, and traditionally it was thought that higher sugar content would naturally correspond with higher caloric content as the latter was linked to increased risk of obesity as well. However, a recent study conducted by researchers Jennifer Erickson and Joanne Slavin, who focused on USDA dietary recommendations, demonstrated that caloric and sugar levels within a food item should not necessarily be correlated. For example, whereas a frosted cake doughnut has 296 calories and 21.4 grams of sugar, _____

Which choice most effectively uses data from the table to complete the statement?

(A) a plain bagel has 271 calories, and a serving of cornflake cereal has 100 calories.

(B) a serving of corn flake cereal has 100 calories and 2.9 grams of sugar.

(C) a blueberry muffin has 470 calories, but a plain bagel only has 271 calories.

(D) a blueberry muffin has 470 calories but only 16.7 grams of sugar.

CONTINUE ➡

14 ☐ Mark for Review

John William Godward (1861–1922) was a British artist known for his *neoclassical* paintings—those that feature subjects from ancient Greece and Rome. His greatest works depict elegant women dressed in brightly colored classical clothing posed in front of stunning ancient architecture. Godward abhorred the modern art movement of the late nineteenth and twentieth centuries, during which avant-garde painters such as Picasso dominated the art world with their nontraditional works. The abstract character of the modern movement lay in stark contrast to Godward's vision of what beauty is and what art should be. One can therefore infer that _____

Which choice most logically completes the text?

Ⓐ Picasso took no inspiration from Godward's work.

Ⓑ modernist painters did not typically use bright colors.

Ⓒ Godward did not approve of developments in the art world towards the end of his life.

Ⓓ famous neoclassical paintings steadily lost their value as the twentieth century progressed.

15 ☐ Mark for Review

High schools in Rhode Island have the highest national average student-teacher ratio of any state at 22:1. While it is reasonable to think that students in Rhode Island should therefore produce similarly higher than average standardized test results, standardized test scores in the state vary wildly. However, the average GPA at Rhode Island high schools is nearly 0.6 higher than the national average GPA of 3.0. Therefore, _____

Which choice most logically completes the text?

Ⓐ high schools in Rhode Island with lower than average standardized test scores must also have lower-than-average GPAs.

Ⓑ the student-teacher ratio at high schools in Rhode Island has a more noticeable effect on standardized test scores than does GPA.

Ⓒ the student-teacher ratio at high schools in Rhode Island may have a stronger correlation with GPA than it does with standardized test scores.

Ⓓ the student-teacher ratio at high schools in Rhode Island is not a critical factor for producing higher standardized test scores or GPAs.

CONTINUE ➤

16 ☐ Mark for Review

Canisia Lubrin published a collection of poems in 2017, *Voodoo Hypothesis*, that _____ the stereotypes that certain demographics of people are inferior to others.

Which choice completes the text so that it conforms to the conventions of Standard English?

- (A) attacking
- (B) to attack
- (C) attacked
- (D) having attacked

17 ☐ Mark for Review

Lorina Naci, a neurologist and psychologist from Albania, studied how to communicate with patients in comas using functional magnetic resonance imagery. Naci aimed to answer a specific question with her research: if patients in a vegetative state were shown a horror film, _____

Which choice completes the text so that it conforms to the conventions of Standard English?

- (A) would they exhibit increased brain activity?
- (B) would they exhibit increased brain activity.
- (C) increased brain activity would be exhibited.
- (D) increased brain activity would be exhibited?

18 ☐ Mark for Review

Zhang Heng was a scientist in China during the Han dynasty who filled the role of astronomer, mathematician, cartographer, and literary expert. Today, Heng _____ considered the equivalent of Ptolemy in terms of academic expertise.

Which choice completes the text so that it conforms to the conventions of Standard English?

- (A) was
- (B) is
- (C) will be
- (D) had been

19 ☐ Mark for Review

In his memoir, *Heavy*, Black southern author Kiese Laymon writes about his complicated relationship with his mother _____ the struggles he experienced as he grew into young adulthood.

Which choice completes the text so that it conforms to the conventions of Standard English?

- (A) is revealing
- (B) to reveal
- (C) reveals
- (D) revealed

CONTINUE ➡

20 ☐ Mark for Review

A respected artist and senior figure in the Kintore women's movements in Australia, Naata Nungurrayi created works that displayed important sites for women and their ceremonies. One of _____ was chosen for an Australian Post International stamp, and she was identified as one of the most collectible artists of Australia in 2004.

Which choice completes the text so that it conforms to the conventions of Standard English?

(A) Nungurrayis painting's

(B) Nungurrayi's painting's

(C) Nungurrayis paintings

(D) Nungurrayi's paintings

21 ☐ Mark for Review

The Perseverance rover, a robotic vehicle, completed the first ground-penetrating survey using radar on _____ layers of magnetic material and buried structures.

Which choice completes the text so that it conforms to the conventions of Standard English?

(A) Mars revealing

(B) Mars; revealing

(C) Mars. Revealing

(D) Mars, revealing

22 ☐ Mark for Review

Using her ambidexterity and ability to use her mouth to complete tasks, physical therapist Bessie Blount Griffin strove to help soldiers who had lost a limb in battle return to a normal life after World War II. She taught veterans how to perform everyday tasks with their feet and teeth and _____ a self-feeding assistive device to feed soldiers who had lost their hands.

Which choice completes the text so that it conforms to the conventions of Standard English?

(A) inventing

(B) invent

(C) invents

(D) invented

23 ☐ Mark for Review

Shen Kuo was a Chinese scientist of the Song dynasty in the 12th century. Kuo explored _____ greatly influenced society, such as mathematics, astronomy, meteorology, and anatomy, throughout his time as the head official for the Bureau of Astronomy. He also invented the first magnetic needle compass.

Which choice completes the text so that it conforms to the conventions of Standard English?

(A) fields that

(B) fields

(C) fields,

(D) fields, that

CONTINUE ➡

24 ⚑ Mark for Review

A folly is a garden building typically built to provide a decorative and extravagant feature to a landscape. Fonthill Abbey, owned by William Thomas Beckford and built in England around the year 1800, is one of the most famous examples. Beckford focused on building the folly as quickly as possible, and, _____ the building was structurally unsound and collapsed in 1825.

Which choice completes the text with the most logical transition?

(A) in contrast,

(B) however,

(C) for example,

(D) as a result,

25 ⚑ Mark for Review

June and Jennifer Gibbons were identical twins born in 1963 who utilized a form of cryptophasia, or twin language, and only communicated with each other. The twins spent years isolated together and created elaborate scenarios with toys and dolls. _____ the twins wrote fictional novels using these scenarios.

Which choice completes the text with the most logical transition?

(A) Nevertheless,

(B) However,

(C) Fortunately,

(D) In addition,

26 ⚑ Mark for Review

Artist Emeka Ogboh creates soundscapes of city life in Nigeria. He uses real recordings of typical city events and activities, such as taxis and crowds at bus stops, and sets up the recordings in museums and art galleries. _____ interested parties are able to visit these locations and use headphones to enjoy an immersive artistic experience.

Which choice completes the text with the most logical transition?

(A) Similarly,

(B) Consequently,

(C) Still,

(D) Regardless,

CONTINUE ➔

27 ☐ Mark for Review

While researching a topic, a student has taken the following notes:

- Preening is a type of behavior that birds engage in to maintain their feathers.
- Feathers are important for flight, insulation, and waterproofing.
- Birds spend time each day preening.
- When preening, birds gather preen oil from a special gland and spread the oil through their feathers.
- Preening can also have secondary functions, such as courtship displays.

The student wants to emphasize the importance of preening. Which choice most effectively uses relevant information from the notes to accomplish this goal?

(A) Birds preen to maintain their feathers, which are important for flight, insulation, and waterproofing.

(B) Preening can have primary and secondary functions.

(C) Preen oil is used by birds to help maintain their feathers.

(D) Birds spend time preening each day and sometimes use the behavior in courtship displays.

CONTINUE

PSAT Prep Test 1—Reading and Writing
Module 2—Harder

Turn to Section 1 of your answer sheet to answer the questions in this section.

---

1 ☐ Mark for Review

According to the opinion of many historians, the 1911 Triangle Shirtwaist Factory fire in the Greenwich Village garment district was _____. For months leading up the incident, workers had been formally complaining to their supervisors about various fire hazards and other unsafe working conditions in the building.

Which choice completes the text with the most logical and precise word or phrase?

(A) disastrous

(B) preventable

(C) routine

(D) dreadful

---

2 ☐ Mark for Review

While many psychosocial phenomena are obvious and even commonsensical, others are _____. For example, the *bystander effect* predicts that the likelihood that one will receive assistance in an emergency is inversely proportional to the number of individuals present at the scene. The larger the crowd, the less personal responsibility each crowd member feels toward the individual or individuals in need.

Which choice completes the text with the most logical and precise word or phrase?

(A) counterintuitive

(B) predictable

(C) unfortunate

(D) falsifiable

CONTINUE ➡

3 ☐ Mark for Review

Richard III is one of the most _____ figures in the history of the British monarchy. Many scholars condemn him as a ruthless villain who usurped the throne for his own self-aggrandizement. Others argue vehemently that he was a noble and selfless character who was tragically misunderstood.

Which choice completes the text with the most logical and precise word or phrase?

(A) polarizing

(B) unifying

(C) wicked

(D) slandered

4 ☐ Mark for Review

Many scholars surmise that Shakespeare had an _____ motive for creating the irreproachable character of Banquo for *The Tragedie of Macbeth*. King James I, who had recently ascended the throne when Shakespeare wrote the play, traced his own ancestry back to the literary Banquo's historical counterpart, and the scholars suggest that Shakespeare thought the inclusion of the character might curry favor with the new king.

Which choice completes the text with the most logical and precise word or phrase?

(A) unimpeachable

(B) unpredictable

(C) artistic

(D) ulterior

CONTINUE

5 ☐ Mark for Review

Historically dismissed as tall tales and the braggadocio of inebriated sailors, gargantuan freak waves known as "rogue waves" were, at least prior to the twentieth century, generally thought to be nonexistent. Modern science then conceded that waves as high as multistory buildings were theoretically possible, but statistically unlikely. Today, oceanographers now believe that as many as ten of these _____ waves could be forming somewhere in the world at any given time.

Which choice completes the text with the most logical and precise word or phrase?

- (A) phantasmic
- (B) colossal
- (C) mythical
- (D) ubiquitous

6 ☐ Mark for Review

Impossible colors are hues that humans are unable to perceive through standard visual observation. Most instances of impossible colors are merely the fabrication of imaginative wordsmiths. For instance, fantasy author Terry Pratchett created the color "octarine," which could only be observed by magicians and cats in his *Discworld* universe. Nevertheless, a certain phenomenon can produce impossible colors in the mind's eye. By concentrating on a single color until some of the eye's cone cells become fatigued and then looking at a significantly dissimilar pigment, an individual can potentially "see" a color irreplicable by the eye under any normal circumstances.

Which choice best describes the function of the underlined sentence in the overall structure of the text?

- (A) It describes a critical oversight in the process used by Pratchett in his novels.
- (B) It demonstrates the imaginative nature of works by Pratchett and other fantasy authors.
- (C) It details the process by which one could observe something that is not typically observable.
- (D) It pinpoints a conflict between fiction and reality that remains unresolved in the scientific community.

CONTINUE →

7 ☐ Mark for Review

Stanley Milgram shocked the world in 1963 when he published the results of his infamous obedience experiments. His ingenious methodology supposedly revealed that human beings will administer potentially lethal shocks (the shocks were actually fake) when instructed to do so by an authority figure. Closer scrutiny, however, compels the conclusion that the accolades for Milgram's work were perhaps too hastily given. It is now evident based on a series of more modern obedience studies that no controlled laboratory environment can precisely recreate real-life conditions or utilize participants who perfectly represent the larger population.

Which choice best describes the function of the fourth sentence in the overall structure of the text?

Ⓐ It provides additional support for the ingenuity of Milgram's work.

Ⓑ It offers context for a dissenting opinion given by the author.

Ⓒ It challenges the credentials of those who still espouse the validity of Milgram's work.

Ⓓ It is the conclusion that the author is attempting to verify through his or her own experimentation.

8 ☐ Mark for Review

When George Washington, the first President of the United States, had his portrait painted by Gilbert Stuart, he initiated a tradition that has persisted to the present. Many of the portraits of iconic presidents, such as Abraham Lincoln and John F. Kennedy, hang on the walls of the White House. Barack Obama, the country's 43rd President, made history as the first African American President, and many considered it only fitting that his portrait was done by African American artist, Kehinde Wiley.

Which choice best states the main purpose of the text?

Ⓐ To contrast historical figures with contemporary political leaders

Ⓑ To show how American presidents have always been supportive of the arts

Ⓒ To juxtapose a long-standing tradition with a groundbreaking development

Ⓓ To explain how an important representation of a nation's leaders originated

CONTINUE ➡

9 ☐ Mark for Review

The following text is from Richard Lovelace's 1649 poem "To Lucasta, Going to the Wars."

> Tell me not (Sweet) I am unkind,
> That from the nunnery
> Of thy chaste breast and quiet mind
> To war and arms I fly.
>
> True, a new mistress now I chase,
> The first foe in the field;
> And with a stronger faith embrace
> A sword, a horse, a shield.
>
> Yet this inconstancy is such
> As you too shall adore;
> I could not love thee (Dear) so much,
> Lov'd I not Honour more.

What is the main idea of the text?

- (A) The speaker no longer loves Lucasta, so he is leaving for the wars.

- (B) The speaker cannot go to war because honor requires that he stay with Lucasta.

- (C) The speaker indicates that he has a duty of greater importance than that of his love for Lucasta.

- (D) The speaker is leaving Lucasta for a woman who supports his military ambitions.

10 ☐ Mark for Review

Established in 1949, Wuxi opera has its roots in Chinese folk songs, but it has evolved into a full operatic genre with string, wind, and percussion instruments to accompany the human voice. Wuxi opera has many of the hallmarks of traditional opera, with long narrative songs and an emphasis on costume and musical performance. However, Chinese experts in Wuxi maintain that a defining feature that separates Wuxi opera from other operatic forms is Huang Tune, a kind of melody with powerful emotions and cheerful rhythms.

Which finding, if true, would most directly support the Chinese experts' argument?

- (A) A series of modern operas stated to be Wuxi operas by their composers each have a Huang Tune within their sheet music.

- (B) A number of Wuxi operas include instrumental accompaniment and narrative songs but do not include Huang tune.

- (C) Most operas, regardless of region of the world, utilize some form of Huang Tune in their composition.

- (D) Most Wuxi operas were not recorded when originally composed and therefore are difficult to examine.

CONTINUE ➡

11 ☐ Mark for Review

Approximate Miles of Highway, in Thousands,
in the United States Over a 20-year Period

Year	Rural interstate	Rural local	Urban interstate	Urban local
0	11.5	7	37.5	32.1
5	12	7.7	38	31.8
10	13.4	8.1	37.4	30.9
15	13.4	8.7	37.7	30.2
20	15.9	10	31.3	29.4

Over a 20-year period, the approximate total length, in miles, of rural highways within the United States generally increased, while the approximate total length, in miles, of urban highways within the United States generally decreased. Interestingly, total urban interstate highway length has decreased more sharply than its local counterpart, which can be seen by examining the changes in _____

Which choice most effectively uses data from the table to complete the statement?

Ⓐ urban interstate and urban local highway mileage from year 0 to year 5.

Ⓑ urban interstate and urban local highway mileage from year 15 to year 20.

Ⓒ rural interstate and rural local highway mileage from year 10 to year 15.

Ⓓ rural interstate and urban interstate highway mileage from year 15 to year 20.

12 ☐ Mark for Review

A team of scientists studying Eurasian jays, members of the corvid family of birds, recently conducted a series of experiments meant to assess the jays' self-control when it comes to food. The jays were each offered mealworms, their favorite food, as well as bread and cheese. The bread and cheese were made immediately available to the jays for consumption, while the jays could see the mealworms but had to wait a period of time before the mealworms were released to them. Because all of the jays in the experiment were willing to wait for the mealworm, the scientists concluded that the Eurasian jays were able to exhibit self-control for a better outcome, which is considered a sign of intelligence in animal biology.

Which finding, if true, would most directly weaken the scientists' conclusion?

Ⓐ The process used in the scientists' study for examining the Eurasian jays is found to be less effective when used to examine other types of animals.

Ⓑ Most bird species prefer mealworms, but they will consume bread and cheese when mealworms are unavailable or difficult to find.

Ⓒ Another bird species is noted as preferring mealworms, bread, and cheese equally in a similar experiment.

Ⓓ A study is released that the aroma in bread and cheese is offensive to Eurasian Jays, unlike that of mealworms.

CONTINUE ➡

13 ☐ Mark for Review

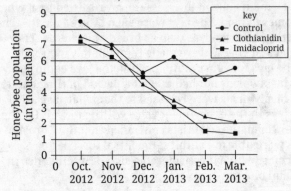

Total Population of Honeybees in Test and Control Colonies, October 2012 to March 2013

In 2007, beekeepers across the globe were shocked when they lost over 30% of the bees in their colonies to colony collapse disorder, or CCD. Five years later, a group of researchers thought they found the culprit: neonicotinoids. They hypothesized that chemicals in this new pesticide caused bees to avoid hibernation, explaining why CCD occurred in the winter. The researchers set up three different apiaries: two experimental groups, one sprayed with Imidacloprid and one with Clothianidin, both of which are neonicotinoids, and a control group, free of neonicotinoids. The data appeared to confirm their hypothesis: bees exposed to neonicotinoids were more vulnerable to CCD, as evidenced by the lower final populations of the two experimental colonies as compared to the control group.

Which choice best describes data from the graph that supports the researchers' conclusion?

(A) The population of the control group declined at roughly the same rate as did those of the experimental group from October 2012 through November 2012.

(B) Neither of the experimental groups experienced a population increase in December 2012.

(C) The rates of CCD for the control group did not consistently follow the pattern for temperature from October 2012 to March 2013.

(D) From December 2012 to January 2013, the population of the experimental groups decreased while the population of the control group mostly increased.

14 ☐ Mark for Review

Some ethicists question whether criminal laws governing "attempts" are reasonable or morally sound. Typically, an attempt to commit a crime is punished less harshly than the successful commission of that same crime. So, connecting with a punch during an altercation may get you jail time, but losing your balance and falling to the ground while intending to deliver a punch during an altercation might not even get you into court. This raises the question: _____

Which choice most logically completes the text?

(A) why should someone avoid consequences merely for lack of physical contact?

(B) why should someone's bad intentions be relevant when the harm that the individual causes is what really matters?

(C) why should someone serve jail time for a simple punch in the nose when more serious crimes occur every day?

(D) why should someone be rewarded by the system for being a skilled fighter?

CONTINUE ➡

15 ☐ Mark for Review

Psychological research studies have consistently shown that early environmental factors, such as parental influence and peer relationships, have a profound effect on a child's developing personality. However, research also suggests that genetics plays a significant role in personality formation as well. So, the question that ought to be considered is _____

Which choice most logically completes the text?

(A) whether early environment or genetics is the sole determining factor regarding personality development.

(B) whether certain personality traits can be created through genetic engineering.

(C) whether genetics or early environmental factors play the greater role in personality development.

(D) whether parental influence or early peer relationships have the greater effect on personality development.

16 ☐ Mark for Review

Victoria Chang is a poet and author from the US who attended the University of Michigan, Harvard University, and Stanford University. Her books of poems have earned many accolades, and one of her books was recognized by *TIME* Magazine and even named one of Electric _____ of 2021.

Which choice completes the text so that it conforms to the conventions of Standard English?

(A) Literature's Favorite Nonfiction Book's

(B) Literatures Favorite Nonfiction Books

(C) Literature's Favorite Nonfiction Books

(D) Literatures Favorite Nonfiction Book's

17 ☐ Mark for Review

Ghost words are words that are accidentally published in an official reference text without any previous intentional _____ they can become widespread as more people use them in everyday language.

Which choice completes the text so that it conforms to the conventions of Standard English?

(A) use,

(B) use

(C) use, yet

(D) use yet

CONTINUE

Elizabeth Woody is a Native American poet who has served in numerous roles in her _____ as a teacher, she taught creative writing for high school and college students, and as an artist, she learned basket weaving and served on multiple multi-disciplinary art committees.

Which choice completes the text so that it conforms to the conventions of Standard English?

(A) field,

(B) field:

(C) field

(D) field and

Scientists have shown that some families are more likely to experience conditions such as kidney failure and diabetes due to mutations in their genetic codes. Armed with this information, _____

Which choice completes the text so that it conforms to the conventions of Standard English?

(A) the disorders of patients within a single family and unrelated patients at risk of developing the same disorders could be treated.

(B) the treatment of both patients within a single family and the treatment of unrelated patients at risk of developing the same disorders could be completed.

(C) scientists could treat both patients within a single family and unrelated patients at risk of developing the same disorders.

(D) scientists' treatments could be applied to both patients within a single family and unrelated patients at risk of developing the same disorders.

CONTINUE

20 ☐ Mark for Review

When Chinese American architect I. M. Pei was hired to renovate the Louvre, an art museum in Paris, France, his proposed design included a large glass and steel pyramid in the courtyard of the museum. Initially, critics and the public reacted negatively. In response, Pei placed a full-size model in the courtyard, which thousands of people visited. By the time the pyramid was built and opened, public opinion _____

Which choice completes the text so that it conforms to the conventions of Standard English?

(A) changed.

(B) had changed.

(C) will change.

(D) changes.

21 ☐ Mark for Review

A chief of the Shawnee people, Tecumseh fought against American expansion onto Native American lands. Tecumseh helped unite Native Americans from many different tribes, including the Shawnee, from the central Ohio River _____ from the shores of Lake Michigan; and the Kickapoo, from Oklahoma.

Which choice completes the text so that it conforms to the conventions of Standard English?

(A) Valley; the Potawatomi,

(B) Valley, the Potawatomi,

(C) Valley, the Potawatomi;

(D) Valley the Potawatomi,

22 ☐ Mark for Review

Rachel Carson was an American marine biologist who wrote numerous respected works, including *Silent Spring*, to promote conservation efforts. Carson's publishers were concerned about being faced with harsh _____ some of her ideas could be interpreted as libel since they contradicted many accepted scientific claims.

Which choice completes the text so that it conforms to the conventions of Standard English?

(A) criticism, however,

(B) criticism. However,

(C) criticism however

(D) criticism, however;

CONTINUE

23 ☐ Mark for Review

Spirit is a Mars rover that launched in 2004 and became inactive in 2010. It used panoramic color imaging technology developed by James F. Bell III. Bell used images from the Mars rover to create a book called *Postcards from Mars*. _____ the general public was able to become more familiar with the work being performed by the rover.

Which choice completes the text with the most logical transition?

Ⓐ As a consequence,

Ⓑ Despite this,

Ⓒ Additionally,

Ⓓ Otherwise,

24 ☐ Mark for Review

Some plants show visible responses to physical contact, such as *Mimosa pudica*, or the sensitive plant. Scientists hypothesize that this reaction is to protect the plant from danger, as the plant can shield its most sensitive areas from a predator or atmospheric threat and reopen to gather sunlight when it is safe to do so. _____ the plant has adapted to respond to its environment when something makes contact with it.

Which choice completes the text with the most logical transition?

Ⓐ In other words,

Ⓑ Moreover,

Ⓒ Also,

Ⓓ Overall,

25 ☐ Mark for Review

While researching a topic, a student has taken the following notes:

- In social mammals, researchers have found a connection between sociality and survival.
- Researchers studied female white-faced capuchin monkeys' social behavior.
- They observed three different behaviors to understand the social relationships.
- The researchers looked at grooming, joining in conflicts, and foraging proximity.
- Female capuchins who groomed and foraged near other females had better survival rates.
- Interactions with male capuchins did not have a positive impact on female survival rates.

The student wants to highlight the difference between female capuchins' relationships with other females and with males. Which choice most effectively uses relevant information from the notes to accomplish this goal?

Ⓐ Female white-faced capuchin monkeys' social behavior is connected to their survival.

Ⓑ Researchers observed three different behaviors—including grooming, joining in conflicts, and foraging proximity—to understand the females' social relationships.

Ⓒ Grooming, joining in conflicts, and foraging proximity with males did not have a positive impact on female survival.

Ⓓ Female capuchins' relationships with other females had a positive impact on their survival, while their relationships with males did not.

CONTINUE ➡

26 🔖 Mark for Review

While researching a topic, a student has taken the following notes:

- The National Oceanic and Atmospheric Administration (NOAA) is a scientific and regulatory agency within the US federal government.
- To track and forecast tropical cyclones, the NOAA gathers data using satellites, buoys, and reconnaissance aircraft.
- Data is entered into the Hurricane Weather Research and Forecasting (HWRF) computer simulation.
- The HWRF produces hurricane forecasts every six hours.
- Computer simulations use mathematical models to analyze data and make predictions about future events.

The student wants to make a generalization about the approach taken by the NOAA to an audience familiar with the HWRF. Which choice most effectively uses relevant information from the notes to accomplish this goal?

(A) The NOAA uses satellites, buoys, and reconnaissance aircraft to gather data for the HWRF.

(B) The Hurricane Weather Research and Forecasting (HWRF) model, which produces hurricane forecasts every six hours, uses computers to analyze data and make predictions about future events.

(C) The HWRF is just one example of a computer simulation: mathematical models used to analyze data and make predictions about future events.

(D) The National Oceanic and Atmospheric Administration (NOAA), a scientific and regulatory agency within the US federal government, tracks and forecasts tropical cyclones by gathering data using satellites, buoys, and reconnaissance aircraft.

27 🔖 Mark for Review

While researching a topic, a student has taken the following notes:

- A study by researchers at the University of Maryland showed that forest fires are getting worse.
- Forest fires recently burned an area almost twice as large as the area burned by forest fires twenty years ago.
- A likely explanation for the increase in forest fires is climate change.
- Climate change and forest fires create a feedback loop.
- In this feedback loop, climate change leads to more frequent heat waves that dry out the land, creating ideal conditions for larger forest fires.
- The forest fires lead to more carbon emissions, which fuel climate change and lead to drier environments.

The student wants to detail the sequence of the climate change and forest fire feedback loop. Which choice most effectively uses relevant information from the notes to accomplish this goal?

(A) Increased forest fires are likely caused by climate change.

(B) Forest fires are getting worse and burning an area twice as large as they burned twenty years ago.

(C) Climate change leads to dry land, which leads to larger forest fires, which leads to more carbon emissions, which leads to more climate change.

(D) Climate change leads to dry land, and forest fires lead to more carbon emissions.

PSAT Prep Test 1—Math
Module 1

Turn to Section 2 of your answer sheet to answer the questions in this section.

DIRECTIONS

The questions in this section address a number of important math skills.
Use of a calculator is permitted for all questions.

NOTES

Unless otherwise indicated:

- All variables and expressions represent real l numbers.
- Figures provided are drawn to scale.
- All figures lie in a plane.
- The domain of a given function f is the set of all real numbers x for which $f(x)$ is a real number.

REFERENCE

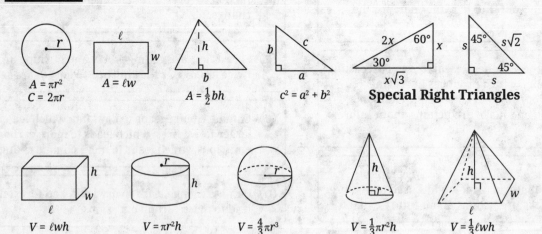

$A = \pi r^2$
$C = 2\pi r$

$A = \ell w$

$A = \frac{1}{2}bh$

$c^2 = a^2 + b^2$

Special Right Triangles

$V = \ell wh$

$V = \pi r^2 h$

$V = \frac{4}{3}\pi r^3$

$V = \frac{1}{3}\pi r^2 h$

$V = \frac{1}{3}\ell wh$

The number of degrees of arc in a circle is 360.
The number of radians of arc in a circle is 2π.
The sum of the measures in degrees of the angles of a triangle is 180.

CONTINUE

‒ ‒

INSTRUCTIONS FOR PRINT TESTS

For multiple-choice questions, solve each problem, choose the correct answer from the choices provided, and then circle your answer in this book. Circle only one answer for each question. If you change your mind, completely erase the circle. You will not get credit for questions with more than one answer circled, or for questions with no answers circled.

For student-produced response directions, solve each problem and write your answer next to or under the question in the test book as described below.

- Once you've written your answer, circle it clearly. You will not receive credit for anything written outside the circle, or for any questions with more than one circled answer.
- If you find **more than one correct answer**, write and circle only one answer.
- You answer can be up to 5 characters for a **positive** answer and up to 6 characters (including the negative sign) for a **negative** answer, but no more.
- If your answer is a **fraction** that is too long (over 5 characters for positive, 6 characters for negative), write the decimal equivalent.
- If your answer is a **decimal** that is too long (over 5 characters for positive, 6 characters for negative), truncate it or round at the fourth digit.
- If your answer is a **mixed number** (such as $3\frac{1}{2}$), write it as an improper fraction (7/2) or its decimal equivalent (3.5).
- Don't enter **symbols** such as a percent sign, comma, or dollar sign in your circled answer

CONTINUE ➔

1 ☐ Mark for Review

When the equation $y = 2x - b$, where b is a constant, is graphed in the xy-plane, the line passes through the point $(3, -1)$. What is the value of b?

Ⓐ −5

Ⓑ −3

Ⓒ 1

Ⓓ 7

2 ☐ Mark for Review

If $-2 \le f \le 3$ and $-5 \le g \le 2$, what is the maximum value of fg?

Ⓐ −15

Ⓑ −4

Ⓒ 6

Ⓓ 10

3 ☐ Mark for Review

Player	A	B	C	D	E	F	G	H	I
Points	5	5	5	17	12	23	3	18	20

The table above shows the number of points scored by each player in a professional basketball game. What is the mean number of points scored by the players in the game?

4 ☐ Mark for Review

$$5\left(\frac{y}{2} + 5\right) = 2y + \frac{1}{2}y + 25$$

Which of the following describes the solution to the equation shown above?

Ⓐ The only solution is $y = 1\frac{1}{2}$.

Ⓑ The only solution is $y = 10$.

Ⓒ The equation has infinitely many solutions.

Ⓓ The equation has no solutions.

CONTINUE ➤

5 ⬚ Mark for Review

Triangles QRS and XYZ are similar right triangles, where $R > Q > S$ and $Y > X > Z$. If the measure of angle X is $63°$, what is the measure of angle S?

Ⓐ 27°

Ⓑ 63°

Ⓒ 90°

Ⓓ 153°

6 ⬚ Mark for Review

A field of soybeans measuring 4.6 square kilometers is being harvested. If the farm workers can harvest 23 hectares per day, how many days will it take to harvest the entire field? (100 hectares = 1 square kilometer).

Ⓐ 5

Ⓑ 20

Ⓒ 100

Ⓓ 500

7 ⬚ Mark for Review

Month	Balance
0	$1,400
1	$1,344
2	$1,290
3	$1,239
4	$1,189
5	$1,142

The table above shows the balance, in dollars, of a bank account. Which of the following best describes the model that fits the data?

Ⓐ Exponential, decreasing by approximately 4% per month

Ⓑ Exponential, decreasing by approximately 8% per month

Ⓒ Linear, decreasing by approximately $47 per month

Ⓓ Linear, decreasing by approximately $56 per month

CONTINUE ➤

8 Mark for Review

$$5x - 3y = 7$$
$$2x + y = 5$$

If (x, y) is the solution to the system of equations above, what is the value of y?

10 Mark for Review

The function h is defined by $h(x) = 9 - |x - 3|$. If $h(n) = -3$, what is the positive value of n?

9 Mark for Review

High School Students' Summer Plans

	Sophomores	Juniors	Total
Travel	15	25	40
Summer job	17	13	30
Relax	33	21	54
Sports	13	9	22
Volunteer	11	14	25
Other	16	13	29
Total	105	95	200

A high school that has a total of 1,200 students surveyed a representative sample of 200 of its students about their summer travel plans. Based on the data in the table above, what is the predicted number of juniors in the entire school who would indicate travel as their summer plans?

(A) 25

(B) 150

(C) 240

(D) 316

11 Mark for Review

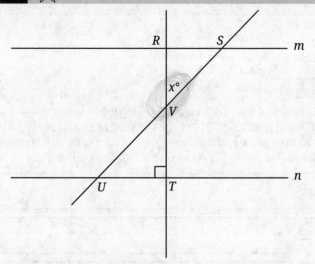

In the figure above, lines m and n cross the lines containing segments $\overline{RT}$ and $\overline{SU}$ such that angle RSV is congruent to angle TUV. If angle UTV is a right angle, and angle TUV measures 65°, what is the value of x?

65

CONTINUE

12 ☐ Mark for Review

$$3x + 2y = 4$$
$$y = \frac{2}{3}x - 2$$

The two equations in the system of equations above each form a line when graphed in the xy-plane. Which of the following statements is true regarding these two lines?

(A) The lines intersect at (3, 2).

(B) The lines are the same line.

(C) The lines are parallel.

(D) The lines are perpendicular.

13 ☐ Mark for Review

Function f, where $y = f(x)$, is graphed in the xy-plane. The graph of the function contains the points (0, 3) and (5, 96). Which of the following could define f?

(A) $f(x) = \frac{1}{2}(3)^x$

(B) $f(x) = 3(2)^x$

(C) $f(x) = 3(3)^x$

(D) $f(x) = 8(2)^x$

14 ☐ Mark for Review

A high school class is selling barrels of popcorn to raise money. The histogram below shows the number of students who sold each quantity of barrels.

Barrels of Popcorn Sold

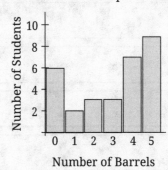

Which of the following is true?

I. The mode number of barrels sold is equal to the median number of barrels sold.

II. The median number of barrels sold is equal to the mean number of barrels sold.

III. The mode number of barrels sold is equal to the range of the number of barrels sold.

(A) I only

(B) III only

(C) I and II only

(D) II and III only

CONTINUE

15 📖 Mark for Review

$$S = 5(bc + 1) - 9$$

In the equation above, which of the following is equivalent to bc?

(A) $\dfrac{S-4}{5}$

(B) $S - 4$

(C) $\dfrac{S+4}{5}$

(D) $\dfrac{S+14}{5}$

16 🔖 Mark for Review

If the equation $y = x^2 - 10x - 75$ is graphed in the xy-plane, what is the y-coordinate of the parabola's vertex?

(A) -100

(B) 0

(C) 5

(D) 100

17 🔖 Mark for Review

$$10x - 62 = 9y$$
$$\frac{1}{4}x = y$$

The equations of two lines are shown above. If the lines are graphed in the xy-plane, they intersect at the point (a, b). What is the value of b?

2.65

18 🔖 Mark for Review

$$\left(a^{\frac{1}{3}}b^{\frac{1}{4}}\right)^3 \left(a^{\frac{1}{3}}b^{\frac{1}{4}}\right)^4 = a^{\frac{k}{3}}b^{\frac{k}{4}}$$

If the equation above, where k is a constant, is true for all positive values of a and b, what is the value of k?

(A) 3

(B) 4

(C) 7

(D) 10

CONTINUE

19 ☐ Mark for Review

$$(3 - y)^2 - (3 + y)$$

Which of the following is an equivalent form of the expression above?

Ⓐ $3 - y$

Ⓑ $y^2 - 7y + 6$

Ⓒ $(3 - y)(2 - y)$

Ⓓ $9 - y^2$

20 ☐ Mark for Review

Function f is defined by $f(x) = 3x$. In the xy-plane, the graph of $y = f(x)$ is parallel to the graph of linear function $y = g(x)$. If $g(0) = 5$ and $g(2) = r$, what is the value of r?

21 ☐ Mark for Review

In a certain marathon, 45 percent of the runners were men, and the rest were women. The official timekeeper determined that 62 percent of the men and 66 percent of the women completed the marathon in under four hours. What percent of the runners who completed the marathon in under four hours were women? (Disregard the percent sign when entering your answer.)

36.3

22 ☐ Mark for Review

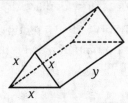

The total surface area of the triangular prism shown above can be calculated using the following formula, where x is the length of the sides of the triangular ends and y is the length of the rectangular faces.

$$SA = 2\left(\frac{\sqrt{3}}{4}x^2\right) + 3xy$$

What must the expression $\frac{\sqrt{3}}{2}x^2$ represent?

Ⓐ The area of one triangular end

Ⓑ The area of one rectangular face and one triangular end

Ⓒ The sum of the areas of the rectangular faces

Ⓓ The sum of the areas of the triangular ends

CONTINUE ➡

PSAT Prep Test 1—Math
Module 2—Easier

Turn to Section 2 of your answer sheet to answer the questions in this section.

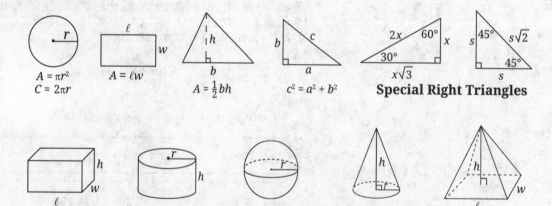
CONTINUE

INSTRUCTIONS FOR PRINT TESTS

For multiple-choice questions, solve each problem, choose the correct answer from the choices provided, and then circle your answer in this book. Circle only one answer for each question. If you change your mind, completely erase the circle. You will not get credit for questions with more than one answer circled, or for questions with no answers circled.

For student-produced response directions, solve each problem and write your answer next to or under the question in the test book as described below.

- Once you've written your answer, circle it clearly. You will not receive credit for anything written outside the circle, or for any questions with more than one circled answer.
- If you find **more than one correct answer**, write and circle only one answer.
- You answer can be up to 5 characters for a **positive** answer and up to 6 characters (including the negative sign) for a **negative** answer, but no more.
- If your answer is a **fraction** that is too long (over 5 characters for positive, 6 characters for negative), write the decimal equivalent.
- If your answer is a **decimal** that is too long (over 5 characters for positive, 6 characters for negative), truncate it or round at the fourth digit.
- If your answer is a **mixed number** (such as $3\frac{1}{2}$), write it as an improper fraction (7/2) or its decimal equivalent (3.5).
- Don't enter **symbols** such as a percent sign, comma, or dollar sign in your circled answer

CONTINUE ▶

1 ☐ Mark for Review

If a certain value is 130, what is 20% of that value?

Ⓐ 26

Ⓑ 65

Ⓒ 104

Ⓓ 110

2 ☐ Mark for Review

$$c + d = 66$$

If $c = 20$ in the given equation, what is the value of d?

3 ☐ Mark for Review

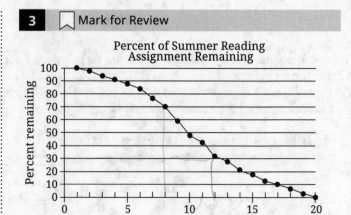

The graph above shows the percent a student had remaining to read for his summer reading assignment each day during the 20 days it took to complete the assignment. On which day had the student completed 30% of the assignment?

Ⓐ Day 3

Ⓑ Day 7

Ⓒ Day 8

Ⓓ Day 12

CONTINUE

4 ☐ Mark for Review

Which of the following is an equivalent form of the expression $30y - 12cy$?

Ⓐ $(5 - 2c)y$

Ⓑ $18(c - 2y)$

Ⓒ $18cy^2$

Ⓓ $(30 - 12c)y$

5 ☐ Mark for Review

A small glass tube used in a scientific lab can hold no more than 8.50 milliliters of liquid needed for a certain experiment. Approximately how many teaspoons can the beaker hold? (1 teaspoon ≈ 4.93 milliliters)

Ⓐ 1.72

Ⓑ 3.57

Ⓒ 6.78

Ⓓ 41.91

6 ☐ Mark for Review

$$4s + 2t = 7$$
$$3s - 2t = -14$$

In the system of equations above, what is the value of s?

| 1 |

$\frac{7s}{7} = \frac{7}{7}$

$s = 1$

- -

7 ☐ Mark for Review

A square has an area of 100 square inches. What is the length of one side of the square, in inches?

(A) 10

(B) 25

(C) 50

(D) 100

8 ☐ Mark for Review

Sydney borrowed money from a friend and is paying back the loan. The remaining amount she owes, A, can be calculated by the equation $A = 870 - 30w$, where w represents the number of weeks since she took the loan. What does the number 870 represent?

(A) The total amount of money Sydney has repaid

(B) The amount of money Sydney repays each week

(C) The number of weeks Sydney has been paying back the loan

(D) The original amount that Sydney borrowed

9 ☐ Mark for Review

Which of the following are the solutions to the equation $3x^2 - 48 = 0$?

(A) −16 and 16

(B) $-\sqrt{48}$ and $\sqrt{48}$

(C) −4 and 4

(D) $-\dfrac{\sqrt{48}}{3}$ and $\dfrac{\sqrt{48}}{3}$

CONTINUE →

10 Mark for Review

$$6(2y + z) = 12y + 18$$

In the equation above, z is a constant. For what value of z does the equation have an infinite number of solutions?

3

11 Mark for Review

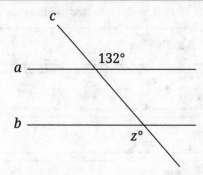

Note: Figure not drawn to scale.

What is the value of z in the figure shown above if line a is parallel to line b?

(A) 48

(B) 66

(C) 132

(D) 264

CONTINUE

12 ☐ Mark for Review

If $w > 3$, then which of the following must be true?

(A) $-w < -3$

(B) $-w > -3$

(C) $w = 4$

(D) w is an integer

13 ☐ Mark for Review

A doctor's office is hiring a medical billing company to type invoices for the patients at the practice. The company charges a one-time fee of $125 plus $80 per invoice typed. Which of the following represents the amount, in dollars, the doctor's office will be charged if the company types 5 invoices each day for y days?

(A) $80y + 125$

(B) $80(5)y + 125$

(C) $80y + 125(5)$

(D) $125(5)y + 80$

14 ☐ Mark for Review

$$P = 2,500 + 135x$$

The population of County Y, <u>in thousands</u>, can be modeled by the above equation, in which x represents the number of years since the 2010 census. What does the number 135 represent in this equation?

(A) Every year the population of County Y increases by 135 people.

(B) Every 135 years that passes, the population of County Y increases by 2,500 people.

(C) Every 135 years that passes, the population of County Y increases by 250,000 people.

(D) Every year the population of County Y increases by 135,000 people.

CONTINUE ➡

15 ☐ Mark for Review

The human population, in billions of people, for the world for the years 1960 through 2010 can be modeled by the function $P(y) = 3.039(1.017)^y$, where y represents the number of years since 1960. According to this model, the human population in 1974 was how many times the human population in 1972?

Ⓐ 1.017

Ⓑ $(1.017)^2$

Ⓒ 3.039(1.017)

Ⓓ $3.039(1.017)^2$

16 ☐ Mark for Review

$$g(x) = 2x^2$$

Function g is defined above. If $g(x) = 288$, what is the positive value of x?

Ⓐ 2

Ⓑ 12

Ⓒ 72

Ⓓ 144

17 ☐ Mark for Review

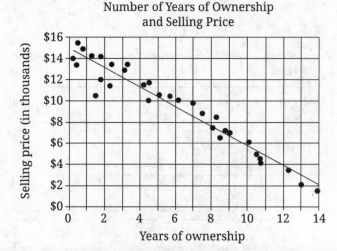

Number of Years of Ownership
and Selling Price

For 32 cars that were identical when new, the scatterplot above shows the number of years of ownership and the selling price when the first owner sold the car. The line of best fit is also shown. For the car that was sold after exactly 7 years of ownership, the actual selling price of the car was approximately how much more than the selling price predicted by the line of best fit?

Ⓐ $650

Ⓑ $1,250

Ⓒ $2,150

Ⓓ $3,350

CONTINUE

18 ◫ Mark for Review

$$t = r$$
$$t = 1.8r - 6$$

The system of equations above has a solution (r, t). What is the value of r?

Ⓐ 4.8

Ⓑ 6.0

Ⓒ 7.5

Ⓓ 10.8

19 ◫ Mark for Review

A certain box has a width that is 2 inches more than its length and a height that is 5 inches less than its length. If each of the two smallest faces of the box has an area of 36 square inches, what is the volume of the box, in cubic inches?

20 ◫ Mark for Review

$$y = x - 6$$
$$y = -x^2 + 7x - 14$$

Which of the following gives all the solutions (x, y) that satisfy the system of equations above?

Ⓐ There is no solution to this system of equations.

Ⓑ $(4, -2)$

Ⓒ $(4, -2)$ and $(2, -4)$

Ⓓ $(4, 2)$ and $(2, -4)$

CONTINUE ➤

21 ☐ Mark for Review

$$p^2 = 3 + q$$
$$3 = p + q$$

A system consisting of a linear equation and a quadratic equation is shown above. If $(p, q) = (x, y)$ is a solution to the system, which of the following could be the value of x?

Ⓐ −3

Ⓑ −2

Ⓒ 0

Ⓓ 3

22 ☐ Mark for Review

If $f(x) = x^k$ for some constant k, and $2f(x) = f(16x)$ for all positive values of x, what is the value of k?

Ⓐ $\frac{1}{8}$

Ⓑ $\frac{1}{4}$

Ⓒ 4

Ⓓ 8

CONTINUE

PSAT Prep Test 1—Math
Module 2—Harder

Turn to Section 2 of your answer sheet to answer the questions in this section.

DIRECTIONS

The questions in this section address a number of important math skills.
Use of a calculator is permitted for all questions.

NOTES

Unless otherwise indicated:

- All variables and expressions represent real l numbers.
- Figures provided are drawn to scale.
- All figures lie in a plane.
- The domain of a given function f is the set of all real numbers x for which $f(x)$ is a real number.

REFERENCE

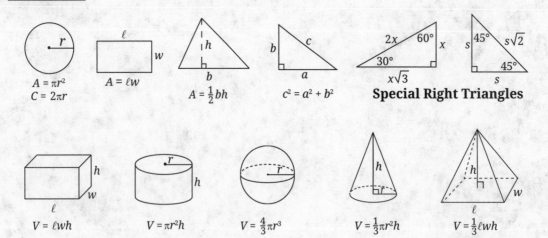

$A = \pi r^2$
$C = 2\pi r$

$A = \ell w$

$A = \frac{1}{2}bh$

$c^2 = a^2 + b^2$

Special Right Triangles

$V = \ell wh$

$V = \pi r^2 h$

$V = \frac{4}{3}\pi r^3$

$V = \frac{1}{3}\pi r^2 h$

$V = \frac{1}{3}\ell wh$

The number of degrees of arc in a circle is 360.
The number of radians of arc in a circle is 2π.
The sum of the measures in degrees of the angles of a triangle is 180.

CONTINUE

INSTRUCTIONS FOR PRINT TESTS

For multiple-choice questions, solve each problem, choose the correct answer from the choices provided, and then circle your answer in this book. Circle only one answer for each question. If you change your mind, completely erase the circle. You will not get credit for questions with more than one answer circled, or for questions with no answers circled.

For student-produced response directions, solve each problem and write your answer next to or under the question in the test book as described below.

- Once you've written your answer, circle it clearly. You will not receive credit for anything written outside the circle, or for any questions with more than one circled answer.
- If you find **more than one correct answer**, write and circle only one answer.
- You answer can be up to 5 characters for a **positive** answer and up to 6 characters (including the negative sign) for a **negative** answer, but no more.
- If your answer is a **fraction** that is too long (over 5 characters for positive, 6 characters for negative), write the decimal equivalent.
- If your answer is a **decimal** that is too long (over 5 characters for positive, 6 characters for negative), truncate it or round at the fourth digit.
- If your answer is a **mixed number** (such as $3\frac{1}{2}$), write it as an improper fraction (7/2) or its decimal equivalent (3.5).
- Don't enter **symbols** such as a percent sign, comma, or dollar sign in your circled answer

CONTINUE ➡

1 ☐ Mark for Review

$$y < \frac{1}{4}(3y - 2)$$

Which of the following values of y would make the above inequality true?

(A) -3

(B) -2

(C) 0

(D) 3

2 ☐ Mark for Review

$$5a^2 - (-3a^2)$$

Which of the following is equivalent to the expression above?

(A) $-15a^2$

(B) $2a^2$

(C) $8a^2$

(D) $8a^4$

3 ☐ Mark for Review

What is the result when 70 is increased by 20%?

(A) 56

(B) 72

(C) 84

(D) 90

4 ☐ Mark for Review

$$9y + 8 = 8 + ky - 5y$$

In the equation above, k is a constant. If the equation has infinitely many solutions, what is the value of k?

CONTINUE

5 ☐ Mark for Review

Right triangle LMN has a right angle at N. If the value of $\cos(L)$ is $\frac{\sqrt{21}}{5}$, what is the value of $\sin(M)$?

Ⓐ $\frac{\sqrt{21}}{21}$

Ⓑ $\frac{5\sqrt{21}}{21}$

Ⓒ $\frac{\sqrt{21}}{5}$

Ⓓ $\sqrt{21}$

6 ☐ Mark for Review

A theater sells student tickets to a play for $24 and regular admission tickets for $36. If the theater sells out the 100-seat theater for opening night and has total ticket sales of $3,144, how many of the tickets sold were student tickets?

☐

7 ☐ Mark for Review

A shoe store is having a sale in which a customer receives a 30 percent discount on a second pair of shoes after purchasing the first at regular price. The tax rate of 6 percent is applied to the whole purchase. If s represents the regular price of each pair of shoes at the store, which of the following expressions gives the total amount that a customer would pay for two pairs during this sale?

Ⓐ $1.7s + 0.06$

Ⓑ $1.06(s - 0.3s)$

Ⓒ $1.06s + 0.7s$

Ⓓ $1.06(s + 0.7s)$

8 ☐ Mark for Review

$$\frac{1}{\dfrac{1}{2y} - \dfrac{1}{y + 3}}$$

For all $y > 3$, which of the following is equivalent to the expression above?

Ⓐ $3 - y$

Ⓑ $\dfrac{2y^2 + 6y}{3 - y}$

Ⓒ $\dfrac{3 - y}{2y^2 + 6y}$

Ⓓ $2y^2 + 6y$

CONTINUE

9 ☐ Mark for Review

At a souvenir shop, the cost of 5 hats and 9 magnets is $72.00, and the cost of 2 hats and 1 magnet is $14.50. If the hats all cost the same price and the magnets all cost the same price, how much does 1 magnet cost?

(A) $3.22

(B) $4.50

(C) $5.50

(D) $5.78

10 ☐ Mark for Review

The function $V(m) = 52(0.91)^{0.5m}$ models the number of cases of a virus in a small country m months after the initial outbreak in January. What is the approximate value of x if, according to the function, the disease cases are predicted to decrease by $x\%$ every 60 days? (Assume 1 month has 30 days.)

(A) 9.0

(B) 9.1

(C) 9.5

(D) 47.3

11 ☐ Mark for Review

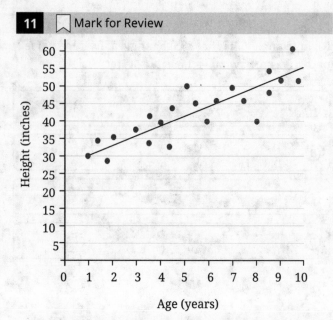

A pediatrician's office collects data on the heights of all its patients. The scatterplot above shows the heights of the male patients seen by the office at various ages less than 10 years. A linear model best describes the data, and the line of best fit is shown. For the patient who is exactly 8 years old, which of the following best estimates the percent increase from his actual height to the height that the model predicts?

(A) 20%

(B) 25%

(C) 75%

(D) 80%

CONTINUE

12 Mark for Review

$$SA = 4\pi r^2$$

The formula for the surface area (SA) of a sphere with radius r is shown above. If the radius of sphere A is 3 times the radius of sphere B, how many times larger is the surface area of sphere A than the surface area of sphere B?

Ⓐ 3

Ⓑ 9

Ⓒ 27

Ⓓ 36

13 Mark for Review

The graph of function f in the xy-plane, where $y = f(x)$, is a parabola. If the graph of function f intersects the x-axis at $(k, 0)$ and $(3, 0)$, and the vertex of f is at $(5, -3)$, what is the value of k?

Ⓐ 1

Ⓑ 5

Ⓒ 7

Ⓓ 9

14 Mark for Review

In the xy-plane above, the graph of $f(x)$ is shown. Which of the following could be the graph of $f(x-4) + 2$?

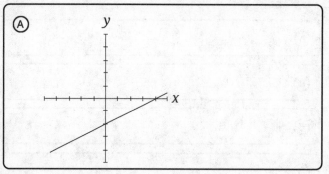

Ⓐ

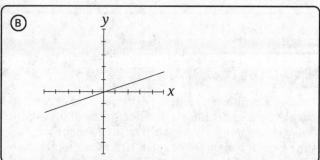

Ⓑ

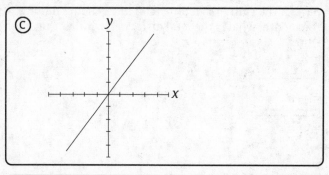

Ⓒ

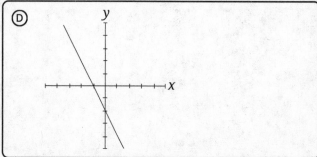

Ⓓ

CONTINUE

15 ☐ Mark for Review

If the equation $5x^2 + bx + 125 = 0$ has no real solutions, which of the following could be the value of constant b?

Ⓐ -50

Ⓑ 25

Ⓒ 50

Ⓓ 130

16 ☐ Mark for Review

During a month of practice, a distance runner ran at a pace of 5 miles per hour at the beginning of the month before increasing her pace to 6 miles per hour for the rest of the month. She spent 70% of her total time jogging at the slower pace, and the rest at the faster pace. If the runner ran for a total of 120 hours during the month, what is the total distance, in miles, that she ran?

☐‾‾‾

17 ☐ Mark for Review

If the function h is defined by $h(x) = 2x^2 - 7x - 3$, what is $h(x + 3)$?

Ⓐ $h(x + 3) = 2x^2 - 7x$

Ⓑ $h(x + 3) = 2x^2 - 7x - 6$

Ⓒ $h(x + 3) = 2x^2 + 5x - 6$

Ⓓ $h(x + 3) = 2x^2 - 23x + 15$

18 ☐ Mark for Review

The function q is defined by $q(x) = 4x^3 - bx^2 + 14x + 12$, where b is a constant. In the xy-plane, the graph of q contains the points $(-\frac{1}{2}, 0)$, $(2, 0)$, and $(n, 0)$. What is the value of b?

☐‾‾‾

CONTINUE ➡

19 ☐ Mark for Review

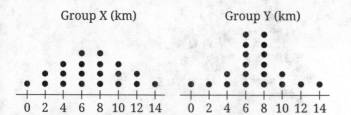

Group X (km)   Group Y (km)

The dot plots above represent two fitness groups at a local gym and the kilometers run by the 20 athletes participating in each group during one week. Which of the following statements correctly compares the means and standard deviations of the two groups?

Ⓐ The mean number of kilometers run by each athlete in group X is less than the mean of group Y, and the standard deviation of the number of kilometers run by each athlete in group X is greater than the standard deviation of group Y.

Ⓑ The mean number of kilometers run by each athlete in group X is more than the mean of group Y, and the standard deviation of the number of kilometers run by each athlete in group X is less than the standard deviation of group Y.

Ⓒ The mean number of kilometers run by each athlete in group X is equal to the mean of group Y, and the standard deviation of the number of kilometers run by each athlete in group X is equal to the standard deviation of group Y.

Ⓓ The mean number of kilometers run by each athlete in group X is equal to the mean of group Y, and the standard deviation of the number of kilometers run by each athlete in group X is greater than the standard deviation of group Y.

20 ☐ Mark for Review

$$kx = -9y + 2$$
$$40x + 8 = 36y - 44x$$

The given system of equations, in which k is a constant, has infinitely many solutions. What is the value of k?

Ⓐ −21

Ⓑ −10

Ⓒ 1

Ⓓ 84

CONTINUE ➡

21 ☐ Mark for Review

At a certain car wash, the first three detailing services cost $60 each, and a discounted amount is charged for each additional detailing service. During one visit, a customer purchased 9 total detailing services and was charged a total of $360. If s is the number of detailing services purchased during one visit, and $s > 2$, which function f gives the total cost, in dollars, of one visit?

Ⓐ $f(s) = 30s + 90$

Ⓑ $f(s) = 30s + 180$

Ⓒ $f(s) = 40s$

Ⓓ $f(s) = 60s$

22 ☐ Mark for Review

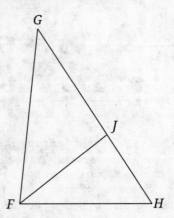

In the figure above, the ratio $\frac{FJ}{FH}$ has the same value as the ratio $\frac{FG}{GH}$. Which of the following angle measures must be congruent?

Ⓐ Angle FGH and angle FHJ

Ⓑ Angle FJG and angle FJH

Ⓒ Angle GFJ and angle HFJ

Ⓓ Angle GFH and angle FJH

STOP
If you finish before time is called, you may check your work on this section only.
Do not turn to any other section.

YOUR NAME: _____
(Print)   Last   First   M.I.

SIGNATURE: _____ DATE: ___ / ___ / ___

HOME ADDRESS: _____
(Print)   Number and Street

_____
                City   State   Zip Code

PHONE NO.: _____
(Print)

DATE OF BIRTH: ___ / ___ / ___
(Print)   Month / Day / Year

Section 1: Module 1
Reading and Writing

1. Ⓐ Ⓑ Ⓒ Ⓓ
2. Ⓐ Ⓑ Ⓒ Ⓓ
3. Ⓐ Ⓑ Ⓒ Ⓓ
4. Ⓐ Ⓑ Ⓒ Ⓓ
5. Ⓐ Ⓑ Ⓒ Ⓓ
6. Ⓐ Ⓑ Ⓒ Ⓓ
7. Ⓐ Ⓑ Ⓒ Ⓓ
8. Ⓐ Ⓑ Ⓒ Ⓓ
9. Ⓐ Ⓑ Ⓒ Ⓓ
10. Ⓐ Ⓑ Ⓒ Ⓓ
11. Ⓐ Ⓑ Ⓒ Ⓓ
12. Ⓐ Ⓑ Ⓒ Ⓓ
13. Ⓐ Ⓑ Ⓒ Ⓓ
14. Ⓐ Ⓑ Ⓒ Ⓓ
15. Ⓐ Ⓑ Ⓒ Ⓓ
16. Ⓐ Ⓑ Ⓒ Ⓓ
17. Ⓐ Ⓑ Ⓒ Ⓓ
18. Ⓐ Ⓑ Ⓒ Ⓓ
19. Ⓐ Ⓑ Ⓒ Ⓓ
20. Ⓐ Ⓑ Ⓒ Ⓓ
21. Ⓐ Ⓑ Ⓒ Ⓓ
22. Ⓐ Ⓑ Ⓒ Ⓓ
23. Ⓐ Ⓑ Ⓒ Ⓓ
24. Ⓐ Ⓑ Ⓒ Ⓓ
25. Ⓐ Ⓑ Ⓒ Ⓓ
26. Ⓐ Ⓑ Ⓒ Ⓓ
27. Ⓐ Ⓑ Ⓒ Ⓓ

Section 1: Module 2 (Easier)
Reading and Writing

1. Ⓐ Ⓑ Ⓒ Ⓓ
2. Ⓐ Ⓑ Ⓒ Ⓓ
3. Ⓐ Ⓑ Ⓒ Ⓓ
4. Ⓐ Ⓑ Ⓒ Ⓓ
5. Ⓐ Ⓑ Ⓒ Ⓓ
6. Ⓐ Ⓑ Ⓒ Ⓓ
7. Ⓐ Ⓑ Ⓒ Ⓓ
8. Ⓐ Ⓑ Ⓒ Ⓓ
9. Ⓐ Ⓑ Ⓒ Ⓓ
10. Ⓐ Ⓑ Ⓒ Ⓓ
11. Ⓐ Ⓑ Ⓒ Ⓓ
12. Ⓐ Ⓑ Ⓒ Ⓓ
13. Ⓐ Ⓑ Ⓒ Ⓓ
14. Ⓐ Ⓑ Ⓒ Ⓓ
15. Ⓐ Ⓑ Ⓒ Ⓓ
16. Ⓐ Ⓑ Ⓒ Ⓓ
17. Ⓐ Ⓑ Ⓒ Ⓓ
18. Ⓐ Ⓑ Ⓒ Ⓓ
19. Ⓐ Ⓑ Ⓒ Ⓓ
20. Ⓐ Ⓑ Ⓒ Ⓓ
21. Ⓐ Ⓑ Ⓒ Ⓓ
22. Ⓐ Ⓑ Ⓒ Ⓓ
23. Ⓐ Ⓑ Ⓒ Ⓓ
24. Ⓐ Ⓑ Ⓒ Ⓓ
25. Ⓐ Ⓑ Ⓒ Ⓓ
26. Ⓐ Ⓑ Ⓒ Ⓓ
27. Ⓐ Ⓑ Ⓒ Ⓓ

Section 1: Module 2 (Harder)
Reading and Writing

1. Ⓐ Ⓑ Ⓒ Ⓓ
2. Ⓐ Ⓑ Ⓒ Ⓓ
3. Ⓐ Ⓑ Ⓒ Ⓓ
4. Ⓐ Ⓑ Ⓒ Ⓓ
5. Ⓐ Ⓑ Ⓒ Ⓓ
6. Ⓐ Ⓑ Ⓒ Ⓓ
7. Ⓐ Ⓑ Ⓒ Ⓓ
8. Ⓐ Ⓑ Ⓒ Ⓓ
9. Ⓐ Ⓑ Ⓒ Ⓓ
10. Ⓐ Ⓑ Ⓒ Ⓓ
11. Ⓐ Ⓑ Ⓒ Ⓓ
12. Ⓐ Ⓑ Ⓒ Ⓓ
13. Ⓐ Ⓑ Ⓒ Ⓓ
14. Ⓐ Ⓑ Ⓒ Ⓓ
15. Ⓐ Ⓑ Ⓒ Ⓓ
16. Ⓐ Ⓑ Ⓒ Ⓓ
17. Ⓐ Ⓑ Ⓒ Ⓓ
18. Ⓐ Ⓑ Ⓒ Ⓓ
19. Ⓐ Ⓑ Ⓒ Ⓓ
20. Ⓐ Ⓑ Ⓒ Ⓓ
21. Ⓐ Ⓑ Ⓒ Ⓓ
22. Ⓐ Ⓑ Ⓒ Ⓓ
23. Ⓐ Ⓑ Ⓒ Ⓓ
24. Ⓐ Ⓑ Ⓒ Ⓓ
25. Ⓐ Ⓑ Ⓒ Ⓓ
26. Ⓐ Ⓑ Ⓒ Ⓓ
27. Ⓐ Ⓑ Ⓒ Ⓓ

YOUR NAME: _____
(Print)   Last   First   M.I.

SIGNATURE: _____   DATE: ___/___/___

HOME ADDRESS: _____
(Print)   Number and Street

_____
City   State   Zip Code

PHONE NO.: _____
(Print)

DATE OF BIRTH: ____/____/____
(Print)   Month / Day / Year

Section 2: Module 1 Math

1. A B C D
2. A B C D
3. _____
4. A B C D
5. A B C D
6. A B C D
7. A B C D
8. _____
9. A B C D
10. _____
11. _____
12. A B C D
13. A B C D
14. A B C D
15. A B C D
16. A B C D
17. _____
18. A B C D
19. A B C D
20. _____
21. _____
22. A B C D

Section 2: Module 2 (Easier) Math

1. A B C D
2. _____
3. A B C D
4. A B C D
5. A B C D
6. _____
7. A B C D
8. A B C D
9. A B C D
10. _____
11. A B C D
12. A B C D
13. A B C D
14. A B C D
15. A B C D
16. A B C D
17. A B C D
18. A B C D
19. _____
20. A B C D
21. A B C D
22. A B C D

Section 2: Module 2 (Harder) Math

1. A B C D
2. A B C D
3. A B C D
4. _____
5. A B C D
6. _____
7. A B C D
8. A B C D
9. A B C D
10. A B C D
11. A B C D
12. A B C D
13. A B C D
14. A B C D
15. A B C D
16. _____
17. A B C D
18. _____
19. A B C D
20. A B C D
21. A B C D
22. A B C D

Chapter 5
Practice Test 1:
Answers and
Explanations

PRACTICE TEST 1 ANSWER KEY

Reading and Writing		
Module 1	**Module 2 (Easier)**	**Module 2 (Harder)**
1. C	1. B	1. B
2. A	2. D	2. A
3. B	3. A	3. A
4. C	4. A	4. D
5. D	5. D	5. B
6. D	6. C	6. C
7. B	7. A	7. B
8. D	8. B	8. C
9. A	9. B	9. C
10. B	10. B	10. A
11. B	11. C	11. B
12. D	12. A	12. D
13. A	13. D	13. D
14. C	14. C	14. A
15. B	15. C	15. C
16. D	16. C	16. C
17. D	17. A	17. C
18. D	18. B	18. B
19. A	19. B	19. C
20. B	20. D	20. B
21. B	21. D	21. A
22. B	22. D	22. D
23. A	23. A	23. A
24. C	24. D	24. A
25. B	25. D	25. D
26. A	26. B	26. C
27. A	27. A	27. C

Math		
Module 1	**Module 2 (Easier)**	**Module 2 (Harder)**
1. D	1. A	1. A
2. D	2. 46	2. C
3. 12	3. C	3. C
4. C	4. D	4. 14
5. A	5. A	5. C
6. B	6. −1	6. 38
7. A	7. A	7. D
8. 1	8. D	8. B
9. B	9. C	9. C
10. 15	10. 3	10. A
11. 25	11. C	11. B
12. D	12. A	12. B
13. B	13. B	13. C
14. B	14. D	14. A
15. C	15. B	15. B
16. A	16. B	16. 636
17. 2	17. B	17. C
18. C	18. C	18. 18
19. C	19. 396	19. D
20. 11	20. C	20. A
21. 56.54	21. A	21. A
22. D	22. B	22. D

PRACTICE TEST 1—READING AND WRITING EXPLANATIONS

Module 1

1. **C** This is a Vocabulary question, so follow the basic approach. Highlight that Fuster's work *has been widely acclaimed*. A good word for the annotation box based off this would be "praised." Eliminate (A) because *criticized* is the opposite of "praised." Eliminate (B) because the text does not support that Fuster was *surprised* by anything the foundation did. Keep (C) because *recognized* is a good synonym for "praised." Eliminate (D) because "worshiped" is too extreme a version of "praised" in this context. The correct answer is (C).

2. **A** This is a Vocabulary question, so follow the basic approach. Highlight that *Mosquito is a multifaceted artist* and his performances *blend art, politics, and entertainment*. A good word for the annotation box based off this would be "varied" or "versatile." Keep (A) because *diverse* is a good match for "varied." Eliminate (B) because *costly* is a Could Be True trap answer: large-scale art installations may be expensive in real life, but the text offers no data for how expensive Mosquito's art is to produce. Eliminate (C) because the text doesn't support that Mosquito's work is meant to be *humorous*, or funny. Eliminate (D) because the text does not state that Mosquito's performances are *brief*, or short. The correct answer is (A).

3. **B** This is a Vocabulary question, so follow the basic approach. Treat *smeared* as if it were a blank and highlight that Mr. Tooter Williams *wore a straw hat with a blue ribbon, an expression of serene content, and a glass amethyst on his third finger*. A good word for the annotation box based off this would be that fortune has "blessed" him with prosperity. Eliminate (A) because it is the opposite tone of "blessed." Keep (B) because *gifted* is a good synonym for "blessed." Eliminate (C) because *assaulted* is the opposite tone of "blessed." Eliminate (D) because *criticized* is the opposite tone of "blessed." The correct answer is (B).

4. **C** This is a Vocabulary question, so follow the basic approach. Highlight that Deer Cloud seems to value *peace and cross-cultural understanding* and that her group has a *mission of hospitality*. A good word for the annotation box based off this would be "inspire." Eliminate (A) because it is too harsh of a tone when compared to "inspire." Eliminate (B) because *fabricate* means "to create with deceitful intent," which is also the opposite of the positive tone of "inspire." Keep (C) because *instill* is a good synonym for "inspire." Eliminate (D) because it is never implied by the text that Deer Cloud is conceding, or giving up, something to achieve her goal. The correct answer is (C).

5. **D** This is a Vocabulary question, so follow the basic approach. Highlight that proponents of the proposal are focusing on *the benefits of the metric system*. A good word for the annotation box based off this would be that metrification would "benefit" or "improve" the competitiveness of American products and services. Eliminate (A) because *refute*, or disprove, is the opposite tone of "benefit." Eliminate (B) because *dilute*, or diminish, is also the opposite tone. Eliminate (C) because the text focuses on the proposal to *convert* the *measurement standards*, so *uphold*, or maintain, does not support the idea of changing, or "improving," American competitiveness. Keep (D) because *buttress* means "strengthen," which is a good synonym for "benefit" or "improve." The correct answer is (D).

6. **D**   This is a Purpose question, so follow the basic approach. Highlight the main points that the author makes in the text that all the other parts of the text relate to: *The modern public is probably more familiar with the wives of Henry VIII than with any other queens in history—or at least with the respective pictures that history has painted of them.* Also highlight the shift in tone used by the author at the end of the text: *one might be surprised to learn* certain facts about these women that are *contrary to their traditional depictions.* In the annotation box, write that the purpose of the text is to "talk about Henry VIII's wives and mention some surprising facts." Eliminate (A) because it is the right answer to the wrong question—it focuses only on the content of the last sentence of the text and ignores all the time the text spent on the traditional depictions of the wives. Eliminate (B) because it is too extreme—while the author notes in the final sentence that a few of Henry VIII's wives possessed traits not associated with their traditional depictions, he does not *deny that all of Henry VIII's wives* possess their traditionally associated character traits. Eliminate (C) because the author does not *criticize* anyone, nor does the author claim anyone views the wives of Henry VIII *solely in terms of their usefulness to Henry*—that part of the answer is extreme. Keep (D) because it is consistent with the annotation. The correct answer is (D).

7. **B**   This is a Dual Texts question, so follow the basic approach. Highlight the *view* referenced in Text 1: *Some scientists caution that…sudden environmental events in a specific region can have global implications.* Highlight what Damany-Pearce and her team in Text 2 say about the same idea or viewpoint: they were *able to establish a causal connection between the ignition of the wildfires and the subsequent rise in mean lower stratosphere temperature.* Write in the annotation box that the two texts "agree—Text 2 provides example of Text 1." Eliminate (A) because *only* is extreme: Text 2 never states that *only* wildfires can affect global temperature. Keep (B) because it is consistent with the annotation. Eliminate (C) because it is Half-Right: Damany-Pearce and her team *have discovered corroborating evidence,* so that would not make the view *dubious,* or doubtful. Eliminate (D) because it is also Half-Right: the theory is indeed appealing, but it is *not* contradictory to what Damany-Pearce and her team found. The correct answer is (B).

8. **D**   This is a Retrieval question, so follow the basic approach. Highlight exactly what the text says about the narrator's uncle: *He was a mean, stooping, narrow-shouldered, clay-faced creature* and *He was long unshaved, but what most distressed and even daunted me* was that *he would neither take his eyes away from me nor look me fairly in the face.* Eliminate (A) because *jovially,* or joyfully, is the opposite of how the uncle is described. Eliminate (B) because it is a Could Be True trap answer: it is logical to assume that someone dressed as the uncle may be *surprised* and *ill-prepared* for a visit, but the text does not state either of these things about the uncle. Eliminate (C) because *pride* is a positive emotion which is the opposite of what the narrator feels. Keep (D) because it is consistent with *what most distressed and even daunted me.* The correct answer is (D).

9. **A**   This is a Claims question, so follow the basic approach. Highlight the researchers' hypothesis: *A team of researchers has posited that, while the influence of DAT on neurodevelopmental disorders such as autism, remains unknown, the therapy is likely beneficial for non-neurodevelopmental disorders, such as anxiety disorder.* The correct answer will be most consistent with this claim. Keep (A) as it shows DAT being beneficial to those with anxiety disorder, which is consistent with the claim. Eliminate (B) as the claim does not address what DAT should or should not do for those with autism; it states

that DAT's influence on autism *remains unknown*. Eliminate (C) because this would weaken the claim by showing that the anxiety levels of those with anxiety disorder would fluctuate and not decrease. Similarly, eliminate (D) because the first half of the answer shows anxiety levels in those with anxiety disorder increasing after DAT, which is the opposite of what the claim says should happen. The correct answer is (A).

10. **B** This is a Charts question, so follow the basic approach. Highlight the claim in the text: *It concluded that, even with the volatility in the market, so long as coffee producers could increase their revenues, their efforts would remain profitable.* Next, read the title, key, variables, and units of the figure. Lastly, head right to the answers and use POE. Eliminate (A) because neither *costs* nor *revenues* increased *every* year from 2008 to 2011. Keep (B) because it shows a positive correlation between revenues and operating profits, just as the claim does. Eliminate (C) because, while it is consistent with the graph, the claim relates only to revenues and operating profits, not *costs*. Eliminate (D) because it's the right answer to the wrong question: it is consistent with the graph, but the claim only mentions the link between *revenues* and *operating profits,* not *costs* and *operating profits.* The correct answer is (B).

11. **B** This is a Claims question, so follow the basic approach. Highlight Carson's claim: she *claimed that Edge's work was instrumental in facilitating her own ornithological research.* The correct answer will be most consistent with this claim. Eliminate (A) because even if Carson and Edge studied some of the same species, there is no explanation of how *Edge's work* on those species was *instrumental in facilitating* Carson's own research. Keep (B) because this shows a direct link between Edge's work and Carson's research. Eliminate (C) because it makes no mention of Carson and how Carson may have benefited from Edge's *knowledge.* Eliminate (D) because it makes no mention of Carson and how Carson may have benefited from Edge's *acclaim.* The correct answer is (B).

12. **D** This is a Claims question, so follow the basic approach. Highlight the claim: *a lady named Marianne experiences unpleasant sights and sounds while having a nightmare.* The correct answer will be most consistent with this claim. Eliminate (A) as it is Half-Right: while unpleasant sights are mentioned (*ghastly-visaged clouds*), no sounds are referenced in these lines. Eliminate (B) as it is also Half-Right: *two dread mountains* are an unpleasant sight, but no sound is referenced in these lines either. Eliminate (C) because while several sights are described, none of them are described as unpleasant, and as with choices (A) and (B), no sounds are mentioned. It would be outside knowledge to assume that the *quivering* referenced in these lines produced a sound. Keep (D) as it mentions *a weight of fear* from the sight of the *Anchor* and *the sound as of a dim low clanging.* The correct answer is (D).

13. **A** This is a Conclusions question, so follow the basic approach. Read the text and highlight the main idea: *The door-in-the-face technique involves initially making an outrageous or unappealing offer, which the other person is likely to refuse, then following up with a more reasonable one.* The concluding sentence to the text must be consistent with this main idea. Keep (A) because the second amount requested is comparatively much smaller than the first. Eliminate (B) because the first request of 3% cannot be considered *outrageous* when compared to 2%. Eliminate (C) because, according to the door-in-the-face technique in the text, the more *outrageous* amount should be asked for first. Eliminate (D) because the two amounts are the same and therefore neither one would be considered *outrageous* compared to the other. The correct answer is (A).

14. **C**   This is a Conclusions question, so follow the basic approach. Read the text and highlight the main idea: *plesiosaurs are believed to have been cold-blooded, and a cold-blooded animal could never survive in the frigid waters of Loch Ness*. Any concluding sentence to the text must be consistent with this main idea. Eliminate (A) because, regardless of whether plesiosaurs were cold-blooded, it would be extreme to say there are *no* undiscovered aquatic animals in Loch Ness. Eliminate (B) for the same reason: the text makes no claim regarding the connection between plesiosaurs and any other aquatic animals. Keep (C) because it is consistent with the claim: the text states that a cold-blooded animal could never survive in Loch Ness, so if plesiosaurs did indeed turn out to be cold-blooded, there would not be any plesiosaurs in Loch Ness today. Eliminate (D) for the same reason as (A) and (B): the status of plesiosaur blood does not allow any claims to be made about any other undiscovered animals in Loch Ness. The correct answer is (C).

15. **B**   In this Rules question, pronouns and apostrophes are changing in the answer choices, so it's testing consistency with pronouns. Find and highlight the word that the pronoun refers back to: *people*. This word is plural, so in order to be consistent, a plural pronoun is needed. Eliminate (C) and (D) because *it* is singular. Next, consider whether a contraction or a possessive pronoun is needed. The sentence refers to the *personalities* of the *people*, so the blank should be possessive. Eliminate (A) as it means "they are." The correct answer is (B).

16. **D**   In this Rules question, punctuation is changing in the answer choices. Some answers contain STOP or HALF-STOP punctuation, so use the Vertical Line Test. Write the words *artists* and *to* on scratch paper with a vertical line in between. The first part of the sentence, *Her theater company strives to provide opportunities for First Nations artists*, is a complete idea, so mark it with a C. The second part of the sentence, *to share their experiences and promote their traditions*, is an incomplete idea, so mark it with an I. In this case, either GO or HALF-STOP punctuation can be used, which is what appears in all four answers. Next, consider whether there is a reason to slow down or separate the ideas. The second part of the sentence is telling what the opportunities are for, so it shouldn't be separated from the first part of the sentence with punctuation. No punctuation is needed here. Eliminate (A), (B), and (C). The correct answer is (D).

17. **D**   In this Rules question, verbs are changing in the answer choices, so it's testing consistency with verbs. All of the answers are consistent with the subject, *she*, so consider tense. Find and highlight any clues in the sentence that would provide an indication of what tense is needed. Highlight the phrase *By 2020* at the beginning of the sentence. Since 2020 is in the past, eliminate (A) and (B). Eliminate (C) because it is also present tense and is not consistent with the phrase *By 2020*. Keep (D) because it is in past tense and correctly implies that this is something that had happened by 2020. The correct answer is (D).

18. **D**   In this Rules question, punctuation is changing in the answer choices. One answer contains STOP punctuation, so use the Vertical Line Test. Write the words *II* and *his* on scratch paper with a vertical line in between. The first part of the sentence, *Charles Drew was a blood transfusion medical researcher and surgeon during World War II*, is a complete idea, so mark it with a C. The second part of the sentence, *his work developed the first blood banks and saved the lives of thousands of Allied soldiers*, is also a complete idea, so mark it with a C. Therefore, STOP or HALF-STOP punctuation is needed. Eliminate (A), (B), and (C) because they are all GO punctuation. The correct answer is (D).

19. **A** In this Rules question, punctuation is changing in the answer choices. Note that only commas are changing, and they are moving around the phrase *developed by Percy Bridgman*, suggesting unnecessary versus necessary information. Try removing the phrase from the sentence: *Modern researchers have improved upon the initial method to make the lab-growing process more efficient.* This works, so the phrase is unnecessary and needs punctuation both before and after. Eliminate (B), (C), and (D) because they lack the two needed commas. The correct answer is (A).

20. **B** In this Rules question, verbs are changing in the answer choices, so it's testing consistency with verbs. Find and highlight the subject for the verb: *Crescent City*. This subject is singular, as it is *one of his most famous operas*, so a singular verb is needed in order to be consistent. Eliminate (A), (C), and (D) as they are all plural. The correct answer is (B).

21. **B** In this Rules question, pronouns are changing in the answer choices, so it's testing consistency with pronouns. Find and highlight the word or phrase that the pronoun refers back to: *the treated eye*. The word *eye* is singular, so in order to be consistent, a singular pronoun is needed. Eliminate (C) and (D) because they are both plural. While (A) is singular, *one* should only be used if it's referring to a single item out of a group, and there's no group. Eliminate (A). The correct answer is (B).

22. **B** This is a transition question, so follow the basic approach. Highlight ideas that relate to each other. The first part of the sentence says *In states with Daylight Saving Time, donations to charities were reduced by 10%*, and the second part of the sentence says *this reduction was not seen in states that do not observe Daylight Saving Time.* These ideas disagree, so an opposite-direction transition is needed. Eliminate (A) because *in addition* is a same-direction transition. Keep (B) because *however* is an opposite-direction transition. Eliminate (C) because *initially* should only be used if it's followed by what happened after the initial results. Eliminate (D) because *otherwise* is used for an exception, and this part of the sentence does not provide an exception. The correct answer is (B).

23. **A** This is a transition question, so follow the basic approach. Highlight ideas that relate to each other. The previous sentence says *She combines* things *to represent historical events and themes.* This sentence says she *created a sculpture…that reimagined Haitian ruins.* These ideas agree, so a same-direction transition is needed. Eliminate (D) because *however* is an opposite-direction transition. Keep (A) because the second sentence is an example of Báez's art. Eliminate (B) because the previous sentence is a generalization and this sentence is a specific example, whereas *Additionally* should be used for another point that is similar. Eliminate (C) because the second sentence is an example, not a consequence of the previous idea. The correct answer is (A).

24. **C** This is a transition question, so follow the basic approach. Highlight ideas that relate to each other. The previous sentence mentions the *9th century* and the *14th century*, and it explains that there was some kind of decline. This sentence states that *the temple was abandoned*, so this follows the decline and thus agrees with the previous sentence. A same-direction transition is needed, but all of the answers are same-direction transitions, so use POE. Eliminate (A) because the second sentence isn't an example of the first. Eliminate (B) because this sentence isn't adding on to a previous point. Keep (C) because it follows the timeline idea in the sentences. Eliminate (D) because this sentence isn't adding to the previous one. The correct answer is (C).

25. **B** This is a Rhetorical Synthesis question, so follow the basic approach. Highlight the goal(s) stated in the question: *highlight the differences between cirrus and cumulus clouds*. Then, go to POE. Eliminate (A) because it doesn't mention *cumulus clouds*. Keep (B) because it mentions both types of clouds and has contrasting ideas (such as *high* and *low*). Eliminate (C) because it doesn't mention *cirrus* or *cumulus*. Eliminate (D) because it doesn't mention *cirrus clouds*. The correct answer is (B).

26. **A** This is a Rhetorical Synthesis question, so follow the basic approach. Highlight the goal(s) stated in the question: *emphasize how Weddell seal mothers provide a benefit to their seal pups*. Then, go to POE. Keep (A) because it mentions *seal pups*, *mothers' milk*, and a benefit—*dive for long periods*. Eliminate (B) because it doesn't mention *mothers*. Eliminate (C) because it doesn't mention any *benefit*. Eliminate (D) because it doesn't mention *pups* or a *benefit*. The correct answer is (A).

27. **A** This is a Rhetorical Synthesis question, so follow the basic approach. Highlight the goal(s) stated in the question: *introduce the timeframe of Lloma de Betxí to an audience unfamiliar with the location of Paterna*. Then, go to POE. Keep (A) because it mentions specific dates, *Lloma de Betxí*, and a *location*. Eliminate (B) because it doesn't mention *Lloma de Betxí* or a *timeframe*. Eliminate (C) because it doesn't state where *Paterna* is, and the goal stated that the audience is *unfamiliar* with it. Eliminate (D) because it doesn't state a *timeframe*. The correct answer is (A).

Module 2—Easier

1. **B** This is a Vocabulary question, so follow the basic approach. Treat *accidental* as if it were a blank and highlight that the passenger is someone Lady Wallace would see *looking out from her window*, not someone she was necessarily expecting to see. A good word for the annotation box based off this would be "unplanned." Eliminate (A) because it is the right answer to the wrong question: Lady Wallace is joyous regarding her husband, but the passenger's emotions are never described. Keep (B) because *random* is a good synonym for "unplanned." Eliminate (C) and (D) because, as with choice (A), the text never states or implies the passenger's emotion, and it would be outside knowledge to assume that individual is *angry* or *jealous* at Lady Wallace and the love she shares with her husband. The correct answer is (B).

2. **D** This is a Vocabulary question, so follow the basic approach. Highlight that there was a *lack of available texts* when Lawson had been *hoping to learn more about African American artists* at her university, indicating that she expected her university to have such texts and it did not. A good word for the annotation box based off this would be "stunned" or "shocked." Eliminate (A) because it is the opposite tone—the lack of texts was not a positive discovery for Lawson. Eliminate (B) because *unaffected* is the opposite of the passage—Lawson was in fact deeply affected by the lack of available texts. Eliminate (C) because, just as with choice (A), this was not a positive discovery for Lawson. While the lack of available texts did ultimately motivate Lawson to *fill this void herself*, the text does not support that she was initially *encouraged* by the lack of texts. Keep (D) because *surprised* is a good synonym for "stunned." The correct answer is (D).

3. **A** This is a Vocabulary question, so follow the basic approach. Highlight that Mawurndjul *tutored his wife and daughter* and *founded his own school to teach the next generation of Aboriginal artists*. A good word for the annotation box based off this would be "teacher." Keep (A) because *mentor* is a good synonym for "teacher." Eliminate (B) because while it Could Be True, this part of the text is not focusing on Mawurndjul's potential art talents but rather his teaching talents. Eliminate (C) and (D) for the same reason—these answers miss that the passage wants to discuss what Mawurndjul is known for *in addition* to being an artist. The correct answer is (A).

4. **A** This is a Vocabulary question, so follow the basic approach. Highlight that *Henley often described the resilience of the human spirit*. A good word for the annotation box based off this would be "persistence." Keep (A) because *tenacity* is a good synonym for "persistence." Eliminate (B) because the author does not go so far as to say that any of Henley's characters would be *cheerful* when facing death. Eliminate (C) because it's Recycled Language—Henley is a poet, but it's never stated that any of his characters were *artists*. Eliminate (D) because while it's logical that a character may experience *sorrow* when faced with death, it's not consistent with the principal focus of Henley's work, which is *resilience*. The correct answer is (A).

5. **D** This is a Vocabulary question, so follow the basic approach. Highlight that *routine examinations may reveal the presence of fibrosis*. A good word for the annotation box based off this would be "indicated." Eliminate (A) because this is the opposite of the relationship between fibrosis and intrauterine adhesion described by the text—one indicates the other, not *diminishes* the other. Eliminate (B) for the same reason, as *nullified* means "canceled." Eliminate (C) because the text does not go so far as to say fibrosis *alters* adhesion, only that it is an indicator of it. Keep (D) because *typified* means categorized, which is a good synonym for "indicated by." The correct answer is (D).

6. **C** This is a Purpose question, so follow the basic approach. Highlight the main points that the author makes in the text that all the other parts of the text relate to: *researchers* were *trying to determine whether distinct colors might deter birds and prevent casualties*. The underlined sentence states that *collisions with unpainted turbines actually increased*, so the researchers *posited that perhaps the birds were avoiding the painted turbines but moving toward the unpainted turbines*. In the annotation box, write that the purpose of the underlined sentence is to show a "surprising result, researchers made new theory." Eliminate (A) because no *earlier studies* are mentioned in the text. Eliminate (B) because *fundamentally flawed* is too extreme: the central hypothesis of the researchers may have not been completely accurate, but the third sentence indicates that bird fatalities for painted turbines did decrease 72%, so there was some merit to painting the turbines. Keep (C) because it is consistent with the annotation. Eliminate (D) because it is Half-Right: the second half of the answer goes beyond the text as it's never stated whether the researchers overcame the hurdle of increased bird fatalities for the unpainted turbines. The correct answer is (C).

7. **A** This is a Purpose question, so follow the basic approach. Highlight the main points that the author makes in the text that all the other parts of the text relate to: Count Kostia *had the misfortune to lose his wife suddenly* and *to mitigate his grief by the distractions of travel, he left his domains near Moscow, never intending to return*. In the annotation box, write that the purpose of the text is "guy loses wife and moves away." Keep (A) because it's consistent with the annotation—the second-to-last sentence mentions that Count Kostia is *accompanied by his twin children*. Eliminate (B) because it is recycled

language—locations are discussed, but the passage is not trying to *highlight popular travel destinations*. Eliminate (C) because the focus of the text is on Count Kostia and his children, not *cultural enrichment*. Eliminate (D) because the author never states whether the *months* that Count Kostia grieved were too short of a time. The correct answer is (A).

8. **B** This is a Retrieval question, so follow the basic approach. Highlight exactly what the text says about the house of Lionel Dacre: *his house was that small one, it had been there long before the avenue was constructed,* it is described as *stained, mildewed,* and *discoloured,* and *it looked a small house from the street…but it deepened into a single long chamber at the back.* Eliminate (A) because it is extreme: the text does not state the house is *one of the oldest houses in Paris.* Keep (B) because it is consistent with the very last sentence since the house *deepened into a single long chamber at the back* and the sentence uses the word *but* to draw a contrast with its *small* appearance. Eliminate (C) because it is Half-Right: it is not stated whether Lionel Dacre's house has a back yard. Eliminate (D) because it is recycled language: the grey tiles on the home are *stained with lichens,* but no other plants are mentioned, nor is it directly stated that the house is *overgrown* with those lichens. The correct answer is (B).

9. **B** This is a Main Idea question, so follow the basic approach. Highlight the person, place, and/or thing that constitutes the main focus of the text. The main individual focused on in the text is *Andy Goldsworthy,* and the main feature of his art discussed is *rock balancing,* which is noted by Goldsworthy in the third sentence as being *relaxing and meditative.* The correct answer should reference as many of these main ideas as possible. Eliminate (A) because it does not mention Goldsworthy and there is no evidence that rock balancing is a *new art form.* Keep (B) because it is consistent with the highlighting. Eliminate (C) because it is too extreme: it is not stated that *Cairns* is unlike *any other piece* of environmental art. Eliminate (D) because it is recycled language: Goldsworthy *compared his style of work* to *picking potatoes,* but the text never states that *picking vegetables* actually *influences* his or any others *environmental artists'* work. The correct answer is (B).

10. **B** This is a Claims question, so follow the basic approach. Highlight the claim: *Mistress Clorinda defends her feelings towards her chosen partner.* The correct answer will be most consistent with this claim. Eliminate (A) because there is no mention of Mistress Clorinda's *chosen partner.* Keep (B) because by stating *"I love my Lord of Dunstanwolde,"* Mistress Clorinda is identifying him as her partner and expressing romantic feelings for him. Eliminate (C) and (D) because, like (A), they do not reference any *partner* of Mistress Clorinda's. The correct answer is (B).

11. **C** This is a Charts question, so follow the basic approach. Highlight the claim in the text: *this led the researchers to conclude that vitamin B12 may be effective in helping patients with NAFLD.* Next, read the title, key, variables, and units of the figure. Lastly, head right to the answers and use POE. Eliminate (A) because, while it is consistent with the graph, the correct answer should reference the group that took vitamin B12, not the placebo group. Eliminate (B) for the same reason: the correct answer should reference the B12 group, not the placebo group. Keep (C) as it is consistent with the setup of the study and the claim made. Eliminate (D) as it is Half-Right: the weight levels of the placebo group did decrease, but the weight levels of the experimental group *decreased* rather than *increased.* The correct answer is (C).

12. **A** This is a Claims question, so follow the basic approach. Highlight the claim: *Jean-Victor…shares one of his only positive memories from his childhood.* The correct answer will be most consistent with this claim. Keep (A) because *the good Sister at the Asylum* and feeling *her warm little hand upon my forehead* would be consistent with a *positive memory* for Jean-Victor. Eliminate (B) because it is the opposite of the claim: it's a negative memory from Jean Victor's childhood. Eliminate (C) as it is a similarly negative memory. Eliminate (D) because, although it shows Jean-Victor making the most of a dismal food situation, it would be too much of an assumption to call this a positive memory. The correct answer is (A).

13. **D** This is a Charts question, so follow the basic approach. Highlight the claim in the text: *Jennifer Erickson and Joanne Slavin…demonstrated that caloric and sugar levels within a food item should not necessarily be correlated.* Next, read the title, key, variables, and units of the figure. Lastly, head right to the answers and use POE. Eliminate (A) because it only references the calorie count of a plain bagel and a serving of corn flake cereal, whereas a correct answer should reference both caloric and sugar content. Eliminate (B) because a serving of corn flake cereal also has less sugar and fewer calories than a frosted cake doughnut, so this would show a correlation as well. Eliminate (C) as this answer only references calories and would not help show that calories and sugar content are not necessarily correlated. Keep (D) as it shows that a *blueberry muffin has 470 calories,* which is more calories than a frosted cake doughnut has, but *only 16.7 grams of sugar,* which is less than a frosted cake doughnut has. This would show that the two measurements are not necessarily correlated. The correct answer is (D).

14. **C** This is a Conclusions question, so follow the basic approach. Read the text and highlight the main idea: *Godward abhorred the modern art movement* and instead focused on *classical, elegant,* and *ancient* depictions. The concluding sentence to the text must be consistent with this main idea. Eliminate (A) because no mention is made of Picasso's feelings towards Godward. Eliminate (B) because this is recycled language using the words *modernist* and *bright colors* differently from how they were used in the story. Keep (C) because it is consistent with the main idea and the text states that *Godward abhorred the modern art movement of the late nineteenth and twentieth centuries* and he died in 1922, so it is reasonable to conclude that the modern art movement came around towards *the end of his life.* Eliminate (D) because it recycles *neoclassical paintings* and *twentieth century* from the text—no mention of the values of paintings is ever made. The correct answer is (C).

15. **C** This is a Conclusions question, so follow the basic approach. Read the text and highlight the main idea: *Rhode Island has the highest national average student-teacher ratio,* yet standardized test scores in the state *vary wildly* while *the average GPA at Rhode Island high schools is nearly 0.6 higher than the national average.* These phrases suggest a possible correlation between student-teacher ratio and GPA but not between student-teacher ratio and standardized test scores. The concluding sentence to the text must be consistent with these ideas. Eliminate (A) because it is recycled language: no connection between *standardized test scores* and *GPA* is ever suggested by the text. Eliminate (B) because it is the opposite of the passage: it is GPA, not standardized test scores, which may be affected by the low student-teacher ratio. Keep (C) because it is consistent with the main ideas. Eliminate (D) because it is Half-Right: while student-teacher ratio seems to not be a critical factor for higher standardized test scores, it may indeed affect GPA. The passage does not have enough evidence for one to judge what "critical" would mean in this context. The correct answer is (C).

16. **C**   In this Rules question, verb forms are changing in the answer choices, so it's testing sentence structure. Eliminate any answer that does not produce a complete sentence. Choices (A) and (D) contain *–ing* verbs, which in this case produce an incomplete sentence. Eliminate (A) and (D). The verb *to attack* also does not produce a complete sentence, so eliminate (B). With (C), the sentence states that the collection *attacked the stereotypes that certain demographics of people are inferior to others*, which does make the sentence complete. The correct answer is (C).

17. **A**   In this Rules question, periods and question marks are changing in the answer choices, so it's testing questions versus statements. The beginning of the sentence states that *Naci aimed to answer a specific question*, so the second part of the sentence should be a question. Eliminate (B) and (C). To make the statement a question, the first part of the verb (*would exhibit*) should come at the beginning. Eliminate (D). The correct answer is (A).

18. **B**   In this Rules question, verbs are changing in the answer choices, so it's testing consistency with verbs. All of the answers are consistent with the subject, *Heng*, so consider tense. Find and highlight any clues in the sentence that would provide an indication of what tense is needed. Highlight the word *Today* at the beginning of this sentence. This word indicates that present tense is needed, so eliminate (A), (C), and (D), which are not in present tense. The correct answer is (B).

19. **B**   In this Rules question, verb forms are changing in the answer choices, so it's testing sentence structure. Eliminate any answer that does not produce a complete sentence. The sentence already has a main subject and verb—*Kiese Laymon writes*. Therefore, this part of the sentence cannot add in another main verb, since it's not part of a clause beginning with a word such as *that* or *which*. Eliminate (A), (C), and (D) because they would all be main verbs and make the full sentence incomplete. Keep (B) because the "to" form of a verb cannot be the main verb in a sentence, and it clearly indicates Laymon's intentions in his memoir. The correct answer is (B).

20. **D**   In this Rules question, apostrophes with nouns are changing in the answer choices. Start with the first word and consider whether it possesses anything. The paintings belong to Nungurrayi, so eliminate (A) and (C), which don't have an apostrophe on that word. Next, consider whether the second word possesses anything. Nothing belongs to *paintings*; it is plural, not possessive. Eliminate (B) because the painting is possessive in that option. The correct answer is (D).

21. **D**   In this Rules question, punctuation is changing in the answer choices. Some answers contain STOP punctuation, so use the Vertical Line Test. Write the words *Mars* and *revealing* on scratch paper with a vertical line in between. The first part of the sentence, *The Perseverance rover, a robotic vehicle, completed the first ground-penetrating survey using radar on Mars*, is a complete idea, so mark it with a C. The second part of the sentence, *revealing layers of magnetic material and buried structures*, is an incomplete idea, so mark it with an I. In this case, GO punctuation is needed. Eliminate (B) and (C) because they are both STOP. Next, consider whether there is a reason to slow down or separate the ideas. The second part of the sentence is a separate idea from the first, so there is a reason to separate them with a comma. Eliminate (A). The correct answer is (D).

22.   **D**   In this Rules question, verbs are changing in the answer choices, so it's testing consistency with verbs. In this case, the verb is part of a list of two things that Griffin did, the first of which is *She taught*. Highlight the word *taught*, which this verb should be consistent with. Eliminate (A), (B), and (C) because they aren't consistent with *taught*. Keep (D) because *invented* is consistent with *taught*. The correct answer is (D).

23.   **A**   In this Rules question, punctuation and connecting words are changing in the answer choices, so it's testing complete sentences. First try reading the sentence without the word *that*: *Kuo explored fields greatly influenced society…* This does not produce a complete sentence, so eliminate (B) and (C). With the word *that*, the sentence says *Kuo explored fields that greatly influenced society…* which does provide a clear meaning and produces a complete sentence. Consider whether a comma is needed. A phrase beginning with *that* is always necessary and should never be surrounded by commas, so eliminate (D). The correct answer is (A).

24.   **D**   This is a transition question, so follow the basic approach. Highlight ideas that relate to each other. The first part of the sentence says *Beckford focused on building the folly as quickly as possible*, and the second part says *the building was structurally unsound and collapsed*. These ideas agree, so a same-direction transition is needed. Eliminate (A) and (B) because they are opposite-direction transitions. Eliminate (C) because the second part of the sentence is not an example of the first; it is the result of the speed of building. Keep (D) because *as a result* matches this relationship. The correct answer is (D).

25.   **D**   This is a transition question, so follow the basic approach. Highlight ideas that relate to each other. The previous sentence says the twins *created elaborate scenarios with toys and dolls*. This sentence says they *wrote fictional novels using these scenarios*. These ideas agree, so a same-direction transition is needed. Eliminate (A) and (B) because they are both opposite-direction. Eliminate (C) because there is no reason to think the fact that they wrote novels is fortunate. Keep (D) because this sentence is another thing the twins did. The correct answer is (D).

26.   **B**   This is a transition question, so follow the basic approach. Highlight ideas that relate to each other. The previous sentence says that Ogboh *sets up the recordings in museums and art galleries*. This sentence says *interested parties are able to visit these locations* to hear the recordings. These ideas agree, so a same-direction transition is needed. Eliminate (C) and (D) because they are both opposite-direction. Eliminate (A) because the two sentences don't describe two different things that share a similarity. Keep (B) because *Consequently* means "As a result," and it's true that people are able to hear the recordings as a result of them being *in museums and art galleries*. The correct answer is (B).

27.   **A**   This is a Rhetorical Synthesis question, so follow the basic approach. Highlight the goal(s) stated in the question: *emphasize the importance of preening*. Then, go to POE. Keep (A) because it mentions *preen* and several reasons preening is *important*. Eliminate (B) because *primary and secondary functions* doesn't necessarily mean preening is important. Eliminate (C) because it doesn't mention the act of *preening*, nor does it necessarily seem important. Eliminate (D) because it merely states that preening is *sometimes* used *in courtship displays*, which doesn't suggest its *importance*. The correct answer is (A).

Module 2—Harder

1. **B** This is a Vocabulary question, so follow the basic approach. Highlight that *for months… workers had been formally complaining to their supervisors about various hazards.* A good word for the annotation box based off this would be "avoidable." Eliminate (A) because it Could Be True: fires are indeed often *disastrous,* but the text gives no indication about the severity of the fire. Keep (B) because *preventable* is a good synonym for "avoidable." Eliminate (C) because nothing in the text suggests that fires were *routine,* or commonplace, at this particular factory. Eliminate (D) for the same reason as (A)—it is often true that fires are *dreadful* in the real world, but the text makes no statement of the severity of the fire. The correct answer is (B).

2. **A** This is a Vocabulary question, so follow the basic approach. Highlight *while many psychosocial phenomena are obvious and commonsensical.* The presence of the opposite-direction transition *while* indicates that a good word for the annotation box would be the opposite of *obvious*: "not obvious." Keep (A) because *counterintuitive* means "contrary to common sense," which is a good synonym for "not obvious." Eliminate (B) because it's the opposite of "not obvious." Eliminate (C) because, while the *bystander effect* could certainly be *unfortunate* for someone needing help in a large crowd, the author never states any opinion towards the effect other than that it goes against common sense. Eliminate (D) because the author never states whether the *bystander effect* could be proven false or not. The correct answer is (A).

3. **A** This is a Vocabulary question, so follow the basic approach. Highlight that *many scholars condemn him as a ruthless villain* and *others argue vehemently that he was a noble and selfless character.* A good word for the annotation box based off this would be "controversial." Keep (A) because *polarizing* is a good synonym for "controversial." Eliminate (B) because *unifying* means "bringing together," which makes it too positive of a word for "controversial." Eliminate (C) similarly because it is too negative of a word for "controversial." Eliminate (D) because *slandered* means "unfairly insulted," but the author never indicates what side of the argument he or she falls on and therefore we cannot know whether the author thinks Richard III has been unfairly attacked. The correct answer is (A).

4. **D** This is a Vocabulary question, so follow the basic approach. Highlight that *Shakespeare thought the inclusion of the character might curry favor with the new king.* A good word for the annotation box based off this would be that Shakespeare had an "additional" motive beyond just wanting to produce solid literature. Eliminate (A) because the text doesn't support that Shakespeare's motives were *unimpeachable,* which means "unable to be doubted." Eliminate (B) because, while the motivation to gain the king's favor may not have been so obvious at the time, the author does not say Shakespeare's motives were *unpredictable* or prone to impulse. Eliminate (C) because it only could be true: Shakespeare likely had *artistic* motives for creating the character as well, but the last sentence of the text indicates that this particular motive was related to gaining the king's favor. Keep (D) because ulterior means "hidden," which is a good synonym for "secret." The correct answer is (D).

5. **B** This is a Vocabulary question, so follow the basic approach. Highlight that it was *conceded that waves as high as multistory buildings were theoretically possible.* A good word for the annotation box based off this would be "huge." Eliminate (A) because it's the right answer to the wrong question: the waves were thought of as *phantasmic,* or unreal, previously but are confirmed to be quite real by the final

sentence. Keep (B) because *colossal* is a good synonym for "huge." Eliminate (C) for the same reason as (A): *today,* the waves are no longer considered *mythical.* Eliminate (D) because *ubiquitous,* which means "seen everywhere," is extreme: just because there may be ten rogue waves forming somewhere in the world at any given time does not mean the waves are found everywhere or appear all over the place. The correct answer is (B).

6. **C** This is a Purpose question, so follow the basic approach. Highlight the main points that the author makes in the text that all the other parts of the text relate to: *Most instances of impossible colors are merely the fabrication of imaginative wordsmiths.* However, the underlined sentences states that there is a way *an individual can potentially "see" a color irreplicable by the eye under any normal circumstances.* In the annotation box, write that the purpose of the underlined sentence is to "show an exception." Eliminate (A) because *Pratchett* is recycled language: the text never states that he made a *critical oversight.* Eliminate (B) because it also recycles *Pratchett* as well as *imaginative*: while these words are used in the text, they have nothing to do with the last sentence of the text. Keep (C) because it is consistent with the annotation. Eliminate (D) because no *conflict* between fiction and reality is discussed in the passage. Rather, the author offers both fictional and realistic situations in which impossible colors can occur. The correct answer is (C).

7. **B** This is a Purpose question, so follow the basic approach. Highlight the main points that the author makes in the text that all the other parts of the text relate to: while the author initially seems to share in the praise for Milgram's work, the third sentence states that upon *closer scrutiny...the accolades for Milgram's work were perhaps too hastily given.* In the annotation box, write that the purpose of the underlined sentence is to "explain why author believes" the accolades were too hastily given. Eliminate (A) because it is the opposite of what the author now believes—the author no longer *supports* the *ingenuity* of Milgram's work. Keep (B) because it is consistent with the annotation. Eliminate (C) because the text challenges Milgram's results, not the *credentials*, or reputation, of other people who support the work. Eliminate (D) because it is Half-Right: while this author would very likely wish to verify the conclusion he or she reaches, the text never states that the author is performing *his or her own experimentation* to do so. The correct answer is (B).

8. **C** This is a Purpose question, so follow the basic approach. Highlight the main points that the author makes in the text that all the other parts of the text relate to: the author states that *George Washington....initiated a tradition that has persisted to the present* and that *Barack Obama...made history as the first African American President.* Additionally, *his portrait is the first by an African American artist.* In the annotation box, write that the purpose of the text is to "discuss a tradition and a milestone for that tradition." Eliminate (A) —no *contrast* between past and present figures is made in the text. Eliminate (B) because *always* is extreme and the only *art* discussed in the passage is portrait-painting. Keep (C) because it's consistent with the annotation, as *juxtapose* means "put next to each other." Eliminate (D) because it is the right answer to the wrong question—it fails to account for the historic milestone achieved by Obama and Wiley. The correct answer is (C).

9. **C** This is a Main Idea question, so follow the basic approach. Highlight the person, place, and/or thing that constitutes the main focus of the text. The citation makes it clear that this poem is being addressed to *Lucasta,* whom the narrator addresses as *Dear, Sweet,* and that he loves her. Yet he makes it clear that *to war and arms I fly* and that *a new mistress I now chase, the first foe in the field.* While annotations are normally not needed for Main Idea questions, on poetry texts, they can be helpful. Write "loves girl, but must go fight" in the annotation box since that seems the easiest conclusion to draw from the poem. Eliminate (A) because it is Half-Right: the narrator is *leaving for war,* but that he *no longer loves Lucasta* is the opposite of what's stated in the poem. Eliminate (B) because it is the opposite of what the narrator has decided: he is indeed going to war. Keep (C) because it is consistent with the annotation. Eliminate (D) because no other woman is mentioned in the text—the *mistress* is a metaphor related to the war that the narrator has chosen over Lucasta. The correct answer is (C).

10. **A** This is a Claims question, so follow the basic approach. Highlight the Chinese experts' argument: *a defining feature that separates Wuxi opera from other operatic forms is Huang Tune.* The correct answer will be most consistent with this claim. Keep (A) as it is consistent with the claim. Eliminate (B) because it is opposite: it would weaken the claim if any Wuxi operas lacked Huang Tune. Eliminate (C) as it would also weaken the claim: Huang Tune would not be a *defining feature* of Wuxi operas if *most* operas utilized it. Eliminate (D) as it would also weaken the claim: if *most* Wuxi operas were not recorded and could not be examined, it would be much harder to demonstrate that Huang Tune is a defining feature for Wuxi opera. The correct answer is (A).

11. **B** This is a Charts question, so follow the basic approach. Highlight the claim in the text: *total urban interstate highway length has decreased more sharply than its local counterpart.* Next, read the title, key, legends, and variables of the figure. Lastly, head straight to the answers and use POE. Eliminate (A) because from year 0 to year 5 urban interstate highway mileage actually increases, not decreases. Keep (B) because from year 15 to year 20 urban interstate highway mileage drops by over 6,000 miles while urban local highway mileage drops by only 800 miles. Eliminate (C) and (D) because the claim references urban, not rural, highway mileage. The correct answer is (B).

12. **D** This is a Claims question, so follow the basic approach. Highlight the scientists' conclusion: they *concluded that the Eurasian jays were able to exhibit self-control for a better outcome, which is considered a sign of intelligence in animal biology.* The correct answer should be LEAST consistent with the claim, as this question wants to weaken the conclusion. Eliminate (A) as it does not matter if *other types of animals* don't perform as well following the same process: the claim is only regarding Eurasian jays. Eliminate (B) as it would also have no effect on the claim: it does not matter if *most* bird species prefer mealworms or not, only whether Eurasian jays held off on eating until the mealworms were available due to self-control. Eliminate (C) because, even if another bird species enjoys all three foods equally, that would not affect the Eurasian jays' preference for mealworms. Keep (D) because, if Eurasian jays found the scent of bread and cheese offensive, this offers a different reason *besides* self-control that they would have waited for the mealworms. The correct answer is (D).

13. **D** This is a Charts question, so follow the basic approach. Highlight the claim in the text: *bees exposed to neonicotinoids were more vulnerable to CCD, as evidenced by their lower populations.* Next, read the title, key, variables, and units of the figure. Lastly, head right to the answers and use POE. Eliminate (A) because the claim states that bees exposed to neonicotinoids should be *more vulnerable to CCD*, not that there was a decline at *roughly the same rate* as the control group. Eliminate (B) because, while it is consistent with the graph, bee colony population not increasing at a specific moment in the graph does not show that the populations may be more vulnerable to CCD. Eliminate (C) because it is recycled language: the graph does not show CCD rates or temperature, only months of the year and populations of bee colonies. Keep (D) because the graph shows the two groups sprayed with neonicotinoids decreasing sharply while the control group's population actually increases, which would be the best evidence that neonicotinoids may play a role in colony collapse disorder. The correct answer is (D).

14. **A** This is a Conclusions question, so follow the basic approach. Highlight the main idea in the text: *an attempt to commit a crime is punished less harshly than the successful commission of that same crime.* The concluding sentence to the text must be consistent with this main idea. Keep (A) because it follows up on *losing your balance and failing to the ground* by referencing a *lack of physical contact* and the concept from earlier in the text that one is punished *less harshly* for an attempted crime than a successfully completed crime. Eliminate (B) because the text does not discuss the distinction between intent and harm, only the distinction between attempt and completion. Eliminate (C) because no other *more serious crimes* are mentioned in the passage. Eliminate (D) because the text does not mention one's fighting skill. As a matter of fact, the more skilled fighter would be more likely to complete the crime and receive a harsher sentence, not a *reward*. The correct answer is (A).

15. **C** This is a Conclusions question, so follow the basic approach. Highlight the main idea in the text: *early environmental factors…have a profound effect on a child's developing* personality and research *also suggests that genetics plays a large role in personality formation as well.* The concluding sentence must be consistent with these ideas. Eliminate (A) because *sole* is too extreme: both genetic and early environment are stated as factors by the text. Eliminate (B) because the passage does not introduce the concept of *genetic engineering*: it is too much of a reach to assume that the author is going to go beyond genetics without evidence. Keep (C) as it references both factors that can influence personality traits and asks a logical question regarding them both. Eliminate (D) as the text has just referenced genetics and does not contrast parental influence with early peer relationships. The correct answer is (C).

16. **C** In this Rules question, apostrophes with nouns are changing in the answer choices. Start with the first word and consider whether it possesses anything. The favorite books belong to *Electric Literature*, so eliminate (B) and (D), which don't have an apostrophe on *Literature*. Next, consider whether the last word possesses anything. The word *Books* is plural, not possessive, so eliminate (A). The correct answer is (C).

17. **C** In this Rules question, punctuation is changing in the answer choices. One answer contains STOP punctuation (comma + FANBOYS), so use the Vertical Line Test. Write the words *use* and *they* on scratch paper with a vertical line in between. The first part of the sentence, *Ghost words are words that are accidentally published in an official reference text without any previous intentional use,* is a complete idea, so mark it with a C. The second part of the sentence, *they can become widespread as more*

people use them in everyday language, is also a complete idea, so mark it with a C. In this case, STOP punctuation is needed. Eliminate (A) and (B) because they are both GO punctuation. A comma + FANBOYS can be used for STOP, so keep (C). A FANBOYS word without the comma can't link two complete ideas, so eliminate (D). The correct answer is (C).

18. **B**   In this Rules question, punctuation is changing in the answer choices. One answer contains HALF-STOP punctuation, so use the Vertical Line Test. Write the words *field* and *as* on scratch paper with a vertical line in between. The first part of the sentence, *Elizabeth Woody is a Native American poet who has served in numerous roles in her field*, is a complete idea, so mark it with a C. The second part of the sentence, *as a teacher, she taught creative writing for high school and college students, and as an artist, she learned basket weaving and served on multiple multi-disciplinary art committees*, is also a complete idea, so mark with a C. In this case, STOP or HALF-STOP punctuation is needed. Eliminate (A), (C), and (D) because they aren't STOP or HALF-STOP. The correct answer is (B).

19. **C**   In this Rules question, the subjects of the answers are changing, which suggests it may be testing modifiers. Look for and highlight a modifying phrase: *Armed with this information*. Whoever is *Armed with* information needs to come immediately after the comma. Eliminate (A) because *disorders* can't be aware of something. Eliminate (B) because *treatment* can't have information. Keep (C) because the *scientists* could be armed with information. Eliminate (D) because their *treatments* aren't the ones with the information. The correct answer is (C).

20. **B**   In this Rules question, verbs are changing in the answer choices, so it's testing consistency with verbs. All of the answers are consistent with the subject, *public opinion*, so consider tense. Find and highlight any clues in the sentence that would provide an indication of what tense is needed. The sentence starts with *By the time the pyramid was built and opened*, so it's referring to something that happened in the past. Eliminate (C) and (D) as they aren't past tense. At a certain time, the pyramid *was built and opened*; however, the change in public opinion took place before that. Thus, keep (B) because *had changed* is the appropriate tense to refer to something that happened before another past event (the pyramid opening). Eliminate (A) because it's not the correct tense for this situation. The correct answer is (B).

21. **A**   In this Rules question, punctuation is changing in the answer choices. Notice that semicolons and commas are the only marks changing, which suggests that this could involve a list. Check the rest of the sentence to see whether there is a list of three or more things. The sentence does contain a list of three groups in the same format: tribe name, comma, location. The first item contains the tribe name, the comma, and the location, so the next thing is a semicolon, since the first item is complete. Eliminate (B), (C), and (D), as they all lack the semicolon after *Valley*. To confirm (A), note that the next item should begin with the tribe name and then a comma, which (A) does correctly. The correct answer is (A).

22. **D**   In this Rules question, punctuation is changing in the answer choices. Some answers contain STOP punctuation, so use the Vertical Line Test. Notice that STOP punctuation appears in two places: before or after *however*. Start by determining whether *however* belongs with the first or the second part of the sentence. The previous sentence states that Rachel Carson *wrote numerous respected works*. This sentence states that *Carson's publishers were concerned about being faced with harsh criticism*. This does contrast with the previous sentence, so the contrast word should go here, with the first part

of the sentence. Eliminate (B) because it puts the contrast word in the second part of the sentence. Write the words *however* and *some* on scratch paper with a vertical line in between. The first part of the sentence, *Carson's publishers were concerned about being faced with harsh criticism*, is a complete idea, so mark it with a C. The second part of the sentence, *some of her ideas could be interpreted as libel since they contradicted many accepted scientific claims*, is also a complete idea, so mark it with a C. In this case, STOP punctuation is needed. Eliminate (A) and (C) because they don't contain STOP punctuation. The correct answer is (D).

23. **A** This is a transition question, so follow the basic approach. Highlight ideas that relate to each other. The previous sentence says *Bell used images from the Mars rover to create a book*. This sentence says *the general public was able to become more familiar* with its work. These ideas agree, so a same-direction transition is needed. Eliminate (B) and (D) because they are contrasting transitions. Keep (A) because the public's familiarity was a *consequence* or result of the book's publication. Eliminate (C) because the second sentence is not an additional point but rather a result of the publication. The correct answer is (A).

24. **A** This is a transition question, so follow the basic approach. Highlight ideas that relate to each other. The previous sentence states that the plant *can shield its most sensitive areas* and *reopen…when it is safe to do so*. This sentence states that *the plant has adapted to respond to its environment*. These ideas agree, so a same-direction transition is needed. All of the answers are same-direction transitions, so use POE. Keep (A) because this sentence is a restatement of the previous one. Eliminate (B) because this transition would be used for an additional point, but instead, this sentence restates what was said in the previous sentence. Eliminate (C) for the same reason. Eliminate (D) because it does not imply a restatement, which is the relationship between the sentences. The correct answer is (A).

25. **D** This is a Rhetorical Synthesis question, so follow the basic approach. Highlight the goal(s) stated in the question: *highlight the difference between female capuchins' relationships with other females and with males*. Then, go to POE. Eliminate (A) because it doesn't mention *relationships with other females and with males*. Eliminate (B) for the same reason. Eliminate (C) because it only mentions their relationships *with males*. Keep (D) because it mentions a *difference* (*positive impact* versus *did not*) and mentions both *females* and *males*. The correct answer is (D).

26. **C** This is a Rhetorical Synthesis question, so follow the basic approach. Highlight the goal(s) stated in the question: *make a generalization about the approach taken by the NOAA to an audience familiar with the HWRF*. Then, go to POE. Eliminate (A) because it doesn't draw a *generalization* about the approach. Eliminate (B) because it explains *HWRF*, but the audience is already *familiar*. Keep (C) because it does not define *HWRF*, since the audience is *familiar*, but it does make a *generalization*, stating that it is *one example of a computer simulation*. Eliminate (D) because it doesn't make a *generalization*. The correct answer is (C).

27. **C** This is a Rhetorical Synthesis question, so follow the basic approach. Highlight the goal(s) stated in the question: *detail the sequence of the climate change and forest fire feedback loop*. Then, go to POE. Eliminate (A) because it doesn't relate to a *feedback loop*. Eliminate (B) because it doesn't mention *climate change*. Keep (C) because it starts and ends with *climate change*, suggesting a *feedback loop*, and it also mentions *forest fires*. Eliminate (D) because it doesn't suggest a *feedback loop*. The correct answer is (C).

PRACTICE TEST 1—MATH EXPLANATIONS

Module 1

1. **D** The question asks for the value of b in the equation when graphed and provides a point on the graph. Plug the point into the equation. Plug $x = 3$ and $y = -1$ into $y = 2x - b$ to get $-1 = 2(3) - b$. Simplify the right side to get $-1 = 6 - b$. Subtract 6 from both sides to get $-7 = -b$. Divide both sides by -1 to get $b = 7$. The correct answer is (D).

2. **D** The question asks for the maximum value of the product of two inequalities. When a question seeks to determine the combination of values for two given inequalities, as here, try all four possible combinations of the limits. If both f and g were at their high ends, the values would be 3 and 2, respectively, and fg would be 6. At the low ends, $f = -2$ and $g = -5$, so $fg = 10$. Next, try the low value of f with the high value of g to get $fg = (-2)(2) = -4$. Lastly, try the high value of f with the low value of g to get $fg = (3)(-5) = -15$. Of the 4 possible combinations, the maximum value for $fg = 10$. The correct answer is (D).

3. **12** The question asks for an average based on data in a table. For averages, use the formula $T = AN$, where T is the total, A is the average, and N is the number of things. Add up the points scored from the second row to get a *Total* of 108. Count the number of players in the table to get a *Number of things* of 9. The formula becomes $108 = (A)(9)$. Divide both sides of the equation by 9 to get $A = 12$. The correct answer is 12.

4. **C** The question asks about the solution to an equation. Two of the answer choices include numbers, and the other two are infinitely many solutions and no solutions. Plug in the easier of the choices with numbers. Plug in $y = 10$ to get $5\left(\dfrac{10}{2} + 5\right) = 2(10) + \dfrac{1}{2}(10) + 25$. The equation becomes $5(5 + 5) = 20 + 5 + 25$ or $5(10) = 50$. Since this is true, $y = 10$ is a solution. Eliminate (A), since $y = 1\dfrac{1}{2}$ cannot be the only solution, and eliminate (D), since there is at least one solution. It is still possible that there are infinitely many solutions. To test, plug in any other number. To make the math as easy as possible, plug in $y = 0$ to get $5\left(\dfrac{0}{2} + 5\right) = 2(0) + \dfrac{1}{2}(0) + 25$. The equation becomes $5(0 + 5) = 0 + 0 + 25$ or $5(5) = 25$. Therefore, $y = 0$ is also a solution. Since $y = 10$ is not the only solution, eliminate (B). The correct answer is (C).

5. **A** The question asks for the measure of an angle in a triangle. Start by drawing two right triangles and labeling the vertices using the information in the question. Triangles are similar when they have the same angle measures. The largest angle in a right triangle is the 90° angle, so label angles R and Y as right angles. Label the next largest angles as Q and X, then label the smallest angles as S and Z.

The drawing should look something like this.

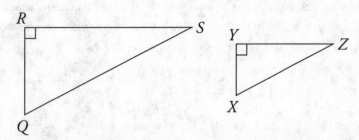

Next, label X as 63°. Since X and Q are the middle-sized angles in the two triangles, also label Q as 63°. All triangles contain 180°, so find S by subtracting the known angles from 180°. Since R is 90° and Q is 63°, S must equal 180° − 90° − 63° = 27°. The correct answer is (A).

6. **B** The question asks for a value based on a rate of work applied to conflicting units of measurement. Start by converting the area of the field into hectares. The question states that the farm workers are harvesting a field *measuring 4.6 square kilometers,* and the note provides the conversion of 100 hectares to 1 square kilometer, so set up a proportion. The proportion is $\dfrac{100 \text{ hectares}}{1 \text{ square km}} = \dfrac{x \text{ hectares}}{4.6 \text{ square km}}$. Cross-multiply to get $x = 460$ hectares. Next, calculate the number of days it will take to harvest 460 hectares. The question states that *the farm workers harvest 23 hectares per day,* so set up another proportion. The proportion is $\dfrac{23 \text{ hectares}}{1 \text{ day}} = \dfrac{460 \text{ hectares}}{x \text{ days}}$. Cross-multiply to get $23x = 460$. Divide both sides of the equation by 23 to get $x = 20$ days. The correct answer is (B).

7. **A** The question asks for the model that best fits the data. Compare the answer choices. Two choices describe a linear decrease, which is a decrease by the same amount each month, and two choices describe an exponential decrease, which is a decrease by the same percent each month. Because linear decreases are easier to work with, first determine whether the relationship is linear with a consistent decrease. From month 0 to month 1, the decrease is $1,400 − $1,344 = $56. Eliminate (C), which indicates a decrease of $47. From month 1 to month 2, the decrease is $1,344 − $1,290 = $54. Eliminate (D), since the decrease is not always $56. Therefore, the decrease must be exponential. To find the percent change between months, use the formula $\dfrac{difference}{original} \times 100$. From month 0 to month 1, the percent decrease is $\dfrac{\$1,400 - \$1,344}{\$1,400} \times 100 = \dfrac{\$56}{\$1,400} \times 100 = 0.04 \times 100 = 4\%$. The correct answer is (A).

8. **1** The question asks for the value of *y* in a system of equations, so solve the system for *y*. Look to eliminate the *x* terms by making the coefficients on *x* in the two equations the same but with opposite signs. Multiply the first equation by 2 to get $10x - 6y = 14$ and multiply the second equation by –5 to get $-10x - 5y = -25$. Stack and add the equations.

$$10x - 6y = 14$$
$$\underline{-10x - 5y = -25}$$
$$-11y = -11$$

Divide both sides by –11 to get *y* = 1. The correct answer is 1.

9. **B** The question asks for the predicted number of juniors in the entire school who plan to travel based on the table. To calculate this, find the percent of the students surveyed who are juniors and planning to travel, then multiply that percent by the total population. There are 25 juniors who plan to travel out of 200 total students surveyed, so the percent is $\dfrac{25}{200} \times 100 = 12.5\%$. There are 1,200 students in the school and, because the survey sample is representative, 12.5% of those can be expected to be juniors who plan to travel. Take 12.5% of 1,200 to get $\dfrac{12.5}{100} \times 1,200 = 150$. The correct answer is (B).

10. **15** The question asks for a value given a function with an absolute value. In this equation, the number inside the parentheses is the *x*-value that goes into the function, or the input, and the value that comes out of the function is the *y*-value, or the output. The question provides an output value of –3, so set the function equal to that value and solve for the input value, *n*. The equation becomes $9 - |n - 3| = -3$. Subtract 9 from both sides of the equation to get $-|n - 3| = -12$. Multiply both sides of the equation by –1 to get $|n - 3| = 12$. With an absolute value, the number inside the value bars can be either positive or negative. Set *n* – 3 equal to 12 and –12 and solve both equations. When *n* – 3 = 12, add 3 to both sides of the equation to get *n* = 15. When *n* – 3 = –12, add 3 to both sides of the equation to get *n* = –9. The question asked for the positive value of *n*, so it cannot be –9. The correct answer is 15.

11. **25** The question asks for the value of *x*, which is a degree measure on a figure. Start by labeling the figure with the given information. Mark that angle *RSV* is congruent to angle *TUV* and that angle *TUV* measures 65°. More information is known about triangle *VUT*, so look for a way to use that to find *x*. Opposite angles are equal, so the measure of angle *UVT* will also be *x*°. There are 180° in a triangle, so angle *UVT* is 180 – 90 – 65 = 25°. Therefore, *x*° also equals 25°. The correct answer is 25.

12. **D** The question asks for a true statement about two equations that each form separate lines. In order to evaluate the answer choices, start by finding the slopes of the two lines. The first equation is in standard form: *Ax* + *By* = *C*. The slope of a line in standard form is $-\dfrac{A}{B}$. For the first equation, *A* = 3 and *B* = 2, so the slope of this line is $-\dfrac{3}{2}$. The second equation is in slope-intercept form: *y* = *mx* + *b*. The slope of a line in slope-intercept form is *m*, so the slope of this line is $\dfrac{2}{3}$. The two slopes are negative reciprocals, which means the lines are perpendicular. The correct answer is (D).

13. **B** The question asks for the definition of a function that represents a graph. The correct function must work with any point on the graph, so test the points given in the question and eliminate answers that don't work. In function notation, the number inside the parentheses is the x-value that goes into the function, and the value that comes out of the function is the y-value. Start with the point (0, 3) and plug $x = 0$ and $y = 3$ into the answer choices. Choice (A) becomes $3 = \frac{1}{2}(3)^0$. Any number raised to the power of zero is 1, so this becomes $3 = \frac{1}{2}(1)$ or $3 = \frac{1}{2}$. This is not true, so eliminate (A). Choice (B) becomes $3 = 3(2)^0$, or $3 = 3(1)$, or $3 = 3$. This is true, so keep (B), but check the remaining answers just in case. Choice (C) becomes $3 = 3(3)^0$, or $3 = 3(1)$, or $3 = 3$. This is true, so keep (C). Choice (D) becomes $3 = 8(2)^0$, or $3 = 8(1)$, or $3 = 8$. This is not true, so eliminate (D). Two answers worked with the first point, so try them again with the second point and plug in $x = 5$ and $y = 96$. Choice (B) becomes $96 = 3(2)^5$, which becomes $96 = 3(32)$, and then $96 = 96$. Keep (B). Choice (C) becomes $96 = 3(3)^5$, which becomes $96 = 3(243)$, and then $96 = 729$. Eliminate (C). The correct answer is (B).

14. **B** The question asks for a true statement based on the data in a histogram. Read the numbered statements carefully and use Process of Elimination. There are various statistical measures in the statements, so start with the easiest to calculate: mode and range. Statement (III) says that the mode is equal to the range. The mode is the most commonly occurring value, so in this case, it will be the bar with the most students, which is 5. The range of a list of values is the greatest value minus the least value, so in this case, that is $5 - 0 = 5$. Because the mode and range are equal, (III) is true. Eliminate (A) and (C), which do not contain statement (III). Compare the remaining answer choices. Choice (D) includes statement (II), which indicates that the median is equal to the mean. The median is the value in the middle of all the values, when all the values are arranged consecutively. There are 6 students who sold 0 barrels of popcorn, 2 who sold 1 barrel, 3 who sold 2, 3 who sold 3, 7 who sold 4, and 9 who sold 5. Therefore, there are $6 + 2 + 3 + 3 + 7 + 9 = 30$ students total. Because there is an even number of students, the median will be average of the 15th and 16th students. Starting from the lower number of barrels of popcorn, there are $6 + 2 + 3 = 11$ students who sold 0 to 2 barrels. The next 3 students sold 3 barrels, bringing the list up to 14 students who sold 0 to 3 barrels. Because 7 students sold 4 barrels of popcorn, the 15th and 16th students both sold 4 barrels of popcorn. Therefore, the median is 4. To find the mean, or average, use the formula $T = AN$, where T is the total, A is the average, and N is the number of things. To find the total number of barrels, multiply the number of students who sold a certain number of barrels by the number of barrels they sold and add up the results. This becomes $(6 \times 0) + (2 \times 1) + (3 \times 2) + (3 \times 3) + (7 \times 4) + (9 \times 5)$, which is $0 + 2 + 6 + 9 + 28 + 45 = 90$. Therefore, $T = 90$ and $N = 30$ for the number of students. The average formula becomes $90 = A(30)$. Divide both sides by 30 to get $3 = A$. This does not match the median, so statement (II) is false. Eliminate (D), which contains statement (II). The correct answer is (B).

15.   **C**   The question asks for an expression that is equivalent to a term in an equation. Although Plugging In is an option, manipulating the equation algebraically will be easier here. The question asks for the product bc, so there is no need to isolate the variables individually. Instead, rearrange the equation to isolate bc. Add 9 to both sides of the equation to get $S + 9 = 5(bc + 1)$. Divide both sides of the equation by 5 to get $\frac{S+9}{5} = bc + 1$. Subtract 1 from both sides of the equation to get $\frac{S+9}{5} - 1 = bc$. To get the left side of the equation into the form of the answer choices, make it into a single fraction. Use 5 as a common denominator and rewrite 1 as $\frac{5}{5}$. The equation becomes $\frac{S+9}{5} - \frac{5}{5} = bc$. Subtract the numerators to get $\frac{S+9-5}{5} = bc$, or $\frac{S+4}{5} = bc$. The correct answer is (C).

16.   **A**   The question asks for the y-coordinate of the vertex of a parabola. One way to find the vertex is to use the built-in calculator. Enter the equation of the graph, then scroll and zoom on the graph to see the vertex. Click in the box with the equation and the vertex will show as a grey dot. Hover over or click on the dot to see that the vertex is at (5, –100). The question asks for the y-coordinate, which is –100. After following those steps, the calculator will look like this:

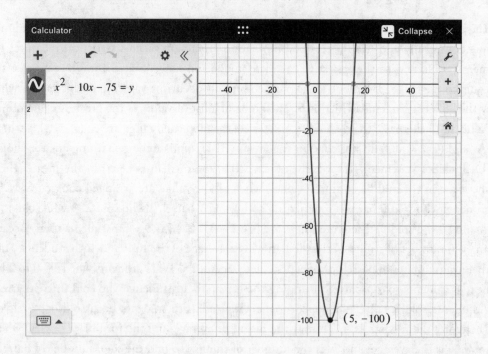

Another option is to solve for h, which is the x-coordinate of the vertex at (h, k). The equation is in standard form, which means $h = -\frac{b}{2a}$. In this case, $a = 1$ and $b = -10$, so the equation becomes $h = -\frac{-10}{2(1)}$. Solve for h to get $h = \frac{10}{2}$, or $h = 5$. Plug that value into the equation to solve for k, the y-value of the vertex. The equation becomes $y = 5^2 - 10(5) - 75$. Solve to get $y = 25 - 50 - 75$, and then $y = -100$. Using either method, the correct answer is (A).

17. **2** The question asks for the y-coordinate of the point of intersection of two graphs. To solve for y, find a way to cancel the x-terms. One way is with substitution: multiply both sides of the second equation by 4 to get $x = 4y$. Substitute $4y$ for x in the first question to get $10(4y) - 62 = 9y$. Simplify the left side of the equation to get $40y - 62 = 9y$. Subtract $9y$ from both sides of the equation to get $31y - 62 = 0$, then add 62 to both sides of the equation to get $31y = 62$. Finally, divide both sides of the equation by 31 to get $y = 2$. The correct answer is 2.

18. **C** The question asks for the value of a constant that appears as part of a fractional exponent. When dealing with questions about exponents, remember the MADSPM rules. The MA part of the acronym indicates that Multiplying matching bases means to Add the exponents. The PM part of the acronym indicates that raising a base with an exponent to another Power means to Multiply the exponents. Use the order of operations to apply the exponents outside the parentheses to the bases inside by multiplying the exponents to get $\left(a^{\frac{3}{3}} b^{\frac{3}{4}} \right) \left(a^{\frac{4}{3}} b^{\frac{4}{4}} \right)$. Although it is possible to reduce some of these exponents, the next step will be to add them together, since the bases are multiplied. Leave the exponents in fractional form to make that easier, getting $a^{\frac{7}{3}} b^{\frac{7}{4}}$. According to the equation, this is equal to $a^{\frac{k}{3}} b^{\frac{k}{4}}$, so k must equal 7. The correct answer is (C).

19. **C** The question asks for an equivalent form of an expression. There are variables in the answer choices, so plug in. Make $y = 2$. The expression becomes $(3 - 2)^2 - (3 - 2)$, which is $(1)^2 - 1$ or 0. This is the target value; circle it. Now plug $y = 2$ into the answer choices to see which one matches the target value. Choice (A) becomes $3 - 2$ or 1. This does not match the target, so eliminate (A). Choice (B) becomes $2^2 - 7(2) + 6$, which is $4 - 14 + 6$ or -4; eliminate (B). Choice (C) becomes $(3 - 2)(2 - 2)$, which is $(1)(0)$ or 0; keep (C), but check (D) just in case. Choice (D) becomes $9 - 2^2$, which is $9 - 4$ or 5; eliminate (D). The correct answer is (C).

20. **11** The question asks for the value of a function in a graph of parallel lines. Parallel lines have the same slope, so find the slope of the line that represents function f. This function is in slope-intercept form, $y = mx + b$, where m represents the slope and b represents the y-intercept. The m term is 3, so the line has a slope of 3. Since the lines are parallel, the slope of the line that represents function g is also 3. In function notation, the number inside the parenthesis is the x-value that goes into the function, and the value that comes out of the function is the y-value. Together, they make an ordered pair, or a point on a graph. The question gives two x-values and two y-values for function g, which means function g has points at $(0, 5)$ and $(2, r)$. Calculate the slope using the formula $slope = \dfrac{y_2 - y_1}{x_2 - x_1}$. The slope is 3, so the formula becomes $3 = \dfrac{r - 5}{2 - 0}$, or $3 = \dfrac{r - 5}{2}$. Multiply both sides of the equation by 2 to get $r - 5 = 6$, then add 5 to both sides of the equation to get $r = 11$. The correct answer is 11.

21. **56.54** The question asks for a percent of women runners completing a marathon based on information also given in terms of percents. Since the question doesn't give an actual number for the runners, but rather percent information about an unknown total, plug in for the unknown total. Make the total number of runners 1,000. The question states that *45 percent of the runners were men*, so $\frac{45}{100} \times 1,000 = 450$ of the runners were men. If the rest of the runners were women, then $1,000 - 450 = 550$ of the runners were women. The question also states that *62 percent of the men* completed the marathon in under four hours, so $\frac{62}{100} \times 450 = 279$ men completed the marathon in under four hours. Similarly, if *66 percent of the women completed the marathon in under four hours*, $\frac{66}{100} \times 550 = 363$ women completed the marathon in under four hours. The total number of runners who completed the marathon in under four hours is $279 + 363 = 642$. If 642 total runners completed the marathon in under four hours and 363 of them were women, the percent of total runners who completed the marathon in under four hours who were women is $\frac{363}{642} \times 100 \approx 56.542$. The fill-in box does not allow percent signs, and there is space for five characters, so enter as many digits after the decimal point as possible. The correct answer is 56.54.

22. **D** The question asks for the meaning of an expression in the context of an equation. Start by reading the final question, which asks for the meaning of the expression $\frac{\sqrt{3}}{2}x^2$. Then label the parts of the equation with the information given. The question states that x is the *length of the sides of the triangular ends* and y is *the length of the rectangular faces*. The equation becomes $SA = 2\left(\frac{\sqrt{3}}{4}(\text{length of sides of triangular ends})^2\right) + 3(\text{length of sides of triangular ends})(\text{length of rectangular faces})$. Next, use Process of Elimination to get rid of answer choices that are not consistent with the labels. Since the expression $\frac{\sqrt{3}}{2}x^2$ only includes the sides of the triangular faces as a variable, it doesn't refer to the rectangular faces; eliminate (B) and (C). Compare the remaining answer choices. The difference between (A) and (D) is the number of triangular faces included. In the equation, the term $\frac{\sqrt{3}}{4}x^2$ is multiplied by 2, which would result in $\frac{\sqrt{3}}{2}x^2$. Therefore, $\frac{\sqrt{3}}{2}x^2$ must represent both the triangular sides. Eliminate (A). The correct answer is (D).

Module 2—Easier

1. **A**   The question asks for a percent of a number. *Percent* means out of 100, so translate 20% as $\frac{20}{100}$.

    Next, multiply the fraction by the number. The result is $\frac{20}{100}(130) = 26$. The correct answer is (A).

2. **46**   The question asks for a value in an equation. The question states that $c = 20$, so plug in 20 for c in the equation. The equation becomes $20 + d = 66$. Subtract 20 from both sides of the equation to get $d = 46$. The correct answer is 46.

3. **C**   The question asks for a certain value on a graph. *Percent remaining* is listed along the vertical axis. However, the question asks for the day when the student had *completed 30% of the assignment*. If 30% is completed, that means 100% – 30% = 70% is remaining. Find 70 on the vertical axis, then trace along the horizontal line representing 70 using the mouse pointer or the edge of your scratch paper to where the graph intersects that line. To find the number of days, trace down to the horizontal axis, where the value is 8. The correct answer is (C).

4. **D**   The question asks for an equivalent form of an expression. There are variables in the answer choices, so plug in. Make $y = 2$ and $c = 3$. The expression becomes $30(2) - 12(3)(2) = 60 - 72 = -12$. This is the target value; circle it. Now plug $y = 2$ and $c = 3$ into the answer choices to see which one matches the target value. Choice (A) becomes $[5 - 2(3)](2) = (5 - 6)(2) = (-1)(2) = -2$. This does not match the target, so eliminate (A). Choice (B) becomes $(18)[3 - 2(2)] = (18)(3 - 4) = (18)(-1) = -18$. Eliminate (B). Choice (C) becomes $(18)(3)(2)^2 = (18)(3)(4) = 216$; eliminate (C). Choice (D) becomes $[30 - 12(3)](2) = (30 - 36)(2) = (-6)(2) = -12$. This matches the target value, so keep (D). The correct answer is (D).

5. **A**   The question asks for the number of teaspoons a glass tube can hold. Begin by reading the question to find information on the glass tube. The question states that a glass tube *can hold no more than 8.50 milliliters of liquid* and that *1 teaspoon = 4.93 milliliters*. Set up a proportion to determine the volume, making sure to match up the units: $\frac{1 \text{ teaspoon}}{4.93 \text{ milliliters}} = \frac{x \text{ teaspoons}}{8.50 \text{ milliliters}}$. Cross-multiply to solve for x: $8.50 = 4.93x$. Divide both sides of the equation by 4.93 to get $x \approx 1.72$ teaspoons. The correct answer is (A).

6. **–1**   The question asks for a value in a system of equations. To find the value of s, look for a way to eliminate the t terms. The t terms have the same coefficient with opposite signs, so stack and add the equations to make t disappear.

    $$\begin{array}{r} 4s + 2t = 7 \\ + \underline{3s - 2t = -14} \\ 7s = -7 \end{array}$$

    Divide both sides of the resulting equation by 7 to get $s = -1$. The correct answer is –1.

7. **A** The question asks for the length of one side of a square. Since the question provides information about the area of the square, write down the formula for the area of a square. The formula is $A = s^2$, where A is the area and s is the side length. Plug in the area given in the question, and the formula becomes $100 = s^2$. Take the square root of both sides of the equation to get $10 = s$. The correct answer is (A).

8. **D** The question asks for the meaning of a number within an equation. Start by reading the full question, which asks for the meaning of the number 870. Then label the parts of the equation with the information given. The question states that A represents the remaining amount she owes, and w represents the number of weeks since she borrowed the money. Because the number 870 is used to calculate A, the remaining amount owed, it must have something to do with money. Next, use Process of Elimination to get rid of answer choices that are not consistent with the labels. Choice (A) describes the total amount Sydney has repaid. However, the amount will change over time, so it cannot be represented by a constant. Eliminate (A). Choice (C) describes w and not 870, so eliminate (C). To check (B) and (D), plug in some numbers. If $w = 1$, then $A = 870 - 30(1) = 840$, so after 1 week, \$840 remains to be paid. If $w = 2$, then $A = 870 - 30(2) = 810$, so after 2 weeks, \$810 remains to be paid. Therefore, between week 1 and week 2, $840 - 810 = 30$ was repaid. Thus, 30 represents the amount Sydney repays each week, so eliminate (B). Only one choice remains. To confirm (D), note that the original amount that Sydney owes is the amount that she owes after 0 weeks. If $w = 0$, then $A = 870 - 30(0) = 870$. The correct answer is (D).

9. **C** The question asks for the solutions to an equation. Solve the equation for x. Start by adding 48 to both sides of the equation to get $3x^2 = 48$. Next, divide both sides by 3 to get $x^2 = 16$. Then, take the square root of both sides to get $x = \pm 4$. The correct answer is (C).

10. **3** The question asks for the value of z for which the equation would have an infinite number of solutions. First, isolate z. Distribute the 6 to get $12y + 6z = 12y + 18$. Subtract $12y$ from both sides to get $6z = 18$. Then divide both sides by 6 to get $z = 3$. If z is set equal to 3, the equation will have infinitely many solutions because the y terms will always be eliminated. The correct answer is 3.

11. **C** The question asks for the value of an angle in a graph of parallel lines. When two parallel lines are cut by a third line, two kinds of angles are created: big and small. All big angles are equal, all small angles are equal, and one small angle and one big angle add up to 180°. Angle z is a big angle, and so is the angle labeled 132°. Thus, the two angles are the same size: 132°. The correct answer is (C).

12. **A** The question asks what must be true in a given inequality. There are variables in the answer choices, so plug in. Make $w = 4$, plug 4 into the answer choices for w, and eliminate any that are not true. Choice (A) becomes $-4 < -3$. This is true, so keep (A), but check the remaining answers since the question asks for what *must* be true. Choice (B) becomes $-4 > -3$. This is not true, so eliminate (B). Choice (C) becomes $4 = 4$; keep (C). Keep choice (D) because 4 is an integer. Since more than one answer worked, plug in a different number. Try a number that is not an integer and make $w = 4.5$. Choice (A) becomes $-4.5 < -3$; keep (A). Choice (C) becomes $4.5 = 4$; eliminate (C). Since 4.5 is not an integer, eliminate (D). The correct answer is (A).

13. **B** The question asks for an equation expressing a billing arrangement in a doctor's office. Translate the information using bite-sized pieces and eliminate after each piece. The question states that there is a *one-time fee of $125*. The correct equation should have + 125 in it. Eliminate (C) and (D), which both multiply 125 by some other value. Compare the remaining answer choices. The difference between (A) and (B) is the 5 in the first term. The company types 5 invoices per day, and *y* represents days, so the correct equation should have (5)*y* in it. This does not appear in (A), so eliminate it. The correct answer is (B).

14. **D** The question asks for the meaning of a number in context. Start by reading the final question, which asks for the meaning of the number 135. Then label the parts of the equation with the information given. The variable *x* is *the number of years since the 2010 census*, so *P* must be the *population of County Y, in thousands*. The equation becomes *population (thousands)* = 2,500 + 135(*years since 2010*). Next, use Process of Elimination to get rid of answer choices that are not consistent with the labels. Choice (A) refers to an increase in population per year, and 135 is multiplied by years in the equation. This is consistent with the labels, so keep (A), but check the remaining answers just in case. Choices (B) and (C) both refer to the population increasing by a certain amount every 135 years, so these answers are not consistent with the labels. Eliminate (B) and (C). Choice (D) also refers to an increase in population per year, so keep (D). The difference between (A) and (D) is the value of the increase. The equation represents the population *in thousands*, so 135 should be multiplied by 1,000 to give 135,000 as the actual population increase. Eliminate (A). The correct answer is (D).

15. **B** The question asks for a comparison of two values of a function. Start by finding both values using the function given in the question. The year 1972 is 12 years after 1960, so plug in 12 for *y*. The equation becomes $P(12) = 3.039(1.017)^{12}$. Put this into the on-screen calculator or a personal calculator to get $P(12) \approx 3.72$. The year 1974 is 14 years after 1960, so plug in 14 for *y*. The equation becomes $P(14) = 3.039(1.017)^{14}$. Put this into a calculator to get $P(14) \approx 3.85$. To find how many times greater the population was in 1974, divide the population in 1974 by the population in 1972. This becomes $\frac{3.85}{3.72} \approx 1.035$. Finally, enter each answer choice into a calculator, and eliminate any that do not equal approximately 1.035. Eliminate (A) since $1.017 \neq 1.035$. Choice (B) becomes 1.034. Keep (B) but check the remaining answers. Choice (C) becomes 3.09; eliminate (C). Choice (D) becomes 3.14; eliminate (D). The correct answer is (B).

16. **B** The question asks for the value of a given function. In function notation, the number inside the parentheses is the *x*-value that goes into the function, and the value that comes out of the function is the *y*-value. The question provides a *y*-value of 288, and the answers have numbers that could represent the *x*-value, so plug in the answers. Start with the easier of the middle numbers and try (B), 12. Plug 12 into the function for *x* to get $g(12) = 2(12)^2$, which becomes $g(12) = 2(144)$, and then $g(12) = 288$. This matches the information in the question, so stop here. The correct answer is (B).

17. **B** The question asks how much more an actual value is than a predicted value on a graph. Specifically, the question asks about a car that *was owned for exactly 7 years*; the graph shows *years of ownership* on the horizontal axis. Find 7 on this axis and use the mouse pointer or edge of your scratch paper to trace up to where the point and the line of best fit intersect $y = 7$. They lie between two gridlines on the vertical axis. Since each interval on the vertical axis is $2,000, the difference between the selling price of the point and the selling price predicted by the line of best fit must be less than $2,000. Eliminate (C) and (D). Since the difference makes up more than half the interval, the difference must be more than $1,000. Eliminate (A). The correct answer is (B).

18. **C** The question asks for the value of a variable in a system of equations. Since both equations are set equal to the same value, setting the right sides of the two equations equal will be the best method to solve the system for r. The new equation becomes $r = 1.8r - 6$. Subtract r from both sides of the equation to get $0 = 0.8r - 6$, then add 6 to both sides of the equation to get $6 = 0.8r$. Divide both sides of the equation by 0.8 to get $7.5 = r$. The correct answer is (C).

19. **396** The question asks for the volume of a geometric figure. The dimensions of the box are described in the word problem, so start by translating English to math. The question states that the *width* is *2 inches more than its length*, so $w = l + 2$. The question also states that the *height* is *5 inches less than its length*, so $h = l - 5$. The two smallest dimensions would be the length and the height, because $l + 2$ is greater than l and $l - 5$. The formula for the area of a rectangle is $A = lw$. The area of the smallest face is 36, so the formula becomes $36 = l(l - 5)$. This simplifies to $36 = l^2 - 5l$. Solve by subtracting 36 from both sides to set the quadratic equal to zero to get $0 = l^2 - 5l - 36$. Factor the quadratic; –9 and 4 add to –5 and multiply to –36, so the quadratic factors to $0 = (l - 9)(l + 4)$. The values of l are 9 and –4, but a length cannot be negative, so use $l = 9$. The width is $l + 2 = 9 + 2 = 11$, and the height is $l - 5 = 9 - 5 = 4$. The formula for the volume of a rectangular box is $V = lwh$, so plug in the values to determine the volume of the box. The formula becomes $V = (9)(11)(4) = 396$. The correct answer is 396.

20. **C** The question asks for all solutions to a system of equations. Because there are numbers in the answer choices that represent these solutions, plug in the answers. The first equation is easier, so start there. Start with the point $(4, -2)$, and plug $x = 4$ and $y = -2$ into the first equation. The first equation becomes $-2 = 4 - 6$, or $-2 = -2$. This is true, so plug the same numbers into the second equation, which becomes $-2 = -(4)^2 + 7(4) - 14$, then $-2 = -16 + 28 - 14$, and finally, $-2 = -2$. This is true, so the correct answer must include $(4, -2)$; eliminate (A) and (D) since they do not include this solution. The difference between (B) and (C) is the point $(2, -4)$, so plug $x = 2$ and $y = -4$ into the first equation. The first equation becomes $-4 = 2 - 6$, or $-4 = -4$. This is true, so plug the same numbers into the second equation. The second equation becomes $-4 = -(2)^2 + 7(2) - 14$, then $-4 = -4 + 14 - 14$, and finally $-4 = -4$. This is true, so $(2, -4)$ is also a solution to the system. Eliminate (B) since it does not contain this solution. The correct answer is (C).

21. **A** The question asks for the *x*-value in a solution to a system of equations. The question states that $(p, q) = (x, y)$ and asks for the value of x, so plug in x for p in the equations. The first equation becomes $x^2 = 3 + q$, and the second equation becomes $3 = x + q$. To solve for x, find a way to cancel the q terms. Multiply the second equation by –1 to get $-3 = -x - q$.

Now the q terms have the same coefficient with opposite signs, so stack and add the equations.

$$x^2 = 3 + q$$
$$\underline{+\ {-3} = -x - q}$$
$$x^2 - 3 = 3 - x$$

To solve the quadratic, move all of the terms to the left and set it equal to 0. Add x to both sides of the equation to get $x^2 + x - 3 = 3$, then subtract 3 from both sides of the equation to get $x^2 + x - 6 = 0$. Factor the quadratic into $(x + 3)(x - 2)$. Set each binomial equal to 0 and solve. When $x + 3 = 0$, subtract 3 from both sides of the equation to get $x = -3$. When $x - 2 = 0$, add 2 to both sides of the equation to get $x = 2$. None of the answer choices are 2, but (A) is -3. The correct answer is (A).

22. **B** The question asks for the value of a constant in a function. The question states that the function is true *for all positive values of x*, so plug in for x. Make $x = 2$. In function notation, the number inside the parentheses is the x-value that goes into the function, and the value that comes out of the function is the y-value. Plug in 2 for x in both functions. The first function becomes $f(2) = 2^k$. Multiply the first function by 2 to get $2f(2) = 2(2^k)$. The second function becomes $2f(2) = f(16 \times 2)$, or $2f(2) = f(32)$. Plug 32 in for x in the first function to get $f(32) = 32^k$. Thus, $2f(2) = 32^k$. Now that both equations are equal to $2f(2)$, set them equal to each other to get $2(2^k) = 32^k$. When dealing with exponents that are applied to different bases, find a way to rewrite the bases so they match. The 32 on the right side of the equation can be written as 2^5. The equation is now $2(2^k) = (2^5)^k$. On the left side of the equation, rewrite 2 as 2^1. The equation is now $2^1(2^k) = (2^5)^k$. When working with exponents, remember the MADSPM rules. On the left side of the equation, the MA part of the acronym indicates that Multiplying matching bases means to Add the exponents. On the right side of the equation, the PM part of the acronym indicates that raising a base with an exponent to another Power means to Multiply the exponents. The equation becomes $2^{1+k} = 2^{5k}$. Since the bases match, the exponents are equal, so $1 + k = 5k$. Subtract k from both sides of the equation to get $1 = 4k$. Divide both sides of the equation by 4 to get $\frac{1}{4} = k$. The correct answer is (B).

Module 2—Harder

1. **A** The question asks for the value of y that makes the inequality true. Solve the inequality for y. Start by multiplying both sides of the inequality by 4 to eliminate the fraction. The inequality becomes $4y < 3y - 2$. Next, subtract $3y$ from both sides to get $y < -2$. Because the value of y must be less than -2, (B), (C), and (D) are all too large. The correct answer is (A).

2. **C** The question asks for an equivalent form of an expression. Both terms have an a^2, so combine the coefficients, keeping in mind that subtracting a negative number is the same thing as adding. Subtract $-3a^2$ from $5a^2$ to get $5a^2 - (-3a^2) = 5a^2 + 3a^2 = 8a^2$. The correct answer is (C).

3. **C**   The question asks for the result when a number is increased by a percent. *Percent* means out of 100, so rewrite 20% as $\frac{20}{100}$. Multiply that by 70 to get $\frac{20}{100}(70) = 14$. Add 14 to the original number to get $70 + 14 = 84$. The correct answer is (C).

4. **14**   The question asks for the value of a constant in an equation with an infinite number of solutions. When an equation has infinitely many solutions, it will be true for any value of y, so plug in a value for y. Make $y = 2$, and the equation becomes $9(2) + 8 = 8 + 2k - 5(2)$, or $18 + 8 = 8 + 2k - 10$. This simplifies to $26 = 2k - 2$. Add 2 to both sides of the equation to get $28 = 2k$, then divide both sides of the equation by 2 to get $14 = k$. The correct answer is 14.

5. **C**   The question asks for the value of a trigonometric function for a particular right triangle. Begin by drawing a triangle and labeling the vertices. Be sure to put N next to the right angle.

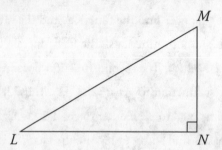

Next, use SOHCAHTOA to remember the trig functions and label the sides. The CAH part of the acronym defines the cosine as $\frac{adjacent}{hypotenuse}$. The question gives the cosine of angle L as $\frac{\sqrt{21}}{5}$, so label the side adjacent to L as $\sqrt{21}$ and the hypotenuse as 5. The figure should look something like this:

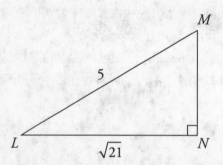

The SOH part of SOHCAHTOA defines the sine as $\frac{opposite}{hypotenuse}$, so find the side opposite angle M. It is already labeled as $\sqrt{21}$, and the hypotenuse is already labeled as 5. Thus, the sine of M is also $\frac{\sqrt{21}}{5}$. It can help to know that this is always true: in a right triangle, the sine of one of the non-90° angles is always equal to the cosine of the other non-90° angle. Either way, the correct answer is (C).

6. **38**   The question asks for the number of student tickets sold. Use Bite-Sized Pieces to translate from English to math and then solve the resulting system of equations. Let s represent the number of student tickets sold and r represent the number of regular tickets sold. Since the *100-seat theater* sold out, $s + r = 100$. *Student tickets* are \$24, *regular admission tickets* are \$36, and *total ticket sales* are \$3,144, so $24s + 36r = 3,144$. The question asks for the number of student tickets sold, so solve for s. Start with the first equation. Subtract s from both sides to get $r = 100 - s$. Substitute this value of r into the second equation to get $24s + 36(100 - s) = 3,144$. Distribute the 36 to get $24s + 3,600 - 36s = 3,144$. Combine like terms on the left side by subtracting to get $-12s + 3,600 = 3,144$. Subtract 3,600 from both sides to get $-12s = -456$. Divide both sides by -12 to get $s = 38$. The correct answer is 38.

7. **D**   The question asks for an expression representing the amount a customer would pay for shoes at sale verses non-sale prices. Translate the English into math in Bite-Sized Pieces and eliminate after each piece. The question states that *the tax rate of 6 percent is applied to the whole purchase*, so everything should be multiplied by 1.06 to represent the total, 1, plus the additional 6 percent, 0.06. Eliminate (A), which does not have 1.06 at all, and (C), which only has 1.06 multiplied by one term. The question also states that the *customer receives a 30 percent discount on a second pair of shoes after purchasing the first at regular price*, so the price of the second pair of shoes should be added to the first, not subtracted from it. Eliminate (B). The correct answer is (D).

8. **B**   The question asks for an equivalent form of an expression. There are variables in the answer choices, so plug in. Since y must be greater than 3, make $y = 4$. The expression becomes $\dfrac{1}{\dfrac{1}{2(4)} - \dfrac{1}{4+3}}$, which is $\dfrac{1}{\dfrac{1}{8} - \dfrac{1}{7}}$. To subtract fractions, make the denominators the same. One common denominator of 7 and 8 is 56. Multiply the numerator and denominator of $\dfrac{1}{8}$ by 7 to get $\dfrac{7}{56}$. Multiply the numerator and denominator of $\dfrac{1}{7}$ by 8 to get $\dfrac{8}{56}$. The expression becomes $\dfrac{1}{\dfrac{7}{56} - \dfrac{8}{56}}$, which is $\dfrac{1}{-\dfrac{1}{56}}$. To divide by a fraction, multiply the numerator by the reciprocal of the denominator to get $1 \times \left(-\dfrac{56}{1}\right)$ or -56. This is the target value; circle it. Now plug $y = 4$ into the answer choices to see which one matches the target value. Choice (A) becomes $3 - 4$ or -1. This does not match the target, so eliminate (A). Choice (B) becomes $\dfrac{2(4)^2 + 6(4)}{3-4}$, which is $\dfrac{2(16) + 24}{-1}$. Multiplying gives $\dfrac{32 + 24}{-1}$, which is -56.

Keep (B) but check the remaining answer choices just in case. Choice (C) is the reciprocal of (B), so it will equal $-\dfrac{1}{56}$. Eliminate (C). Choice (D) is the numerator of (B), so it will equal 56. Eliminate (D). The correct answer is (B).

9. **C** The question asks for the cost of an individual magnet at a souvenir shop when the individual cost of items is unknown. Translate the English to math, then solve the resulting system of equations for the price of 1 magnet. Let m represent the cost of one magnet and h represent the cost of one hat. The question states that *the cost of 5 hats and 9 magnets is $72.00*, which translates to $5h + 9m = 72$. The question also states that *the cost of 2 hats and 1 magnet is $14.50*, which translates to $2h + m = 14.50$. To solve for m, which is the cost of 1 magnet, find a way to cancel the h terms. Multiply the equations so the coefficients on the price of hats are the same but with opposite signs. Multiply the first equation by 2 to get $10h + 18m = 144.00$. Multiply the second equation by –5 to get $-10h - 5m = -72.50$. Now stack and add the equations.

$$
\begin{aligned}
10h + 18m &= 144.00 \\
+ \underline{(-10h - 5m} &= \underline{-72.50)} \\
13m &= 71.50
\end{aligned}
$$

Divide both sides of the resulting equation by 13 to get $m = 5.50$. The correct answer is (C).

10. **A** The question asks for a percent decrease. The function is in the form of the exponential growth or decay formula, which is *final amount = original amount*$(1 \pm \text{rate})^{\text{number of changes}}$. To find the percent decrease over 60 days, start by converting days into months. The question says to assume that *1 month has 30 days*. This means that 60 days = 2 months. The question also states that m represents the number of months, so $m = 2$. Plug 2 into the function for m to get $V(2) = 52(0.91)^{0.5(2)}$, which becomes $V(2) = 52(0.91)^1$. Since the number of changes is 1, the percent decrease only occurs once. The value inside the parentheses is $1 \pm \text{rate}$, so $0.91 = 1 \pm \text{rate}$. The rate is thus $1 - 0.91 = 0.09$. Since *percent* means out of 100, 0.09 is the same as 9%. The correct answer is (A).

11. **B** The question asks for the percent increase from a patient's actual height to that predicted by the line of best fit. Percent change is defined as $\dfrac{\text{difference}}{\text{original}} \times 100$. The child who is *exactly 8 years old* is 40 inches tall, and the line of best fit indicates that someone with an age of 8 will have a height of 50 inches. The difference in heights is $50 - 40 = 10$ inches. Because the question asks for a *percent increase*, use the smaller number as the original. The percent change is $\dfrac{10}{40} \times 100 = 25\%$. The correct answer is (B).

12. **B** The question asks how many times larger the surface area of sphere A is compared to the surface area of sphere B. Because the question asks for the relationship between the two surface areas, plug in values. Make the radius of sphere B equal to 2 and plug $r = 2$ into the surface area formula. The formula becomes $SA = 4\pi(2)^2$, or $SA = 16\pi$. The radius of sphere A is three times the radius of sphere B, so the radius of sphere A is $(3)(2) = 6$. Plug $r = 6$ into the surface area formula to get $SA = 4\pi(6)^2$, or $SA = 144\pi$. To find how many times larger the surface area of sphere A is, divide the surface area of sphere A by the surface area of sphere B: $\dfrac{144\pi}{16\pi} = 9$. The correct answer is (B).

13. **C** The question asks for the value of k, which is the x-coordinate of one of the x-intercepts of a parabola. The graph of parabola f has vertical symmetry and the axis of symmetry goes through the vertex. Since the vertex is at $(5, -3)$, the axis of symmetry is $x = 5$. Since one of the x-intercepts is $(3, 0)$, the other must be equidistant from the axis of symmetry. Since the distance from 3 to 5 is 2, the distance from 5 to k must also be 2. Therefore, $k = 5 + 2 = 7$. The correct answer is (C).

14. **A** The question asks for the graph of a function after it has been transformed. Adding or subtracting outside the parenthesis shifts the graph up or down. Thus, $+ 2$ means the graph of $f(x - 4) + 2$ is shifted 2 units up from the graph of $f(x)$. Adding or subtracting inside the parenthesis shifts the graph left or right. Thus, $- 4$ means the graph of $f(x - 4) + 2$ is shifted 4 units right from the graph of $f(x)$. Pick a point on the graph of $f(x)$ and make both transformations. The graph of $f(x)$ has a point at $(0, -2)$. Move this point 2 units up and 4 units to the right to get a point at $(4, 0)$. The graph in (A) includes this point, but the graphs in (B), (C), and (D) do not. The correct answer is (A).

15. **B** The question asks for the value of a constant. To determine when a quadratic equation has no real solutions, use the discriminant. The discriminant is the part of the quadratic formula under the square root sign, and can be written as $D = b^2 - 4ac$. When the discriminant is positive, the quadratic has two real solutions; when the discriminant is 0, the quadratic has exactly one real solution; and when the discriminant is negative, the quadratic has no real solutions. Thus, the discriminant of this quadratic must equal a negative number. The quadratic is given in standard form, $ax^2 + bx + c = 0$, so $a = 5$, $b = b$, and $c = 125$. Plug these into the discriminant formula to get $D = b^2 - 4(5)(125)$, or $D = b^2 - 2,500$. Plug in the values from the answer choices to see which value of b makes the discriminant negative. Start with a middle answer and try (C), 50. If $b = 50$, the discriminant becomes $D = 50^2 - 2,500$, or $D = 2,500 - 2,500$, or $D = 0$. This is not negative, so eliminate (C). A smaller value is needed, so try (B), 25. If $b = 25$, the discriminant becomes $D = 25^2 - 2,500$, or $D = 625 - 2,500$, or $D = -1,875$. This is negative, so stop here. The correct answer is (B).

16. **636** The question asks for the total distance run when a runner ran at different paces over time. The question states that the runner *ran for a total of 120 hours* and *spent 70% of her total time jogging at the slower pace*. Therefore, she spent $\dfrac{70}{100}(120) = 84$ hours running at the slower pace, which was 5 miles per hour. To find the distance, multiply the rate by the time to get $(5)(84) = 420$ miles. The runner

spent the rest of her time running at the faster rate of 6 miles per hour. The remaining time is 120 – 84 = 36 hours. Running at a pace of 6 miles per hour for 36 hours gives a distance of (6)(36) = 216 miles. The total distance traveled for the month is 420 + 216 = 636 miles. The correct answer is 636.

17. **C**   The question asks for $h(x + 3)$. There are variables in the answer choices, so plug in. Let $x = 2$. If $x = 2$, then $h(x + 3) = h(2 + 3) = h(5) = 2(5)^2 - 7(5) - 3 = 2(25) - 35 - 3 = 50 - 38 = 12$. Therefore, the target is 12; circle it. Plug $x = 2$ into each choice and eliminate any for which $h(5)$ is not equal to 12. In (A), $h(2 + 3) = 2(2^2) - 7(2)$, so $h(5) = 2(4) - 14 = 8 - 14 = -6$. Eliminate (A). In (B), $h(2 + 3) = 2(2^2) - 7(2) - 6$, so $h(5) = 2(4) - 14 - 6 = 8 - 20 = -12$. Eliminate (B). In (C), $h(2 + 3) = 2(2^2) + 5(2) - 6$, so $h(5) = 2(4) + 10 - 6 = 8 + 4 = 12$. Keep (C), but check (D) just in case. In (D), $h(2 + 3) = 2(2^2) - 23(2) + 15$, so $h(5) = 2(4) - 46 + 15 = 8 - 31 = -23$. Eliminate (D). The correct answer is (C).

18. **18**   The question asks for the value of a constant in a function. The question provides three points on the graph, so plug in one of the points. Start with (2, 0) because it will make the math easier. Plug $x = 2$ and $y = 0$ into function q to get $0 = 4(2)^3 - b(2)^2 + 14(2) + 12$. This becomes $0 = 4(8) - 4b + 28 + 12$. Simplify the equation to get $0 = 32 - 4b + 40$, and then $0 = 72 - 4b$. Next, add $4b$ to both sides of the equation to get $4b = 72$. Lastly, divide both sides of the equation by 4 to get $b = 18$. The correct answer is 18.

19. **D**   The question asks for a comparison of the means and standard deviations of two data sets. It might be possible to estimate based on the dot plots. Standard deviation is a measure of how close together the data points are in a group of numbers. A list with numbers close together forms a steeper curve and has a small standard deviation, whereas a list of numbers spread out forms a shallower curve and has a large standard deviation. The values in group Y are clustered around the middle with fewer off to the sides, so the standard deviation of group Y is less than the standard deviation of group X. Eliminate (B) since it gets this piece backwards. Eliminate (C) since it says the standard deviations are equal. The difference between (A) and (D) is whether the mean in group X is less than the mean in group Y or the two means are equal. From the figures, it looks like the means are equal: the range of numbers is the same, and they appear to be evenly split on either side of 7. If there's time, check using the formula $T = AN$, where T is the total, A is the average, and N is the number of things. The question states that there are *20 athletes participating in each group*, so the number of things is 20. To find the total, one method is to carefully enter the value for every dot in a calculator and add them. Another method is to multiply each value by the number of dots for that value. In group X, for example, 1 zero = 0, 2 twos = 4, 3 fours = 12, etc. Using either method, the total of group X is 140, and the total of group Y is 140. Because the totals and numbers of things are equal, the averages will also be equal: $140 = (A)(20)$, and $A = 7$. This confirms the estimate made by looking at the figures. Eliminate (A) since it does not say that the means are equal. The correct answer is (D).

20. **A**   The question asks for the value of a constant in a system of equations with infinite solutions. When two linear equations have infinitely many solutions, they are the same line when graphed, and the two equations are equivalent to each other. Since k is a coefficient of x, look for a way to cancel the y-terms. Start by combining like terms in the second equation: add $44x$ to both sides of the equation to get $84x + 8 = 36y$. Subtract 8 from both sides of the equation to get $84x = 36y - 8$. Now that both equations have the terms in the same order, work with the first equation so that the y-term has the

same coefficient as it does in the second equation but with the opposite sign. Multiply the first equation by 4 to get $4kx = -36y + 8$.

Now stack and add the equations.

$$4kx = -36y + 8$$
$$+ \underline{84x = 36y - 8}$$
$$4kx + 84x = 0$$

Subtract $84x$ from both sides of the resulting equation to get $4kx = -84x$. Divide both sides of the equation by $4x$ to get $k = -21$. The correct answer is (A).

21.　**A**　The question asks for the function that represents the cost of car detailing services when the cost of services is discounted after a certain number of services are ordered. There are variables in the answer choices, and the question asks about the relationship between the number of detailing services and the cost, so plug in. The question provides information about a visit with 9 detailing services, so plug in $s = 9$. The total cost of the visit is $360, so that is the target value; write it down and circle it. When $s = 9$, (A) becomes $f(9) = 30(9) + 90$, then $f(9) = 270 + 90$, then $f(9) = 360$. This matches the target value of 360, so keep (A) but check the remaining answers just in case. Choice (B) becomes $f(9) = 30(9) + 180$, then $f(9) = 270 + 180$, then $f(9) = 450$. This does not match the target value, so eliminate (B). Choice (C) becomes $f(9) = 40(9)$, or $f(9) = 360$; keep (C). Choice (D) becomes $f(9) = 60(9)$, or $f(9) = 540$; eliminate (D). Since two answers worked, try plugging in a different value and make $s = 10$. In the original scenario, the first 3 detailing services cost $(60)(3) = \$180$ total, so the remaining $9 - 3 = 6$ services cost the remaining $\$360 - \$180 = \$180$. That means each additional detailing service costs $\frac{180}{6} = \$30$. If a customer purchases 10 detailing services, the first 3 still cost $180 combined. The remaining $10 - 3 = 7$ are $30 each, for a cost of $(7)(30) = \$210$. The total cost is $\$180 + \$210 = \$390$. This is the new target value; circle it. Now plug $s = 10$ into the remaining answer choices. Choice (A) becomes $f(10) = 30(10) + 90$, then $f(10) = 300 + 90$, then $f(10) = 390$. This matches the new target value; keep (A). Choice (C) becomes $f(10) = 60(10)$, or $f(10) = 600$; eliminate (C). The correct answer is (A).

22.   **D**   The question asks for a pair of congruent angles in a figure containing triangles. When given two or more triangles and information about the ratios of the sides, look for similar triangles. Sides $\overline{FJ}$ and $\overline{FH}$ are both on the smallest triangle, while $\overline{FG}$ and $\overline{GH}$ are both on the largest triangle. Redraw the two triangles side-by-side to better see the similarities. Start with triangle *FHJ*, redrawing it by itself with the same orientation it currently has, labeling the vertices.

Then draw a bigger triangle next to it with the same shape as triangle *FHJ*, like this:

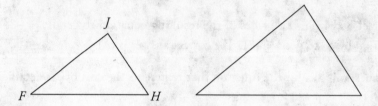

Since the ratio of $\dfrac{FJ}{FH}$ is equal to $\dfrac{FG}{GH}$, label the sides of this new triangle correspondingly. Make sure to keep angle *FGH* as the smaller angle and angle *GFH* as the larger one, like this:

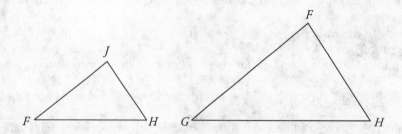

Now it is easier to check corresponding angles. Choice (A) gives the angles on the lower left of the big triangle and the lower right of the small triangle. These are not necessarily congruent, so eliminate (A). Choice (B) gives an angle that does not appear on either triangle and the angle at the top of the small triangle. These are not necessarily congruent, so eliminate (B). Choice (C) gives an angle that does not appear on either triangle and the angle on the lower left of the small triangle. These are not necessarily congruent, so eliminate (C). Choice (D) gives the angles at the tops of both triangles, so these angles are congruent. The correct answer is (D).

Part III
PSAT/NMSQT Prep

Chapter 6
Reading and Writing Introduction

Now that you've learned some general strategies for the PSAT and taken and analyzed your first test, it is time to dive into some content chapters. This chapter will introduce you to the Reading and Writing section of the PSAT.

FIND YOUR STRENGTHS AND WEAKNESSES

As you may recall from the Introduction, your PSAT is going to have two Reading and Writing modules, each consisting of 27 questions. Of those 54 total verbal questions, 25–33 will be Reading questions and 19–31 will be Writing questions. You'll have 32 minutes for each module, which gives you a little more than a minute for each question.

While College Board jams the topics of Reading and Writing into the same section, you may have recognized that they really represent two different sets of skills. The Reading questions ask you to either answer a question about a text you have read (such as what its main idea is or why the author included a certain piece of information) or choose an answer that completes the text based on the inferences that can be made. On the other hand, the Writing questions will ask you to choose the best construction of a sentence, based on such aspects as punctuation, grammar, and style. These questions will also ask you to connect ideas with transitions or to fit certain rhetorical goals.

This distinction is important because you may find that you are stronger at Reading or stronger at Writing. Recognizing your strengths and weaknesses will help you follow POOD most effectively, and as you practice it will allow you to identify what areas you need to focus on during your study time.

THE LESSER OF TWO (OR THREE) EVILS

We think you'll find it most helpful to think of each Reading and Writing module as having 3 parts, displayed visually below.

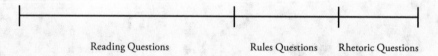

Reading Questions   Rules Questions   Rhetoric Questions

This is the same order and rough proportion of questions you will see in each module. (It's worth keeping in mind that the Reading actually has two parts according to College Board. However, there isn't a strong difference in the types of questions you'll see in both parts, so we don't think you need to notice when the section switches. See the Reading lesson for more on that.) If you are stronger or faster at Writing questions, you may find that it makes more sense for you to start about halfway through the section when those questions start. Of course, if Reading questions are easier for you, it's fine to start at the beginning of the module. Either way, it's helpful to be able to recognize these three categories of questions so that you'll notice when the module switches from one to the next and be able to apply the right set of steps to each question type. Let's take a look at the characteristics of each category.

Reading Questions

Any question with text in the form of a poem or a work of fiction is going to be in the Reading portion. The same is true for dual texts (which have a Text 1 and a Text 2), passages that involve graphs, and questions that ask you to fill in the blank with the most appropriate word. The rest of the Reading questions will generally ask you for the meaning or purpose of some or all of the text.

Rules Questions

It should be easy to spot when the module switches from Reading questions to Rules questions. That's because all Rules questions ask the same thing: *Which choice completes the text so that it conforms to the conventions of Standard English?* Only Rules questions ask this, so if you're planning to start with the Rules questions, you can skip to about the middle of the section and click ahead until you see the first one with that question. It's worth noting that Rules questions will be some of the fastest ones for many students, as you typically only need to read a single sentence and will be tested on basic punctuation and grammar rules, rather than comprehension.

Rhetoric Questions

Once again, it should be easy to spot when the Rules questions end. That's because the rest of the questions, Rhetoric questions, will not ask the standard question you saw above for Rules questions. If you want to start with these questions, go about three-quarters of the way into the section and continue until you stop seeing the question about the conventions of Standard English. Furthermore, Rhetoric questions come in only two formats. The first involves transition words, and the second has bullet points instead of a passage. So, these should be relatively easy to identify by looking for those two unique attributes, but you will learn more about these distinctions in later chapters.

As you prepare for the PSAT, try to identify which of these three categories makes sense for you to begin with. It's best to start with the category in which you will be able to get the questions right quickly and easily.

STARTING OFF ON THE RIGHT SIDE…OF THE SCREEN

As you saw earlier in this introduction, it's the question, rather than the text, that will give you a clue as to what category of question you are dealing with. Once you've established that, you'll be able to execute the appropriate strategy for that specific type of question. To that end, we've developed a basic approach for all Reading and Writing questions:

Reading and Writing Basic Approach

1. Read the question.
2. Identify the question type.
3. Follow the basic approach for that question type.

As we discussed earlier, you are free (and encouraged!) to start with the types of questions at which you excel and to leave for last the ones you struggle with most or that you expect to take the most time. For each question, skip over the text initially and go straight to the question. That will help you to confirm whether it is a Reading question, Rules question, or Rhetoric question. In some cases, such as with most Reading questions, reading the question first will also give you an idea of what you need to find in the text, which will allow you to do double duty as you read: you can already start to look out for what the question will be asking you about as you read the text.

In the chapters that follow, we'll show you our basic approach for each type of question that we expect you to see on the Reading and Writing section. Once you have learned and practiced these approaches, you'll know exactly what to do once you identify the type of question you are looking at. It's worth noting that we have put the verbal chapters in the same order that we expect the questions to be in for both modules of the Reading and Writing section, so you can use them as a guide for approximately where each question type will appear. Let's dive in!

Chapter 7
Reading Comprehension

Reading questions will account for 25–33 of the 54 RW questions and will always appear before the Writing questions in each module. The Reading questions will ask you to do many different tasks, including selecting the best vocabulary word to fill in a blank, understanding the function of portions of the text, comparing multiple texts, finding the main idea of a text, determining which answer would best support the author's argument, and completing the text based on data from tables and graphs. Each text will range from 25 to 150 words and be accompanied by just a single question, so efficiency will be of the essence. The purpose of this chapter is to introduce you to how the Reading and Writing Basic Approach can be adapted to each of the Reading question types. This will help you streamline how you take the test and keep you focused on what information you need in order to get your points.

PSAT READING: CRACKING THE TEXTS

Answering Reading questions is exactly like taking an open-book test: all of the information that you could be asked about is right in front of you, so you never have to worry about any history, literature, or chemistry that you may (or may not) have learned in school. Of course, you will use the text to answer the question, but your *primary* goal is to find the information that helps answer the question, NOT to understand every last word of the text perfectly. What you need is a way to get in and get out of this section with as little stress and as many points as possible.

To put it another way, think of the process you go through when planning a trip. You start by selecting where you most want to visit before you plan anything else, and then you find the best route to your destination. The PSAT Reading questions are the same: for each of them, your first job is to understand the specific question you are answering, then to locate the specific evidence in the text that either provides a direct answer to the question or offers support as to what the answer to the question should be.

Your Mission:

Identify what you are being asked to do for each question and locate the answer or support in the text as efficiently as possible. Get as many points as you can.

Okay…so how do you get those points? Let's start with the instructions for the Reading and Writing section as a whole.

DIRECTIONS

The questions in this section address a number of important reading and writing skills. Each question includes one or more passages, which may include a table or graph. Read each passage and question carefully, and then choose the best answer to the question based on the passage(s).

All questions in the section are multiple-choice with four answer choices. Each question has a single best answer.

Notice that the directions clearly state the correct answer is based on the passage(s). This is great news! You do not have to rely on your outside knowledge here. All the College Board cares about is whether you can read a text and understand it well enough to answer some questions about it. Unlike in Math or the Writing questions, there are no formulas to memorize, no comma rules to learn. You just need to know how to efficiently process the text, the question, and the answer choices in order to maximize your score.

Your POOD and the Reading Questions

You will get one question with its text (or occasionally, with two texts) on screen at a time. While it's tempting to do the questions in the order they appear, you will sometimes be confronted with a question or text that seems difficult or confusing to you for one reason or another. In that situation, Mark the question for review, use your LOTD, and move on to the next question. You can always come back to your marked questions later after you've tackled every question you knew how to do for certain.

How do you decide which ones to do and which ones to skip? Consider these concepts:

- **Topic:** You may be able to tell from glancing at the passage whether it is about science, history, the arts, or another topic area. If you have significant topic-based strengths and weaknesses, use that knowledge to decide your POOD.
- **Literature:** Most, if not all, fictional passages will contain a blurb introducing the author and title. This will help you quickly decide when to do these passages. You'll also spot poems quickly, and your strengths and weaknesses will tell you when to do those.
- **Question Type:** In this lesson, you'll learn how to identify the different types of questions as well as the order they come in. Determine which ones will be fastest and easiest for you and start with those.

> Don't forget: On any questions that you skip, always fill in your LOTD!

Basic Approach for the Reading Questions

To tackle the Reading questions, we'll expand on the Reading and Writing Basic Approach that you learned previously. No matter what type of question you are confronted with, you will follow the same five basic steps. We'll adapt these steps for each question type as we go through this chapter.

1. **Read the Question**. As with all Reading and Writing questions, you need to first understand what you are being asked to do before you dive into any text.

2. **Identify the Question Type**. Each question has a phrase that indicates a very specific task that you are being asked to accomplish for that question. This also affects how you will adapt the rest of the approach and is lastly a chance to apply your POOD, marking and using LOTD on question types you'd rather deal with later, or not at all.

3. **Read the Text(s)**. Read the text(s) thoroughly, keeping the question task in mind. Remember that you are looking for an answer to the question, or at the very least, evidence that can help answer the question. You don't need to memorize, or even understand, every detail!

4. **Highlight What Can Help (and Annotate if Needed)**. Within the text, you'll want to highlight a phrase or sentence that can help answer the question. It could be a direct answer to the question or a piece of information that the question wants you to do something with. On certain question types, such as Vocabulary or Purpose, you'll also make an annotation that will help you nail the correct answer.

5. **Use POE**. Eliminate anything that isn't consistent with your highlighting (and annotation if you made one). Don't necessarily try to find the right answer immediately, because there is a good chance you won't see anything that you like. If you can eliminate answers that you know are wrong, though, you'll be closer to the right answer. If you can't eliminate three answers with your prediction, use the POE criteria (which we'll talk about on the next page).

Where the Money Is

A reporter once asked notorious thief Willie Sutton why he robbed banks. Legend has it that his answer was, "Because that's where the money is." While reading comprehension is safer and slightly more productive than larceny, the same principle applies. Concentrate on the questions and answer choices because that's where the points are. The text is just a place for the College Board to stash facts and details. You'll find them when you need to. Think of the Reading questions as an open-book test. The correct answer is correct because the text says so, not because of any deep understanding or interpretation of the story.

Before we see these steps in action, we should revisit POE. You saw earlier in this book how POE, or Process of Elimination, is an effective way to earn points on multiple-choice questions. On Reading, there are very specific types of traps. If you catch them, your accuracy will improve dramatically!

POE Criteria

On most of the easy and medium questions, you'll be able to eliminate three of the four answers simply by using your highlighting and annotation. On other questions, usually the Harder questions, your prediction will help you get rid of one or two answers, and then you'll need to consider the remaining answers a little more carefully. If you're down to two answers, and they both seem to make sense, you're probably down to the right answer and the trap answer. Luckily, there are some common traps that the College Board will set for you, and knowing them can help you figure out which is the trap answer and which is the right answer. Here are the main types of traps you will see:

When to use the POE Criteria?
Use these criteria if you have multiple answers remaining after comparing the answers to what you highlighted/annotated in the text.

- **Recycled Language:** These answer choices repeat exact words and phrases from the text but use those words and phrases incorrectly. They often establish relationships between the words and phrases that do not exist in the text.
- **Could Be True**: These answers might initially look good because they make sense or seem logical based on outside reasoning, but they lack support within the text itself.
- **Extremes**: These answers look just about perfect except for a word or phrase that goes too far beyond what the text can support. This also includes answers that could be called insulting or offensive to a person or a group.
- **Right Answer, Wrong Question:** These answer choices are true based on the text, but they don't answer the question asked. They can also miss the author's purpose in including information and focus on the content of the information instead.
- **Opposites:** These answer choices use a single word or phrase that make the answer convey a tone, viewpoint, or meaning not intended by the author. This can include using a word such as "not" in the answer or using a negative vocabulary word when the tone of the text was positive.
- **Half-Right:** These answers address part but not all of the question task. They can also have one half of the answer address the question perfectly and the other half contain at least one of the traps mentioned previously.

QUESTION TYPES AND FORMATS

Now that you know the steps of the Basic Approach, let's consider the different types of questions you'll be answering. It's not important that you can identify the question types by the names we give them. But it is extremely important that you can read a question and know how to respond. Is the question asking you what the author says, why the author included something, what a particular word means, which answer best supports a claim, etc.? The next section of this chapter will help you decode those question types and formats. Your score will depend on your ability to figure out if a question is asking you what, why, how, or which. Luckily, you can understand what you are being asked by learning and adapting the Basic Approach to each of the question types.

Question Types and Formats

- Vocabulary
- Purpose
- Dual Texts
- Retrieval

- Main Idea
- Claims
- Charts
- Conclusions

VOCABULARY

The first group of questions you will see will ask you to choose an appropriate vocabulary word to fill in a blank or determine what the meaning of a word is in the context of the paragraph it's in. The PSAT tests a blend of common words with multiple meanings and slightly more advanced vocabulary words, but the important thing to remember is that the context of the sentence(s) surrounding the word will provide a clue that you can highlight. This will allow you to annotate, or write down, your own word for the blank, which will help your POE.

Kuei-Chih Lee's landscape artistry can best be described as _____ : his large-format installations make use of raw materials collected on-site in order to blend his created work with the natural environment.

1 🔖 Mark for Review

Which choice completes the text with the most logical and precise word or phrase?

Ⓐ beautiful

Ⓑ harmonious

Ⓒ jarring

Ⓓ acclaimed

Here's How To Crack It

If you **read the question** and see "most logical and precise word or phrase," you can **identify the question type** as a **Vocabulary** question.

As you **read the text,** look for something you can **highlight** to help understand what word should go in the blank. The text says after the colon that the materials that Kuei-Chih Lee collects are used to *blend his created work with the natural environment.* A good word to write down in your **annotation** box based on the highlighting would be "blended" or "made to fit together."

Use POE! Choice (A), *beautiful,* is a **Could Be True** trap answer: while Lee's landscape art may indeed very be beautiful if seen in real life, the author never states how aesthetically pleasing Lee's art actually is. Eliminate (A). Choice (B), *harmonious,* is a good synonym for "blended," so keep (B). Choice (C), *jarring,* is the **Opposite** of what we annotated, so eliminate (C). Choice (D), *acclaimed,* is another **Could Be True** trap: it's very possible Lee is a well-known artist and is celebrated by others, but the text does not say so one way or the other. Eliminate (D). The correct answer is (B).

VOCABULARY (*The Second Format*)

The Basic Approach for Vocabulary works equally well even if a word is provided instead of a blank—you'll highlight a clue in the text and then write down your own word, treating the word given as if it weren't there. Do not give in to the temptation to simply answer the question without following all of the steps. It's very common for College Board to include 1–2 Could Be True traps on each Vocabulary question, so thinking too much can make you jump to those traps. Read, highlight, and annotate on vocabulary questions, and you will be trap, and stress, free!

The following text is adapted from Thomas Love Peacock's 1818 novel *Nightmare Abbey.* Marionetta, a young woman, is reflecting on her relationship with a young man named Scythrop.

> Scythrop grew every day more reserved, mysterious, and distrait; and gradually lengthened the duration of his diurnal seclusions in his tower. Marionetta thought she perceived in all this very manifest symptoms of a warm love cooling.

2 ⬜ Mark for Review

As used in the text, what does the word "reserved" most nearly mean?

(A) Agreeable

(B) Observant

(C) Withdrawn

(D) Hostile

Here's How To Crack It

If you **read the question** and see "most nearly mean," you can **identify the question type** as a **Vocabulary** question.

As you **read the text,** look for something you can **highlight** to help understand what a good synonym for *reserved* would be. The text states that Scythrop is lengthening his *seclusions in his tower* and Marionetta feels that a *warm love* is *cooling.* A good word to write down in your **annotation** box based on the highlighting would be that Scythrop is "less available" or "not around as much."

Use POE! Choice (A), *agreeable*, is a positive word that is the **Opposite** of the tone of "less available," which is negative. Eliminate (A). Choice (B), *observant*, is **Right Answer, Wrong Question**: it's a good synonym for *perceived* later in the text but not for *reserved*. Eliminate (B). Choice (C), *withdrawn*, is a good synonym for "less available," so keep (C). Choice (D), *prearranged*, is a **Could Be True** trap as it's another definition of *reserved* that doesn't match what we highlighted, so eliminate (D). The correct answer is (C).

VOCABULARY (*Try it out!*)

Use all of the skills you've learned to this point on this Vocabulary question.

Improper drainage of water in pools and spas used for personal recreation has led to widespread contamination that can cause immense environmental damage and even kill plant and animal life. Chemicals in pool water may not _____ local habitats completely but will continue to cause great harm unless disposed of properly.

3	🔖 Mark for Review

Which choice completes the text with the most logical and precise word or phrase?

(A) decimate

(B) buttress

(C) overlook

(D) refute

Here's How To Crack It

If you **read the question** and see "most logical and precise word or phrase," you can **identify the question type** as a **Vocabulary** question.

As you **read the text,** look for something you can **highlight** to help understand what word should go in the blank. The text states that the chemicals from pool water *can cause immense environmental damage and even kill plant and animal life* and *will continue to cause great harm*. A good word to write down in your **annotation** box based on the highlighting would be "destroy" or "wipe out."

Use POE! Choice (A), *decimate,* meaning "kill or "remove a large percentage of" is a good synonym for "destroy," so keep (A). Choice (B), *buttress,* actually means "support," so it is the **Opposite** of what we are looking for. Eliminate (B). Choice (C), *overlook,* is a **Could Be True** trap because it seems likely that at least some pool and spa owners are overlooking the damage that pool chemicals can cause, but it doesn't match "destroy," so eliminate (C). Choice (D), *refute,* which means "disprove," is negative, but it doesn't match "destroy," so eliminate (D). The correct answer is (A). **It's worth noting that some answers won't have a clearly defined trap, such as choice (D)—they simply won't be consistent with the word we write down or the situation described in the text.**

One last thing: if you do well enough on your first Reading and Writing module, the harder second Reading and Writing module will likely test some more difficult words than those you've seen here. You may need to start brushing up on some vocabulary as you continue to prepare for the PSAT in order to keep your score progressing. As you work your way through this book, whenever you come across a word that you don't know, add it to a word list. Continue adding new words and definitions, and study the list to keep improving your score.

PURPOSE

The second group of questions you may see ask you why the author wrote the text or how a sentence functions in the text. The PSAT isn't looking for any outside reasoning on these questions, as it's not possible to know why any author does anything without asking him or her! Instead, you're being asked for the *most likely, best supported* reason that the text or sentence was written or included. Highlight main ideas in the text or connecting ideas between sentences and annotate when needed. Lastly, don't forget the power of using POE—some answers will contain words or phrases that simply don't match what happened in the text regardless of what the author's purpose was.

In 1978, British biochemist Sir Philip Cohen was experimenting with a type of enzyme to understand how calcium activated that enzyme. He noticed a faint blue smear occurring at the bottom of the gel used in his experiments but had assumed it to be of little importance. After hearing another scientist's lecture, Cohen realized that calmodulin, a calcium-binding protein, was the source of the blue smear. His next experiments confirmed that calmodulin still appeared in his gels even after the gels had been boiled and was therefore heat stable. He correctly concluded that calmodulin mediated the activity of calcium within the enzyme.

---

4 ☐ Mark for Review

Which choice best states the main purpose of the text?

(A) To explain how misunderstood calmodulin is

(B) To describe Cohen's realization regarding calmodulin

(C) To illustrate how calcium-binding proteins function

(D) To place emphasis on the importance of calcium within enzymes

Here's How To Crack It

If you **read the question** and see "main purpose of the text" you can **identify the question type** as a **Purpose** question.

As you **read the text,** look for something you can **highlight** to help understand why the text was written. At the end of the text, Cohen *concluded that calmodulin mediated the activity of the calcium within the enzyme,* which relates back to what Cohen was trying *to understand* at the start of the text. Write in your **annotation** box that the purpose here is "role of calmodulin in Cohen's work" since both Cohen and calmodulin are the main focuses of the text.

Use POE! Choice (A) is **Extreme**: just because Cohen didn't realize its importance at first, the text doesn't indicate that the protein is *misunderstood* by Cohen or anyone else. Eliminate (A). Choice (B) is consistent with the annotation, so keep (B). Choice (C) is **Right Answer, Wrong Question.** We do learn a little about how calmodulin, one calcium-binding protein, functions, but this can't be the main purpose because it does not mention Cohen, who is a central figure in the text. Eliminate (C). Choice (D) is **Recycled Language.** It borrows *calcium within the enzyme* from the very end of the text, but the text doesn't ever stress exactly how important calcium is to an enzyme, nor does this answer mention calmodulin or Cohen. Eliminate (D). The correct answer is (B).

PURPOSE

The same approach can be used when a question asks how a sentence functions in the text. Generally, if you focus on the sentences before and/or after the indicated sentence, you'll be able to highlight connections between ideas that keep the sentence flowing. From this logical flow, you'll be able to annotate the role that the indicated sentence performs.

The following text is from Alexandre Dumas's 1850 novel *The Black Tulip*. Cornelius, the main character, is in jail and is guarded by a turnkey, an older word for jailer.

Cornelius saw nothing but the golden brocade cap, tipped with lace, such as the Frisian girls wore; he heard nothing but someone whispering into the ear of the turnkey. <u>But the latter put his heavy keys into the white hand which was stretched out to receive them, and, descending some steps, sat down on the staircase which was thus guarded above by himself, and below by the dog.</u> The headdress turned round, and Cornelius beheld the face of Rosa, blanched with grief, and her beautiful eyes streaming with tears.

5   🔖 Mark for Review

Which choice best describes the function of the underlined sentence in the text as a whole?

(A) It details the outcome of a conversation mentioned in the previous sentence.

(B) It describes the specifics of the construction of the jailhouse.

(C) It explains that an individual is debating his obligations to duty.

(D) It introduces a claim that the following sentence further explains.

Here's How To Crack It

If you **read the question** and see "function of the _____ sentence" you can **identify the question type** as a **Purpose** question.

As you **read the text,** look for something you can **highlight** to help understand why the sentence was included. The text mentions that someone was *whispering into the ear of the turnkey,* or jailer. The turnkey then *put his heavy keys into the white hand* of the other individual and descends the staircase, leaving Cornelius alone with that other individual, Rosa. Write in your **annotation** box that the function of the sentence here is "to describe what happened after the whisper."

Use POE! Choice (A) is consistent with the annotation because it does indeed describe what happens after the whisper, so keep (A). Choice (B) is **Right Answer, Wrong Question.** It's true that we now know something about the layout of this particular part of the jailhouse, but this ignores the question of WHY the sentence was included in the context of the sentences before and after it. Eliminate (B). Choice (C) **Could Be True**: while we can imagine that a jailer would debate giving his jail keys to someone, we get no insight into any turmoil or debate going on in the jailer's mind. Eliminate (C). Choice (D) is **Half-Right:** The following sentence may further explain what happens next in the story, but no *claim* is introduced in the underlined sentence. Eliminate (D). The correct answer is (A).

One last thing: you can also be asked for the overall structure of the text. Don't panic! You are still being asked for the purpose of the text as a whole. Once you write down what the purpose is, the correct answer will describe what the author did in the text to accomplish that goal. An example of one of these questions is included in the drill for this chapter.

DUAL TEXTS

The next question type you may see will offer you two texts rather than one and ask how someone from the second text would respond to an idea, person, or group from the first text. These can seem intimidating at first, but all you are looking for is a single idea mentioned in the first text that is commented upon by the second. It will be pretty obvious when you are faced with a Dual Texts question (after all, there will be two texts!), so we won't need to **Identify the Question Type.** Instead, you'll slightly modify the Reading Basic Approach to focus on what you need in order to understand the link between these texts!

Dual Texts Basic Approach

1. Read and understand the question.
2. Read Text 1 and highlight the idea or viewpoint referenced in the question.
3. Read Text 2 and highlight the main idea or viewpoint towards the same information from Text 1.
4. If necessary, write the relationship between the texts down in your Annotation box.
5. Use POE and eliminate answers that are inconsistent with one or both texts.

Text 1

Anxiety has long been considered a critical area of focus for those involved in both psychological analysis and behavior management. The traditional treatment for anxiety has been prescription medication. But what about situations when medication is ineffective or ill-advised? Psychologists continue to explore possible alternative treatments for anxiety to this day.

Text 2

Professor Spike W. S. Lee and his team have demonstrated a possible link between self-cleansing and anxiety reduction. They conducted a study of 1,150 adults and showed each of them one of three different videos: how to properly wash hands, how to properly peel an egg, and how to properly draw a circle. The subjects were then all exposed to a series of situations meant to induce anxiety. Those individuals who had seen the handwashing video demonstrated consistently lower levels of anxiety than those who had seen either of the other two videos.

6 ☐ Mark for Review

Based on the texts, how would Lee and his team (Text 2) most likely respond to the "traditional treatment" discussed in Text 1?

(A) By noting that it may not be the only possible treatment by which an individual may reduce anxiety

(B) By claiming that those who prescribe medication for anxiety completely ignore the emotional benefits of frequent hand-washing

(C) By stating that his team's findings help establish handwashing as an alternative treatment to prescribed medication

(D) By calling for other psychologists to focus their own efforts on how handwashing frequency increases with exposure to instructional videos

Here's How To Crack It

When you **read and understand the question,** you can see that it's asking for what Text 1 says about the "traditional treatment" and how Lee in Text 2 would respond to the discussion of that treatment.

As you **read Text 1,** look for something you can **highlight** regarding the traditional treatment. The text states that the *traditional treatment for anxiety has been prescription medication.* As you **read Text 2,** look for something you can **highlight** related to treatment, anxiety, or prescription medication. The text states that there is *a possible link between self-cleansing and anxiety reduction* and that those who watched the handwashing video *demonstrated consistently lower levels of anxiety.*

Write in your **annotation** box that Lee and his team would reply by saying "there's something else that may help reduce anxiety." You may even feel confident enough to move forward with just your highlighting—it depends on how clear the link is to you when you read!

Use POE! Choice (A) is consistent with the highlighting and annotation: self-cleansing is mentioned in Text 2 as reducing anxiety levels, so keep (A). Choice (B) is **Extreme** because of the phrase *completely ignores.* Text 1 never makes any comment regarding handwashing's emotional benefits nor does it ever claim prescription medication is the only treatment, just the traditional one. Eliminate (B). Choice (C) is also **Extreme**: Lee and his team never state that handwashing is now an *established alternative treatment* to prescription medication, just that it may lower anxiety levels. Eliminate (C). Choice (D) is **Recycled Language.** It misuses *handwashing* and *videos* from Text 2 and establishes a link between them (*increases*) that Text 2 never states. Additionally, Text 2 never calls for any *other psychologists* to research this area. Eliminate (D). The correct answer is (A).

DUAL TEXTS (*Try it out!*)

Use all of the skills you've learned to this point on this Dual Texts question.

Text 1

Plant species need to be able to ensure their own survival just as animals do. But when a plant species invades a new region and is able to ward off predators, this raises questions as to what could be responsible for such protection. Scientists have been looking into this mostly to discover how to control the spread of invasive plant species and why local animal populations meet with such difficulty in doing so. Though many scientists know of soil microbiota, a type of bacteria found in a plant's root nodule, they believe some other organism must be responsible for the plants' invasiveness and hardiness.

Text 2

Researcher Satu Ramula and her team in Finland planted a mixture of North American and Finnish garden lupines (*lupinus polyphyllus)* into Finnish soil to examine the impact of soil microbiota on the plant's growth and development. One crop was planted into nutrient-poor soil that contained microbiota from local lupine populations while the other crop was planted into nutrient-poor soil that contained no microbiota. Regardless of the country of origin, the crop of garden lupines in the soil containing microbiota not only grew much larger than the other crop's lupines, but also secreted a much stronger scent that is a natural deterrent to snails, the garden lupine's most common predator.

---

7 ☐ Mark for Review

Based on the texts, what would the author of Text 2 most likely say about the scientists' belief regarding soil microbiota from Text 1?

(A) It is overly celebratory given the evidence that Ramula and her team have found to the contrary.

(B) It is understandable given that Ramula and her team have demonstrated that soil microbiota is not linked to plant growth.

(C) It is prematurely dismissive given the experiments run by Ramula and her team.

(D) It is surprising considering that Ramula and her team's research was able to control plant spread.

Here's How To Crack It

When you **read and understand the question,** you can see that it's asking for what the scientists in Text 1 would say about the soil microbiota and how the author of Text 2 would respond to their statement.

As you **read Text 1,** look for something you can **highlight** regarding soil microbiota. The text states that the *scientists know of soil microbiota* but *believe some other organism must be responsible for the plant's invasiveness and hardiness.* As you **read Text 2,** look for something you can **highlight** related to soil microbiota's role in plant growth. The text states that *the crop of garden lupines containing soil microbiota not only grew much larger* but also *secreted a much stronger scent* than the crop without.

Write in your **annotation** box that the author of Text 2 would "disagree" with the scientists regarding soil microbiota.

Use POE! Choice (A) is **Half-Right:** Ramula and her team have indeed found evidence contrary of the scientists' belief, but there's no *celebratory* tone in Text 1. Eliminate (A). Choice (B) is the **Opposite** of what we annotated—Ramula and her team HAVE demonstrated that soil microbiota is linked to plant growth and the author of Text 2 would NOT find the scientists' belief *reasonable.* Eliminate (B). Choice (C) is consistent with what we annotated by showing a disagreement, so keep (C). Choice (D) is **Recycled Language.** It misuses *control, plant,* and *spread* from Text 1: Text 2 never states that Ramula and her team were able to control plant spread with the research they conducted. Eliminate (D). The correct answer is (C).

RETRIEVAL

The next group of questions you may see switches up the focus of the Reading and Writing section substantially. Up until this point, the questions have all been about structure—the right vocabulary word for a blank, the reason something was included, how one text relates to another, etc. Starting with Retrieval questions, you'll be focusing on what the text actually says rather than why the author included something or how someone would respond. This means that many times, you'll be able to go right to using POE once you highlight something in the text. As we move forward through this chapter, we will still mention when you should be annotating.

The following is adapted from George Eliot's 1871 novel *Middlemarch*. The author is describing Dorothea Brooke, one of the central characters in the novel.

It had now entered Dorothea's mind that Mr. Casaubon might wish to make her his wife, and the idea that he would do so touched her with a sort of reverential gratitude. How good of him—nay, it would be almost as if a winged messenger had suddenly stood beside her path and held out his hand towards her! For a long while she had been oppressed by the indefiniteness which hung in her mind, like a thick summer haze, over all her desire to make her life greatly effective.

---

8 ☐ Mark for Review

According to the text, what is true about Miss Brooke?

- (A) She is skeptical of Mr. Casaubon's career as a messenger.

- (B) She wants to know Mr. Casaubon's feelings towards summer.

- (C) She is enthused by the prospect of marriage to a particular individual.

- (D) She prefers marriage over other types of relationships.

Here's How To Crack It

If you **read the question** and see "according to the text" or "based on the text" you can **identify the question type** as a Retrieval question. It's not looking for anything fancy—it wants to know exactly WHAT the text says, and which answer says the same thing using slightly different words.

As you **read the text,** look for what you can **highlight** about Miss Brooke. The text states that the idea of Mr. Casaubon wanting to marry her *touched her with a sort of reverential gratitude* and the idea was *almost as if a winged messenger had suddenly stood beside her path and held out his hand towards her*. It also states that *she had been oppressed by the indefiniteness*. You don't know what the answers will say until you see them, so underline anything relevant to the person or thing in question and understand that the answers could be consistent with any of the above highlighting.

Use POE! Choice (A) is **Recycled Language** as it misuses the word *messenger* from the text. Eliminate (A). Choice (B) is also **Recycled Language:** the word *summer* is used to describe Miss Brooke's mental state before realizing Mr. Casaubon may propose, not the season. Eliminate (B). Choice (C) is consistent with the positive feelings Miss Brooke expresses in your highlighting. Keep (C). Choice (D) **Could Be True:** Miss Brooke may indeed prefer marriage over any other types of relationship, but no other types of relationships are mentioned in the text. Eliminate (D). The correct answer is (C).

One last thing: you can also be asked why something happens in the text. Why something happens is not a Purpose question—it's still Retrieval because it actually wants to know what reason the author gave for something occurring in the text. You only need to find and highlight that reason, and you're ready to use POE. An example of one of these questions is included in the drill for this chapter.

MAIN IDEA

Quite similar to Retrieval questions, Main Idea questions also want to know what the author said. The difference is that Main Idea questions are looking for the single sentence or idea that is the main focus of the text rather than a detail about a character or thing. This should be the sentence or idea that all of the other sentences and ideas are connected to. Many times, this will be the first or last sentence of the paragraph, but College Board can place the main idea anywhere. As you read, ask yourself, "Which sentence does all of the other sentences build to or build off of?"

Fire photography, the practice of taking photographs of firefighting operations, has numerous applications in both occupational safety and criminal investigation. Fire photographers can also work with fire departments directly. Despite their numerous job prospects, all fire photographers must first and foremost undergo rigorous safety training before setting foot into the field.

9 ☐ Mark for Review

Which choice best states the main idea of the text?

(A) Advanced cameras can now take pictures from a much safer distance than fire photographers can.

(B) Although there are numerous possible career paths for fire photographers, they must prioritize safety given the nature of their jobs.

(C) While there are many possible career paths, most fire photographers prefer working directly with fire departments.

(D) Fire photographers have been charged with documenting fires for a century.

Here's How To Crack It

If you **read the question** and see "main idea" you can **identify the question type** as a **Main Idea** question. It's looking for the sentence that all of the other sentences are building up to.

As you **read the text,** look for a main idea that you can **highlight**. While sentences 1 and 2 both discuss job prospects of fire photographers, sentence 3 mentions that no matter what field they choose, *all fire photographers must first and foremost undergo rigorous safety training.* Highlight sentence 3: it's the sentence the correct answer should be consistent with.

Use POE! Choice (A) **Could Be True:** while this is probably true in real life, there is no mention of *advanced cameras* in the text. Eliminate (A). Choice (B) is consistent with the highlighting and written with slightly different words as College Board will almost always do. Keep (B). Choice (C) is **Half-Right:** there are indeed many possible career paths according to the text, but the second half of the answer is **Extreme.** We don't know that *most* fire photographers prefer any particular field. This half of the answer is also **Recycled:** College Board is hoping you'll see the words *directly, working,* and *with fire departments* and choose them because they match the text. Eliminate (C). Choice (D) **Could Be True:** it's possible the career of fire photography has been around for decades, but we have no proof of that in the text. Eliminate (D). The correct answer is (B).

CLAIMS

The next group of questions you will see ask which answer would best illustrate, support, or weaken a claim made by the author. Note that these questions are often interspersed with the next question type, **Charts,** but luckily, the skills you need for these two question types are similar. As with Retrieval and Main Idea questions, your main job here will be to identify the claim made by the author in the text without any regard to the structure or purpose of the text. However, you'll need to perform the exact task required by the question and keep a razor-sharp eye as you use POE: it only takes one word or phrase to make an answer do the opposite of what was intended!

"A Dry Spell" is a 1905 short story by Einar H. Kvaran. In the story, the narrator and his companions wait out an ongoing rain torrent in a store where they work as clerks. In his musings, the narrator expresses a desire for the presence of individuals that he formerly considered an annoyance: _____

10 ☐ Mark for Review

Which quotation from the narrator's musings best illustrates the claim?

(A) "We sat there and smoked, staring vacantly at the half-empty shelves, and all but shivering in the damp room."

(B) "We made clever comments to the effect that the farmers were now getting plenty of moisture for the hay-fields, and that it would be a pity if rain should set in now, right at the beginning of the haying season."

(C) "We were tired of the store—indeed, I should like to know who would have enjoyed it."

(D) "We had often cursed their lengthy visits, but now that they had hired themselves out during the haymaking, we suddenly realized that they had often been entertaining."

Here's How To Crack It

If you **read the question** and see the word "which" along with "claim," "hypothesis," or "argument," you can **identify the question type** as a **Claims** question.

Sometimes, as in this example, the text will be quite short with one single claim, so **read the text** and **highlight** the claim: the right answer must show that the narrator *expresses a desire for the presence of individuals he formerly considered an annoyance.*

Use POE! Choice (A) only mentions that the narrator and his companions are miserable in the store and makes no mention of any individuals they now miss, so eliminate (A). Choice (B) is **Half-Right:** the narrator and his companions seem to be poking fun at the farmers by making *clever comments* about them, but the answer does not express any desire to see these farmers back in the store or that the farmers were ever customers in the store in the first place. Eliminate (B). Choice (C) expresses negative emotions towards the store but not towards any individuals, so eliminate (C). Choice (D) is consistent with both halves of the claim: the narrator and his companions have *suddenly realized* the people referred to here *had often been entertaining*, but previously, the narrator and his companions *had cursed their lengthy visits*. Keep (D). The correct answer is (D).

CLAIMS (*Poetry*)

While poetry can be tested on Purpose, Retrieval, and Main Idea questions, Claims questions are where you will most often see poetry. The nice thing about it showing up on Claims questions is that you don't need to read and attempt to understand an entire poem. Instead, just like the previous question, your main job is to understand the claim in the question stem and then read through the couplets in the answer choices extremely carefully, eliminating answers that only address part of the claim or miss it entirely.

"A Ballad of Evesham" is a 1933 poem by Francis T. Palgrave. The poem demonstrates a character's ignorance of a deception created by his enemy:

11 Mark for Review

Which quotation from the poem most effectively illustrates the claim?

- (A) "Earl Simon on the Abbey tower / In summer sunshine stood, / While helm and lance o'er Greenhill heights / Come glinting through the wood."

- (B) 'My son!' he cried, 'I know his flag / Amongst a thousand glancing':— / Fond father! no!—'tis Edward stern / In royal strength advancing."

- (C) "The Prince fell on him like a hawk / At Al'ster yester-eve, / And flaunts his captured banner now / And flaunts but to deceive:—"

- (D) "—Look round! for Mortimer is by, / And guards the rearward river:— / The hour that parted sire and son / Has parted them for ever!"

Here's How To Crack It

If you **read the question** and see the word "which" along with "claim," "hypothesis," or "argument," you can **identify the question type** as a Claims question.

As with our previous example, the text will often be quite short with one single claim, so **read the text** and **highlight** the claim: the right answer must show *a character's ignorance of a deception created by his enemy.*

Use POE! Choice (A) introduces the main character, Earl Simon, but does not yet indicate that the approaching army he sees is a *deception*. Eliminate (A). Choice (B) is consistent with the claim: the earl believes his son has returned because he sees his son's flag, but another of his sons warns him that it is an impostor who carries the son's banner, meaning that the Earl did not know about the deception. Keep (B). Choice (C) is **Half-Right:** it references the deception and the circumstances that led to the capture of the son's banner, but there is no evidence in this answer that the Earl is ignorant of this fact. Eliminate (C). Choice (D) indicates that the Earl and his son will not meet again but does not address either the Earl's ignorance of the deception or the deception itself, so eliminate (D). The correct answer is (B).

CLAIMS (*Try it out!*)

Use all of the skills you've learned to this point on this Claims question. Note that this question is asking you to support the claim and is accompanied by significantly more text. Don't panic: treat it just like looking for and highlighting a main idea on a Main Idea question, and then make sure the answer is as consistent with what you highlighted as possible!

Artificial sweeteners offer an appealing alternative to sugar, but they may carry unintended consequences for the body because of their effect on the gut microbiome. It has been demonstrated that the bacteria that make up the gut microbiome affect glucose tolerance and appetite. Researchers at the Weizmann Institute of Science claim that the consumption of artificial sweeteners such as sucralose can lower glucose tolerance and increase appetite in humans. The researchers conducted a study comparing the glucose tolerance and appetite levels of people who had been fed sucralose against a control group who was not fed sucralose.

12 🔖 Mark for Review

Which finding from the researchers' study, if true, would most directly support their hypothesis?

(A) Both the individuals who consumed sucralose and the control group had much higher glucose tolerance levels at the conclusion of the study.

(B) At the conclusion of the study, individuals who consumed sucralose had lower glucose tolerance levels but also lower appetite levels than the control group.

(C) Individuals who consumed sucralose had lower glucose tolerance levels and higher appetite levels at the conclusion of the study than the control group.

(D) When individuals who consumed sucralose were interviewed, they were found to also have consumed large quantities of water, which is known to decrease appetite.

Here's How To Crack It

If you **read the question** and see the word "which" along with "claim," "hypothesis," or "argument," you can **identify the question type** as a Claims question.

As you **read the text,** look for and **highlight** the researchers' claim: they claim that *the consumption of artificial sweeteners such as sucralose can lower glucose tolerance and increase appetite.* The right answer should offer a finding that is as consistent with this claim as it possibly can be.

Use POE! Choice (A) is the **Opposite** of the claim, as those who consumed sucralose should have *lower* glucose tolerance levels, not *higher.* Eliminate (A). Choice (B) is **Half-Right:** those who consume sucralose should indeed have *lower glucose tolerance levels* but they should have *higher,* not *lower,* appetite levels than the control group, according to the claim. Eliminate (B). Choice (C) is consistent with the claim: it is exactly what the researchers claimed should happen in the text. Keep (C). Choice (D) mentions that those who consumed sucralose also consumed *large quantities of water*. Not only does the researchers' claim not mention the consumption of water, but this answer does not even comment on the whether or not the appetite levels of those who consumed sucralose increased or decreased. Eliminate (D). The correct answer is (C).

One last thing: These questions can also ask you to weaken or undermine a claim or hypothesis. When confronted with weaken or undermine, you will still highlight the claim, and then look for an answer that contradicts as much as possible without introducing anything irrelevant to the claim (like water consumption.) An example of one of these questions is included in the drill for this chapter.

CHARTS

As mentioned before, Charts questions are interspersed with Claims questions, and you won't necessarily see both on the same module. The biggest difference here is that you'll be reading some information from a table or graph in addition to the text. As with Dual Texts, it will be pretty clear when you are asked a Charts question, so we'll once again modify the Reading Basic Approach slightly to make sure you catch everything needed to earn these points!

Charts Basic Approach

1. Read and understand the question.
2. Read the title, key/legend, variables, and units from the table or graph.
3. Read the text and look for the same information you saw in the table or graph.
4. Highlight the claim made by the text regarding the information in the table or graph.
5. Use POE and eliminate answers that are inconsistent with one or both texts.

Nutritional Information for Skim Cow's Milk and Unsweetened Oat Milk Based on a 1 Cup Serving

Milk type	Skim cow's milk	Unsweetened oat milk
Calories	90	90
Fat (g)	0	1.5
Sodium (mg)	130	120
Sugars (g)	12	4

In the field of nutrition, skim cow's milk and unsweetened oat milk are two popular substitutions for whole milk, which can be too high in fat and cholesterol for some individuals. Each whole milk substitute goes through different processes that affect its final nutritional value. For instance, unsweetened oat milk is made by straining a blend of rolled oats (which have less sugar than cow's milk) and water. A scientist theorized that because skim milk is whole milk that has been run through a centrifuge to separate out all of the fat droplets, it would likely have less fat content but higher sugar content than would unsweetened oat milk.

13 Mark for Review

Which choice most effectively uses data from the table that supports the scientist's hypothesis?

(A) The skim cow's milk has higher sugar content than fat content, but it also contains more sodium than does unsweetened oat milk.

(B) Both the skim cow's milk and the unsweetened oat milk's sodium contents were over 100 milligrams per cup.

(C) The skim cow's milk and unsweetened oat milk both contain 90 calories in an average 1 cup serving.

(D) The unsweetened oat milk has lower sugar content but higher fat content than does the skim cow's milk.

Here's How To Crack It

As you **read and understand the question**, you'll notice the words "which" and "table" or "graph" indicate this is a Charts question. You are looking for the scientist's hypothesis regarding the information in the table.

As you **read the titles, key/legend, etc.** from the table, you'll want to note that table shows two different *milk types* and four different nutritional units (*calories, fat, sodium,* and *sugar*), 3 of which are in *grams*. As you **read the text,** look for a claim the text makes regarding these terms specifically. **Highlight** the last sentence, which states that skim milk *would likely have less fat content but higher sugar content than unsweetened oat milk.* The answer should be as consistent as possible with this claim.

Use POE! Choice (A) is **Half-Right:** the information is consistent with the table, but it mentions sodium, which is not related to the sugar and fat content referenced by the claim in the text. Eliminate (A). Choice (B) is also **Half Right** for the exact same reason: any mention of sodium is not relevant to the claim. Eliminate (B). Choice (C) is **Right Answer, Wrong Question.** It's 100% true but would not support the scientist's hypothesis as the theory does not mention calories. Eliminate (C). Choice (D) is exactly consistent with the scientist's hypothesis as stated in the text. Keep (D). The correct answer is (D).

---○---

CHARTS (*Text Completions*)

Charts questions can also ask you to complete an example or statement made by the text. Following the Charts Basic Approach is critical because you are looking for what the text and chart say about the exact same data. Above all else, the answer you choose must be consistent with the data in the table or graph and be relevant to the sentence that you are completing.

---○---

Approximate Appearance Percentage for Three Blood Types in Four Regions

Region	O+	A+	B+
Asia	37%	28%	25%
Americas	55%	28%	9%
Africa	47%	27%	17%
Oceania	42%	33%	11%

Blood is critical to the function of the human body, as it delivers nutrients to vital organs, exchanges carbon dioxide and oxygen, and moves white blood cells through the circulatory system to fight infections. Blood is often categorized by one of eight blood types, which are referred to first by a letter or letter combination (A, B, AB, or O) and then a positive or negative marker (such as O+ or AB−.) Researcher Anshool Deshmukh compiled blood type data from thousands of individuals and re-organized the data by region to better understand the distribution of the blood types O+, A+, and B+ by region. His research shows that type O+ blood has the highest frequency of occurrence in all four regions researched, while type B+ blood in turn has the lowest frequency of occurrence. For example, whereas the approximate appearance percentage for type O+ blood in Asia was 37%, the approximate appearance percentage for _____

14 ☐ Mark for Review

Which choice most effectively uses data from the table to complete the example?

(A) type O+ blood in the Americas was 55%.

(B) type B+ blood in Africa was 17%.

(C) type O+ blood in Oceania was 42%.

(D) type B+ blood in Asia was 25%.

Here's How To Crack It

As you **read and understand the question**, you'll notice the words "which" and "table" or "graph" indicate this is a Charts question.

As you **read the titles, key/legend, etc.** from the table, you'll want to note that the table shows *approximate appearance percentage* for *three blood types* in *four regions*. As you **read the text,** look for a claim the text makes regarding these terms specifically. **Highlight** the second-to-last sentence, which states that *type O+ blood has the highest frequency of occurrence in all four regions researched, while type B+ blood in turn has the lowest frequency of occurrence.* The text wants to give an example of this, and the first half of the example states that *the average appearance for type O+ blood in Asia was 37%.* So, the correct answer should complete this example while staying consistent with the table and the claim.

Now use **POE!** Choice (A) focuses on the wrong blood type and the wrong region: we want to support the claim that type O+ is the most common of the three types shown while B+ is the least common. Furthermore, we should focus on the region mentioned in the example, Asia, so that the two percentages discussed in the example have a common link. Eliminate (A) and use this to inform the rest of your POE. Choice (B) is **Half-Right** because it focuses on the correct blood type, B+, but the wrong region. Choice (C), like (A), gets both region and blood type incorrect. Eliminate (C). Choice (D) focuses on the correct blood type, B+, which is contrasted with O+ in the text's claim, as well as the same region, Asia, that the example discusses. Keep (D). The correct answer is (D).

CONCLUSIONS

The last question type you will see is very similar to the Charts question you just saw: it will ask you to complete the text. However, Conclusions questions are text only and are always asking you the same thing: which of the four answers is a logical conclusion based on all of the other sentences given in the text? Like Claims and Charts questions, you just need to read the main claim made or investigated by the author and choose an answer consistent with the statements regarding that same claim from the text.

Western honeybees (*Apis mellifera*) are social insects that live inside rigid colonial nests made from wax, which can make it difficult to observe bee behavior within the colony. Bees typically form colonies with thousands to tens of thousands of bees, the weight of which would seem to place immense strain on the nest structure. Using an *x*-ray machine, researchers at CU Boulder have observed that swarms of *A. mellifera* inside the nest will form pyramids of bees, with larger numbers of bees at the base of the pyramid and fewer bees in each level as you move up the swarm. These researchers therefore imply that _____

15 🔖 Mark for Review

Which choice most logically completes the text?

(A) the pyramids formed by *A. mellifera* swarms may reduce strain on the nest structure.

(B) any individual *A. mellifera* bee can be in danger of suffocation by the rest of the bee swarm.

(C) improving the numbers of *A. mellifera* requires Western intervention.

(D) colonial nests enable *A. mellifera* to produce high quantities of wax.

Here's How To Crack It

If you **read the question** and see "which choice most logically completes the text," you can **identify the question type** as Conclusions: that is the prompt you will see on these questions.

As you **read the text,** look for the main focus of the text. The text focuses on *western honeybees (Apis mellifera).* You should **highlight** the main points made about these bees: the bees *live in rigid colonial nests,* the bees' *weight would seem to place immense strain on the nest,* and the bees *will form pyramids of bees* inside their nests, *with larger numbers of bees at the base.* The right answer should ideally reference all these points: the nest structure, the strain on the nest structure, and the pyramids the bees form within the nest.

Use POE! Choice (A) is consistent with the main points of the other sentences and references all three ideas. Keep (A). Choice (B) **Could Be True:** it's logical to think any bee could be *in danger of suffocation* with that many bees in the colony, but the text never makes this claim. Eliminate (B). Choice (C) is **Recycled Language:** it misuses the words *Western* and the numbers of bees mentioned in the text. Eliminate (C). Choice (D) is also **Recycled Language:** the author says the bees make the nests from wax, not that the nests enable them to make wax, even if that **Could Be True** in real life. Eliminate (D). The correct answer is (A).

CONCLUSIONS (*Try it out*!)

Conclusions questions are pretty common and it's almost a guarantee you'll see at least 1 of them on each module you complete. Use all of the skills you've learned to this point on this Conclusions question.

Barefoot running, the act of running without footwear, has increased in popularity since the year 2000, with exercise enthusiasts looking to reduce the repetitive stress injuries caused by padded running footwear. However, the practice dates back thousands of years, with some long-established Latin American and African groups utilizing barefoot running even up to the present day despite the availability of modern footwear in those regions. This suggests that before the year 2000, _____

16 ☐ Mark for Review

Which choice most logically completes the text?

- Ⓐ certain practitioners of barefoot running in different regions of the world may have discovered its benefits before the year 2000.

- Ⓑ barefoot running has made exercise more accessible to those who cannot afford expensive footwear.

- Ⓒ exercise enthusiasts speculated that barefoot running would soon surpass other methods of exercise as awareness of its benefits becomes more prevalent.

- Ⓓ footwear manufacturers could increase profits if they created region-specific running shoe designs.

Here's How To Crack It

If you **read the question** and see "which choice most logically completes the text," you can **identify the question type** as Conclusions: we want a sentence or phrase that references as many ideas from the text correctly as possible.

As you **read the text,** look for the main focus of the text. The text focuses on *barefoot running*. You should **highlight** the main points made about this activity: barefoot running *has increased in popularity since the year 2000* among exercise enthusiasts as a way to prevent injury, *but the practice dates back thousands of years*. Also, *Latin American and African groups* have apparently used barefoot running for a long time and continue to use it *despite the availability of modern footwear in those regions*. The right answer should ideally reference both these points: barefoot running becoming more popular with exercise enthusiasts since the year 2000 as a way to prevent injury, and Latin American and African groups using it for a much longer period of time even when given the option to change to modern footwear.

Use POE! Choice (A) is consistent with the main points of the other sentences and references both main ideas. Keep (A). Choice (B) is **Extreme:** there is no support given to conclude that people in Latin America and Africa cannot afford the footwear. It is directly implied that they choose not to wear it. Eliminate (B). Choice (C) **Could Be True:** while it's likely at least some exercise enthusiasts correctly predicted the trend, no support for this is given in the text. Eliminate (C). Choice (D) also **Could Be True:** region-specific footwear sounds like a logical way to boost sales to regions that may have passed on modern footwear, but nothing about footwear manufacturers or their practices is mentioned in the text. Eliminate (D). The correct answer is (A).

One last thing: These questions will occasionally ask you to "best describe something as presented in the text." The skills for this prompt are identical: identify the main focus of the text and highlight each idea regarding that focus!

Reading Drill

Below, you'll find an assessment featuring one of each of the eight question types you've learned in this chapter, in the common order in which they would typically appear on a Reading module. Use all of the skills you've learned and be ready for some of the different question variations that we promised you earlier in the chapter. Answers can be found in Part IV.

---

1 ☐ Mark for Review

In many cultures, dogs and elderly humans share a type of bond known as a true symbiotic relationship: in this positive feedback loop, the dog can help the elderly person complete simple tasks and grants the person a true companion with which to communicate. In return, the person _____ by providing the dog with shelter, food, medical care, and affection, all of which it would respond to warmly based on its natural instincts as a pack animal.

Which choice completes the text with the most logical and precise word or phrase?

- (A) diverges
- (B) exaggerates
- (C) reciprocates
- (D) counters

---

2 ☐ Mark for Review

The following text is adapted from Jane Porter's 1809 novel *The Scottish Chiefs*. The narrator opens the novel by providing the setting within which the action of the story will take place.

Bright was the summer of 1296. The war which had desolated Scotland was then at an end. Ambition seemed satiated; and the vanquished, after having passed under the yoke of their enemy, concluded they might wear their chains in peace. Such were the hopes of those Scottish noblemen who, early in the preceding spring, had signed the bond of submission to a ruthless conqueror, purchasing life at the price of all that makes life estimable—liberty and honor.

Which choice best describes the overall structure of the text?

- (A) It explains one group's strategy for winning a war and then emphasizes the despair that another group feels about not having won the war.
- (B) It details the outcome of a war and then explains a group's reasoning for accepting that outcome.
- (C) It emphasizes that a group is distraught about the current situation and then speculates as to why allies have yet to assist the group.
- (D) It describes one group's concerns about foreign leadership and then specifies the government of that leadership.

---

3 ☐ Mark for Review

Text 1

In the 1990s, anecdotal evidence was compiled by a group of independent researchers studying animal behavior who announced a surprising conclusion: <u>domesticated felines, commonly known as cats, did not respond when called by their owners</u>. The group concluded that this was most likely due to a cat's more independent natural instincts—because most feral cats are solitary predators, they likely do not see their owners as protectors and therefore may not heed their vocal instructions.

Text 2

A French team of animal behaviorists led by Charlotte de Mouzon has recently investigated how 16 different cats responded to pre-recorded voice samples from their owners versus how the same 16 cats responded to pre-recorded voice samples from strangers. De Mouzon and her team monitored the cats' behaviors as they listened to the audio samples and noted that the cats increased their behavior intensity when directly addressed by the voice on their owners' audio samples but either did not react or decreased their behavior intensity when called by the voice samples of the strangers.

How would the author of Text 2 most likely respond to the underlined claim in Text 1?

Ⓐ By stating that while the claim may seem accurate, the findings of de Mouzon's team imply a stronger link between cats and their owners' voices than the independent researchers do

Ⓑ By strongly concurring with the claim but noting that the connection it assumes conflicts with the findings of the anecdotal analysis run by the independent researchers

Ⓒ By praising the claim for indicating that domesticated cats would have inherited the predator-like nature of their feral feline ancestors

Ⓓ By criticizing the claim for being based on the premise that before being domesticated, cats responded to the human voice

4 ☐ Mark for Review

Once the native language of the region of Cornwall, the Cornish language today has only about 557 practitioners. Cornish can trace its roots back nearly 2,000 years, but the language experienced a sharp decline in users from 1300 to 1800, after which no record of any living user could be found for decades. The efforts of linguists and etymologists over the last hundred years have gone a long way to reviving Cornish, which had its "extinct" status removed by UNESCO in 2010.

According to the text, why was the Cornish language declared extinct?

Ⓐ Its complex syntax discourages any new practitioners.

Ⓑ Its rate of growth slowed down more than linguists expected.

Ⓒ Its active users died or became difficult to verify.

Ⓓ It stopped spreading into new regions because it was surpassed by other languages.

5 ☐ Mark for Review

The following text is from Archibald Lampman's 1899 poem "The Mystery of a Year." In this poem, the speaker is describing a woman whom he has known for some time.

A little while, a year agone,
  I knew her for a romping child,
A dimple and a glance that shone
  With idle mischief when she smiled.

To-day she passed me in the press,
  And turning with a quick surprise
I wondered at her stateliness,
  I wondered at her altered eyes.

Which choice best states the main idea of the text?

Ⓐ The speaker is reminiscing about a past romantic relationship with a woman.

Ⓑ The speaker is astonished at the changes within a certain individual.

Ⓒ The speaker is an expert in observing subtle changes in others.

Ⓓ The speaker uses intricate and complex thought processes to impress those around him.

6 ☐ Mark for Review

While grazing on grass, cows suffer immense discomfort from biting flies. Across the world, many societies rely on cows for meat and dairy, yet biting flies account for over $2 billion a year in losses for the U.S. cattle industry alone, as cows succumb to disease or infection caused by the bites. To combat this, a team of Japanese researchers painted zebra stripes onto six Japanese Black cows and then observed the cows for three days. Noting that the number of bites on the zebra-striped cows were far less than those on unpainted cows, the team theorized that the zebra stripes must confuse the biting flies' landing and biting patterns; this, in turn, reduces the number of bites each cow receives.

Which finding, if true, would most directly undermine the team's hypothesis?

Ⓐ For the cows observed in the study, the number of bites caused by insects other than biting flies was not reduced by the presence of the zebra stripes.

Ⓑ For the cows observed in the study, biting flies were more prevalent near cows that did not have the zebra stripes.

Ⓒ For some cows observed in a different study, the presence of zebra stripes reduced the number of bites by biting flies nearly to zero.

Ⓓ For some cows observed in a different study, the number of bites caused by biting flies increased on cows painted with zebra stripes.

7 ⚑ Mark for Review

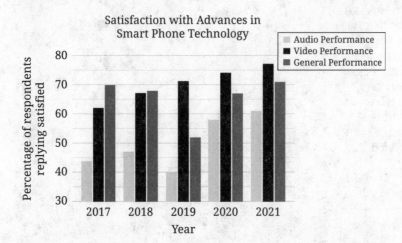

A steep curve of innovation in the domain of smart phone technology can lead to unrealized expectations and unsatisfied consumers, but detailed information regarding consumer satisfaction is not always readily accessible to the public. Recently, a group of researchers from an online technology website released its findings after polling the same tech-savvy smart phone users over the last five years and measuring their general satisfaction with their smart phone performance that year as well as measuring their more specific satisfaction with their phones' audio and video performance. One notable aspect of this publication is that consumer satisfaction with general performance does not necessarily correlate with satisfaction with specific performance areas, as is the case in the group's poll, where general performance satisfaction _____

Which choice most effectively uses data from the graph to illustrate the claim?

Ⓐ was roughly correlated with video performance satisfaction in 2018 but deviated significantly from video performance satisfaction in 2019.

Ⓑ was consistently higher than video performance satisfaction each year from 2017 to 2021.

Ⓒ reached its lowest level in 2019, which also had the lowest recorded level of satisfaction in audio performance.

Ⓓ was notably higher than video performance satisfaction in 2017 but significantly lower than video performance satisfaction in 2019.

8 ☐ Mark for Review

Hobby tunneling, or carving a tunnel by hand, is a form of recreation for individuals wishing to test their physical or emotional fortitude. In a poll of tunnel hobbyists, a large percentage reported that their tunnel started as something useful such as a wine cellar or evacuation route, and then they simply continued digging once the initial job was completed. An even larger percentage of those polled stated that the effort required to make their tunnels seemed disproportionate to the stated purpose. These replies suggest that _____

Which choice most logically completes the text?

(A) many tunnel hobbyists are uncertain of why they started their tunnels.

(B) many tunnel hobbyists believe they should only tunnel on their own properties.

(C) hobby tunneling may be about more than simply accomplishing a goal.

(D) hobby tunneling can improve a practitioner's mental conditioning more than it improves the practitioner's physical conditioning.

Summary

- The Reading questions on the PSAT make up just over 50 percent of your Reading and Writing Section score.

- Reading questions are presented in order of difficulty (which resets with each question type) but because some question types appear may appear once, twice, or not at all on each module, it's important to rely on your POOD to pick up the points you can get, and don't forget LOTD on the rest!

- Reading is an open-book test! Use that to your advantage by focusing only on the text you need to get each point.

- After you read the text, highlight the phrase or sentence that most addresses the question task. Annotate if you need to—sometimes, writing down a word or phrase will help you use POE more effectively.

- If you have more than one answer left after you eliminate the ones that don't match what you highlighted and annotated, compare the remaining answers to see if any of them are **Recycled Language; Could Be True; Extreme; Right Answer, Wrong Question; Opposite; or Half-Right.**

- Tackle Dual Texts questions using the Dual Texts Basic Approach. Highlight the information, claim, or theory that both texts make a comment on and annotate if needed.

- Tackle Charts questions using the Charts Basic Approach. Highlight the statement or claim in the text that uses as much terminology in the chart as possible. Always familiarize yourself with the chart first before reading any of the text,

- Practice, practice, practice—with eight question types, most of which with 2–3 different formats, it can feel at first like it's too much to keep track of. But the more you use the Reading Basic Approach and see that it is the same steps EVERY single time, the more comfortable you will be no matter what the PSAT throws at you!

- Remember most of all to not let a question bog you down. If you find yourself stuck or running low on time, LOTD and move on!

Question Types Review Chart		
Type	**Question Word**	**Common Question Phrasing**
Vocabulary	What?	• Which choice completes the text with the most logical or precise word or phrase? • As used in the text, what does the word X most nearly mean?
Purpose	Why or How?	• Which choice best describes the function of the X sentence in the overall structure of the text? • Which choice best states the main purpose of the text? • Which choice best describes the overall structure of the text?
Dual Texts	How?	• Based on the texts, how would X (Text 2) most likely respond to X (Text 1)?
Retrieval	What?	• According to/based on the text, what is true about X? • According to the text, why did X happen? • Based on the text, how does X respond to Y?
Main Idea	What?	• What is the main idea of the text?
Claims	Which?	• Which quotation from the poem most effectively illustrates the claim? • Which quotation from X most effectively illustrates X's claim? • Which statement/finding, if true, would most directly/strongly support X's claim/hypothesis/argument/prediction? • Which finding, if true, would most directly weaken/undermine X's claim/hypothesis/argument?
Charts	Which?	• Which choice most effectively uses data from the table/graph to complete the text/statement/example? • Which choice most effectively uses data from the table/graph to illustrate the claim? • Which choice best describes data from the table/in the graph that support X's suggestion/claim/hypothesis/conclusion?
Conclusions	Which?	• Which choice most logically completes the text? • Which choice best describes X as presented in the text?

Chapter 8
Rules Questions:
Punctuation

After the Reading portion of the RW section, you'll see
a set of questions that we call Rules questions. These
questions encompass various punctuation and grammar topics, and rather than being grouped by topic,
they are in order of difficulty only. This means you'll
see a mix of topics, and you may notice the questions
getting harder from the first Rules question to the last
one. In this chapter, you'll learn the punctuation rules
that are tested in questions throughout this portion of
the RW module.

WAIT; THE PSAT WANTS ME TO KNOW
HOW TO USE A SEMICOLON?

Kurt Vonnegut once wrote, "Here is a lesson in creative writing. First rule: Do not use semi-colons…All they do is show you've been to college." Unfortunately, the writers of the PSAT don't quite agree. They want you to know how to use the semicolon and a few other types of weird punctuation as well. In this chapter, we're going to talk about the varieties of punctuation that the PSAT wants you to know how to use. Learn these few simple rules, and you'll be all set on the punctuation questions.

As you may recall, punctuation questions fall under the Rules category. This category also includes grammar questions. Remember, you can easily spot the Rules questions by their question stem: *Which choice completes the text so that it conforms to the conventions of Standard English?*. How can you tell whether it's testing sentence structure or grammar? Ask yourself the following question:

> What's changing in the answer choices?

Look at the answer choices. If you see punctuation marks—commas, periods, apostrophes, semicolons, colons—changing, then the question is testing punctuation. Then, as you work the question, make sure to ask the big question:

> Does this punctuation need to be here?

The particular punctuation mark you are using—no matter what it is—must have a specific role within the sentence. You wouldn't use a question mark without a question, would you? Nope! Well, all punctuation works that way, and in what follows, we'll give you some basic instances in which you would use some type of punctuation. Otherwise, let the words do their thing unobstructed!

The Rules questions are in order of difficulty—NOT by type. So, you'll see a mix of punctuation and grammar questions, going from easy to hard, until you get to the Rhetoric questions.

COMPLETE AND INCOMPLETE IDEAS

In order to decide what type of punctuation is needed to connect ideas in a sentence, you must be able to identify whether the ideas being connected are complete or incomplete. A complete idea can stand on its own. It might be its own sentence, or it might be part of a longer sentence, but it's allowed to be by itself. Here are some examples.

> *The view is beautiful.*
> *Look at that sunset!*
> *How high is the summit?*
> *I gazed at the majestic mountains before me.*

As you can see, commands and questions can be complete ideas. However, they are rarely tested on the PSAT. Most complete ideas on the PSAT will be statements. In general, a complete idea must have a subject and a verb. Sometimes it needs more than that. Consider the following idea:

> *The tour guide told us we will need*

This idea has a subject (*tour guide*) and a verb (*told*), but it's missing the rest of the idea—what *we will need*. Therefore, this idea is incomplete. An incomplete idea could also be missing the subject, verb, or both, as in the examples below.

> *Bought hiking boots*
> *To get to the top of the mountain*
> *The people in our group*

In addition, some transition words and conjunctions can make an idea incomplete even when it has a subject and a verb. Consider the following statement.

> *We began to descend into the canyon*

The idea above is complete. It has a subject (*we*) and a verb (*began*). However, look at what happens when we add some transition words.

> *Because we began to descend into the canyon*
> *When we began to descend into the canyon*
> *Though we began to descend into the canyon*
> *As we began to descend into the canyon*

All of the ideas above are incomplete. Even though each has a subject and a verb, the transition word at the beginning makes each idea incomplete.

There is one more aspect of complete sentences that you will need to understand for the PSAT. Not only does a complete sentence need a verb, but that verb must be in a form that allows it to be the main verb in a sentence. Here are some examples:

> Complete: *We enjoy the outdoors*
> Incomplete: *We enjoying the outdoors*
> *Incomplete:* We to enjoy the outdoors

The rule to know is that an *-ing* verb or a "to" verb cannot be the main verb in a sentence. It makes the idea incomplete.

Now that we have established the difference between complete and incomplete ideas, let's take a look at the different types of punctuation that can connect two ideas.

STOP, GO, AND THE VERTICAL LINE TEST

Let's get the weird ones out of the way first. Everyone knows that a period ends a sentence, but even particularly nerdy grammarians can get lost when things get more complicated. Because of this confusion, we've come up with a basic chart that summarizes the different times you might use what could be called "end-of-sentence" and "middle-of-sentence" punctuation.

FANBOYS stands for **F**or, **A**nd, **N**or, **B**ut, **O**r, **Y**et, and **S**o.

STOP
- Period (.)
- Semicolon (;)
- Comma + FANBOYS
- Question mark (?)
- Exclamation Mark (!)

HALF-STOP
- Colon (:)
- Long dash (—)

GO
- Comma (,)
- No punctuation

Semicolons can also be used to separate complicated lists that would otherwise include too many commas. We'll talk about that a little later.

STOP punctuation can link *only* complete ideas.

HALF-STOP punctuation must be *preceded* by a complete idea.

GO punctuation can link anything *except* two complete ideas.

Let's see how these work. Here is a complete idea:

Samantha studied for the PSAT.

Notice that we've already used one form of STOP punctuation at the end of this sentence: a period.

Now, if we want to add a second complete idea, we'll keep the period.

Samantha studied for the PSAT. She ended up doing really well on the test.

In this case, the period is linking these two complete ideas. But the nice thing about STOP punctuation is that you can really use any of the punctuation in the list to do the same thing, so we could also say this:

Samantha studied for the PSAT; she ended up doing really well on the test.

What the list of STOP punctuation shows us is that, essentially, a period and a semicolon are the same thing. We could say the same for the use of a comma plus one of the FANBOYS words.

Samantha studied for the PSAT, and she ended up doing really well on the test.

You can also use HALF-STOP punctuation to separate two complete ideas, so you could say

Samantha studied for the PSAT: she ended up doing really well on the test.

Or

Samantha studied for the PSAT—she ended up doing really well on the test.

There's a subtle difference, however, between STOP and HALF-STOP punctuation: for STOP, both ideas have to be complete, but for HALF-STOP, only the first one does.

Let's see what this looks like. If we want to link a complete idea and an incomplete idea, we can use HALF-STOP punctuation as long as the complete idea is first. For example,

Samantha studied for the PSAT: both sections of it.

Or

Samantha studied for the PSAT: the silliest test in all the land.

When you use HALF-STOP, there has to be a complete idea before the punctuation, so these examples wouldn't be correct:

> *Samantha studied for: the PSAT, the SAT, and every AP test in between.*

> *Studying for the PSAT—Samantha created a schedule and a plan.*

When you are not linking two complete ideas, you can use GO punctuation. So, you could say, for instance,

> *Having studied for the PSAT, Samantha was confident going into the test.*

Or

> *Samantha studied for the PSAT, both sections of it.*

These are the three types of mid-sentence or end-of-sentence punctuation: STOP, HALF-STOP, and GO. You'll notice that there is a bit of overlap between the concepts, but the writers of the PSAT couldn't possibly make you get into the minutiae of choosing between, say, a period and a semicolon. If you can figure out which of the big three (STOP, HALF-STOP, and GO) categories you'll need, that's all you need to be able to do.

In the following exercise, choose the type of punctuation that will correctly work in the blank. Some questions have more than one answer! Check your answers on page 182.

	STOP	HALF-STOP	GO
The other day I went to the stadium _____ and bought a ticket.			
I had saved up all week _____ I couldn't think of anything better to spend the money on!			
Some of my favorite sports include _____ hockey, baseball, and tennis.			
There's always something _____ for me to see at the stadium.			
When I arrived _____ I was thrilled to see that I had bought great seats.			
Some people from my school were sitting next to me _____ we're all in the same math class.			
The game was exciting _____ a goal in the first five minutes!			
The crowd was extremely diverse _____ men, women, and children in the stands.			
I didn't want to go home _____ even though I had school the next day.			
You can be sure of one thing _____ I'll be back as soon as I can.			

	STOP	HALF-STOP	GO
The other day I went to the stadium _____ and bought a ticket.			X
I had saved up all week _____ I couldn't think of anything better to spend the money on!	X	X	
Some of my favorite sports include _____ hockey, baseball, and tennis.			X
There's always something _____ for me to see at the stadium.			X
When I arrived _____ I was thrilled to see that I had bought great seats.			X
Some people from my school were sitting next to me _____ we're all in the same math class.	X	X	
The game was exciting _____ a goal in the first five minutes!		X	X
The crowd was extremely diverse _____ men, women, and children in the stands.		X	
I didn't want to go home _____ even though I had school the next day.			X
You can be sure of one thing _____ I'll be back as soon as I can.	X	X	

Let's see what this will look like on the PSAT.

Ted Ellis, a native of New Orleans and an artist, was examining his mother's home in the wake of Hurricane Katrina when he saw a man repairing the roof of his _____ he was so inspired by this image of hope amidst devastation that he began painting a series of pieces that became the collection *Katrina: The Hope, Healing, and Rebirth of New Orleans.*

---

1 ☐ Mark for Review

Which choice completes the text so that it conforms to the conventions of Standard English?

- Ⓐ house,
- Ⓑ house;
- Ⓒ house
- Ⓓ house and

Here's How to Crack It

The question tells you that this is a Rules question. Next, look at the answers to see what's changing: punctuation. Notice the types of punctuation that appear here— STOP and GO.

When you see STOP or HALF-STOP punctuation changing in the answer choices, you can do something that we like to call the Vertical Line Test on your scratch paper.

On your paper, write down the two words surrounding the punctuation, with a line between them where the punctuation may go. Here's how that should look:

house | he

Now, read up to the vertical line: *Ted Ellis, a native of New Orleans and an artist, was examining his mother's home in the wake of Hurricane Katrina when he saw a man repairing the roof of his house.* That's Complete. Add a C to your paper. Now, read after the vertical line: *he was so inspired by this image of hope amidst devastation that he began painting a series of pieces that became the collection Katrina: The Hope, Healing, and Rebirth of New Orleans.* That's also Complete, so put a second C on your paper.

By the time you're done, your page should look like this:

C | C
house | he

So, let's think; we've got two complete ideas here. What kind of punctuation do we need? STOP or HALF-STOP. Eliminate (A) and (C) because they are both GO punctuation. Choice (D) may look appealing, but remember that the FANBOYS word needs a comma before it in order for it to qualify as STOP punctuation. Thus, eliminate (D) and choose (B), the only answer with STOP punctuation.

Let's try another.

A recent study of fossilized dinosaur eggs in the Shanyang Basin in China provides more evidence that dinosaurs were in decline before the extinction event. The 1,000 fossilized eggs studied by researchers belonged to only three dinosaur _____ *Macroolithus yaotunensis, Elongatoolithus elongatus,* and *Stromatoolithus pinglingensis.*

---

2 🔖 Mark for Review

Which choice completes the text so that it conforms to the conventions of Standard English?

(A) species.

(B) species;

(C) species:

(D) species

Here's How to Crack It

Identify the category—Rules—by the question, and then use the answers to see that this is a punctuation question. The answers include STOP and HALF-STOP punctuation, so use the Vertical Line Test. On your scratch paper, write the words *species* and *Macroolithus* with a vertical line in between.

> Remember, a semicolon and a period function the same way. If you see both in the answers, neither one could be correct.

What's before the vertical line? *The 1,000 fossilized eggs studied by researchers belonged to only three dinosaur species* is complete, so mark it with a C, for Complete. Then, *Macroolithus yaotunensis, Elongatoolithus elongatus, and Stromatoolithus pinglingensis* is not, so mark it with an I, for Incomplete. Therefore, because we have one complete idea (the first) and one incomplete idea (the second), we can't use STOP punctuation, thus eliminating (A) and (B).

Now, what's different between the last two? Choice (C) has HALF-STOP, while (D) has GO. Consider the link between the ideas. The first part explains that there were *three dinosaur species,* and the second part tells what those species were. There should be separation between the ideas, so eliminate (D). Choice (C) is appropriate because it follows the HALF-STOP rule and also uses a colon in the right way: to explain or elaborate on the idea in the first part of the sentence. Thus, the correct answer is (C).

Let's see one more.

In 1894, during the first wave of feminism in the Netherlands, Betsy Bakker-Nort joined the Dutch Association for Women's Suffrage and traveled extensively to advocate for women's rights. Women finally gained the right to vote in the 1922 general election. Bakker-Nort's work for women's rights was not _____ she became the first woman to represent the Free-thinking Democratic League political party in the House of Representatives, where she continued to advocate for women's rights around marriage and labor for twenty years.

---

3 ▢ Mark for Review

Which choice completes the text so that it conforms to the conventions of Standard English?

Ⓐ over however

Ⓑ over. However,

Ⓒ over, however,

Ⓓ over, however;

Here's How to Crack It

After identifying that this is a Rules question, look at the answers to see what's changing: punctuation. Note the STOP punctuation in some of the answers. This is your cue to do the Vertical Line Test. In this case, the test becomes a little tricky. Choice (B) has STOP punctuation after *over*, but choice (D) has it after *however*. This means that in addition to punctuation, this question is also testing you on where a transition should go. Before using the Vertical Line Test, determine whether *however* belongs with the first or the second part of the sentence.

The first part says *Bakker-Nort's work for women's rights was not over*. Does that contrast with what came before? Yes! The previous sentence states that *Women finally gained the right to vote in the 1922 general election*, which suggests that Bakker-Nort's campaign succeeded. This first part of the sentence is a contrast because although her work succeeded, she wasn't finished. Thus, *however* belongs with the first part of the sentence. Eliminate (B) because it puts *however* in the second part of the sentence.

Now, do the Vertical Line Test by writing the words *however* and *she* on your scratch paper with a vertical line between them. The first part of the sentence, *Bakker-Nort's work for women's rights was not over, however*, is a complete idea, so mark it with a C. The second part of the sentence, *she became the first woman to represent the Free-thinking Democratic League political party in the House of Representatives, where she continued to advocate for women's rights around marriage and labor for twenty years*, is also a complete idea, so mark it with a C. Because both parts are complete, STOP punctuation is needed. Eliminate (A) and (C) because they are both GO punctuation. Choice (D) uses STOP punctuation and correctly puts *however* in the first part of the sentence. The correct answer is (D).

A SLIGHT PAUSE FOR COMMAS

In the real world, you may think of commas as signifying when to take a breath or as something that authors just put whenever they feel like it. There's some truth to these ideas, but the more ambiguous or arbitrary uses of commas are NOT tested on the PSAT. The PSAT only tests commas that are used for specific purposes. Make it your goal to learn the specific reasons to use a comma that are tested on the PSAT, and you won't have much difficulty with these questions. Here are the rules to know when it comes to commas:

On the PSAT, there are only four reasons to use a comma:

- in STOP punctuation, with one of the FANBOYS words
- in GO punctuation, to separate incomplete ideas from complete ideas, in some cases
- in a list of three or more things
- before and after unnecessary information

If you can't cite a reason to use a comma, *don't use one*.

We've already seen the first two concepts, so let's look at the third and fourth.

Try this one.

Many children dream of being veterinarians. Working all day with animals just like one's dog, cat, _____ like a dream come true. For some reason, though, kids seem to grow out of this fantasy as they get older, with fewer than 3,000 veterinary school graduates each year in the United States.

4 🔖 Mark for Review

Which choice completes the text so that it conforms to the conventions of Standard English?

(A) fish or horse seems,

(B) fish, or, horse seems

(C) fish, or horse seems

(D) fish or, horse seems

Here's How to Crack It

Based on the question, identify the category as Rules. Then, look to see what's changing in the answers: commas, so this question is testing commas. It will help to know that the PSAT wants a comma after every item in a series with three or more things (except for the last item). Does this sentence have a list? Yes, and the items in the list are *dog, cat, fish*, and *horse*. Thus, there should be a comma after *fish*, so eliminate (A) and (D). Should there be a comma after *or*? No, there isn't any reason to put a comma there, so eliminate (B). Thus, the correct answer is (C).

It's worth noting that the comma after *fish* here (the comma that comes before the word *and* or *or* in a list) is a disputed punctuation rule. According to the PSAT, there should be a comma there. That being said, College Board does not actually test this rule. You'll notice that (A) and (D) had additional errors besides the lack of comma before *or*—each has an extra comma elsewhere that doesn't need to be there.

Note as well that we did not use the Vertical Line Test on this question. Only use it when you see STOP or HALF-STOP punctuation. You might be thinking, what about the comma + FANBOYS? Isn't *or* one of the FANBOYS words? Yes! However, it is not treated as STOP punctuation in this case, since the comma + *or* is part of a list. When you see the comma + *or* or comma + *and* in the answers, look for a list. If there isn't a list, then in that case be sure to use the Vertical Line Test.

———○———

Let's try another.

———○———

American author and MacArthur Fellow Jacqueline Woodson's body of work includes *Brown Girl Dreaming*, her memoir in _____ a picture book about a Black girl and a white girl becoming friends in a segregated town; and *Harbor Me*, a uniquely structured novel that examines the lives and fears of middle school students.

5 🔖 Mark for Review

Which choice completes the text so that it conforms to the conventions of Standard English?

Ⓐ verse; *The Other Side*

Ⓑ verse, *The Other Side*:

Ⓒ verse; *The Other Side*,

Ⓓ verse, *The Other Side*,

Here's How to Crack It

Identify the category, Rules, and then the topic—punctuation. This question appears to test STOP and GO punctuation. However, look a little closer at the sentence: it's explaining what Woodson's work *includes*, and there are three works mentioned (one in the answer choices). So, this is actually a list. That might make you think that the answer with only commas is correct but hold on—there's another rule related to lists that you need to know for this question. Take a look at the following example:

The committee members are Alex, a parent, Taylor, a teacher, and Ali, a community member.

Can you spot what's a little confusing about that list? It's unclear whether the committee has three people on it (the ones with the names) or more people, some of whose names aren't given. In this case, the intention is to provide the names and titles of the three committee members. We can make that clearer by doing this:

The committee members are Alex, a parent; Taylor, a teacher; and Ali, a community member.

By using semicolons to separate the three parts of the list, we can make it clear what each item in the list is. This use of a semicolon may also appear on the PSAT, so when you see a semicolon in the answer choices, confirm that the question doesn't involve lists before using the Vertical Line Test. In this case, there is a list, so don't use it.

The hard part is recognizing that this rule is being tested. Once we've established that, we only need to figure out where to separate the items in the list. Start by looking at the last item, since it's not near the blank and is a complete item. It says *Harbor Me, a uniquely structured novel that examines the lives and fears of middle school students.* Therefore, the items in the list should be in this same format—title, comma, description.

The first item in the list has its title, a comma, and the description, so at that point we're finished with that one and ready to move on to the next item. This means that a semicolon should follow the word *verse*—eliminate (B) and (D). In the next item, we know that a comma should follow the title so that all of the items in the list are in the same format. Eliminate (A) because it doesn't follow this format. Therefore, the answer is (C).

Let's see another comma rule.

Jellyfish Lake, a marine lake located on the island of Eil Malk in Palau, sees millions of golden jellyfish migrate each day. The golden _____ sustain themselves through symbiotic algae and zooplankton.

6 ⬚ Mark for Review

Which choice completes the text so that it conforms to the conventions of Standard English?

(A) jellyfish, similar to the spotted jellyfish,

(B) jellyfish, similar to the spotted jellyfish

(C) jellyfish similar to the spotted jellyfish,

(D) jellyfish similar to the spotted jellyfish

Here's How to Crack It

After identifying the category as Rules, use the answers to determine that this is a punctuation question. Specifically, it's testing commas. Note that the commas are moving around the phrase *similar to the spotted jellyfish*. This is a great clue that the question is probably testing on necessary versus unnecessary information. The rule is that unnecessary information should be separated from the sentence with punctuation both before and after the idea—that could be two commas, two dashes, or two parentheses.

If you've noticed this, you can start by eliminating (B) and (C) because the rule is either two commas or no commas—we can't put a comma only before the phrase and not after or vice versa. Next, determine whether the phrase is necessary or unnecessary.

A good way to test whether the idea is necessary to the meaning of the sentence is to take it out. Read the original sentence again. Now read this one: *The golden jellyfish sustain themselves through symbiotic algae and zooplankton.* Does it still work? Yes! Did the meaning of the sentence change? No, we just lost a little extra information about the golden jellyfish.

Therefore, this information is unnecessary and should be surrounded by commas, as it is in (A). Eliminate (D). The correct answer is (A).

———————◯———————

Let's try a few more. Try to figure out whether the word or idea in italics is necessary to the meaning of the sentence.

1. The student *with the highest score* has a good chance at a National Merit scholarship.
2. Katie wants to go to Bennington *which has a really good theater program.*
3. The team *that scored five touchdowns* won the game in a landslide.
4. The National Merit competition *which began in 1955* has approximately 1.5 million applicants each year.
5. Rising senior *Liam* is hoping to be one of the chosen few this year.

Answers are on page 194.

Let's put it all together in this question.

People _____ and people with a fear of negative feedback from those around them tend to display a more developed connection between their artistic potential and their actual artistic production.

7 | Mark for Review

Which choice completes the text so that it conforms to the conventions of Standard English?

(A) who identify, as creative types,

(B) who identify as creative types,

(C) who identify as creative types

(D) who, identify, as creative types

Here's How to Crack It

Identify the question type—Rules—and the topic—punctuation, specifically commas. There are varying numbers of commas in varying places. Remember, the rule of thumb with commas is that if you can't cite a reason to use a comma, *don't use one*.

In (A), *as creative types* is being set off by commas. Let's see whether it's necessary or unnecessary information. Without the phrase, the sentence would read *People who identify and people with a fear...* This no longer works, as it's necessary to explain how these people identify. Since this information is necessary, it shouldn't be surrounded by commas. Eliminate (A).

Choice (D) does something similar, but of course removing *identify* from the sentence makes the sentence incomplete, so eliminate (D).

Choice (B) puts a comma after *types*. Notice that this comma would come before the word *and*. That can only happen in two cases: if you have two complete ideas (because comma + FAN-BOYS is STOP) or if you have a list of three or more things. Here, the first part is definitely not complete (it says *People who identify as creative types*), and this is a list of only two things. So, there is no reason to put a comma after *types*. Therefore, eliminate (B) and choose (C), which is the correct answer. No punctuation is needed here.

YOUR GOING TO BE TESTED ON APOSTROPHE'S (AND INTERNET SPELLING IS A TERRIBLE GUIDE!)

As with commas, apostrophes have only a very limited set of applications. Apostrophes are a little trickier, though, because you can't really hear them in speech, so people misuse them all the time. Think about the header of this section. The apostrophes are wrong there. Here's the correct way of punctuating it: *You're going to be tested on apostrophes*. Can you hear the difference? Neither can we.

Therefore, as with commas,

> If you can't cite a reason to use an apostrophe, *don't use one*.
>
> On the PSAT, there are only two reasons to use an apostrophe:
>
> - possessive nouns (NOT pronouns)
> - contractions

Here are some examples.

While many humans and animals have influenced the history of the United States and Canadian border, one _____ has been as significant as it is overlooked. Although Michigan eventually became a powerhouse in the later part of the Industrial Revolution, it was initially attractive to settlers who wanted to cash in on the fur trade, and beaver pelts were some of the hottest commodities.

8 ▢ Mark for Review

Which choice completes the text so that it conforms to the conventions of Standard English?

- Ⓐ animals influence, the beavers
- Ⓑ animal influence, the beavers,
- Ⓒ animals' influence, the beaver's,
- Ⓓ animal's influence, the beaver's,

Here's How to Crack It

Start by identifying the category, which is Rules, and then the specific topic, punctuation. Even more specific than that, apostrophes are changing in the answers. The apostrophes are on nouns, so consider whether those nouns should be possessive.

Does something belong to the *animal* or *animals*? Yes, it's the *influence* of the *animal(s)*, so eliminate (A) because it lacks an apostrophe in *animals*. Next, consider whether something belongs to the *beaver* or *beavers*. The sentence is referring also to the *influence* of the *beaver(s)*, so there does need to be an apostrophe there. Eliminate (B) because it says *beavers* with no apostrophe.

Next, compare (C) and (D). The difference is that (C) means *animals*, plural, while (D) is *animal*, singular. The part before the blank says *one*, so the word should be singular. Eliminate (C) and choose (D).

———○———

Let's see another example of how the PSAT tests apostrophes.

———○———

In the absence of light, people report seeing a dark gray background color that has been called *Eigengrau*, which means "intrinsic gray." Scientists have suggested that different people have _____ own perceptions of Eigengrau, however.

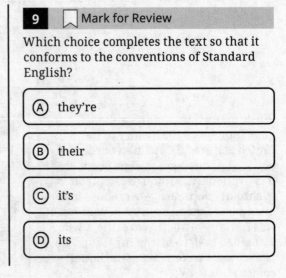

9 🔖 Mark for Review

Which choice completes the text so that it conforms to the conventions of Standard English?

(A) they're

(B) their

(C) it's

(D) its

Here's How to Crack It

Start by identifying the category as Rules. Then, look at the answers to determine that the topic is punctuation, and specifically apostrophes. Here, the apostrophes appear on pronouns, which would signify a contraction—in this case "they are" or "it is." The other options are possessive pronouns, which have no apostrophes.

Start by determining whether a form of "they" or a form of "it" is needed. In this case, the perceptions belong to the *people*, which is a plural noun. Eliminate (C) and (D) because any form of *it* is singular. Next, do you want to say, "they are own perceptions?" No, so eliminate (A). Since this is the perception of the people, a possessive pronoun is needed, and *their* is the correct spelling. The correct answer, therefore, is (B).

———○———

Phew! These apostrophes can get a little tricky, so let's try a few more. On these (as on many parts of the PSAT), you'll find that using your ear, sounding things out, doesn't really help all that much.

Circle the option that works. The big question is this: apostrophes or no apostrophes?

1. *Salims/Salim's* teacher said *hes/he's* allowed to miss next *Tuesdays/Tuesday's* exam.
2. *Its/It's* really not going to hurt my feelings if you don't want to go to *they're/their* party with me.
3. Whatever the *justification's/justifications* for *your/you're* attitude, *there/they're* is no reason to be so obnoxious about it.
4. *Were/We're* going to get back to you as soon as your *application's/applications* are processed.
5. *They're/Their they're/their* nachos, but they *wont/won't* share any unless *its/it's* absolutely necessary or we share *ours/our's*.

Answers are on page 194.

CONCLUSION

In sum, we've looked at all the punctuation you'd ever need on the PSAT. It's really not so much, and you probably knew a lot of it already. In general, checking what's changing in the answer choices can help you determine what rule or rules are being tested, and POE can help you narrow those answers down.

Punctuation rules are easy to learn, as is the biggest rule of all about punctuation.

> Know why you are using punctuation, whether that punctuation is STOP, HALF-STOP, GO, commas, or apostrophes. If you can't cite reasons to use these punctuation marks, don't use them!

In the last few pages of this chapter, try out these skills on a drill.

Answers to Questions on Page 189:

1. NECESSARY to the meaning of the sentence (no commas). If you remove the italicized part, the sentence is not adequately specific.
2. UNNECESSARY to the meaning of the sentence (commas). If you remove the italicized part, the sentence is still complete and does not change meaning.
3. NECESSARY to the meaning of the sentence (no commas). If you remove the italicized part, the sentence is not adequately specific.
4. UNNECESSARY to the meaning of the sentence (commas). If you remove the italicized part, the sentence is still complete and does not change meaning.
5. NECESSARY to the meaning of the sentence (no commas). If you remove the italicized part, the sentence is no longer complete.

Answers to Questions on Page 193:

1. Salim's, he's, Tuesday's
2. It's, their
3. justifications, your, there
4. We're, applications
5. They're, their, won't, it's, ours

Punctuation Drill

Time: 12 minutes. Note that these questions have been placed in order of difficulty, as they will appear on the test, although on the test they will be interspersed with grammar questions. Check your answers in Part IV.

---

1 🔖 Mark for Review

Juan José Soler and his team noticed that the preen oil of spotless starlings changes color as the starlings age. If the chicks have a brighter color oil, _____ Soler and his team designed a study to find out.

Which choice completes the text so that it conforms to the conventions of Standard English?

(A) they could use that color to attract their parents' attention?

(B) could they use that color to attract their parents' attention?

(C) could they use that color to attract their parents' attention.

(D) they could use that color to attract their parents' attention.

---

2 🔖 Mark for Review

Doris Lessing received the Nobel Prize in Literature in 2007 for her literary oeuvre, including her novel *The Golden Notebook*, which _____ the inner life and complexities of the main character, Anna Wulf.

Which choice completes the text so that it conforms to the conventions of Standard English?

(A) exploring

(B) to explore

(C) having explored

(D) explores

3 ☐ Mark for Review

The Servicemen's Readjustment Act was signed into law in 1944. More than twenty years earlier, after the conclusion of World War I, the veterans of the bloodiest war on record were more or less forgotten by the US government. Many of them were given little more than a $60 allowance and a train ticket home. While _____ was some talk of military bonuses, those bonuses were not easily obtained.

Which choice completes the text so that it conforms to the conventions of Standard English?

Ⓐ they're

Ⓑ it

Ⓒ their

Ⓓ there

4 ☐ Mark for Review

Cristina Ibarra's documentary *Las Marthas* follows two girls who are preparing to participate in the Colonial _____ over 100 years the ball in Laredo, Texas, has been part of the celebration of George Washington's birthday.

Which choice completes the text so that it conforms to the conventions of Standard English?

Ⓐ Ball for

Ⓑ Ball and for

Ⓒ Ball, for

Ⓓ Ball. For

5 ▢ Mark for Review

The Nobel Prize winners in most categories come from the elite research institutions in the United States and abroad. Not, however, the winners of the Nobel Prize in Literature. These winners share an average age (64) and geographical diversity with those in other _____ they have not attended the same schools—not by a long shot.

Which choice completes the text so that it conforms to the conventions of Standard English?

(A) categories, though

(B) categories; though

(C) categories, though,

(D) categories. Though

6 ▢ Mark for Review

Maintaining the public face of a company has created a new job: Chief Listening Officer. While a Social Media Manager might be in charge of a _____ on social media websites, a Chief Listening Officer is on the other side. A CLO scours review sites as well as social media to make sure that a company's public image is under control.

Which choice completes the text so that it conforms to the conventions of Standard English?

(A) companies posts

(B) companies' posts

(C) company's posts

(D) company's post's

7 ☐ Mark for Review

For many years, veterinarians have provided a series of basic services for household _____ basic check-ups and shots to neutering and defanging. Today, however, pets have a longer life expectancy than in the past, and veterinarians are required to perform more and more procedures involving animal cancers, skin abscesses, and torn ligaments and cartilage.

Which choice completes the text so that it conforms to the conventions of Standard English?

Ⓐ pets. From

Ⓑ pets—from

Ⓒ pets; from

Ⓓ pets from,

8 ☐ Mark for Review

Stephanie Kwolek, a Polish American chemist, is credited with inventing _____ while working at the DuPont chemical company during the 1950s and 1960s.

Which choice completes the text so that it conforms to the conventions of Standard English?

Ⓐ Kevlar—a high-strength material used in personal armor, sports equipment, and musical instruments—

Ⓑ Kevlar, a high-strength material used in: personal armor, sports equipment, and musical instruments,

Ⓒ Kevlar—a high-strength material—used in personal armor, sports equipment, and musical instruments,

Ⓓ Kevlar, a high-strength material used in personal armor, sports equipment, and musical instruments

9 ⚑ Mark for Review

As World War II neared its end, the US government sought to avoid conflict with veterans. Indeed, for many, the goal was not idealistic: the _____ was seen as accelerating the economic collapse of the Great Depression.

Which choice completes the text so that it conforms to the conventions of Standard English?

- (A) tremendous unemployment, among World War I veterans,

- (B) tremendous unemployment among World War I veterans

- (C) tremendous, unemployment among, World War I veterans

- (D) tremendous unemployment among World War I veterans,

10 ⚑ Mark for Review

Hanif Abdurraqib, an American essayist, poet, and cultural critic, published a poetry collection, *The Crown Ain't Worth* _____ *They Can't Kill Us Until They Kill Us*, in 2017; and a non-fiction book, *Go Ahead in the Rain: Notes on A Tribe Called Quest*, in 2019.

Which choice completes the text so that it conforms to the conventions of Standard English?

- (A) *Much*, in 2016, an essay collection,

- (B) *Much*, in 2016; an essay collection,

- (C) *Much*; in 2016, an essay collection,

- (D) *Much*; in 2016; an essay collection;

Chapter 9
Rules Questions:
Grammar

THE WORDS CHANGE, BUT THE SONG REMAINS THE SAME

In the last chapter, we looked at what to do when the PSAT is testing punctuation. In this chapter, we're going to look at what to do when the PSAT is testing the parts of speech—mainly verbs, nouns, and pronouns.

Our basic strategy, however, has remained the same. As we saw in the previous chapter, when faced with a PSAT Rules question, you should always

> Check what's changing in the answer choices and use POE.

Remember that the grammar questions and punctuation questions will be mixed up together in the Rules portion, organized from easy to hard.

As you will notice, throughout this chapter, we talk a lot about certain parts of speech, but we don't really use a lot of grammar terms. That's because we find that on the PSAT grammar questions, there is really one main idea to keep in mind: **consistency**. Correct answers must be consistent with the rest of the sentence and the text as a whole.

Let's look at some examples of how consistency relates to the grammar topics you can expect to see on the test.

VERBS

The circumstances of musician Jimmie Rodgers's birth _____ obscure, but legend has it that he was born in Meridian, Mississippi, in 1897.

1 Mark for Review

Which choice completes the text so that it conforms to the conventions of Standard English?

(A) is

(B) are

(C) has been

(D) was

Here's How to Crack It

First, identify the question type. Since the question mentions Standard English, this is a Rules question. Next, look at the answers to determine the topic. The answers contain verbs, so this question is testing consistency with verbs.

When you see verbs changing in the answer choices, the first thing to check is the subject of the sentence. Look for and highlight the one-word subject—who or what is doing the action. What is *obscure*? The *circumstances* of his birth. Highlight the word *circumstances*, as that is the subject of the sentence.

Because *circumstances* is plural, the verb must also be plural, in order to be consistent. Therefore, (A), (C), and (D) have to be eliminated because they are all singular. So, (B) must be the correct answer.

Thus, when you see verbs changing in the answer choices, check the subject first. Subjects and verbs need to be consistent with each other. You might assume that the question is testing tense when you see verbs, but as with this question, typically only one answer will agree with the subject when the question is testing subject-verb agreement. Therefore, this strategy saves you a lot of time since you don't have to consider tense on this type of question.

Of course, sometimes tense will be tested. Let's see an example.

In 1947, veterans on the G. I. Bill accounted for 49 percent of college admissions. By 1956, of the 16 million World War II veterans, nearly half had used the G.I. Bill for some kind of training. Therefore, by the early 1960s, college training _____ drastically.

2 ☐ Mark for Review

Which choice completes the text so that it conforms to the conventions of Standard English?

- (A) had changed
- (B) changes
- (C) will change
- (D) has changed

Here's How to Crack It

Identify the question type first. The question reveals that this falls under the Rules category, so look at the answers to see what's changing. Verbs are changing in the answers, so this is a grammar question testing consistency of verbs. The subject is *training*, so highlight that word. All of the answers work with that subject, so this question is testing tense, not subject-verb agreement.

Look for clues in the text to determine whether past, present, or future tense is needed. This sentence is describing what happened by *the early 1960s*, so some form of past tense should be used. Eliminate (B), which is present tense, and (C), which is future tense. The verb in the previous sentence is *had used*, so keep (A) because it is consistent with that verb. Choice (D), *has changed*, is actually a form of present tense, as it would suggest something that has changed going up until right now. However, the text is referring to something that had changed by *the early 1960s*, not going up to the present day. So, eliminate (D) and choose (A), which is the correct answer.

As you can see, verbs are all about consistency.

When you see verbs changing in the answer choices, make sure those verbs are:

- CONSISTENT with their subjects
- CONSISTENT with other verbs in the sentence and surrounding sentences

Let's try one more on a related topic.

It was ultimately not medical science that saved the day during the 1793 Yellow Fever Epidemic in Philadelphia. Doctors tried various treatment approaches, but they were stalled by their inability to figure out both how the disease originated and how it _____ It therefore seemed a godsend when the frost came in November and the number of deaths tapered off. Medical historians now know that the disease was spread by mosquitoes, but this was not verified until nearly a century after the disease had come and gone.

3 ☐ Mark for Review

Which choice completes the text so that it conforms to the conventions of Standard English?

(A) was spreading.

(B) spread.

(C) had been spread.

(D) spreads.

Here's How to Crack It

Identify the category, which is Rules. Then, look to the answers to see what's changing: the form of the verbs. This lets us know that the question is testing consistency of verbs. Look at the rest of the context to determine what this verb needs to be consistent with.

In this case, the verb is part of a list of two things that doctors had an *inability to figure out*. The first thing is *how the disease originated*, so this verb should be in the same tense. Highlight *originated*. The verb *originated* is in past tense, so eliminate (D) because it's in present tense. Next, eliminate any other past tense verbs that aren't in the correct form. Choices (A) and (C) are not in the same type of past tense as *originated* (the simple past), so they must be eliminated. Choice (B), *spread*, is consistent with *originated*. Therefore, (B) is the correct answer.

Consistency applies across the grammar questions. Let's see another topic in which the idea of Consistency might help us.

PRONOUNS

What are pronouns? Pronouns are words that stand in for nouns. They make writing less repetitive, because they prevent us from having to use the same nouns over and over. On the PSAT, you'll be tested on which pronoun agrees with the noun (or sometimes another pronoun) that it is referring back to. Let's see an example.

A traditional form of Japanese theater, Nōgaku involves masks, costumes, and props. Although its popularity peaked in the fourteenth and fifteenth centuries, _____ actually originated in the eighth century.

4	🔖 Mark for Review

Which choice completes the text so that it conforms to the conventions of Standard English?

(A) they

(B) one

(C) those

(D) it

Here's How to Crack It

Start by identifying the question type: Rules. Next, look at the answers to determine what topic is being tested. Since pronouns are changing in the answer choices, the question is testing consistency with pronouns.

Since a pronoun refers back to a noun or another pronoun, determine who or what *actually originated in the eighth century*. The sentence is talking about *its popularity*, referring to that of Nōgaku. Highlight the existing pronoun, *its*. Since the blank refers to the same thing, the pronoun that is needed is "it." Eliminate (A), (B), and (C). The correct answer is (D).

That one may have seemed pretty easy. Let's take a look at a tougher way pronouns can be tested.

The fact that winners of the Nobel Prize in Literature have come from diverse educational backgrounds should remind us that creativity can strike anywhere. One of the Nobel committee's great merits is that _____ been willing to identify great talent outside of the typical places.

---

5 ☐ Mark for Review

Which choice completes the text so that it conforms to the conventions of Standard English?

(A) they have

(B) we have

(C) it has

(D) you have

Here's How to Crack It

Begin by identifying the category of question. Since it mentions Standard English, this is a Rules question. Next, look to see what's changing in the answers: pronouns. Therefore, this question is testing consistency of pronouns.

Identify who or what the pronoun refers back to. The sentence discusses one of the *merits* of *the Nobel committee*. Therefore, the blank refers to the *committee* being willing to do something. Highlight that word and be careful! The word *committee* is singular, which you can note with an annotation. Therefore, a singular pronoun is needed. Eliminate (A) and (B) because *they* and *we* are plural. Keep (C) because *it* is singular. While *you* can be singular, it isn't appropriate to describe the *committee* as *you* because this isn't directed toward the committee. Eliminate (D). The correct answer is (C).

As you can see, you may not be able to use your ear for all of these questions. We may think of a committee as a "they," since it is composed of multiple people, but the word itself is singular and thus must be referred to with a singular pronoun. Think about it this way—you would say "the committee is," not "the committee are." So, that shows that the noun is singular. You can also think about the fact that "committees" is plural, so "committee" must be singular.

MODIFIERS

Let's take a look at a type of question that students often have difficulty with.

A recent study helps explain why animals continue to live after they are no longer able to reproduce. After watching over 750 hours of video and observing the behavior of pods of whales, _____ The older female whales were the most likely to lead younger whales to salmon feeding grounds, particularly in the periods where the usually plentiful salmon were sparse. This knowledge is particularly useful for whale pods because the abundance of salmon is typically what determines whale life cycles, both reproduction and mortality.

| 6 | 🔖 Mark for Review |

Which choice completes the text so that it conforms to the conventions of Standard English?

(A) whale grandmothers were observed to have teaching behaviors by the scientists.

(B) scientists observed that many of the teaching behaviors were performed by whale grandmothers.

(C) whale grandmothers were the most likely to exhibit teaching behaviors.

(D) teaching behaviors were observed from whale grandmothers that were shown to scientists.

Here's How to Crack It

Look at the question to determine the category: Rules. Next, look at the answers to see what's changing. You'll probably notice right away that the beginnings of the answer choices (which you could call the subjects) are changing. This is a big clue that the question could be testing modifiers. Look for a describing phrase, which often comes at the beginning of a sentence, followed by a comma.

Did you spot it? We have the describing phrase, known as a modifier, at the beginning: *After watching over 750 hours of video and observing the behavior of pods of whales*. Highlight that phrase. Whom is that describing? Take a look at the subjects in the answers and use POE.

It can't be the *whale grandmothers* who were watching the videos, so eliminate (A) and (C). The *scientists* could have watched the videos, so keep (B). As for (D), it doesn't make sense that *teaching behaviors* could have watched videos, so eliminate that answer. Therefore, the answer must be (B). You don't even need to read the rest of the answer choice.

For modifier questions, the toughest part is identifying the error. Once you've spotted it, all you need to do is eliminate answers that don't match with what the phrase is intended to describe.

Let's have a look at some more of these modifiers. Rewrite each sentence below so the modifier and what it is referring to are *consistent*.

1. Given all its logical twists and turns, many people struggle with philosophy.
2. Readers in different times tend to gravitate toward different philosophers and places.
3. Once cracked, you can find incredible guidance and solace in philosophy.
4. I first learned about Pragmatism from a professor in college at 20.
5. Boring and uninteresting, Jack didn't care much for the work of William James.

Answers are below.

Consistency

- When verbs are changing in the answer choices, make sure those verbs are consistent with their subjects and with other verbs.

- When pronouns are changing in the answer choices, make sure those pronouns are consistent with the nouns or other pronouns that they refer back to.

- When the subjects are changing in the answer choices, look for a modifier. The modifier must come as close as possible to the person or thing it's describing.

As we have seen in this chapter, when the PSAT is testing grammar (i.e., any time the words are changing in the answer choices), make sure that those words are **consistent** with the rest of the sentence and text.

Answers to Questions above:

1. Many people struggle with philosophy given all its logical twists and turns.
2. Readers in different times and places tend to gravitate toward different philosophers.
3. Once cracked, philosophy can provide incredible guidance and solace.
4. I first learned about Pragmatism from a college professor when I was 20 years old.
5. Jack didn't care much for the work of William James, which he found boring and uninteresting.

Note: these are just examples of ways to fix the modifier errors. It's fine if you rewrote the sentence differently, as long as your version makes the intended meaning clear.

Grammar Drill

Time: 12 minutes. Note that these questions have been placed in order of difficulty, as they will appear on the test, although on the test they will be interspersed with punctuation questions. Check your answers in Part IV.

1 ▢ Mark for Review

Co-commissioned by the Metropolitan Opera and the Los Angeles Opera, *Eurydice* had its world premiere in 2020. Its co-writers, composer Matthew Aucoin and librettist Sarah Ruhl, _____ multiple significant awards.

Which choice completes the text so that it conforms to the conventions of Standard English?

Ⓐ has won

Ⓑ was winning

Ⓒ has been winning

Ⓓ have won

2 ▢ Mark for Review

Ugandan writer Doreen Baingana earned a law degree from Makerere University before she studied creative writing and _____ her MFA in that subject. Afterward, she became the writer-in-residence at the Jiménez-Porter Writers House and published quite a few short stories, novels, and works of non-fiction.

Which choice completes the text so that it conforms to the conventions of Standard English?

Ⓐ obtained

Ⓑ obtaining

Ⓒ to obtain

Ⓓ having obtained

3 ☐ Mark for Review

Hikaye is a Turkish narrative genre, performed by a singer-poet, which is primarily prose but interspersed with poems that the artist will sing. A hikaye centers around the performer's romantic exploits, and _____ the poems to express the performer's emotions.

Which choice completes the text so that it conforms to the conventions of Standard English?

Ⓐ they use

Ⓑ it uses

Ⓒ one uses

Ⓓ you use

4 ☐ Mark for Review

Trịnh Xuân Thuận, a Vietnamese American astrophysicist, has focused his research on compact blue dwarf galaxies, the chemical composition of the universe, and the evolution of galaxies. He is a professor at the University of Virginia and _____ astronomy there since 1976.

Which choice completes the text so that it conforms to the conventions of Standard English?

Ⓐ has taught

Ⓑ had taught

Ⓒ taught

Ⓓ teaches

5 ☐ Mark for Review

The nutrient-poor soil and extremely salty water have posed a challenge to the possibility that one day people might work or even live on Mars. A study led by then-high school student Pooja Kasiviswanathan has demonstrated that alfalfa, a plant that is often used for hay to feed cattle, could grow well in Mars's soil and even _____ vegetables such as radishes, lettuces, and turnips to help them survive.

Which choice completes the text so that it conforms to the conventions of Standard English?

Ⓐ fertilizing

Ⓑ fertilize

Ⓒ fertilized

Ⓓ fertilizes

6 ☐ Mark for Review

Navajo Nation member Annie Dodge Wauneka became the second woman elected to the Tribal Council, after she saw the poverty and lack of medical care around the reservation and vowed to do what she could to address these problems. Wauneka worked to eradicate tuberculosis within her nation and authored a dictionary that translated English medical terms into the Navajo language. Her interest in public health _____ in part inspired by her experience as a child caring for other students during the 1918 influenza epidemic.

Which choice completes the text so that it conforms to the conventions of Standard English?

Ⓐ is

Ⓑ will be

Ⓒ was

Ⓓ has been

7 ☐ Mark for Review

The long, stiff plumes known as flight feathers primarily assist in generating thrust and lift, enabling birds to fly. In addition, some birds use their flight feathers to present _____ as potential mates as part of a courtship ritual.

Which choice completes the text so that it conforms to the conventions of Standard English?

Ⓐ them

Ⓑ it

Ⓒ itself

Ⓓ themselves

8 ☐ Mark for Review

Beaver skins were once popular in stylish clothes of the 1700s, particularly hats. Although silks had become more popular than animal skins in the early 1800s, by that time the beaver had been hunted to the point that _____ nearly eliminated from the region altogether.

Which choice completes the text so that it conforms to the conventions of Standard English?

Ⓐ it was

Ⓑ this was

Ⓒ they were

Ⓓ one was

9 ☐ Mark for Review

Work in economics, medicine, or the sciences _____ a vibrant, collaborative atmosphere, with the best minds in the field working together toward solutions.

Which choice completes the text so that it conforms to the conventions of Standard English?

(A) requires

(B) require

(C) do require

(D) have required

10 ☐ Mark for Review

A global team of 49 researchers wanted to determine the evolution of the donkey. Where and when was it domesticated? Analyzing the genomes of existing populations and fossil DNA, _____ came from Africa about 7,000 years ago and quickly spread into Europe and Asia.

Which choice completes the text so that it conforms to the conventions of Standard English?

(A) donkeys

(B) the research demonstrated that donkeys

(C) the scientists determined that donkeys

(D) the genetic information revealed that donkeys

Chapter 10
Rhetoric
Questions

After all of the Rules questions, you'll see the last category of RW questions, which we call Rhetoric. You'll see Transitions questions, from easy to hard, and then Rhetorical Synthesis questions, from easy to hard. In this lesson, you'll learn how to approach both types of questions that fall into this category.

The last portion of each Reading and Writing module will include two types of questions: Transitions and Rhetorical Synthesis, in that order. We call these Rhetoric questions because they relate to the purpose or quality of the writing. These questions will not test your understanding of the rule-based punctuation and grammar topics. In fact, for these questions, all four answer choices will be or will produce complete sentences that are grammatically correct. Instead, you will need to consider the *content* of the writing and how the answers fulfill certain meaning-related or rhetorical goals. Let's take a look at the first type of question in this category.

A SMOOTH TRANSITION

Transition questions will be easy to spot. Let's look at an example.

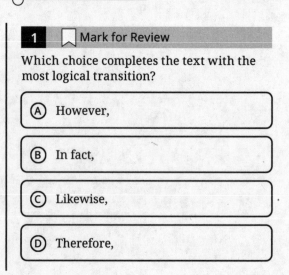

Pragmatism may be rooted in the German philosophers Immanuel Kant and Georg Friedrich Hegel, but it has found more popularity in Anglo-American communities than in German or French ones. _____ the term "Pragmatism" was first used by Americans—philosophers William James and Charles Sanders Peirce.

1 Mark for Review

Which choice completes the text with the most logical transition?

(A) However,

(B) In fact,

(C) Likewise,

(D) Therefore,

Like the question above, all transition questions will ask you the same thing: *Which choice completes the text with the most logical transition?* As soon as you see that question, you'll know you're dealing with a transition question. Let's take a look at the basic approach for transition questions and apply it to this one.

Transition Questions Basic Approach

1. Read the text and highlight any ideas that support or contradict each other.
2. Make an annotation indicating whether the ideas surrounding the blank agree or disagree.
3. Eliminate any answers that go the wrong direction. Then, use POE on any remaining options.

Here's How to Crack It

Highlight anything that is the same in both sentences. The first sentence mentions that Pragmatism *has found more popularity in Anglo-American communities than in German or French ones*. The second sentence repeats a word, *American*, so highlight the phrase in that sentence: *the term "Pragmatism" was first used by Americans*. These two ideas agree, so make an annotation that says "agree." Then, eliminate any opposite-direction transitions, since we need a same-direction transition here. Eliminate (A).

Now, compare the remaining answers. *In fact* can be used to support the previous idea, so keep (B). *Likewise* is used to compare two different things that have something in common. In this case, there isn't a separate thing being compared to the previous sentence, so eliminate (C). Eliminate (D) because *therefore* comes before a conclusion, and this sentence doesn't draw a conclusion from previously stated evidence. Therefore, (see what we did there?) the correct answer is (B).

Let's try another example.

Camille Henrot's installation *The Pale Fox* is a collection of objects that at first glance appears to be random. For example, a sculpture of Buddha props up a copy of a modern magazine. There is an organization, _____ that is revealed as the audience spends time in the space.

2 ☐ Mark for Review

Which choice completes the text with the most logical transition?

- (A) likewise,
- (B) specifically,
- (C) though,
- (D) rather,

Here's How to Crack It

Start by highlighting ideas that relate to each other. The first sentence says that the collection *at first glance appears to be random*. The third sentence says *There is an organization*. These ideas disagree, so write that in an annotation. Next, eliminate any same-direction transitions: (A) and (B). Compare (C) and (D). *Though* works well, so keep (C). While *rather* is an opposite-direction transition, it means something more like "instead," so it doesn't fit correctly in this sentence. The correct answer is (C).

Let's try one more.

Sandra Welner, a medical professor, wanted to make medical care more accessible for patients with disabilities. _____ she invented an examination table that could be lowered for easier access to and from a wheelchair and called it the Universally Accessible Examination Table.

3 🔖 Mark for Review

Which choice completes the text with the most logical transition?

Ⓐ To that end,

Ⓑ Additionally,

Ⓒ Not surprisingly,

Ⓓ Rather,

Here's How to Crack It

First, highlight any phrases that draw a connection. The first sentence states that Welner *wanted to make medical care more accessible for patients with disabilities*. The second sentence says she *invented* the *Universally Accessible Examination Table*. These ideas agree, so make an annotation saying "agree" and eliminate any opposite-direction transitions. In this case, (D) can be eliminated.

Next, consider the link between the highlighted phrases. The first sentence states Welner's goal, while the second sentence states what she did. Use POE. Choice (A) is a good match because an *end* is a goal, and this transition essentially means "with that goal in mind." Keep (A). Eliminate (B) because *additionally* is used to add on to the previous point, but this would suggest that the sentences are two separate things, when instead the second sentence explains what she did in pursuit of her goal. Eliminate (C) because there is no evidence that her invention was *not surprising*; one could be surprised or not that she was able to accomplish her goal. The correct answer is (A).

READY, SET... SYNTHESIZE

Now, let's move on to the other type of question in the Rhetoric category, the one that will appear at the very end of each verbal module: Rhetorical Synthesis. The word *synthesize* means "put together," so these questions are asking you to put together two or more bullet points in order to fulfill a certain rhetorical goal. Let's see an example.

While researching a topic, a student has taken the following notes:

- Robin Wall Kimmerer is a writer, educator, and scientist working in the field of biocultural restoration.

- She is also a member of the Citizen Potawatomi Nation.

- Her first book, *Gathering Moss*, published in 2003, contained a series of essays about mosses that mixed scientific writing and personal reflection together.

- In her second book, *Braiding Sweetgrass*, Kimmerer's writing weaves together different types of knowledge: the Western scientific tradition, Traditional Ecological Knowledge, and lessons that plants themselves can teach.

---

4 ☐ Mark for Review

The student wants to emphasize a similarity between the two books Kimmerer wrote. Which choice most effectively uses relevant information from the notes to accomplish this goal?

Ⓐ *Gathering Moss* is about moss, and *Braiding Sweetgrass* is about lessons from plants.

Ⓑ *Gathering Moss* and *Braiding Sweetgrass* both include scientific writing.

Ⓒ *Gathering Moss* combines science and personal reflection, while *Braiding Sweetgrass* combines three different types of knowledge.

Ⓓ Published in 2003, *Gathering Moss* was written by Robin Wall Kimmerer, who has worked in the field of biocultural restoration.

Here's How to Crack It

First, identify the type of question. Rhetorical Synthesis questions are extremely easy to identify: they are the only question type to use bullet points instead of text in the form of a paragraph. Then, like with all Reading and Writing questions, determine what the question is asking. Rhetorical Synthesis questions always contain the same question: *Which choice most effectively uses relevant information from the notes to accomplish this goal?* The key part to notice is *this goal*. You MUST read the sentence before the question to determine what the goal is.

Here, the stated goal is to *emphasize a similarity between the two books*. Now, your impulse might be to read the bullet points and identify a similarity. However, we've found that you probably don't need to do this. Instead, highlight the task or tasks of the question and then go straight to the answer choices and eliminate anything that doesn't completely fulfill the task.

In this case, highlight *similarity* and *two books*. Any answer that does not mention *two books* or draw a comparison can be eliminated. Let's go to POE.

Choice (A) mentions the two books, and *moss* and *plants* are somewhat similar, so keep (A). Choice (B) mentions the two books and uses the word *both* to state a similarity. Keep (B). Choice (C) mentions both books, but the word *while* and the types of content in the books indicate a contrast, not a *similarity*. Eliminate (C). Choice (D) only mentions one of the books, so eliminate it because the question asked about *two books*.

Finally, compare (A) and (B). Choice (A) does not clearly state that this is a similarity between the two; it merely presents information about the content of both books. Eliminate (A). On the other hand, (B) clearly states that there is a similarity between the two books: they both contain *scientific writing*. Therefore, the correct answer is (B).

Of course, we can also confirm that this information is in the bullet points: the third bullet point states that *Gathering Moss* contains *scientific writing*, and the fourth bullet point mentions that the *Western scientific tradition* is part of the book's content, which clearly indicates that *scientific writing* is a component of the book.

Here's the basic approach for these questions:

Rhetorical Synthesis Basic Approach

1. Read the question and highlight each goal that is mentioned.
2. Eliminate any answer choice that does not completely fulfill the goal or goals.
3. Read the bullet points to confirm the answer if needed.

It's very unlikely that you will see an answer choice that is inconsistent with what is stated in the bullet points. That is, you won't see the kind of wrong answers that you will see on the Reading questions—ones that could be arrived at through misreading or making assumptions. Instead, the wrong answers will simply not completely fulfill the goal or goals stated in the question. This is why you can save yourself some time by not reading the bullet points first; you generally won't need to prove that the information is supported. It's also worth remembering that these questions do NOT test you on punctuation, grammar, style, being concise, or any other Rules topics. Focus on the content of the sentence in each answer choice and how well it does or does not fulfill the goal or goals.

Let's try another one.

While researching a topic, a student has taken the following notes:

- Large animals known as megafauna have substantial impacts on their environments.
- However, many native megafauna are extinct, so their effects on the ecosystem are unknown.
- Bison are a type of megafauna that used to be dominant in the United States.
- Reintroducing bison to their native environments doubled plant diversity.
- The presence of cattle, a domesticated megafauna, in the same environments produced a significantly lower increase in plant diversity.

5 ☐ Mark for Review

The student wants to present one impact that native megafauna have on their environments. Which choice most effectively uses relevant information from the notes to accomplish this goal?

(A) Bison, a type of native megafauna, doubled plant diversity in their native environments.

(B) Bison and cattle are two types of megafauna that live in the United States.

(C) Although many native megafauna are extinct, bison were reintroduced to their native environment.

(D) Native and domesticated megafauna can have impacts on their environments.

Here's How to Crack It

Once you've established that you're dealing with a Rhetorical Synthesis question, highlight the goal or goals in the question. Here, you should highlight *one impact that native megafauna have on their environments*. The correct answer should relate to *native megafauna* and a specific environmental *impact*. Move on to POE.

Choice (A) mentions *a type of native megafauna* and describes an environmental *impact* (*doubled plant diversity*), so keep (A). Choice (B) mentions *megafauna*, but there's no environmental impact. Eliminate (B). Choice (C) mentions *native megafauna* but does not say the *impact* of reintroducing bison; eliminate it. Choice (D) mentions *impacts* but does not *present one impact*; it's not specific about what that impact might be. Eliminate (D). The correct answer is (A).

Let's try one more.

While researching a topic, a student has taken the following notes:

- R. Murray Schafer was a Canadian composer, writer, and environmentalist.
- Schafer created many soundscapes during his career.
- Soundscapes are the sounds that arise from a location.
- Soundscapes include animal sounds, natural sounds such as weather, and human-created sounds.
- Schafer wrote *The Tuning of the World* and *The Soundscape*, which are books on soundscapes.

6 🔖 Mark for Review

The student wants to introduce soundscapes to an audience familiar with Schafer. Which choice most effectively uses relevant information from the notes to accomplish this goal?

Ⓐ Canadian composer, writer, and environmentalist R. Murray Schafer created and wrote about the collections of animal sounds, natural sounds such as weather, and human-created sounds known as soundscapes.

Ⓑ *The Tuning of the World* and *The Soundscape* were written by R. Murray Schafer, a Canadian composer, writer, and environmentalist.

Ⓒ R. Murray Schafer, a Canadian composer, writer, and environmentalist, created many soundscapes during his career.

Ⓓ Schafer wrote about and created soundscapes, which are sounds that arise from a location, including animal sounds, natural sounds such as weather, and human-created sounds.

Here's How to Crack It

Identify that this is a Rhetorical Synthesis question, and then highlight the goal or goals in the question. In this case, you should highlight *introduce soundscapes* and *audience familiar with Schafer*. It's common for Rhetorical Synthesis questions to specify whether the audience is familiar or unfamiliar with something. If the audience is unfamiliar, the answer should explain who or what the person or thing is, while if the audience is familiar, the answer should not. Let's go to POE.

Eliminate (A) because it describes Schafer—the audience is *familiar* with Schafer, so he should not be introduced. Eliminate (B) and (C) for the same reason. No description of Schafer is needed if the audience is familiar. Check (D). This answer does not describe Schafer, but it does *introduce soundscapes* by defining what they are. Therefore, this answer fulfills all parts of the question. The correct answer is (D).

CONCLUSION

While the term Rhetoric might have sounded scary initially, we hope you're feeling more confident now that you know how to approach the two types of questions in this category. Remember, you choose the order of questions—practice Rhetoric questions on the following drill and use the results to help determine when to attempt them.

Take a Breather
You've made it through the entire Reading and Writing section! Next up is Math, so feel free to take a break before diving in. Grab a snack, relax with a book, go for a walk—anything that will help you refresh before reviewing more content. Remember that study breaks can make you more productive, so don't deprive yourself of some needed relaxation time.

Rhetoric Questions Drill

Time: 12 minutes. Note that these questions have been placed in order of difficulty for each of the two question types, as they will appear on the test. Check your answers in Part IV.

1 ☐ Mark for Review

The popular board game *Monopoly* rewards players who compete with each other, act aggressively, and acquire as much money as possible. _____ the original version of *Monopoly*, *The Landlord's Game*, had a much different objective. *The Landlord's Game*, created by Lizzie Magie in 1903, was designed to demonstrate the negative effects of monopolies and included a second set of rules, called Prosperity, in which players were encouraged to cooperate with each other.

Which choice completes the text with the most logical transition?

Ⓐ Likewise,

Ⓑ Regardless,

Ⓒ By contrast,

Ⓓ In effect,

2 ☐ Mark for Review

The play *The 7 Stages of Grieving*, written by Wesley Enoch and Deborah Mailman, was directed by Enoch and performed by Mailman for the first time in 1995. The title of the play references seven phases of Aboriginal history in Australia as well as the stages of grieving as developed by Elisabeth Kübler-Ross. Since then, the play has gone on to become a classic of Australian theater and has been updated with each production. _____ the current version added an epilogue that introduces seven actions of healing for the audience to engage in.

Which choice completes the text with the most logical transition?

Ⓐ For instance,

Ⓑ Moreover,

Ⓒ Similarly,

Ⓓ Subsequently,

3 ☐ Mark for Review

Researchers interested in how nanoplastics can move up the food chain planted lettuce in soil contaminated with nanoplastics. They fed some of the lettuce to black soldier fly larvae and then fed some of the larvae to an insectivorous fish. When the researchers examined the larvae, they found nanoplastics in the mouths and guts of the larvae. _____ when they examined the fish, they also found nanoplastics in different parts of the fish.

Which choice completes the text with the most logical transition?

- (A) To that end,

- (B) Specifically,

- (C) Similarly,

- (D) Nevertheless,

4 ☐ Mark for Review

Dugongs, a species of marine mammal similar to manatees, may be extinct in China. Dugongs rely on seagrass, a type of habitat that is particularly vulnerable to pollution. Although conservation efforts have been enacted, it may be too late. _____ hope is not lost, as there are populations of dugongs in other parts of the world.

Which choice completes the text with the most logical transition?

- (A) Therefore,

- (B) Still,

- (C) Instead,

- (D) For example,

5 ☐ Mark for Review

Located in Millennium Park in Chicago, Illinois, *Cloud Gate* is a sculpture by Anish Kapoor. The sculpture is constructed of stainless steel plates and has a 12-foot-high arch in the middle, making it look like a large, silver bean. _____ the sculpture has been nicknamed "The Bean," a name that Kapoor initially disliked.

Which choice completes the text with the most logical transition?

(A) Though,

(B) Indeed,

(C) In conclusion,

(D) Nonetheless,

6 ☐ Mark for Review

While researching a topic, a student has taken the following notes:

- Researchers in the Ugandan rainforest have found that wild chimpanzees drum on tree roots to communicate.
- Each chimpanzee has a distinct drumming pattern that scientists could use to identify and locate the chimp.
- The drumming could help explain why scientists observed chimpanzees greeting each other when meeting but not "saying goodbye" when they parted.
- The chimpanzees may not "say goodbye" because they can still communicate with each other over long distances.

The student wants to present a possible explanation for chimpanzees not "saying goodbye." Which choice most effectively uses relevant information from the notes to accomplish this goal?

(A) Chimpanzees have distinct drumming patterns that they use to greet each other when meeting, but they do not "say goodbye."

(B) Chimpanzees may not "say goodbye" because they can use their distinct drumming patterns to communicate with each other over long distances.

(C) Scientists can use the distinct drumming patterns to identify and locate chimps even if the chimpanzees may not "say goodbye."

(D) Chimpanzees drum on tree roots to communicate their identity and location.

7 ☐ Mark for Review

While researching a topic, a student has taken the following notes:

- Louise Erdrich is an American novelist and an enrolled member of the Turtle Mountain Band of Chippewa.
- She frequently writes stories about the contemporary Native American experience and is recognized as one of the writers in the second wave of the Native American Renaissance.
- Her early novels, including *Love Medicine* and *Four Souls*, tell the story of the same three families who live in and around a reservation in North Dakota.
- Her novel *The Round House*, published in 2012, won the National Book Award for Fiction.
- Another one of her novels, *The Night Watchman*, won her the Pulitzer Prize for Fiction in 2021.

The student wants to highlight the various literary accolades that Erdrich has received. Which choice most effectively uses relevant information from the notes to accomplish this goal?

(A) Erdrich received a Pulitzer Prize for her novel *The Night Watchman*.

(B) Erdrich has written many stories about the contemporary Native American experience, including *Love Medicine*, *Four Souls*, *The Round House*, and *The Night Watchman*.

(C) Erdrich received a National Book Award for *The Round House* and a Pulitzer Prize for *The Night Watchman*.

(D) Erdrich is part of the second wave of the Native American Renaissance and has won the National Book Award.

8 ☐ Mark for Review

While researching a topic, a student has taken the following notes:

- Crème brûlée is a custard-based dessert.
- Typically, crème brûlée is made with heavy cream, eggs, sugar, and vanilla.
- These ingredients are mixed together, baked, and then cooled.
- A defining feature of crème brûlée is a caramelized sugar surface.
- Caramelization is the use of heat to change the chemical structure of sugar.
- Caramelized sugar is darker in color and nuttier in flavor than white sugar.

The student wants to introduce crème brûlée to an audience familiar with caramelization. Which choice most effectively uses relevant information from the notes to accomplish this goal?

(A) Caramelization, which is the use of heat to change the chemical structure of sugar, is a defining feature of the custard-based dessert crème brûlée.

(B) Crème brûlée is a custard-based dessert featuring a caramelized sugar surface.

(C) Crème brûlée is made with heavy cream, eggs, sugar, and vanilla, ingredients that are mixed together, baked, and then cooled.

(D) Sugar that is darker in color and nuttier in flavor can be made by caramelization, a process that uses heat to change the chemical structure of sugar.

9 🔖 Mark for Review

While researching a topic, a student has taken the following notes:

- Many place names in the US have French origins.

- Some city names are French words or phrases, such as Detroit and Baton Rouge.

- Some city names are translations of French phrases, such as Little Rock and Green Bay.

- Some state names are French words, such as Louisiana and Vermont.

- Some state names are French interpretations of Native American words, such as Illinois and Wisconsin.

The student wants to introduce the main point to an audience unfamiliar with US city and state names. Which choice most effectively uses relevant information from the notes to accomplish this goal?

(A) Many place names in the US, from Little Rock to Wisconsin, have French origins.

(B) From cities such as Detroit and Green Bay to states such as Illinois and Wisconsin, many places in the US have names with French origins.

(C) Many cities in the US, such as Baton Rouge and Little Rock, have names with French origins.

(D) Many states in the US, such as Louisiana and Wisconsin, have names with French origins.

10 🔖 Mark for Review

While researching a topic, a student has taken the following notes:

- Green spaces in urban areas can help support biodiversity.

- However, the maintenance and mowing of lawns in urban areas can negatively affect arthropods (animals such as insects and spiders).

- Researchers analyzed a group of studies that looked at the impact of reduced mowing on arthropods.

- The analysis showed that reduced mowing was connected to an increase in the abundance of arthropods.

- The analysis also showed that reduced mowing was connected to an increase in the taxa richness (or diversity) of arthropods.

The student wants to emphasize the two results of the study. Which choice most effectively uses relevant information from the notes to accomplish this goal?

(A) Green spaces in urban areas can help support biodiversity, but mowing lawns can negatively affect arthropods.

(B) Reduced mowing was connected to an increase in taxa richness.

(C) Researchers analyzed studies about arthropod abundance and taxa richness.

(D) Reduced mowing was connected to an increase in abundance and diversity of arthropods.

Chapter 11
Math Basics

Although we'll show you which mathematical concepts are most important to know for the PSAT, this book relies on your knowledge of basic math concepts. If you're a little rusty, this chapter is for you. Read on for a review of the math basics you'll need to know before you continue.

HOW TO CONQUER PSAT MATH

So, what do you need to do? There are three important steps:

1. **Know the basic content.** Obviously you do need to know the basics of arithmetic, algebra, and geometry. We'll cover what you need to know in this chapter.
2. **Learn some PSAT-specific problem-solving skills.** Since these basic concepts appear in ways you're probably not used to from math class, you need to prepare yourself with a set of test-specific problem-solving skills designed to help you answer PSAT Math questions. We'll cover the most important ones in the next chapter.
3. **Have a sound overall testing strategy.** This means knowing what to do with difficult questions and having a plan to pace yourself to get the maximum number of points in the time allotted. Be sure to read carefully the material in Chapter 3 to make sure you're using the strategy that will get you the greatest number of points in the time you have.

KNOW THE STRUCTURE

The Math section of the Digital PSAT is split into two modules. Each module contains 22 questions, of which 16 or 17 are multiple-choice questions and the rest are student-produced response questions (SPR), meaning that you fill in your own answer instead of choosing from four answers. Questions on the second module are, on average, easier or harder based on performance on the first module. Each module has two "pre-test" questions that do not count towards your score, but they are not identified, so treat every question as if it counts.

The Math section is further broken down by question type and content area, as follows.

By Question Type	
70% Problem Solving	15–16 questions per module
30% Word Problems	6–7 questions per module

By Content Area	
35% Algebra	7–8 questions per module
32.5% Advanced Math	7–8 questions per module
20% Problem-Solving & Data Analysis	4–5 questions per module
12.5% Geometry and Trigonometry	2–3 questions per module

(PERSONAL) ORDER OF DIFFICULTY

The questions on each module in the Math section of the Digital PSAT have a loose order of difficulty. You may notice the questions getting harder as the section progresses. More important than any question format, math content, or official order of difficulty is your own Personal Order of Difficulty. Though the last questions of each module are likely to be the hardest, use your own personal strengths and weaknesses to decide which questions to do and which to skip.

USING THE ONLINE TOOLS AND SCRATCH PAPER

Online Tools

Several of the on-screen features of the Digital SAT will be useful on the Math section.

- Mark for review tool to mark questions to come back to later
- Built-in calculator, which can be accessed at any time
- Reference sheet with common math formulas, which can be accessed at any time
- The annotate tool is NOT available on the Math section, so you will not be able to underline or highlight parts of the question.

Scratch Paper

The proctor at the test center will hand out three sheets of scratch paper, and you can use your own pen or pencil. Plan ahead about how to use the scratch paper in combination with what's on the screen.

Use the Tools Effectively!

Online Tools
- Eliminate wrong answers
- Work steps on the calculator
- Look up geometry formulas

Scratch Paper
- Rewrite key parts of the question
- Write out every calculation
- Redraw geometric figures and label them
- Rewrite answer choices as needed

The Calculator Guide in your Online Student Tools will show you how to get the most out of the built-in calculator. Refer to it as you work through the Math chapters in this book.

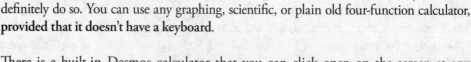

USING YOUR CALCULATOR

You are allowed to use a calculator on all Math questions on the PSAT, and you should definitely do so. You can use any graphing, scientific, or plain old four-function calculator, **provided that it doesn't have a keyboard.**

There is a built-in Desmos calculator that you can click open on the screen at any time. If you plan to use the built-in calculator instead of bringing your own, be sure to practice with it. Download the Bluebook app from the College Board website, where you can do untimed practice to get used to the built-in calculator. It will make many questions, especially ones dealing with functions and graphs, easier than they would be by hand.

There are a few simple rules to remember when dealing with your calculator:

1. Use the calculator you're most comfortable with. You definitely don't want to be trying to find the right button on test day. Ideally, you should be practicing with the same calculator you'll use on test day.
2. Change or charge your batteries the week before the test. If they run out during the test, you can use the built-in Desmos calculator instead.
3. Be sure to hit the "clear" or "on/off" button after each calculation to reset the calculator after an operation. A common mistake to make when using your calculator is to forget to clear your last result.
4. Your calculator is very good at calculating, but watch out for mis-keying information. (If you type the wrong numbers in, you'll get the wrong result.) Check each number on the display as you key it in.
5. For the most part, you'll use your calculator for the basic operations of addition, subtraction, multiplication, and division; the ability to convert fractions to decimals, and vice versa; and the ability to do square roots and exponents. Don't forget, though, that it likely has handy buttons for things like sine, cosine, and absolute value, should you encounter those on the test.
6. Then, there's one really big, important rule whenever you think about using your calculator:

> A calculator can't think; it can only calculate.

What does this mean? It means that a calculator can't think through a question for you. You have to do the work of understanding and setting up the problem correctly to make sure you know what the right calculation will be to get the answer. Only then can you use the calculator to calculate the answer.

So, use your paper and pencil to practice your problem-solving skills on all Math questions. You should always be sure to set up the question on your scratch paper—writing it down is still the best method—which will help you catch any errors you might make and allow you to pick up where you left off if you lose focus. Then, move quickly to your calculator or the built-in calculator to chug your way through the calculations, and be careful to enter each number and operator correctly. Remember, using your calculator is already saving you time on these questions—don't rush and lose the advantage that it gives you.

Not sure whether your calculator is acceptable? Check College Board's website for a list of approved calculators.

Drill 1

DEFINITIONS

One of the reasons that good math students often don't get the credit they deserve on the PSAT is that they've forgotten one or more of these definitions—or they read too fast and skip over these "little" words. Be sure you know them cold and watch out for them!

Match the words with their definitions, and then come up with some examples. Answers can be found in Part IV.

1. integers

2. positive numbers

3. negative numbers

4. even numbers

5. odd numbers

6. factors

7. multiples

8. prime numbers

9. distinct

10. digit

a. numbers that a certain number can be divided by, leaving no remainder
   Examples: _____

b. integers that cannot be divided evenly by 2
   Examples: _____

c. numbers that have no fractional or decimal parts
   Examples: _____

d. numbers that are greater than zero
   Examples: _____

e. having a different value
   Examples: _____

f. integers that can be divided by 2 evenly (with no remainder)
   Examples: _____

g. numbers that are less than zero
   Examples: _____

h. numbers that have exactly two distinct factors: themselves and 1
   Examples: _____

i. numbers that can be divided by a certain number with no remainder
   Examples: _____

j. a numerical symbol from 0 through 9 that fills a place in a number
   Examples: _____

11. consecutive numbers

12. divisible

13. remainder

14. sum

15. product

16. difference

17. quotient

18. absolute value

k. the result of addition
    Examples: _____

l. a whole number left over after division
    Examples: _____

m. the result of subtraction
    Examples:_____

n. can be divided with no remainder
    Examples: _____

o. a number's distance from zero; always a
    positive value or 0
    Examples: _____

p. numbers in sequential order
    Examples: _____

q. the result of division
    Examples: _____

r. the result of multiplication
    Examples: _____

EXPONENTS AND SQUARE ROOTS

Exponents are just shorthand for multiplication. Instead of writing $3 \times 3 \times 3 \times 3$, you can write 3^4. Thus, you can handle exponents by expanding them out if necessary.

$$y^2 \times y^3 = y \times y \times y \times y \times y = y^5$$

$$\frac{y^4}{y^2} = \frac{y \times y \times y \times y}{y \times y} = \frac{\cancel{y} \times \cancel{y} \times y \times y}{\cancel{y} \times \cancel{y}} = y \times y = y^2$$

$$(y^2)^3 = (y \times y)^3 = (y \times y)\,(y \times y)\,(y \times y) = y^6$$

However, you can also multiply and divide exponents that have the same base using a shortcut called MADSPM. MADSPM also helps you remember how to deal with raising exponents to another power. Let's see the breakdown:

- **MA** means when you see a Multiplication sign between like bases, Add the exponents. So, $y^2 \times y^3 = y^{2+3} = y^5$.

- **DS** means when you see a Division sign (or fraction), Subtract the exponents. So, $\frac{y^5}{y^2} = y^{5-2} = y^3$.

- **PM** means when you see a base with an exponent raised to a Power, Multiply the exponents. So, $(y^2)^3 = y^{2 \times 3} = y^6$. (This is really easy to confuse with multiplication, so watch out!)

Here are some additional rules to remember about exponents:

> **Warning**
> The rules for multiplying and dividing exponents do not apply to addition or subtraction:
> $2^2 + 2^3 = 12$
> $(2 \times 2) + (2 \times 2 \times 2) = 12$
> It does not equal 2^5
> or 32.

- Anything to the zero power equals 1: $3^0 = 1$. Mathematicians argue about whether 0^0 is 1 or is undefined, but that won't come up on the PSAT.
- Anything to the first power equals itself: $3^1 = 3$.
- 1 to any power equals 1: $1^{3876} = 1$.
- A **negative exponent** means to take the reciprocal of what would be the result as if the negative weren't there: $2^{-2} = \frac{1}{2^2} = \frac{1}{4}$.

- A **fractional exponent** has two parts (like any other fraction): the numerator is the power the base is raised to, and the denominator is the root of the base. For example, $8^{\frac{2}{3}} = \sqrt[3]{8^2} = \sqrt[3]{64} = 4$.

Remember that in calculating the value of a root, you're looking for what number multiplied by itself results in the number under the radical. In the above example, $\sqrt[3]{64} = 4$ because $4 \times 4 \times 4 = 64$.

When you see the square root sign, that means to take the positive root only. So, $\sqrt{9} = 3$, but not -3.

Square roots work just like exponents: you can *always* multiply and divide roots, but you can add and subtract only with the *same* root.

Multiplication and Division:

$$\sqrt{8} \times \sqrt{2} = \sqrt{8 \times 2} = \sqrt{16} = 4$$

$$\sqrt{\frac{1}{4}} = \frac{\sqrt{1}}{\sqrt{4}} = \frac{1}{2}$$

$$\sqrt{300} = \sqrt{100 \times 3} = \sqrt{100} \times \sqrt{3} = 10\sqrt{3}$$

Addition and Subtraction:

$$2\sqrt{2} + 3\sqrt{2} = 5\sqrt{2}$$

$$4\sqrt{3} - \sqrt{3} = 3\sqrt{3}$$

$2\sqrt{3} + 3\sqrt{2}$ *Cannot be added without a calculator since the terms do not have the same root.*

Drill 2

Answers can be found in Part IV.

a. $3^3 \times 3^2 = $ _____

b. $\dfrac{3^3}{3^2} = $ _____

c. $\left(3^3\right)^2 = $ _____

d. $x^6 \times x^2 = $ _____

e. $\dfrac{x^6}{x^2} = $ _____

f. $\left(x^6\right)^2 = $ _____

g. $\sqrt{8} = $ _____

h. $\sqrt[3]{-64} = $ _____

i. $\sqrt{12} + 5\sqrt{3} = $ _____

j. $\sqrt{y^3} = $ _____

k. $\sqrt[3]{-y^3} = $ _____

l. $\sqrt{x^2 y} + 5x\sqrt{y} = $ _____

1 ☐ Mark for Review

If $3^4 = 9^x$, what is the value of x?

Ⓐ 2

Ⓑ 3

Ⓒ 4

Ⓓ 5

2 ☐ Mark for Review

If $\left(3^x\right)^3 = 3^{15}$, what is the value of x?

Ⓐ 3

Ⓑ 5

Ⓒ 7

Ⓓ 9

3 ☐ Mark for Review

If $\sqrt{s} - 3 = 9$, which of the following is a possible value of s?

(A) 12

(B) 36

(C) 81

(D) 144

4 ☐ Mark for Review

Which of the following is equivalent to the expression $x^6 y^{-3} z^{\frac{1}{2}}$?

(A) $\dfrac{x^6 \sqrt{z}}{3y}$

(B) $\dfrac{x^6 \sqrt{2z}}{y^3}$

(C) $\dfrac{6x\sqrt{z}}{y^3}$

(D) $\dfrac{x^6 \sqrt{z}}{y^3}$

5 ☐ Mark for Review

The function $f(x) = k^{0.3x}$, where k is a constant, can also be expressed as $f(x) = k^{\frac{Bx}{9}}$ for what value of B?

(A) 2.7

(B) 9.3

(C) 27

(D) 30

6 ☐ Mark for Review

$$\sqrt{m^2 + 39} = 8$$

In the equation above, what is a possible value of m?

(A) 3

(B) 4

(C) 5

(D) 6

7 ⬚ Mark for Review

If $x^y x^6 = x^{54}$ and $\left(x^3\right)^z = x^9$, what is the value of $y + z$?

(A) 11

(B) 12

(C) 48

(D) 51

8 ⬚ Mark for Review

Which of the following expressions is equivalent to $\sqrt[4]{81b^3 c}$?

(A) $3b^{\frac{3}{4}} c^{\frac{1}{4}}$

(B) $3b^3 c$

(C) $20.25 b^{\frac{3}{4}} c^{\frac{1}{4}}$

(D) $20.25 b^3 c$

9 ⬚ Mark for Review

If $x^{\frac{5}{2}} = 8x$, which of the following could be the value of x?

(A) 2

(B) 4

(C) 6

(D) 8

10 ⬚ Mark for Review

Which of the following expressions is equivalent to $\left(3m^2 n^{-3}\right)^{\frac{2}{3}}$?

(A) $2m^{\frac{4}{3}} n^{-2}$

(B) $\sqrt[3]{9} m^{\frac{4}{3}} n^{-2}$

(C) $3m^{\frac{4}{3}} n^{-2}$

(D) $3m^4 n^{-6}$

EQUATIONS AND INEQUALITIES

An **equation** is a statement that contains an equals sign, such as $3x + 5 = 17$.

To solve an equation, you must get the variable x alone on one side of the equals sign and everything else on the other side.

The first step is to put all of the variables on one side of the equation and all of the numbers on the other side, using addition and subtraction. As long as you perform the same operation on both sides of the equals sign, you aren't changing the value of the variable.

Then you can divide both sides of the equation by the *coefficient,* which is the number in front of the variable. If that number is a fraction, you can multiply everything by its reciprocal.

For example,

$$3x + 5 = 17$$
$$\underline{\quad -5 \quad\; -5 \quad}$$ Subtract 5 from each side.
$$3x \quad\;\; = 12$$
$$\underline{\div 3 \qquad \div 3 \quad}$$ Divide each side by 3.
$$x \quad\;\; = \;\; 4$$

Always remember this rule of equations:

> Whatever you do to one side of the equation, you must also do to the other side.

The example above was fairly simple. The PSAT may test this idea with more complex equations and formulas, though. Just keep trying to isolate the variable in question by undoing the operations that have been done to it. Here's an example.

1 📑 Mark for Review

Doyle's Log Rule is used to estimate the amount of usable lumber, in board feet B, that can be milled from logs. The rule is defined as $B = L\left(\dfrac{d-4}{4}\right)^2$, where d is the diameter inside the bark measured in inches at the small end of the log and L is the log length measured in feet. Which of the following gives the value of d, in terms of B and L?

Ⓐ $d = \dfrac{1}{4}\left(\sqrt{\dfrac{B}{L}} + 16\right)$

Ⓑ $d = 4\left(\sqrt{BL} + 1\right)$

Ⓒ $d = 4\left(\sqrt{\dfrac{B}{L}} - 1\right)$

Ⓓ $d = 4\left(\sqrt{\dfrac{B}{L}} + 1\right)$

Here's How to Crack It

The question asks for an equation that gives the value of d in terms of the other variables. Ignore all of the words describing what the variables stand for, and focus on isolating the correct variable.

To isolate d, start with the L on the outside of the parentheses on the right. Divide both sides by L to get $\dfrac{B}{L} = \left(\dfrac{d-4}{4}\right)^2$. Now undo the power of 2 outside the parentheses. Take the square root of both sides of the equation to get $\sqrt{\dfrac{B}{L}} = \dfrac{d-4}{4}$. Multiply both sides by 4 to get $4\sqrt{\dfrac{B}{L}} = d - 4$. Add 4 to both sides to get $4\sqrt{\dfrac{B}{L}} + 4 = d$. Factor out the 4 to get $4\left(\sqrt{\dfrac{B}{L}} + 1\right) = d$. The correct answer is (D).

An **inequality** is any statement with one of these signs:

> <   (less than)
>
> \>   (greater than)
>
> ≤   (less than or equal to)
>
> ≥   (greater than or equal to)

You can solve inequalities in the same way you solve equations, with one exception: whenever you multiply or divide an inequality by a negative value, you must change the direction of the sign: for example, > becomes <, and ≤ becomes ≥.

For example,

$$3x + 5 > 17$$
$$\underline{-5 \quad -5}\qquad \text{Subtract 5 from each side.}$$
$$3x \quad > \quad 12$$
$$\underline{\div 3 \qquad \div 3}\qquad \text{Divide each side by 3.}$$
$$x \quad > \quad 4$$

In this case, we didn't multiply or divide by a negative value, so the direction of the sign didn't change. However, if we were to divide by a negative value, we would need to change the direction of the sign.

$$-4x + 3 > 15$$
$$\underline{-3 \quad -3}\qquad \text{Subtract 3 from each side.}$$
$$-4x \quad > \quad 12$$
$$\underline{\div -4 \qquad \div -4}\qquad \text{Divide each side by } -4.$$
$$x \quad < \quad -3$$

Now let's look at how the PSAT may make things more complicated with a question about a range of values.

---

2 ☐ Mark for Review

Which of the following is equivalent to $-12 \leq 3b + 3 \leq 18$?

Ⓐ $-5 \leq b \leq 5$

Ⓑ $-5 \leq b \leq 6$

Ⓒ $-4 \leq b \leq 6$

Ⓓ $3 \leq b \leq 5$

Here's How to Crack It

The question asks for an inequality that is equivalent to the one given. Like many questions on the PSAT, this question will be difficult if you try to do it all at once. Instead, break it down into Bite-Sized Pieces. Start with just part of the inequality, $-12 \leq 3b + 3$. Remember that you can solve inequalities just like equations—provided that if you multiply or divide by a negative value, you swap the direction of the inequality sign. To solve this part of the inequality, though, you just need to subtract 3 from each side (giving you $-15 \leq 3b$) and then divide each side by 3, which leaves you with $-5 \leq b$. Now you can eliminate any choices that you know won't work: (C) and (D) don't have $-5 \leq b$ in them. Now take the other part of the inequality: $3b + 3 \leq 18$. If you subtract 3 from each side and then divide by 3, you get $b \leq 5$. Now you can eliminate (B), and you're left with (A).

ABSOLUTE VALUES

PSAT Smoke and Mirrors

When you're asked to solve an equation involving an absolute value, it is very likely that the correct answer will be the negative result. Why? Because the test-writers know that you are less likely to think about the negative result! Another way to avoid mistakes is to do all the math inside the absolute value symbols first, and then make the result positive.

Absolute value is just a measure of the distance between a number and 0. Since distances are always positive, the absolute value of a number is also always positive. The absolute value of a number is written as $|x|$.

When solving for the value of a variable inside the absolute value bars, it is important to remember that variable could be either positive or negative. For example, if $|x| = 2$, then $x = 2$ or $x = -2$ since both 2 and -2 are a distance of 2 from 0.

Here's an example.

---○---

| 3 | 🔖 Mark for Review |

$$|x + 3| = 6$$

The value of one solution to the equation above is 3. What is the value of the other solution?

> [　　　]

Here's How to Crack It

The question asks for a solution to an equation with an absolute value. Since the value inside the absolute value bars can be positive or negative, set that value equal to 6 and −6 to find both solutions. When $x + 3 = 6$, $x = 3$. This solution was already given, so try the other one. When $x + 3 = -6$, $x = -9$. To check, substitute −9 for x to get $|-9 + 3| = |-6| = 6$. The correct answer is −9.

---○---

SIMULTANEOUS EQUATIONS

Simultaneous equations occur when you have two or more equations at the same time. Occasionally, all you have to do is stack the equations and then add or subtract them, so try that first. Sometimes, it won't get you exactly what you want, but it will get you close to it.

---

4 ☐ Mark for Review

$$x + 2x = 12$$
$$2x + x = 9$$

Given the system of equations above, what is the value of $x + y$?

Ⓐ 3

Ⓑ 7

Ⓒ $\frac{21}{2}$

Ⓓ 21

Here's How to Crack It

The question asks for the value of $x + y$ given a system of equations. When solving simultaneous equations, you can sometimes get what you need by adding the equations together. Even getting closer to $x + y$, such as getting a multiple of that expression, would be useful.

Let's see what happens when you add the equations:

$$\begin{array}{r} x + 2y = 12 \\ + \underline{2x + y = 9} \\ 3x + 3y = 21 \end{array}$$

Now all you need to do is divide both sides of the equation by 3 to get the expression you're being asked for, $x + y$, and you end up with the answer, 7. The correct answer is (B).

That was pretty simple, but simultaneous equations on the PSAT can be tougher. Let's look at a really challenging one.

---

5 ☐ Mark for Review

Two restaurants sell hamburgers at the same price and french fries at the same price. Restaurant A's lunchtime sales can be modeled as $40h + 70f = \$260.00$, where h is the cost of a hamburger and f is the cost of an order of french fries. If restaurant B sells 80 hamburgers and 60 orders of french fries over the same period and outsells restaurant A by \$100, what is the total cost of three hamburgers and three orders of french fries at either restaurant?

Ⓐ $5.00

Ⓑ $9.00

Ⓒ $11.00

Ⓓ $15.00

Here's How to Crack It

The question asks for the total cost of three hamburgers and three orders of fries at either restaurant. The sales equation at restaurant A is given in the question. Create an equation for restaurant B's lunchtime sales so you can solve the two equations. Restaurant B's sales can be modeled as $80h + 60f = 260 + 100 = 360$. Adding these equations together or subtracting one from the other won't give you the 3 burgers and 3 fries that you want. Instead, you need to create a common coefficient for one of the variables and then add or subtract the two equations from each other to get rid of that variable. In this case, multiply the restaurant A equation by -2 to get $-80h - 140f = -520$. Place the two equations on top of each other and add:

$$
\begin{aligned}
-80h - 140f &= -520 \\
+80h + 60f &= 360 \\
\hline
-80f &= -160
\end{aligned}
$$

Divide both sides by -80 to get $f = 2$. Plug 2 into the restaurant A equation to get $40h + 70(2) = 260$. Solve for h to get $40h + 140 = 260$, or $40h = 120$, so $h = 3$. Therefore, the total cost of 3 hamburgers and 3 orders of french fries is $3(3) + 3(2) = 9 + 6 = 15$. The correct answer is (D).

WRITING YOUR OWN EQUATIONS

For the most part, we've been looking at solving equations given to you in questions. That last question, though, required you to create one of your own. The PSAT Math section tests not only your math skills but also, and possibly even more important to your score improvement, your reading skills. On word problems, it is imperative that you read the questions carefully and translate the words in the question into math.

ENGLISH	MATH EQUIVALENTS
is, are, were, did, does, costs	=
what (or any unknown value)	*any variable* (*x, y, k, b*)
more, sum	+
less, difference	−
of, times, product	× (*multiply*)
ratio, quotient, out of, per	÷ (*divide*)

Sometimes you'll be asked to take a word problem and create equations or inequalities from that information. Usually, they will not ask you to solve these equations/inequalities, so if you are able to locate and translate the information in the question, you have a good shot at getting the correct answer. Always start with the most straightforward piece of information. What is the most straightforward piece of information? Well, that's up to you to decide. Consider the following question.

---

6 ☐ Mark for Review

Elom joined a gym that charges a monthly fee of $35. A one-time enrollment fee of $40 is charged when he joins. Which of the following represents the total amount of fees that Elom has paid to his gym after *m* months, in dollars?

Ⓐ $35m + 40$

Ⓑ $35 + 40m$

Ⓒ $35m - 40$

Ⓓ $(35 + 40)m$

Here's How to Crack It

The question asks for an expression to represent a situation. Read the question carefully and translate the information. The question states that there is a monthly fee of $35 and that the variable m represents the number of months. Therefore, the correct answer should include $35m$, so you can eliminate (B). The one-time enrollment fee of $40 has nothing to do with the number of months, so the 40 should be by itself. Eliminate (D), which multiplies the 40 by m. The fee should be added on, so the correct answer is (A).

Use Your Tools!

We showed you in the introduction how important it is to utilize the online tools and scratch paper frequently and effectively. This question is a great example. You worked the question one piece at a time and eliminated answers as you went. Use your scratch paper to rewrite parts of the question and translate them into math, and then use the Answer Eliminator tool to eliminate answers that don't match that piece. Take a look below at an example of what your screen and scratch paper should look like at the end of a question like this.

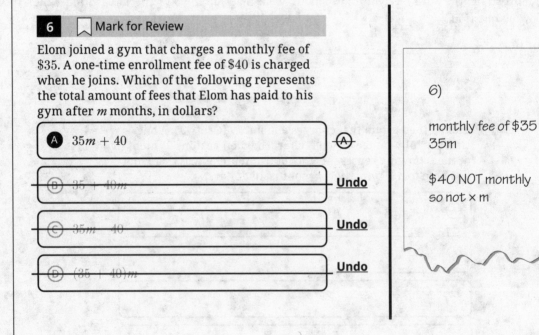

6   🔖 Mark for Review

Elom joined a gym that charges a monthly fee of $35. A one-time enrollment fee of $40 is charged when he joins. Which of the following represents the total amount of fees that Elom has paid to his gym after m months, in dollars?

A $35m + 40$

B $35 + 40m$

C $35m - 40$

D $(35 + 40)m$

6)

monthly fee of $35
35m

$40 NOT monthly
so not × m

Now let's look at a harder one. The following question has a lot more words and more than one inequality in each answer choice. This makes it even more important to translate one piece at a time and eliminate after each step.

---

7 ☐ Mark for Review

Kai has two different after-school jobs, one at a bookstore and one at a grocery store. He can only work a total of 10 hours each week. When he works at the bookstore, he earns $10 per hour, and when he works at the grocery store, he earns $13 per hour. He never earns less than $100 in a week, and he always works more hours at the bookstore. Solving which of the following systems of inequalities yields the number of hours at the bookstore, b, and the number of hours at the grocery store, g, that Kai can work in one week?

Ⓐ $b - g \leq 10$
$b < g$
$10b + 13g \geq 100$

Ⓑ $b + g \leq 10$
$b > g$
$10b + 13g \geq 100$

Ⓒ $b + g \leq 10$
$b > g$
$13b + 10g \geq 100$

Ⓓ $bg \leq 10$
$b > g$
$10b + 10g \geq 100$

Here's How to Crack It

The question asks for a system of inequalities that represents a situation. Start with a straightforward piece of information to translate. If you start with the fact that Kai works more hours at the bookstore than at the grocery store, you can translate that into $b > g$. This would eliminate (A). If you start with the fact that Kai works no more than 10 hours each week, you can translate that into $b + g \leq 10$. This would eliminate (D). Now, to decide between (B) and (C), compare the answers and see what the differences are. Choice (B) has a coefficient of 10 in front of the variable b. Check the question to see if 10 should be associated with b. Since b is the number of hours Kai works at the bookstore, and he earns $10 per hour there, the correct answer should have $10b$, not $13b$. Eliminate (C) and choose (B).

Drill 3

Answers can be found in Part IV.

---

1 🔖 Mark for Review

The number a is 2 more than one-fourth of the number b. Which of the following represents the relationship between a and b?

(A) $a = \frac{1}{4}b - 2$

(B) $a = \frac{1}{4}b + 2$

(C) $a = 4b - 2$

(D) $a = 4b + 2$

---

2 🔖 Mark for Review

If $\frac{3a}{4b} = \frac{5c}{6d}$, then which of the following is equal to bc?

(A) $\frac{a}{2d}$

(B) $\frac{5a}{8d}$

(C) $\frac{9ad}{10}$

(D) $18ad$

---

3 🔖 Mark for Review

A ski resort is renting skis for $30 and snowboards for $20 over a weekend. On Friday, 40 skis and snowboards were rented, and the resort collected $1,100 in rental fees. On Saturday, 55 skis and snowboards were rented, and the resort collected $1,400 in rental fees. On Sunday, the resort rented 85 skis and snowboards and collected $2,100 rental fees. Solving which of the following systems of equations yields the number of skis, s, and the number of snowboards, b, that were rented over the three-day weekend?

(A) $s + b = 50$
$30s + 20b = 180$

(B) $s + b = 180$
$30s + 20b = 460$

(C) $s + b = 180$
$30s + 20b = 4,600$

(D) $s + b = 4,600$
$30s + 20b = 180$

---

4 🔖 Mark for Review

$$-4(h + 5) = -3(2 - h) + 14$$

In the equation above, what is the value of h?

(A) -18

(B) -4

(C) $\frac{18}{7}$

(D) 18

---

5 ☐ Mark for Review

$$10(3x + a) - a(4x + 2) = 2a(x + 4)$$

If the equation above has infinitely many solutions for x, what is the value of a?

Ⓐ 1

Ⓑ 3

Ⓒ 4

Ⓓ 5

6 ☐ Mark for Review

If a certain number is 3 more than 7 times itself, what is the number?

Ⓐ -3

Ⓑ $-\frac{3}{2}$

Ⓒ $-\frac{1}{2}$

Ⓓ $-\frac{3}{8}$

7 ☐ Mark for Review

Ann is writing a book that will include up to 98 recipes. She currently has 32 main dish recipes and 18 dessert recipes. If r represents the number of additional recipes that Ann could include in her book, which of the following inequalities represents all possible values of r?

Ⓐ $r - 50 \geq 98$

Ⓑ $r - 50 \leq 98$

Ⓒ $98 - (32 + 18) - r \leq 0$

Ⓓ $98 - (32 + 18) - r \geq 0$

8 ☐ Mark for Review

$$\frac{m + 9}{3} + 2 = \frac{m - 2}{7} + 3$$

In the equation above, what is the value of m?

Ⓐ -17

Ⓑ -12

Ⓒ 5

Ⓓ 10

9 ☐ Mark for Review

A group of students sells different types of cookies at a bake sale. When the students sell two snickerdoodle cookies, s, and seven cinnamon cookies, c, they raise $14.00. When the students sell eight snickerdoodle cookies and three cinnamon cookies, they raise $17.50. Assuming the price per cookie does not change, which of the following equations represents a sale the students could make during the bake sale?

Ⓐ $2s + 3c = \$8.00$

Ⓑ $4s + 6c = \$16.25$

Ⓒ $6s + 5c = \$17.36$

Ⓓ $8s + 7c = \$24.50$

10 ☐ Mark for Review

Laura has a recipe for cake that calls for both eggs and cups of flour. Laura can purchase five eggs and four cups of flour for $5.50 and nine eggs and eight cups of flour for $10.50. Based on these costs, what is the cost of the ten eggs that Laura will need for her recipe?

Ⓐ $5.00

Ⓑ $5.50

Ⓒ $7.50

Ⓓ $10.50

THE COORDINATE PLANE

You will definitely see some questions on the coordinate plane, or *xy*-plane, on the PSAT. Let's start by covering the basics here. You'll see more advanced concepts in the Advanced Math chapter. So, let's just review:

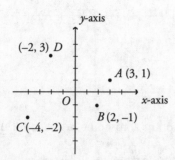

The *x*-axis is the horizontal axis, and the *y*-axis is the vertical axis. Points are given on the coordinate plane with the *x*-coordinate first. Positive *x*-values go to the right, and negative ones go to the left; positive *y*-values go up, and negative ones go down. So, point *A* (3, 1) is 3 points to the right on the *x*-axis and 1 point up from the *y*-axis. Point *B* (2, –1) is 2 points to the right on the *x*-axis and 1 point down from the *y*-axis.

Slope is a measure of the steepness of a line on the coordinate plane. On most slope questions, you need to recognize only whether the slope is positive, negative, or zero. A line that goes up and to the right has positive slope; a line that goes down and to the right has negative slope, and a flat line has zero slope. In the figure below, ℓ_1 has positive slope, ℓ_2 has zero slope, and ℓ_3 has negative slope.

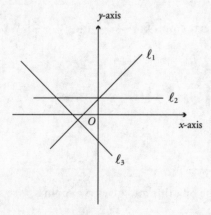

If you do need to calculate the slope, and the graph is drawn for you, here's how: slope = $\frac{y_2 - y_1}{x_2 - x_1}$. The *slope* of a line is equal to $\frac{rise}{run}$. To find the slope, take any two points on the line and count off or calculate the distance you need to get from one of these points to the other.

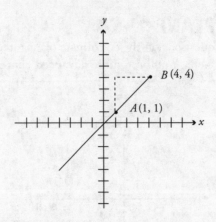

In the graph above, to get from point A to point B, we count up (rise) 3 units, and count over (run) 3 units. Therefore, the slope is $\dfrac{rise}{run} = \dfrac{3}{3} = 1$. Always remember to check whether the slope is positive or negative when you use $= \dfrac{rise}{run}$.

If you're not given a figure and you can't draw one easily using the points given, you can find the slope by plugging the coordinates you know into the slope formula. Just remember to plug the numbers into the formula carefully!

Here's an example.

⊖

<table>
<tr><td>8</td><td>🔖 Mark for Review</td></tr>
</table>

Line l contains the points $\left(-3, \dfrac{7}{3}\right)$ and $\left(2, -\dfrac{5}{3}\right)$. What is the slope of line l?

> We will talk more about Fill-In questions like this one later in this chapter.

Here's How to Crack It

The question asks for the slope of a line and gives two points. Use $\dfrac{rise}{run}$ to find the slope, being careful to start with the same point for both A and B. The equation $slope = \dfrac{y_2 - y_1}{x_2 - x_1}$ becomes $slope = \dfrac{-\dfrac{5}{3} - \dfrac{7}{3}}{2 - (-3)}$, which simplifies to $slope = \dfrac{-\dfrac{12}{3}}{5}$ and then $slope = \dfrac{-4}{5}$. This can be entered as $-4/5$ or in decimal form as -0.8.

The equation of a line can take multiple forms. One is known as the **standard form**. In this form, $Ax + By = C$, the slope is $-\dfrac{A}{B}$ and the y-intercept is $\dfrac{C}{B}$. Knowing these shortcuts can help you avoid having to convert a line equation into the more common form known as the **slope-intercept form**. A slope-intercept equation takes the form $y = mx + b$, where m is the slope and b is the y-intercept.

Knowing how to find the slope is useful for solving questions about perpendicular and parallel lines. **Perpendicular lines** have slopes that are negative reciprocals of one another. **Parallel lines** have the same slope and no solutions. You may also be given two equations that have infinitely many solutions.

Take a look at an example.

---

9   🔖 Mark for Review

$$gx - hy = 78$$
$$4x + 3y = 13$$

In the system of equations above, g and h are constants. If the system has infinitely many solutions, what is the value of $\dfrac{g}{h}$?

(A) $-\dfrac{4}{3}$

(B) $-\dfrac{3}{4}$

(C) $\dfrac{3}{4}$

(D) $\dfrac{4}{3}$

> **To Infinity…and Beyond!**
> When given two equations with infinitely many solutions, find a way to make them equal. The equations represent the same line.

Here's How to Crack It

The question asks for the value of a fraction given a system of equations. This question may have you scratching your head and moving on to the next question, but you may be surprised by how easy it is to solve.

When equations have infinitely many solutions, it means they are the same equation, or one is a multiple of the other. In other words, these two equations represent the same line. If it's the same line, it has the same slope. Both equations are in standard form, $Ax + By = C$, in which the slope is $-\dfrac{A}{B}$. In the first equation, $A = g$ and $B = -h$, so the slope is $-\dfrac{g}{-h}$, or $\dfrac{g}{h}$. In the second equation, $A = 4$ and $B = 3$, so the slope is $-\dfrac{4}{3}$. Set the two slopes equal to get $\dfrac{g}{h} = -\dfrac{4}{3}$. Knowing how to work with different forms of linear equations made this much simpler than it would have been with simultaneous equations. The correct answer is (A).

Let's look at a question for which the slope-intercept form is useful.

10 ☐ Mark for Review

If c is a constant less than 0, which of the following could be the graph of $y = c(x + y)$ in the xy-plane?

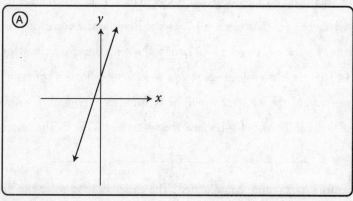

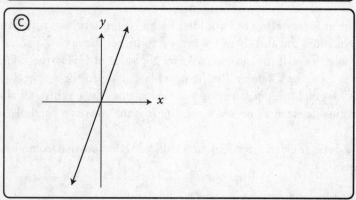

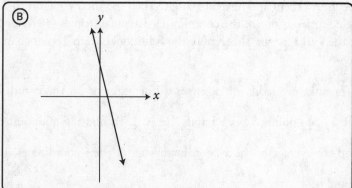

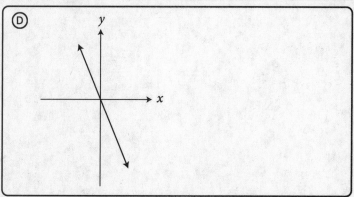

Here's How to Crack It

The question asks for the graph of the equation of a line. No points are labeled on the graphs in the answers, and the equation of the line has a mysterious c in it. If you knew the slope or y-intercept of the equation, you could use Process of Elimination. To see what is going on with this question, make up a value for c that is less than 0. Let's say that $c = -2$, in which case $y = -2(x + y)$. Distribute the -2 to get $y = -2x - 2y$. Rewrite the equation so that it is in the slope-intercept form, $y = mx + b$, to get $3y = -2x$ or $y = -\dfrac{2}{3}x$. Therefore, the slope is $-\dfrac{2}{3}$ and the y-intercept is 0. In fact, no matter what value you picked for c, if c is a constant less than 0, the slope will be negative, and the y-intercept will be 0. Eliminate (A) and (C) since both of these lines have positive slopes. Eliminate (B) because the y-intercept is not 0. The correct answer is (D).

The **distance formula** looks quite complicated. The easiest way to solve the distance between two points is to connect them and form a triangle. Then use the Pythagorean Theorem. Many times, the triangle formed is one of the common Pythagorean triples (3-4-5 or 5-12-13). We'll talk more about the Pythagorean Theorem in the Additional Math Topics chapter.

The **midpoint formula** gives the midpoint of a line segment on the coordinate plane. For example, the line ST has points $S(x_1, y_1)$ and $T(x_2, y_2)$. To find the midpoint of this line segment, simply find the average of the x-coordinates and of the y-coordinates. In our example, the midpoint would be $\left(\dfrac{x_1 + x_2}{2}, \dfrac{y_1 + y_2}{2} \right)$.

To find the **point of intersection** of two lines, find a way to set them equal and solve for the variable. If the equations are already in $y = mx + b$ form, set the $mx + b$ part of the two equations equal and solve for x. If the question asks for the value of y, plug the value of x back into either equation to solve for y. It may also be possible to Plug In the Answers (see Chapter 12 for more on this) or graph the equations on your calculator. These skills will also help find the points of intersection between a line and a non-linear graph such as a parabola.

Sometimes, it's a little trickier. Let's look at a difficult question that combines several of the previous concepts.

---

11 🔖 Mark for Review

Line 1 contains the points (2, 1) and (1, –2), and line 2 contains the points (–2, 9) and (10, –3). What is the y-coordinate of the point of intersection of lines 1 and 2?

Ⓐ –1

Ⓑ 3

Ⓒ 4

Ⓓ 7

Here's How to Crack It

The question asks for the y-coordinate of a point of intersection. To answer this question, first you need to find the equations of the two lines in order to set the equations equal to each other and find the value of x. Given two points on a line, you can find the slope using $\frac{y_2 - y_1}{x_2 - x_1}$. Therefore, the slope of line 1 can be calculated as $\frac{-2 - 1}{1 - 2} = \frac{-3}{-1} = 3$. Plug this and the coordinates of the easier point, (2, 1), into $y = mx + b$ to find the value of b. The equation for line 1 becomes $1 = 3(2) + b$. Solve for b to find that the value is –5, so line 1 is $y = 3x - 5$. The slope of line 2 can be calculated as $\frac{-3 - 9}{10 - (-2)} = \frac{-12}{12} = -1$. Find the value of b: $9 = -1(-2) + b$, so $b = 7$. The equation for line 2 is $y = -x + 7$. Set the two equations equal to each other to get $3x - 5 = -x + 7$. Solve for x to get $4x - 5 = 7$ or $4x = 12$, so $x = 3$. Finally, plug x into one of the equations to solve for y. Plug x into the equation $y = -x + 7$, to get $y = -3 + 7 = 4$. Therefore, the correct answer is 4, which is (C).

Drill 4

Answers can be found in Part IV.

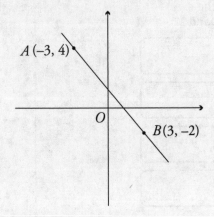

A (–3, 4)

O

B (3, –2)

a.   What is the change in *y* (rise)?
_____

b.   What is the change in *x* (run)?
_____

c.   What is the slope of the line above?
_____

(Remember, the line is going down to the right, so it must have a negative slope.)

d.   What would be the slope of a line parallel to *AB*? _____

e.   What would be the slope of a line perpendicular to *AB*? _____

f.   What is the distance from point *A* to point *B*? _____

g.   What is the midpoint of line segment *AB*? _____

1 ☐ Mark for Review

If $y = 6x + 3$ and $y = cx + 3$ are the equations of perpendicular lines, then what is the value of c?

Ⓐ -6

Ⓑ $-\frac{1}{6}$

Ⓒ $\frac{1}{6}$

Ⓓ 6

2 ☐ Mark for Review

What is the y-intercept of the line with equation $2x + 3y = 12$?

Ⓐ $\frac{1}{4}$

Ⓑ 2

Ⓒ 3

Ⓓ 4

3 ☐ Mark for Review

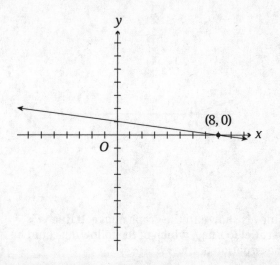

Which of the following could be the equation of the line in the graph above?

Ⓐ $2y - x = -8$

Ⓑ $4y + x = -8$

Ⓒ $8y - 3x = 8$

Ⓓ $8y + x = 8$

4 ☐ Mark for Review

$$y = 4x^2 - 6x + 4$$
$$y = 2x + 4$$

The equations above intersect at two points. What is the sum of the x-coordinates of the two points of intersection?

☐☐☐
___

5   🔖 Mark for Review

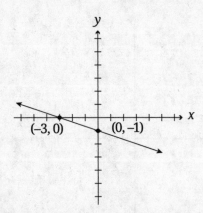

Line *l* is shown in the graph above. If line *m* is parallel to line *l*, which of the following could be the equation of line *m*?

Ⓐ $y = -3x - 1$

Ⓑ $y = -\frac{1}{3}x + 2$

Ⓒ $y = \frac{1}{3}x - 3$

Ⓓ $y = 3x + 2$

6   🔖 Mark for Review

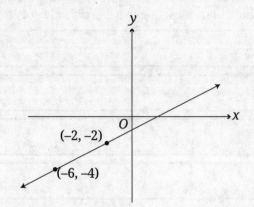

What is the *x*-intercept of the line in the graph above?

Ⓐ -1

Ⓑ 0

Ⓒ 1

Ⓓ 2

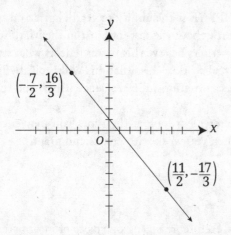

Which of the following is the slope of the line in the graph above?

Ⓐ $-\dfrac{11}{6}$

Ⓑ $-\dfrac{11}{9}$

Ⓒ $-\dfrac{9}{8}$

Ⓓ $-\dfrac{9}{11}$

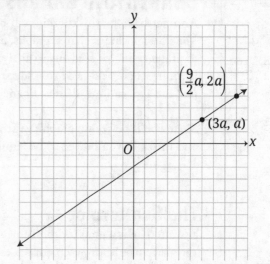

The graph of a line is shown in the xy-plane above. It contains the points $(3a, a)$ and $\left(\dfrac{9}{2}a, 2a\right)$, where a is a positive constant. Which of the following could be the equation of this line?

Ⓐ $y = \dfrac{2}{3}x - 2$

Ⓑ $y = \dfrac{2}{3}x + 2$

Ⓒ $y = \dfrac{4}{3}x - 2$

Ⓓ $y = \dfrac{3}{2}x - 2$

CHARTS AND GRAPHS

Another basic math skill you will need for the PSAT is the ability to read charts and graphs. The PSAT includes charts, graphs, and tables throughout the test (not just in the Math section) to present data for students to analyze. The test-writers believe this better reflects what students learn in school and need to understand in the real world. The situations will typically include real-life applications, such as finance and business situations, social science issues, and science.

Since you'll be seeing graphics throughout the test, let's look at the types you may encounter and the skills you'll need to be familiar with when you work with charts and graphs.

The Scatterplot

A scatterplot is a graph with distinct data points, each representing one piece of information. On the scatterplot below, each dot represents the number of televisions sold at a certain price point.

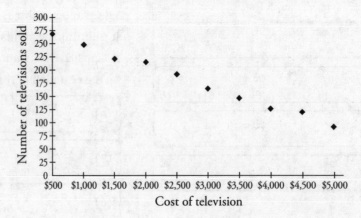

Here's How to Read It

To find the cost of a television when a certain number of televisions are sold, start at the number of televisions sold on the vertical axis and imagine a horizontal line to the right until you hit a data point. You can't draw on the figures on the Digital PSAT, but you can move the mouse pointer to the right starting from the number on the vertical axis. Once you hit a point, trace with the mouse pointer a straight line down from it to the horizontal axis and read the number the line hits. To determine the number of televisions sold when they cost a certain amount, reverse the steps—start at the bottom, trace up until you hit a point, and then move left until you intersect the vertical axis. You can also hold your scratch paper up to the screen and use it as a ruler.

The Line Graph

A line graph is similar to a scatterplot in that it shows different data points that relate the two variables. The difference with a line graph, though, is that the points have been connected to create a continuous line.

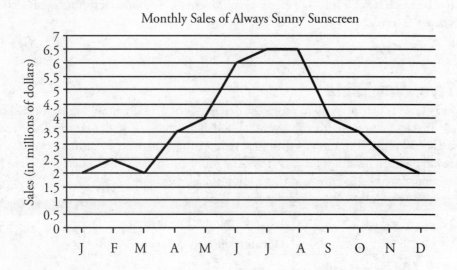

Monthly Sales of Always Sunny Sunscreen

Here's How to Read It

Reading a line graph is very similar to reading a scatterplot. Start at the axis that represents the data given and trace a straight line with the mouse pointer up or to the right until you intersect the graph line. Then move left or down until you hit the other axis. For example, in February, indicated by an F on the horizontal axis, Always Sunny Sunscreen had 2.5 million in sales. Make sure to notice the units on each axis. If February sales were only $2.50, rather than $2.5 million, then this company wouldn't be doing very well!

The Bar Graph (or Histogram)

Instead of showing a variety of different data points, a bar graph will show how many items belong to a particular category. If the variable at the bottom is given in ranges, instead of distinct items, the graph is called a histogram, but you read it the same way.

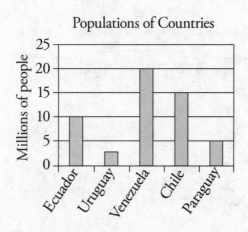

Populations of Countries

Here's How to Read It

The height of each bar corresponds to a value on the vertical axis. In this case, the bar above Chile hits the line that intersects with 15 on the vertical axis, so there are 15 million people in Chile. Again, watch the units to make sure you know what the numbers on the axes represent. On this graph, horizontal lines are drawn at 5-unit intervals, making the graph easier to read. If the bar isn't exactly at a line—or if the graph doesn't have horizontal lines at all—use your scratch paper as a ruler.

The Two-Way Table

A two-way table is another way to represent data without actually graphing it. Instead of having the variables represented on the vertical and horizontal axes, the data will be arranged in rows and columns. The top row will give the headings for each column, and the left-most column will give the headings for each row. The numbers in each box indicate the data for the category represented by the row and the column the box is in.

	Computer Production	
	Morning Shift	Afternoon Shift
Monday	200	375
Tuesday	245	330
Wednesday	255	340
Thursday	250	315
Friday	225	360

Here's How to Read It

If you wanted to see the number of computers produced on Tuesday morning, you could start in the Morning Shift column and look down until you found the number in the row that says "Tuesday," or you could start in the row for Tuesday and look to the right until you found the Morning Shift column. Either way, the result is 245. Some tables will give you totals in the bottom row and/or the right-most column, but sometimes you will need to find the totals yourself by adding up all the numbers in each row or in each column. More complicated tables will have more categories listed in rows and/or columns, or the tables may even contain extraneous information.

The Box Plot

A box plot shows data broken into quartiles, as follows:

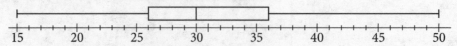

Here's How to Read It

Here is what all the parts of the box plot represent.

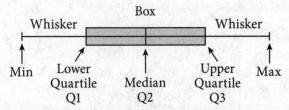

The line in the middle of the box shows the median value of the data, which is 30 in the example above. The "whiskers," which give this figure the alternate name "box-and-whisker plot," represent the highest value on the list with the end of the whisker on the right and the lowest value with the end of the whisker on the left. Thus, the minimum value of this data set is 15, and the maximum is 50. Then the data between the median and these minimum and maximum values is broken into two parts on each side, creating four "quartiles." The median of the lower half of the data is the Q1 value on the left side of the box, at about 26, and the median of the upper half of the data is the Q3 value on the right side of the box, at about 36.

The Stem-and-Leaf Plot

A stem-and-leaf plot shows data according to a common first digit.

$$
\begin{array}{c|l}
2 & 0\ 1\ 7 \\
3 & 2\ 2\ 4 \\
4 & 0\ 1\ 5\ 7\ 7\ 8 \\
5 & 1\ 1\ 4\ 5\ 5\ 7\ 9 \\
6 & 2\ 5\ 8\ 8\ 9 \\
7 & 0
\end{array}
$$

A book club took a survey of the age, in years, of its members. The data is shown in the stem-and-leaf plot above.

Here's How to Read It

The numbers on the left of the vertical line are the initial digit of each age, and the numbers to the right of the vertical line are the following digits corresponding to the given first digit. This means that the ages of the members of the book club are 20, 21, 27, 32, 32, 34, etc. Questions using stem-and-leaf plots often ask for things like the range of the data, the median of the data, or the probability of selecting a certain number. We will look at all those statistical measures in the Math Techniques chapter.

From a stem-and-leaf plot or a box plot, you can determine the median and range of the set of data. It is also possible to calculate the mode and mean from a stem-and-leaf plot and the interquartile range from a box plot.

Figure Facts

Every time you encounter a figure or graphic on the PSAT, you should make sure you understand how to read it by checking the following things:

- What are the variables for each axis or the headings for the table?
- What units are used for each variable?
- Are there any key pieces of information (numbers, for example) in the legend of the chart that you should note?
- What type of relationship is shown by the data in the chart? For instance, if the chart includes curves that show an upward slope, then the graph exhibits a *positive association*, while curves that show a downward slope exhibits a *negative association*.
- You can use the mouse pointer or the edge of your scratch paper to make sure you are locating the correct data in the graph.

FILL-INS: THE BASICS

You will see 10–12 questions in the Math section of the PSAT that ask you to enter your own numerical answer in a box, rather than answer a multiple-choice question. The test-writers call these Student-Produced Response questions, but we're going to keep things simple and call them fill-ins.

The only difficulty with fill-ins is getting used to the way in which you are asked to answer the question. For each fill-in question, you will have a box like this:

To enter your answer, click inside the box and start typing. The numbers you enter will automatically appear left to right, and the computer will show a preview of your answer, so you can make sure it looks right.

The fill-in instructions appear on the left side of the screen for every fill-in question. You can click in the center and drag left to shrink the fill-in instructions and focus on the question.

You don't want to have to spend time re-reading the instructions every time, so here is some additional information about entering a fill-in answer:

1. There is space to enter 5 characters if the answer is positive and 6 characters—including the negative sign—if the answer is negative.

2. You can enter your answer as either a fraction or a decimal. For example, .5, 0.5, and 1/2 are all acceptable answers. Use the forward slash for fractions.

3. If your answer is a fraction, it must fit within the space. Do not try to enter something like $\frac{200}{500}$ as a fraction: either reduce it or convert it to a decimal.

4. Fractions do not need to be in the lowest reduced form. As long as it fits, it's fine.

5. You cannot fill in mixed numbers. Convert all mixed numbers to ordinary fractions or decimals. If your answer is $2\frac{1}{2}$, you must convert it to 5/2 or 2.5. If you enter 21/2, the computer will read your answer as $\frac{21}{2}$.

6. You do not need to type the comma for numbers longer than three digits, such as 4,200. In fact, the computer will not allow it.

7. The computer also will not allow symbols such as %, $, or π. Additionally, square roots, units, and variables cannot be entered.

8. If your answer is a decimal that will not fit in the space provided, either enter as many digits as will fit or round the last digit. The fraction $-\frac{2}{3}$ can be entered in decimal form as −0.666, −0.667, −.6666, or −.6667.

9. Some questions will have more than one right answer. Any correct answer you enter will count as correct; do not try to enter multiple answers.

Drill 5

Answers can be found in Part IV.

1 ▢ Mark for Review

If $5x^2 = 125$, and $x < 0$, what is the value of $5x^3$?

2 ▢ Mark for Review

$$z = 5 - 5[5z - 2(1 - z)]$$

In the equation above, what is the value of z?

3 ▢ Mark for Review

If $3a + 2b = 37$ and $7a + 4b = 85$, what is the value of b?

4 ▢ Mark for Review

A scientist is making a new sugar-water solution by combining two solutions. Solution 1 has a sugar content of 25%, and Solution 2 has a sugar content of 10%. The scientist mixes 50 ounces of Solution 1 with some quantity of Solution 2 to make Solution 3, which has a sugar content of 15%. How many ounces of Solution 2 did the scientist use to make Solution 3?

5 Mark for Review

If $5 - \sqrt{z} = \sqrt{z-5}$, what is the value of z?

---

6 Mark for Review

In a certain city, the predicted temperatures for the next 2 days are 95 degrees and 86 degrees Fahrenheit, respectively. A traveler wants to convert these temperatures from Fahrenheit to Celsius, so he subtracts 32 from the degrees in Fahrenheit for each day and multiplies the difference by $\frac{5}{9}$. How many degrees higher is the predicted temperature for the first day than the predicted temperature for the second day, in degrees Celsius?

---

7 Mark for Review

Mathew and Moriah purchased a tandem bicycle for $540. If the amount Moriah paid was $30 less than twice the amount Mathew paid, how much, in dollars, did Moriah pay? (Disregard the dollar sign when entering your answer.)

Summary

o   Each Math module is arranged in a loose Order of Difficulty, which can make it easier to spot the less difficult questions. However, remember that the test-writers' idea of "easier" questions is not necessarily the same as your idea. Let your Personal Order of Difficulty be your guide.

o   Write on your scratch paper to set up your work, and then use your calculator or the built-in calculator to figure out solutions. And remember to type carefully—a calculator won't check for mistakes.

o   Review basic definitions again before the test to make sure you don't get stuck on the "little words."

o   When you have to manipulate exponents, remember the MADSPM rules.

o   To solve equations for a variable, isolate the variable. Make sure you perform the same operations on both sides of the equation.

o   Inequalities can be worked just like equations until you have to multiply or divide by a negative number. Then you need to flip the inequality sign.

o   The absolute value of a number is the positive distance from zero, or practically, making the thing inside the | | sign positive. Everything inside the | | is equal to the positive and the negative value of the expression to which it is equal. Also remember that | | work like ( ); you need to complete all the operations inside the | | before you can make the value positive.

o   To solve simultaneous equations, simply add or subtract the equations. When the simultaneous equation question asks for a single variable and addition and subtraction don't work, try to make something disappear. Multiply the equations by a constant to make the coefficient(s) of the variable(s) you want go to zero when the equations are added or subtracted.

o   When writing a system of equations, start with the most straightforward piece of information.

o   You can also use the equations or inequalities in the answer choices to help you narrow down the possibilities. Eliminate any answers in which an equation or inequality doesn't match a piece of information in the question.

o   Parallel lines have the same slope and no solutions. If two lines have the same slope and infinitely many solutions, they are actually the same line. Perpendicular lines have slopes that are negative reciprocals of each other.

o   Rather than worrying about the distance formula, connect the two points and make the resulting line the hypotenuse of a right triangle. Then you can use the Pythagorean Theorem to find the distance.

o   The coordinates of the midpoint of a line segment with endpoints (x_1, y_1) and (x_2, y_2) will be $\left(\dfrac{x_1 + x_2}{2}, \dfrac{y_1 + y_2}{2}\right)$.

o   When you encounter charts, carefully check the chart for information you should note, and use the mouse pointer or edge of your scratch paper to locate information.

o   When answering fill-in questions, don't bother reducing fractions or rounding decimals if they fit in the allotted space. Check the answer preview on the screen before moving on.

Chapter 12
Math Techniques

In the previous chapter, we mentioned that one of the keys to doing well on the PSAT is to have a set of test-specific problem-solving skills. This chapter discusses some powerful strategies, which—though you may not use them in school—are specifically designed to get you points on the PSAT. Learn them well!

PLUGGING IN

One of the most powerful problem-solving skills on the PSAT is a technique we call Plugging In. Plugging In will turn nasty algebra questions into simple arithmetic and help you through the particularly twisted problems that you'll often see on the PSAT. There are several varieties of Plugging In, each suited to a different kind of question.

Plugging In Your Own Numbers

The problem with doing algebra is that it's just too easy to make a mistake.

> Whenever you see a question with variables in the answer choices, use Plugging In.

Start by picking a number for the variable in the question (or for more than one variable, if necessary), solve the problem using your number, and then see which answer choice gives you the correct answer.

Take a look at the following question.

---

1 ☐ Mark for Review

A triangle has a base of x units and a height that is 4 times the base. In terms of x, what is the area of the triangle?

Ⓐ $2x$

Ⓑ $5x$

Ⓒ $2x^2$

Ⓓ $4x^2$

Here's How to Crack It

The question asks for the area of a geometric figure. The other dimensions are given in terms of a variable, so pick a number and plug it in. Make $x = 2$. The triangle now has a base of 2 and a height of $4(2) = 8$. The equation for the area of a triangle is $\frac{1}{2}\ base \times height$. Plug the values for the base and the height into the equation to get $Area = \dfrac{1}{2}(2)(8)$, or $Area = 8$. This is the target value; circle it.

Now plug $x = 2$ into each answer choice and eliminate any answer that does not equal your target value of 8.

A) $2(2) = 4$ Not 8; eliminate!

B) $5(2) = 10$ Not 8; eliminate!

C) $2(2)^2 = 2(4) = 8$ Is 8; keep!

D) $4(2)^2 = 4(4) = 16$ Not 8; eliminate!

Notice that the wrong answers are all the result of simple mistakes, like forgetting to take one-half or adding the base and height instead of multiplying them. When you use real numbers instead of variables, you're much less likely to make that kind of mistake. Here, you did some basic arithmetic and got (C) as the right answer.

Use Your Tools!

Plugging In offers a fantastic opportunity to make full use of the online tools and your scratch paper. See all those notes above that helped find the target value and check each answer choice? Those go on your scratch paper. Instead of writing down "eliminate," use the Answer Eliminator tool on the screen.

Plugging In is such a great technique because it turns hard algebra questions into medium and sometimes even easy arithmetic questions. Remember this when you're thinking of your POOD and looking for questions to do among the hard ones; if you see variables in the answers, there's a good chance it's one to try.

Don't worry too much about what numbers you choose to plug in; just plug in easy numbers (small numbers like 2, 5, or 10 or numbers that make the arithmetic easy, like 100 if you're looking for a percent). Also, be sure your numbers fit the conditions of the questions (for example, if they say $x \leq 11$, don't plug in 12).

Also, be sure to check all four answers. Once in a while, the numbers you plug in work for more than one answer. In those cases, pick a new number or numbers, get a new target value, and plug into the remaining answers until you are down to one.

Now let's try one with two variables.

---

2 ☐ Mark for Review

If $2x + x + \frac{1}{x} = y$, what is the value of $xy - 1$, in terms of x?

Ⓐ $\dfrac{3x^2 + 1}{x}$

Ⓑ $3x^2 - 1$

Ⓒ $3x^2 + 1$

Ⓓ $3x^2$

When to Plug In

- phrases like "in terms of" or "equivalent form" in the question
- variables in the question and/or answer choices

Here's How to Crack It

The question asks for the value of $xy - 1$ in terms of x. Let's try to avoid algebra by Plugging In. First, start by choosing a value for one of the variables. Here, all the action is happening to the x, so choose a value for x. Make $x = 2$. Next, work the question in Bite-Sized Pieces until you've come up with a numerical answer for the question. If $x = 2$, then the equation becomes $2(2) + 2 + \frac{1}{2} = y$. Multiply, then add on the left side: $4 + 2 + \frac{1}{2} = y$; $\frac{13}{2} = y$. Note that the question doesn't want the value of y, but rather $xy - 1$. Because $x = 2$ and $y = \frac{13}{2}$, $xy - 1 = (2)\left(\frac{13}{2}\right) - 1 = 13 - 1 = 12$. This is the target number; circle it.

Now that you have a target number, work your answer choices using Process of Elimination. Make $x = 2$ in each answer choice and eliminate any choice that doesn't equal your target number of 12:

A) $\dfrac{3(2)^2 + 1}{2} = \dfrac{13}{2}$ Not 12; eliminate!

B) $3(2)^2 - 1 = 11$ Not 12; eliminate!

C) $3(2)^2 + 1 = 13$ Not 12; eliminate!

D) $3(2)^2 = 12$ Is 12; keep!

Only (D) matches your target number, so it must be the answer!

As you can see, Plugging In can turn messy algebra questions into more straightforward arithmetic questions. Here are the steps to follow.

Plugging In

1. When you see *in terms of* or *equivalent* and there are variables in the answer choices, you can Plug In.
2. Pick your own number(s) for the variable(s) in the question.
3. Do the necessary math to find the answer to the question, which is the target number. Circle the target number.
4. Use POE to eliminate every answer that doesn't match the target number.

You've seen two questions using the phrase "in terms of." Plugging In is also a powerful technique when the question asks you to find an equivalent form of an expression. Here's an example.

---

3   🔖 Mark for Review

Which of the following is equivalent to $\dfrac{f}{f-2} - \dfrac{5}{f+3}$?

(A) $\dfrac{f-5}{2f+1}$

(B) $\dfrac{-5f}{f^2-6}$

(C) $\dfrac{f^2-2f+10}{f^2+f-6}$

(D) $\dfrac{f^2+8f-10}{f^2+f-6}$

Here's How to Crack It

The question asks for an expression that is equivalent to the given one. A question that has a

variable and asks about an equivalent expression is a good chance to plug in your own number

for the variable. If $f = 2$, the denominator of the first fraction will be 0, so make $f = 3$ instead.

Plug 3 into the expression in the question in place of f and solve for a numerical answer. The expression becomes $\dfrac{3}{3-2} - \dfrac{5}{3+3}$, which simplifies to $\dfrac{3}{1} - \dfrac{5}{6}$. Use 6 as a common denominator and write $\dfrac{3}{1}$ as $\dfrac{18}{6}$, then subtract the fractions to get $\dfrac{18}{6} - \dfrac{5}{6} = \dfrac{13}{6}$. You can also use your calculator to get a decimal answer. Either way, the result is the target value; circle it.

The fact that the target number is sort of ugly is OK since all that matters is finding an answer choice that does *not* equal the target number. Plug 3 into each answer choice for f and eliminate any choice that doesn't equal your target value of $\dfrac{13}{6}$.

A) $\dfrac{3-5}{2(3)+1} = \dfrac{-2}{6+1}$ It's going to be negative, so eliminate!

B) $\dfrac{-5(3)}{3^2-6} = \dfrac{-15}{9-6}$ It's going to be negative, so eliminate!

C) $\dfrac{3^2-2(3)+10}{3^2+3-6} = \dfrac{9-6+10}{9+3-6} = \dfrac{13}{6}$ Is $\dfrac{13}{6}$; keep!

D) $\dfrac{3^2+8(3)-10}{3^2+3-6} = \dfrac{9+24-10}{9+3-6} = \dfrac{23}{6}$ Not $\dfrac{13}{6}$; eliminate!

Only (C) matches your target value, so it's the answer!

What If There's No Variable?

Sometimes you'll see a question that doesn't contain an x, y, or z, but which contains a hidden variable. If your answers are percents or fractional parts of some unknown quantity (total number of marbles in a jar, total miles to travel in a trip), try Plugging In.

4 ☐ Mark for Review

Ratio of Students in a Club

	Male	Female	Total
Junior	18%	27%	45%
Senior	24%	31%	55%
Total	42%	58%	100%

The two-way table above shows the percentages of male students and female students and juniors and seniors in a particular club. If a male student is chosen at random, what is the probability that he will be a junior?

We'll cover probability in more detail later in this chapter.

Ⓐ $\frac{9}{50}$

Ⓑ $\frac{3}{7}$

Ⓒ $\frac{27}{58}$

Ⓓ $\frac{3}{4}$

Here's How to Crack It

The question asks for the probability that a male student chosen at random will be a junior. The total percentage of students is 100%, so plug in for the total number of students. Make the number of students 100. To find the number of students in each category, you only need to remove the percent sign. For example, 18% of 100 is 18. This gives you the following:

	Male	Female	Total
Junior	18	27	45
Senior	24	31	55
Total	42	58	100

You're asked to find the probability of choosing a junior if you choose from the male students.

Probability is $\frac{number\ of\ outcomes\ you\ want}{number\ of\ possible\ outcomes}$. There are 18 male juniors and 42 total male students, making the probability of choosing a junior from the male students $\frac{18}{42}$, which reduces to $\frac{3}{7}$. This matches (B).

Drill 1

Answers can be found in Part IV.

1 ☐ Mark for Review

The expression $-2x - (3x - 8x)$ is equivalent to which of the following?

Ⓐ $-13x$

Ⓑ $-7x$

Ⓒ $3x$

Ⓓ $9x$

2 ☐ Mark for Review

If $a = \dfrac{b}{c^2}$ and $c \neq 0$, what is the value of $\dfrac{1}{b^2}$?

Ⓐ ac^2

Ⓑ a^2c^4

Ⓒ $\dfrac{1}{ac^2}$

Ⓓ $\dfrac{1}{a^2c^4}$

3 ☐ Mark for Review

If $p \neq 0$, what is the value of $\dfrac{\frac{1}{8}}{2p}$?

Ⓐ $\dfrac{1}{16p}$

Ⓑ $\dfrac{p}{4}$

Ⓒ $\dfrac{4}{p}$

Ⓓ $4p$

4 ☐ Mark for Review

A certain standardized test has 50 questions. A student receives 1 point for each correct answer and loses $\frac{1}{4}$ of a point for each incorrect answer. Which of the following equations best models the net score, S, in points, for a student who completes all 50 questions and answers c of the questions correctly?

Ⓐ $S = 50 - 0.25c$

Ⓑ $S = 50 - 0.75c$

Ⓒ $S = c - 0.25(50 - c)$

Ⓓ $S = c - 0.75(50 - c)$

5 ☐ Mark for Review

David acquired a data plan for his smart phone. Every month he pays a flat rate of $25 and an additional $0.05 for every megabyte he goes over his monthly limit. Which of the following represents David's monthly data bill when he goes over his limit by m megabytes?

Ⓐ $25 + 1.05m$

Ⓑ $25 + 0.05m$

Ⓒ $0.05(25 + m)$

Ⓓ $1.05(25 + m)$

6 ☐ Mark for Review

The expression $x^2 + 4x - 4$ is written in the equivalent form $(x + 2)^2 - a$. What is the value of a?

Ⓐ -2

Ⓑ 2

Ⓒ 4

Ⓓ 8

7 ☐ Mark for Review

Jodi has x dollars in her bank account. She withdraws $\frac{1}{6}$ of the money in her account to pay her rent and another $\frac{1}{6}$ of the money in her account to make her car payment. Jodi then deposits her paycheck of y dollars into her account. A week later, she withdraws $\frac{1}{2}$ of the money in her account. In terms of x, how many dollars are left in Jodi's account?

Ⓐ $\dfrac{(4x - 3y)}{6}$

Ⓑ $\dfrac{(3x - 5y)}{6}$

Ⓒ $\dfrac{(3x - y)}{6}$

Ⓓ $\dfrac{(2x + 3y)}{6}$

PLUGGING IN THE ANSWERS (PITA)

You can also plug in when the answer provided to a question is an actual value, such as 2, 4, 10, or 20. Why would you want to do a lot of complicated algebra to solve a question, when the answer is right there on the page? All you have to do is figure out *which* choice it is.

How can you tell which is the correct answer? Try every choice *until you find the one that works*. Even if this means you have to try all four choices, PITA is still a fast and reliable means of getting the right answer.

If you work strategically, however, you almost never need to try all four answers. If the question asks for either the greatest or the least answer, start there. Otherwise, start with one of the middle answer choices. If that answer works, you're done. If the answer you started with was too big, try a smaller answer. If the answer you started with was too small, try a bigger answer. You can almost always find the answer in two or three tries this way. Let's try PITA on the following question.

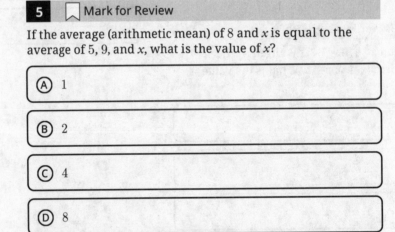

5 ☐ Mark for Review

If the average (arithmetic mean) of 8 and x is equal to the average of 5, 9, and x, what is the value of x?

Ⓐ 1

Ⓑ 2

Ⓒ 4

Ⓓ 8

PITA = Plugging In the Answers

Don't try to solve problems like this by writing equations and solving for x or y. Plugging In the Answers lets you use arithmetic instead of algebra, so you're less likely to make errors.

Here's How to Crack It

The question asks for the value of x based on an average. Rather than doing complicated algebra, try out the answers. Let's start with (C) and plug in 4 for x. The question now reads:

If the average (arithmetic mean) of 8 and 4 is equal to the average of 5, 9, and 4 . . .

Does this work? The average of 8 and 4 is 6, and the average of 5, 9, and 4 is also 6. Therefore, (C) is the answer.

Neat, huh? Of course, the first answer you choose won't always be the correct one. Let's try one more.

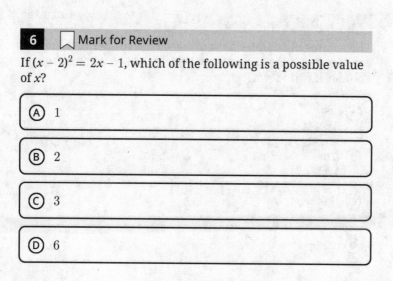

6 ☐ Mark for Review

If $(x - 2)^2 = 2x - 1$, which of the following is a possible value of x?

Ⓐ 1

Ⓑ 2

Ⓒ 3

Ⓓ 6

Here's How to Crack It

The question asks for the value of x, and there are numbers in the answer choices. Try PITA any time the question asks for a specific value like this. If we try plugging in (C), 3, for x, the equation becomes $1 = 5$, which is false. So, (C) can't be right. If you're not sure which way to go next, just pick a direction. It won't take very long to figure out the correct answer. If we try plugging in (B), 2, for x, the equation becomes $0 = 3$, which is false. If we try plugging in (A), 1, for x, the equation becomes $1 = 1$, which is true. There's no need to try the remaining answer because there are no variables in the answers; only one answer choice can work. So, the answer is (A).

PITA also works great when the question is about geometry but still asks for a specific value and has numbers in the answer choices.

Here's an example.

───────────────◯───────────────

> **7** 🔖 Mark for Review
>
> The volume of cylinder A is twice that of cylinder B. If the combined volume of the two cylinders is 114π, what is the volume of cylinder A?
>
> Ⓐ 38π
>
> Ⓑ 76π
>
> Ⓒ 114π
>
> Ⓓ 228π

Don't panic if you don't remember much about geometry. We'll review everything you need to know in Chapter 14.

Here's How to Crack It

The question asks for a specific value, and there are numbers in the answer choices. Rather than writing and solving equations, recognize that one of the four answers has to be the volume of cylinder A, and try them until one of them fits the information in the question. Eliminate (C) and (D) because they don't make sense: the volume of one cylinder cannot be equal to or greater than the combined volume of both cylinders. Try (B), 76π. The question states that *the volume of cylinder A is twice that of cylinder B*, which also means that the volume of cylinder B is half the volume of cylinder A. If the volume of cylinder A is 76π, the volume of cylinder B is 38π. The question also states that the combined volume is 114π. It is true that $76\pi + 38\pi = 114\pi$, so all of the math checks out. It's impossible for a second volume to also work, so stop here. The correct answer is (B).

───────────────◯───────────────

Use Your Tools!

Be sure to let your scratch paper and the Answer Eliminator tool help on PITA questions. Rewrite the answers in order to try them out one by one. Label what the answers represent: one of them is the answer to the question. Then label each step along the way and check whether the result matches the information in the question. If it doesn't, cross out that answer on the screen. Here's what your screen and scratch paper should look like after finishing the previous question.

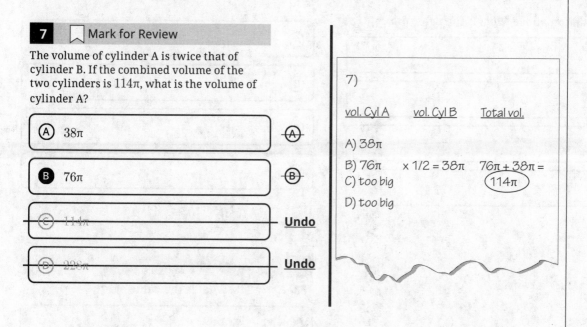

Plugging In

- When to Use PITA
- When the questions asks for a specific amount
- When there are numbers in the answer choices
- When you are tempted to write your own equation

PITA Pointers

- Keep your work neatly organized on you scratch paper
- Start with one of the middle values and work through the problem
- Eliminate answers that are too big or too small
- When one answer works, stop! That's the correct answer.

Drill 2

Answers can be found in Part IV.

1 ☐ Mark for Review

$$2(n + 5) = 3(n - 2) + 8$$

In the equation above, what is the value of n?

- Ⓐ 1
- Ⓑ 3
- Ⓒ 4
- Ⓓ 8

2 ☐ Mark for Review

$$2x - y > -3$$
$$4x + y < 5$$

Which of the following points is in the solution set of the system of inequalities above?

- Ⓐ $(-4, -1)$
- Ⓑ $(-3, -2)$
- Ⓒ $(-1, -1)$
- Ⓓ $(3, -5)$

3 ☐ Mark for Review

If $\frac{24x}{4} + \frac{1}{x} = 5$, what is one possible value of x?

- Ⓐ $-\frac{1}{6}$
- Ⓑ $\frac{1}{6}$
- Ⓒ $\frac{1}{4}$
- Ⓓ $\frac{1}{2}$

4 ☐ Mark for Review

If $3^{x + 2} = 243$, what is the value of x?

- Ⓐ 1
- Ⓑ 2
- Ⓒ 3
- Ⓓ 4

5 ▢ Mark for Review

$$-\frac{5}{7} - \frac{11}{7}u = -v$$
$$2v = 7 + 5u$$

Based on the system of equations above, what is the value of v?

(A) −4

(B) −3

(C) −1

(D) 0

7 ▢ Mark for Review

In a certain game, enchanted items are worth 15 points each and normal items are worth 4 points each. If a player has 9 items worth 102 points, how many enchanted items does the player have?

(A) 3

(B) 4

(C) 5

(D) 6

6 ▢ Mark for Review

The system of inequalities $x < 21$ and $x - 7y \geq -12$ is graphed in the xy-plane. If $(8, y)$ is a point in the graph of the system, what is one possible value of y?

(A) 2

(B) 5

(C) 12

(D) 44

DATA ANALYSIS

The PSAT has questions that ask you to work with concepts such as averages, percentages, and unit conversions. Luckily, The Princeton Review has you covered! The rest of this chapter will give you techniques and strategies to help you tackle these questions.

Averages and *T = AN*

You probably remember the average formula from math class, which says **Average** (arithmetic mean) = $\dfrac{\text{total}}{\text{\# of things}}$. However, the PSAT rarely will ask you to take a simple average. Of the three parts of an average question—the average, the total, and the number of things—you're usually given the average and the number of things, and you'll need to use the total to answer the question. If you multiply both sides of the average formula by the number of things, you get (average) × (# of things) = total. You can remember this as *T = AN*. Plug the information into the formula and solve.

Let's try this example.

---

8 ☐ Mark for Review

The average (arithmetic mean) of 3 numbers is 22 and the smallest of these numbers is 2. If the remaining two numbers are equal, what are their values?

Ⓐ 22

Ⓑ 32

Ⓒ 40

Ⓓ 64

Total
When calculating averages, always find the total. It's the one piece of information that PSAT loves to withhold.

Here's How to Crack It

The question gives the value of one number and the average of all three numbers and asks for the value of the two remaining numbers. Use *T = AN*. The average is 22, and there are 3 numbers. Therefore, *T* = (22)(3), so *T* = 66. If the smallest number is 2, the remaining two numbers equal 66 – 2 = 64. Finally, the remaining two numbers are equal, so divide: 64 ÷ 2 = 32. The answer is (B).

Try one more.

---

9 🔖 Mark for Review

Caroline scored 85, 88, and 89 on three of her four history tests. If her average (arithmetic mean) score for all four tests was 90, what did she score on her fourth test?

Ⓐ 90

Ⓑ 93

Ⓒ 96

Ⓓ 98

Here's How to Crack It

The question asks for the score Caroline received on her fourth test. Let's start with what we know: we know that the average of all four of her tests was 90. Putting these into the formula $T = AN$ gives us $T = (90)(4)$, which means the total is 360. Since three of these tests have a sum of $85 + 88 + 89$, or 262, we know that the score on the fourth test must be equal to $360 - 262$, or 98. This makes the answer (D).

Median and Mode

Another two terms that are often tested along with average are median and mode.

The **median** of a group of numbers is the number in the middle, just as the "median" is the large divider in the middle of a road. To find the median, here's what you do:

- First, put the elements in the group in numerical order from lowest to highest.
- If the number of elements in the group is *odd*, find the number in the middle. That's the median.
- If you have an *even* number of elements in the group, find the two numbers in the middle and calculate their average (arithmetic mean).

> **Finding a Median**
> To find the median of a set containing an even number of items, take the average of the two middle numbers after putting the numbers in order.

Try this on the following question.

---◯---

10 🔖 Mark for Review

If the 5 students in Ms. Jaffray's math class scored 91, 83, 84, 90, and 85 on their final exams, what is the median score for her class on the final exam?

Ⓐ 84

Ⓑ 85

Ⓒ 86

Ⓓ 88

Here's How to Crack It

First, let's place these numbers in order from lowest to highest: 83, 84, 85, 90, 91. There are an odd number of elements in the group, and the number in the middle is 85, so the median of this group is 85 and the answer is (B).

---◯---

The **mode** of a group of numbers is the number that appears the most. (Remember: *mode* sounds like *most*.) To find the mode of a group of numbers, simply see which element appears the greatest number of times.

---

11 🔖 Mark for Review

Score on final paper	Frequency
85	4
86	2
87	6
88	3
89	4
90	7
91	11
92	6
93	5
94	2

An English professor graded the final papers of the 50 students in her Honors courses and recorded the information in the frequency table above. For this data, how much greater is the mode than the median?

[　　　]

Here's How to Crack It

The question asks for the difference between the mode and the median of a list of data. On a frequency table, the mode is easy to see—it is the data with the greatest number in the Frequency column. On this table, the greatest number in that column is 11, and it is associated with the score of 91. Therefore, the mode is 91. The median is a little more difficult to find. You don't want to take the time to list out all 50 scores, but the median will be the average of the 25th and 26th scores. If you can find those, you are all set. Start at the top of the chart and add up the numbers in the Frequency column until you get to 25. The first three scores, 85–87, account for $4 + 2 + 6 = 12$ of the students. The scores of 88 and 89 account for another $3 + 4 = 7$ students, so now we are up to the 19th student on the list. The next 7 students received a score of 90, so the 25th and 26th scores are both 90. The average of 90 and 90 is 90, so the median is 90. The difference between the mode and the median is $91 - 90 = 1$. This is the correct answer.

Range

Another measure of the spread of data is range. The **range** of a list of numbers is the difference between the greatest number on the list and the least number on the list. For the list 4, 5, 5, 6, 7, 8, 9, 10, 20, the greatest number is 20 and the least is 4, so the range is 20 − 4 = 16.

Let's look at a question.

---

12 ▢ Mark for Review

184	176	181	157	168
154	148	165	190	162

A group of patients is recruited for a clinical trial. Their heights, recorded in centimeters, are listed in the table above. Two more patients are recruited to the study. After these patients join, the range of the heights is 42 cm. Which of the following could NOT be the heights of the two new patients?

(A) 154 cm and 186 cm

(B) 146 cm and 179 cm

(C) 150 cm and 188 cm

(D) 148 cm and 185 cm

Here's How to Crack It

The question asks for the values that cannot be the heights of two new patients given information about the range of the data. To determine the current range, take the difference of the greatest and least values: 190 − 148 = 42 cm. If the range is to remain 42 cm, then the new patients' heights cannot be greater than 190 cm or less than 148 cm tall. Choice (B) violates this restriction. Because the question wants what could NOT be the heights of the new patients, the answer is (B).

PROBABILITY

Probability refers to the chance that an event will happen, and it is given as a percent or a fractional value between 0 and 1, inclusive. A probability of 0 means that the event will never happen; a probability of 1 means that it is certain to happen.

$$\text{Probability} = \frac{\text{number of outcomes you want}}{\text{number of possible outcomes}}$$

For instance, if you have a die with faces numbered 1 to 6, what is the chance of rolling a 2? There is one face with the number 2 on it, out of 6 total faces. Therefore, the probability of rolling a 2 is $\frac{1}{6}$.

What is the chance of rolling an even number on one roll of this die? There are 3 faces of the die with an even number (the sides numbered 2, 4, and 6) out of a total of 6 faces. Therefore, the probability of rolling an even number is $\frac{3}{6}$, or $\frac{1}{2}$.

Let's look at how this concept will be tested on the PSAT.

13 🔖 Mark for Review

A survey was conducted among a randomly chosen sample of full-time salaried workers about satisfaction in their current jobs. The table below shows a summary of the survey results.

Reported Job Satisfaction by Education Level (in thousands)

Highest level of education	Satisfied	Not satisfied	No response	Total
High school diploma	17,880	12,053	2,575	32,508
Bachelor's degree	24,236	8,496	3,442	36,174
Master's degree	17,605	5,324	1,861	24,790
Doctoral degree	12,210	2,081	972	15,263
Total	71,931	27,954	8,850	108,735

All persons who have earned a Master's or Doctoral degree must have previously earned a Bachelor's degree. Which of the following is closest to the probability that a full-time salaried worker does NOT have a Bachelor's degree?

Ⓐ 29.9%

Ⓑ 33.3%

Ⓒ 36.8%

Ⓓ 66.7%

Here's How to Crack It

The question asks for the probability that a full-time worker does not have a bachelor's degree.

If everyone with a master's or doctoral degree has a bachelor's degree, then the only people who do NOT have a bachelor's degree are those whose highest level of education is a high school diploma. Find the probability of choosing someone with a high school diploma out of the total: $\frac{32,508}{108,735} \approx 0.299 = 29.9\%$, which is (A).

RATES

Rate is a concept related to averages. Cars travel at an average speed. Work gets done at an average rate. Because the ideas are similar, you can use Distance = Rate × Time ($D = RT$) or Work = Rate × Time ($W = RT$) to tackle these questions.

Of course, you might use the simple definitions of speed or rate to answer some questions.

Let's look at an example of a PSAT rate question.

---

14 ⬜ Mark for Review

A machine produces 100 screws per minute. How many <u>seconds</u> will it take the machine to produce 450 screws?

Here's How to Crack It

The question asks for time in seconds but gives the rate in screws per minute. Write out Work = Rate × Time ($W = RT$) and fill in the numbers given. The Work is 450 screws, and the Rate is 100 screws per minute, so the equation becomes $450 = (100)(T)$. Divide both sides of the equation by 100 to get $T = 4.5$ minutes. There are 60 seconds in 1 minute, so multiply by 60 to get $4.5 \text{ minutes} \left(\dfrac{60 \text{ seconds}}{1 \text{ minute}} \right) = 270 \text{ seconds}$. It's also possible to convert the rate to screws per second before figuring out how long in seconds it will take to make 450 screws. No matter which order you do the steps in, write out everything to make sure you keep the units straight. The correct answer is 270.

PERCENTS

Percent just means "divided by 100." So, 20 percent = $\dfrac{20}{100} = \dfrac{1}{5}$, or 0.2.

Likewise, 400 percent = $\dfrac{400}{100} = \dfrac{4}{1} = 4$.

Any percent question can be translated into algebra—just use the following rules:

percent	÷ 100
of	×
what	x (or any variable)
is, are, equals	=

Take a look at some examples of phrases you might have to translate on the PSAT:

8 percent of 10		$\dfrac{8}{100}(10) = 0.8$
10 percent of 80		$\dfrac{10}{100}(80) = 8$
5 is what percent of 80?	becomes	$5 = \dfrac{x}{100} \times 80$
5 is 80 percent of what number?		$5 = \dfrac{80}{100}x$
What percent of 5 is 80?		$\dfrac{x}{100} \times 5 = 80$

Percent Increase/Decrease

Percent Increase or *Percent Decrease* = $\dfrac{\textit{difference}}{\textit{original}} \times 100$

For example, if an $80 item is reduced to $60 during a sale, the percent decrease is the change in price ($80 − $60 = $20) divided by the original amount ($80), which gives us 0.25. Multiply by 100 to get 25 percent.

On the other hand, if a $60 item is increased to $80, the percent increase is the change in price ($80 − $60 = $20) divided by the original amount ($60), which gives us $0.\overline{33}$. Multiply by 100 to get approximately 33%. The numerical change is the same ($20), but the percent change is different because the original is different.

Try a question.

---

15 ⬚ Mark for Review

Estimated Numbers of Cell Phone Users by Type
(in millions)

	Prepaid users	Contracted users	Totals
2008	45	225	270
2012	75	250	325
Total	120	475	595

By how much greater was the percent increase in prepaid users from 2008 to 2012 than the percent increase in contracted users over the same period, to the nearest percent?

Ⓐ 6%

Ⓑ 10%

Ⓒ 30%

Ⓓ 56%

Here's How to Crack It

The question asks for a comparison of the percent increase in prepaid users over time to the percent increase in contracted users over time. First, find the percent increase in each group. Remember that percent increase is $\frac{difference}{original} \times 100$. For prepaid users, the equation would be $\frac{75-45}{45} \times 100 = 66\frac{2}{3}\%$. For contracted users, $\frac{250-225}{225} \times 100 = 11\frac{1}{9}\%$. Finally, subtract: $66\frac{2}{3} - 11\frac{1}{9} = 55\frac{5}{9}\%$, which is closest to (D).

GROWTH AND DECAY

Another aspect of percent questions may relate to things that increase or decrease by a certain percent over time. This is known as "growth and decay." Real-world examples include population growth, radioactive decay, and credit payments, to name a few. While Plugging In can help on these, it is also useful to know the growth and decay formula.

When the growth or decay rate is a percent of the total population:

$$\text{final amount} = \text{original amount} \ (1 \pm \text{rate})^{\text{number of changes}}$$

When the growth or decay is a multiple of the total population:

$$\text{final amount} = \text{original amount} \ (\text{multiplier})^{\text{number of changes}}$$

Let's see how this formula can make quick work of an otherwise tedious question.

---

16 ☐ Mark for Review

The population of a certain city is currently 61,000 and is growing at a rate of 2.5% every three months. If the city's population, P, is a function of time in years, t, then which of the following functions represents the city's population growth?

(A) $P(t) = 61{,}000(1.025)^t$

(B) $P(t) = 61{,}000(1.1)^t$

(C) $P(t) = 61{,}000(1.025)^{4t}$

(D) $P(t) = 61{,}000(1.1)^{3t}$

Here's How to Crack It

The question asks for a function to represent population growth over time. Carefully translate the information in the question in Bite-Sized Pieces. Because the rate of growth is 2.5%, you need to add 0.025 (2.5% in decimal form) to 1 within the parentheses. This would be $1 + 0.025 = 1.025$. Eliminate (B) and (D) because they do not have this piece. The only difference between (A) and (C) is the exponent, which represents the number of changes. Here, t is in years, but the population increases every 3 months, which is 4 times a year. This means you want 4 changes when $t = 1$; this gives you (C) as your answer.

RATIOS AND PROPORTIONS

Some questions will ask about ratios and proportions. With the strategies that you'll learn on the next few pages, you'll be well prepared to tackle these concepts on the PSAT.

Ratios

Ratios are about relationships between numbers. Whereas a fraction is a relationship between a part and a whole, a ratio is about the relationship between parts. So, for example, if there were 3 boys and 7 girls in a room, the fraction of boys in the room would be $\frac{3}{10}$. But the ratio of boys to girls would be 3:7 or $\frac{3}{7}$. Notice that if you add up the parts, you get the whole: $7 + 3 = 10$.

Ratio questions usually aren't difficult to identify. The question will tell you that there is a "ratio" of one thing to another, such as a 2:3 ratio of boys to girls in a club. Often, the PSAT will ask you to compare different ratios or to find the greatest or least ratio. To do so, divide the first part of the ratio by the second and compare the resulting values.

Try this one.

$$\text{Fraction} = \frac{\text{part}}{\text{whole}}$$

$$\text{Ratio} = \frac{\text{part}}{\text{part}}$$

Filling In
A ratio is usually expressed as 2:3 or 2 to 3, but on a fill-in question, enter it as 2/3.

17   🔖 Mark for Review

Reported Favorite Ice Cream Flavor by Age Group

Age	Vanilla	Chocolate	Mint chocolate chip	Cookies and cream	Coffee
3–6	8,534	7,835	6,135	4,526	254
7–10	9,250	10,936	4,019	7,530	497
11–15	5,093	7,591	9,495	1,076	760
16–18	11,024	7,345	2,026	4,620	1,062

The ice cream flavor preferences of a randomly selected group of young Americans aged 3–18 are represented in the table above. Survey participants were asked to choose their favorite flavor among the following five: Vanilla, Chocolate, Mint Chocolate Chip, Cookies and Cream, and Coffee.

According to the data in the table, the ratio of survey participants whose favorite flavor is vanilla to those whose favorite flavor is cookies and cream is least for which age category?

(A) 3–6

(B) 7–10

(C) 11–15

(D) 16–18

Here's How to Crack It

The question asks which ratio is the least based on the data in the table. Ignore all flavors other than vanilla and cookies and cream and compare the ratios for those two flavors. One method is to estimate: the vanilla to cookies and cream ratio for the 3–6 age group is a little less than 2:1. The same ratio for the 7–10 age group is close to 9:7. This is a smaller ratio than 2:1; eliminate (A) since it cannot be the least. The ratio for the 11–15 age group is nearly 5:1. The ratio in (B) is still smaller, so eliminate (C). The ratio for the 16–18 age group is roughly 11:4; the ratio in (B) is still smaller, so eliminate (D). Only (B) is left.

Another option is to use a calculator to find the decimal form of each ratio:

A) $\dfrac{8,534}{4,526} \approx 1.89$

B) $\dfrac{9,250}{7,530} \approx 1.23$

C) $\dfrac{5,093}{1,076} \approx 4.73$

D) $\dfrac{11,024}{4,620} \approx 2.39$

Compare the ratios to see that the one in (B) is the least. Using either approach, the correct answer is (B).

Direct Variation

Direct variations or proportions occur when two variables increase together or decrease together. These questions generally ask you to make a conversion (such as from ounces to pounds) or to compare two sets of information and find a missing piece. For example, a proportion question may ask you to figure out the amount of time it will take to travel 300 miles at a rate of 50 miles per hour.

To answer proportion questions, just set up two equal fractions. One will have all the information you know, and the other will have a missing piece that you're trying to figure out.

$$\frac{50 \text{ miles}}{1 \text{ hour}} = \frac{300 \text{ miles}}{x \text{ hours}}$$

Be sure to label the parts of your proportion so you'll know you have the right information in the right place; the same units should be in the numerator on both sides of the equals sign and the same units should be in the denominator on both sides of the equals sign. Notice how using a setup like this helps us keep track of the information we have and to find the information we're looking for, so we can use Bite-Sized Pieces to work through the question.

Now we can cross-multiply and then solve for x: $50x = 300$, so $x = 6$ hours.

> ## Formula for Direct Variation (Proportions)
>
> $$\frac{x_1}{y_1} = \frac{x_2}{y_2}$$

Let's try the following question.

○

18	🔖 Mark for Review

John receives $2.50 for every 4 pounds of berries he picks. How much money will he receive if he picks 90 pounds of berries?

(A) $36.00

(B) $42.25

(C) $48.50

(D) $56.25

Here's How to Crack It

The question gives a relationship between two variables and asks for a value based on that relationship. To solve this, set up a proportion.

$$\frac{\$2.50}{4\,\text{pounds}} = \frac{x}{90\,\text{pounds}}$$

Now we can cross-multiply: $4x = 2.50 \times 90$, so $4x = 225$, and $x = 56.25$. The answer is (D).

○

Occasionally, you may see a question that tells you there are two equal ratios. For example, if a question says that the ratio of 24 to 0.6 is equal to the ratio of 12 to y, you can solve for y by setting up a proportion. A proportion, after all, is really just two ratios set equal to each other.

$$\frac{24}{0.6} = \frac{12}{y}$$

Then you can cross-multiply and solve to get 0.3 for your answer.

Inverse Variation

Inverse variation is simply the opposite of direct variation, or proportion. In a proportion, when one variable increases, the other variable also increases. With inverse variation, when one variable increases, the other variable decreases, or vice versa. These types of questions are generally clearly labeled and all you have to do is apply the inverse variation formula:

> **Formula for Inverse Variation**
>
> $$x_1 y_1 = x_2 y_2$$

Once you memorize the formula, applying it will become second nature to you.

Now try this one.

─────────○─────────

19 ☐ Mark for Review

On a particular test, the percentage of people answering a question with the same response is inversely proportional to the number of the question. If 80% of test-takers answered the 8th question correctly, then approximately what percentage of test-takers gave the correct response to the 30th question?

Ⓐ 3%

Ⓑ 13%

Ⓒ 18%

Ⓓ 21%

Here's How to Crack It

The question asks for the percentage of test-takers that correctly answered the 30th question. The question tells us that the numbers are inversely proportional, so we need to figure out what to put into the formula. The first piece of information is that 80 percent of the people answered the 8th question correctly; we need to know the percent of people who answered the 30th question correctly. Let's make x the percent and y the question number. Your equation should look like this:

$$(80)(8) = (x_2)(30)$$

When you solve the equation, you should end up with $\frac{640}{30}$ or $21\frac{1}{3}$, which is (D) (remember, when the question says "approximately," you'll probably have to round up or down).

Drill 3

Answers can be found in Part IV.

a. If a student scores 70, 90, 95, and 105, what is the average (arithmetic mean) for these tests? _____

b. If a student has an average (arithmetic mean) score of 80 on 4 tests, what is the total of the scores received on those tests? _____

c. If a student has an average of 60 on tests, with a total of 360, how many tests has the student taken? _____

d. If the average of 2, 8, and x is 6, what is the value of x? _____

        2, 3, 3, 4, 6, 8, 10, 12

e. What is the median of the group of numbers above? _____

f. What is the mode of the group of numbers above? _____

g. What is the range of the group of numbers above? _____

h. What percent of 5 is 6? _____

i. 60 percent of 90 is the same as 50 percent of what number? _____

j. Jenny's salary increased from $30,000 to $33,000. By what percent did her salary increase? _____

k. In 1980, factory X produced 18,600 pieces. In 1981, factory X produced only 16,000 pieces. By approximately what percent did production decrease from 1980 to 1981? _____

The amount of money in a savings account after m months is modeled by the function $f(m) = 1{,}000(1.01)^m$.

l. What was the original amount in the bank account? _____

m. By what percent does the amount in the account increase each month? _____

n. In a certain bag of marbles, the ratio of red marbles to green marbles is 7:5. If the bag contains 96 marbles, how many green marbles are in the bag? _____

o. One hogshead is equal to 64 gallons. How many hogsheads are equal to 96 gallons? _____

p. The pressure and volume of a gas are inversely related. If the gas is at 10 kPa at 2 liters, then what is the pressure when the gas is at 4 liters? _____

1 🔖 Mark for Review

If 10 pecks are equivalent to 2.5 bushels, then 4 bushels are equivalent to how many pecks?

Ⓐ 4

Ⓑ 10

Ⓒ 12.5

Ⓓ 16

2 🔖 Mark for Review

A forest fire is burning an area of forest that is 10 square miles. An air squad is able to reduce the size of the fire by 7% every 12 hours. If $F(t)$ is the area being burned by the fire, which expression for $F(t)$ represents the area of forest still on fire after t hours?

Ⓐ $10 - (0.93)^{12t}$

Ⓑ $10 \times (1 - 0.07)^{\frac{t}{12}}$

Ⓒ $10 - 93^{12t}$

Ⓓ 0.93^{10-12t}

3 🔖 Mark for Review

A student took five tests. He scored an average (arithmetic mean) of 80 on the first three tests and an average of 90 on the other two. What was the student's average score on all five tests?

4 🔖 Mark for Review

Esther is paying off her student loans. She currently owes $20,000, and she will reduce the amount due by $\frac{1}{2}$ every 5 years. How much will she owe after 20 years?

Ⓐ $625

Ⓑ $1,000

Ⓒ $1,250

Ⓓ $5,000

5 🔖 Mark for Review

In a political poll, 500 voters were first asked whether they were registered as Democrat, Republican, or Independent. The voters were then asked whether they planned to vote for Candidate A, for Candidate B, or were Undecided. The table below shows the results of the poll.

	Candidate A	Candidate B	Undecided	Total
Democrat	24	56	70	150
Republican	117	70	50	237
Independent	15	18	80	113
Total	156	144	200	500

The number of registered Republicans who plan to vote for Candidate B is what percent greater than the number of registered Democrats who plan to vote for Candidate B?

Ⓐ 14%

Ⓑ 20%

Ⓒ 25%

Ⓓ 28%

6 🔖 Mark for Review

When Everett drives home from college to visit his parents, he drives at an average speed of 66 miles per hour. When his parents go to visit him, they drive at an average speed of 54 miles per hour. If each trip is 594 miles long, approximately what percent less is the time Everett spends driving than the time his parents spend driving?

Ⓐ 2

Ⓑ 8

Ⓒ 18

Ⓓ 22

7 🔖 Mark for Review

Estimated Numbers of Cell Phone Users by Type (in millions)

	Prepaid users	Contracted users	Total
2022	45	225	270
2023	75	250	325
Total	120	475	595

If a cell phone user from 2022 is selected at random, what is the probability that the user is a contracted user?

8 🔖 Mark for Review

Marcia can type 18 pages per hour, and David can type 14 pages per hour. If they work together, how many minutes will it take them to type 24 pages?

Summary

○ The test is full of opportunities to use arithmetic instead of algebra—just look for your chances to use Plugging In and Plugging In the Answers (PITA).

○ If a question has *in terms of* or variables in the answer choices, it's a Plugging In question. Plug in your own number, do the math, find the target number, and use POE to get down to one correct answer.

○ If a question doesn't have variables but asks for a fraction or a percent of an unknown number, you can also plug in. Just substitute your own number for the unknown and take the rest of the question step by step.

○ If a question has an unknown and asks for a specific amount, making you feel like you have to write an equation, try PITA instead.

○ When a question asks about an average or arithmetic mean, use $T = AN$, plug in the values given in the question, and solve for what you need.

○ The median is the middle value in a list of numbers in order. If there is an even number of elements, the median is the average of the two middle values.

○ The mode is the most commonly occurring value in a list of numbers.

○ The range is the difference between the greatest and least values in a list of numbers.

○ Probability is a fractional value between 0 and 1 (inclusive), and it is equal to the number of outcomes the question is asking for divided by the total number of possible outcomes. It can also be expressed as a percent.

○ Rates are closely related to averages. Use $D = RT$ or $W = RT$ just like you use $T = AN$. Remember that the PSAT likes to make you find the totals (distance or work in rate questions).

○ Percent simply means "per 100." Many percent questions can be tackled by translating English to math.

o   Percent increase or decrease is $\dfrac{difference}{original} \times 100$.

o   Growth and decay are given by the formulas *final amount = original amount*$(1 \pm rate)^{number\ of\ changes}$ and *final amount = original amount* $(multiplier)^{number\ of\ changes}$.

o   Set up ratios like fractions. Take care to put the first term of the ratio in the numerator and the second term in the denominator.

o   Sometimes you'll need to treat ratios like fractions or decimals. Use your calculator to turn the numbers into the easiest form to work the question.

o   Direct variation or proportion means as one value goes up, the other goes up. The formula is $\dfrac{x_1}{y_1} = \dfrac{x_2}{y_2}$.

o   Inverse variation means as one value goes up, the other goes down. The formula is $x_1 y_1 = x_2 y_2$.

Chapter 13
Advanced Math

There will be 7 or 8 questions on each Math module of the PSAT that test what College Board calls "Advanced Math." This category includes topics such as functions and quadratics. If you've learned these topics already in school, great! You'll have a step up on the PSAT. If not, fear not—this chapter will give you the foundation needed for tackling these questions on the PSAT. You will also find information on how to tackle Meaning in Context questions.

FUNCTIONS

In the Math Basics chapter, we looked at some concepts related to the *xy*-plane. Here, we will look at some more complicated topics involving functions and graphs. The functions on the PSAT mostly look like this:

$$f(x) = x^2 + 6x + 24$$

Most questions of this type will give you a specific value to plug in for *x* and then ask you to find the value of the function. Each function is just a set of instructions that tells you what to do to *x*—or the number you plug in for *x*—in order to find the corresponding value for *f(x)* (a fancy name for *y*). Just plug your information into that equation and follow the instructions.

Let's try an easy one.

Just Follow the Instructions
Functions are like recipes. Each one is just a set of directions for you to follow. The College Board provides the ingredients and you work your magic.

---

1 ☐ Mark for Review

If $f(x) = x^2 + 3x - 3$, what is the value of $f(7)$?

(A) 14

(B) 20

(C) 32

(D) 67

Fundamental facts about functions
$f(x) = y$
x is the input
y is the output

Here's How to Crack It

The question asks for the value of $f(7)$ given the definition of $f(x)$. Function questions are just trying to see if you can follow the directions, so follow them! The instructions, in this case, are in the equation. The question gives an input value of 7, so plug 7 into the equation and it should look like this: $f(7) = (7)^2 + 3(7) - 3$. Do the math and $f(7) = 67$. Therefore, the answer is (D).

Sometimes you'll get more complicated questions. As long as you know that when you put in x, your function will spit out another number, you'll be fine. Try this next one.

---

2 ☐ Mark for Review

$$f(x) = 5x^3$$

The function f is defined above. If $f(x) = 135$, what is the value of x?

Ⓐ 3

Ⓑ 5

Ⓒ 27

Ⓓ 125

Here's How to Crack It

The question asks for a value given a function. If you remember your functions basics, you know that x is the value that goes into the function, or the input, and y is the value that comes out of the function, or the output. The question gives an output value of 135 and asks which input, or x, will produce that value. It must be one of the answer choices, so plug in the answers!

Start with one of the middle values and try (B), 5. Plug $x = 5$ into the function to get $f(5) = 5(5)^3$. Simplify the right side of the equation to get $f(5) = 5(125)$, and then $f(5) = 625$. This is too big, so eliminate (B).

Since (C) and (D) will also be too big, the answer has to be (A), but try it just in case. Plug $x = 3$ into the function to get $f(3) = 5(3)^3$. Simplify the right side of the equation to get $f(3) = 5(27)$, and then $f(3) = 135$. This matches the output value given in the question, so stop here. The correct answer is (A).

Another way the PSAT can make functions more complicated is to give you two functions to deal with together. If you approach these questions one piece at a time, they will be easier to handle.

Here's an example.

---

3 🔖 Mark for Review

If $f(x) = x + \dfrac{1}{x}$ and $g(x) = x^2 - 7$, what is the value of $f(g(-2))$?

> [ ]

Here's How to Crack It

The question asks for the value of $f(g(-2))$ given the definitions of $f(x)$ and $g(x)$. With compound functions like this one, start from the inside and work your way out. Plug -2 into the g function to get $g(-2) = (-2)^2 - 7 = 4 - 7 = -3$. Plug this value into the f function to get $f(-3) = -3 + \dfrac{1}{-3}$, which becomes $f(-3) = -3\dfrac{1}{3}$. You can't enter a mixed fraction in the fill-in box, so convert the answer to the improper fraction $-\dfrac{10}{3}$ or the decimal -3.333 or -3.334. Any of these would be acceptable answers.

Sometimes the PSAT will use a word problem to describe a function, and then ask you to "build a function" that describes that real-world situation.

Try one of those.

---

4 ☐ Mark for Review

A scientist noted that the rate of growth of a tree which he had been observing is directly proportional to time. The scientist first measured the height of the tree to be 20 feet; two years later, the tree was 21 feet tall. If the tree continues to grow at a constant rate, which of the following represents the height of the tree in feet, y, as a function of time, x, in years since the scientist's first measurement?

Ⓐ $y(x) = 0.5x + 20$

Ⓑ $y(x) = 21x + 20$

Ⓒ $y(x) = x + 20$

Ⓓ $y(x) = 20x + 21$

Here's How to Crack It

The question asks for the function that represents the height of the tree over time. Instead of trying to write your own equation, use the ones in the answer choices. According to the question, 2 years after the first measurement, the tree was 21 feet tall. Therefore, when $x = 2$, $y(x) = 21$. Plug these points into the answers to see which answer works. Choice (A) becomes $21 = 0.5(2) + 20$. Solve the right side of the equation to get $21 = 1 + 20$, or $21 = 21$. The correct answer is (A).

Roots of a Function

You may also be asked about the roots of a function. These are the solutions for x that you get when you solve the function or the places where the graph of the function crosses the x-axis. Here's how this concept may be tested on the PSAT.

---

5 ⬚ Mark for Review

The graph of the function f in the xy-plane has exactly three x-intercepts at $(-3, 0)$, $(0, -2)$, and $(4, 0)$. Which of the following is a factor of function f?

(A) $x - 2$

(B) $x + 2$

(C) $x + 3$

(D) $x + 4$

Here's How to Crack It

The question asks for a factor of a function given points on the graph of the function. The factors are used to find the roots of a function, which are also known as the x-intercepts or the solutions. At the x-intercept, $y = 0$. Therefore, the point $(0, -2)$ is not a root, so that point cannot be used to determine the factors of the function. You can eliminate (A) and (B) because they include 2. According to the question, one of the x-intercepts is at $(-3, 0)$. This means that one solution to the function can be found by $x + 3 = 0$, and one of the factors of the function is $x + 3$. The other factor would be $(x - 4)$, but that's not a choice. The correct answer is (C).

Drill 1

Answers can be found in Part IV.

1 ☐ Mark for Review

Which of the following equivalent forms of the equation $x^2 + 8x + 15 = 0$ would be the most useful for finding the x-intercepts of the equation?

Ⓐ $x(x) + 8(x) + 15 = 0$

Ⓑ $x^2 + 3x + 5x + 15 = 0$

Ⓒ $(x + 3)(x + 5) = 0$

Ⓓ $x^2 + 8x + 4 + 11 = 0$

2 ☐ Mark for Review

A car dealership leases a new truck for a down payment of \$3,200 plus monthly payments of \$380 per month for 36 months. Which of the following functions, f, represents the total amount paid, in dollars, after m months, where $0 \le m \le 36$?

Ⓐ $f(m) = 380 + 3{,}200m$

Ⓑ $f(m) = 3{,}200 + 36m$

Ⓒ $f(m) = 3{,}200 + 380m$

Ⓓ $f(m) = 10{,}480 - 380m$

3 ☐ Mark for Review

The number of bonus points, $B(p)$, that a credit card holder receives is given by the function $B(p) = ap + 7$, where p represents the number of purchases made and a is a constant. If the number of purchases is increased by 4, the number of bonus points increases by 25. What is the value of a?

Ⓐ 4

Ⓑ 4.5

Ⓒ 6.25

Ⓓ 11

4 ☐ Mark for Review

x	-1	j	5
$f(x)$	2	j	-6

The table above shows selected values for the linear function $f(x)$. What is the value of j?

Ⓐ $-\dfrac{1}{6}$

Ⓑ $\dfrac{2}{7}$

Ⓒ $\dfrac{5}{7}$

Ⓓ $\dfrac{7}{6}$

5 ☐ Mark for Review

If $f(x) = x^{-\frac{2}{3}}$, what is the value of $\dfrac{f(8)}{f(3)}$?

Ⓐ $\dfrac{4}{\sqrt[3]{9}}$

Ⓑ $\dfrac{8}{3}$

Ⓒ $\sqrt{\dfrac{512}{27}}$

Ⓓ $\dfrac{\sqrt[3]{9}}{4}$

6 ☐ Mark for Review

Which of the following could be the equation of linear function f if $f(2) = -5$, and $f(4) = 15$?

Ⓐ $f(x) = 5x - 25$

Ⓑ $f(x) = 10x - 25$

Ⓒ $f(x) = 10x - 5$

Ⓓ $f(x) = 10x$

7 ☐ Mark for Review

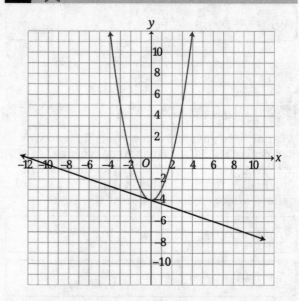

In the above graph, parabola $f(x)$ is represented by the equation $f(x) = x^2 - 4$ and line $g(x)$ is represented by the equation $g(x) = -\frac{1}{3}x - 4$. Line $g(x)$ intersects parabola $f(x)$ at point $(0, -4)$. For $x = 12$, how much greater is the value of $f(x)$ than $g(x)$?

EXTRANEOUS SOLUTIONS

Sometimes solving a rational or radical expression makes funny things happen. Let's look at an example.

$$\frac{1}{z+2} + \frac{1}{z-2} = \frac{4}{(z+2)(z-2)}$$

Given the equation above, what is the value of z?

To add the fractions on the left side, you need a common denominator. Multiply the numerator and the denominator of the first fraction by $(z-2)$ and the numerator and denominator of the second fraction by $(z+2)$. Now the fractions can be added together.

The equation becomes

$$\frac{(z-2)+(z+2)}{(z+2)(z-2)} = \frac{4}{(z+2)(z-2)}$$

Since the denominators are equal, the numerators are equal. This gives you

$$(z-2)+(z+2) = 4$$

When you simplify the left side, you get $2z = 4$, so $z = 2$. Sounds great, right? However, you need to plug this solution back into the original equation to make sure that it works. You get

$$\frac{1}{2+2} + \frac{1}{2-2} = \frac{4}{(2+2)(2-2)}$$

Once simplified, two of the three denominators become zero. That is not allowed, so the solution you found isn't really a solution at all. It is referred to as an "extraneous solution." That term refers to any answer you get to an algebraic equation that results in a false statement when plugged back into the original equation.

> **Extra Answers**
> Any time you are solving for a variable, make sure your solutions actually work. If they do not, they are "extraneous," or extra.

Here's how it might look on the PSAT.

---

6 🔖 Mark for Review

$$\frac{3p}{p-2} = \frac{6}{p-2}$$

Which of the following is a true statement about the equation above?

Ⓐ There are no solutions to the equation.

Ⓑ The solution is $p = 2$.

Ⓒ The solution is $p = 3$.

Ⓓ There are infinitely many solutions to the equation.

Here's How to Crack It

The question asks for a true statement based on an equation. When given two fractions set equal to one another, you often have to cross-multiply to solve. In this case, though, the fractions have the same denominator. This tells you that their numerators are equal. Therefore, $3p = 6$, so $p = 2$, right? But what if you put that value back into the denominators? They become 0, which can't happen. Therefore, 2 is an extraneous solution and the answer is (A).

An answer like (D) would occur if literally any value for a variable would make the equation true, such as would be the case in $x + 3 = x + 3$.

Extraneous solutions also show up on questions about quadratic equations, so let's look at those next.

QUADRATIC EQUATIONS

Ah, quadratics. You're likely to see several questions on the PSAT that require you to expand, factor, or solve quadratics. You may even need to find the vertex of a parabola or the points of intersection of a quadratic and a line. So, let's review, starting with the basics.

Expanding

Most often you'll be asked to expand an expression simply by multiplying it out. When working with an expression of the form $(x + 3)(x + 4)$, multiply it out using the following rule:

> FOIL = First Outer Inner Last

Start with the *first* figure in each set of parentheses: $x \times x = x^2$.

Now do the two *outer* figures: $x \times 4 = 4x$.

Next, the two *inner* figures: $3 \times x = 3x$.

Finally, the *last* figure in each set of parentheses: $3 \times 4 = 12$.

Add them all together, and we get $x^2 + 4x + 3x + 12$, or $x^2 + 7x + 12$.

Factoring

If you ever see an expression of the form $x^2 + 7x + 12$ on the PSAT, there is a good chance that factoring it will be the key to cracking it.

The key to factoring is figuring out what pair of numbers will multiply to give you the constant term (12, in this case) and add up to the coefficient of the x term (7, in this case).

Let's try an example:

$$x^2 + 7x + 12$$

Step 1: Draw two sets of parentheses next to each other and fill an x into the left side of each. That's what gives us our x^2 term.

$$(x \quad)(x \quad)$$

Step 2: 12 can be factored a number of ways: 1×12, 2×6, or 3×4. Which of these adds up to 7? 3 and 4, so place a 3 on the right side of one set of parentheses and a 4 in the other.

$$(x \quad 3)(x \quad 4)$$

Step 3: Now we need to figure out what the correct signs should be. They should both be positive in this case, because that will sum to 7 and multiply to 12, so fill plus signs into each parentheses.

$$(x + 3)(x + 4)$$

If you want to double-check your work, try expanding out $(x + 3)(x + 4)$ using FOIL and you'll get the original expression.

Now try the following question.

⎯⎯⎯⎯⎯⎯◯⎯⎯⎯⎯⎯⎯

7 🔖 Mark for Review

Travis determines that the average speed of his kayak traveling down the river when he is not paddling can be calculated using the formula $4r^2 - 40r + 100$, where r represents the strength of the river's current in feet per second. Which of the following expressions would be an equivalent formula that Travis could use to determine his kayak's speed?

Ⓐ $(2r + 10)^2$

Ⓑ $(2r + 10)(2r - 10)$

Ⓒ $4(r + 5)^2$

Ⓓ $4(r - 5)^2$

> You can also plug in on a question like this. The question has the word *equivalent*, and there are variables in the answers.

Here's How to Crack It

The question asks for an equivalent formula that can be used to determine Travis's speed. To compare the equation in the question with the answer choices, you need to either factor the equation in the question or expand out the answer choices. The first option is probably faster. Start by factoring a 4 out of the entire equation to get $4(r^2 - 10r + 25)$. Now, determine what two numbers can be added to get −10 and multiplied to get 25. In this case, it's −5 and −5. The equation becomes $4(r - 5)(r - 5)$ or $4(r - 5)^2$, which is (D).

⎯⎯⎯⎯⎯⎯◯⎯⎯⎯⎯⎯⎯

Solving Quadratic Equations

Sometimes you'll want to factor to solve an equation. In this case, there will be two possible values for x, called the roots of the equation. To solve for x, use the following steps:

Step 1: Make sure that the equation is set equal to zero.
Step 2: Factor the equation.
Step 3: Set each parenthetical expression equal to zero. So, if you have $(x + 2)(x - 7) = 0$, you get $(x + 2) = 0$ and $(x - 7) = 0$. When you solve for each, you get $x = -2$ and $x = 7$. Therefore, -2 and 7 are the solutions or roots of the equation.

Try the following question.

---

8 ⬜ Mark for Review

If $b^2 + 2b - 8 = 0$, and $b < 0$, what is the value of b?

(A) -6

(B) -4

(C) -2

(D) 0

Here's How to Crack It

The question asks for the value of b in a quadratic equation. Begin by using Process of Elimination. Since the question states that $b < 0$, eliminate (D). Now follow the steps:

1. The equation is already set equal to zero.
2. You can now factor the left side of the equation to get $(b + 4)(b - 2) = 0$.
3. When you set each parenthetical expression equal to zero, you get $b = -4$ and $b = 2$. Since $b < 0$, the answer is (B).

An alternative approach to this question is to plug in the answers. For (A), plug $b = -6$ into the equation to get $(-6)^2 + 2(-6) - 8 = 0$. Solve the left side of the equation to get $36 - 12 - 8 = 0$, or $16 = 0$. Since this statement is not true, eliminate (A). For (B), plug $b = -4$ into the equation to get $(-4)^2 + 2(-4) - 8 = 0$. Solve the left side of the equation to get $16 - 8 - 8 = 0$, or $0 = 0$. Since this statement is true, the correct answer is (B).

Sometimes, solving will get a little trickier. When quadratics do not factor easily and there are no answer choices to plug in, you can use the quadratic formula to solve.

> The values of x for a quadratic equation in the form $y = ax^2 + bx + c$ are
> $$x = \frac{-b \pm \sqrt{b^2 - 4ac}}{2a}$$

Let's try one.

9　☐ Mark for Review

If $y = x^2 - 4x + 3.75$, what is one possible value of x?

Here's How to Crack It

The question asks for the value of x in a quadratic equation. This one is not easy to factor, so try the quadratic formula. In the given equation, $a = 1$, $b = -4$, and $c = 3.75$. Therefore,

$$x = \frac{-(-4) \pm \sqrt{(-4)^2 - 4(1)(3.75)}}{2(1)} = \frac{4 \pm \sqrt{16 - 15}}{2} = \frac{4 \pm 1}{2}.$$

So, x equals $\frac{5}{2}$ (or 2.5) and $\frac{3}{2}$ (or 1.5). Any of these 4 options could be entered into the fill-in box.

Another option for this one would be to graph the equation with the built-in calculator to determine the x-intercepts, which are the roots, or solutions, to the equation.

Other Quadratic Questions

Sometimes, quadratic equations will be tested with word problems or charts. Let's look at these types of questions.

---

10   🔖 Mark for Review

An Olympic shot-putter throws a heavy spherical object that follows a parabolic trajectory. The equation describing the trajectory of the shot-putter's throw is $y = -0.04x^2 + 2.02x + 5.5$, where y represents the height of the object in feet and x represents the horizontal distance in feet traveled by the object. What is the original height of the object, in feet, immediately before it leaves the shot-putter's hand?

Here's How to Crack It

The question asks for the original height of an object based on an equation for the object's trajectory. According to the question, x represents the horizontal distance in feet traveled by the object, and y represents the height. Before the shot-putter throws the object, $x = 0$. Plug 0 into the equation and solve for y. The equation becomes $y = -0.04(0^2) + 2.02(0) + 5.5 = 0 + 0 + 5.5 = 5.5$. The correct answer is 5.5.

Now look at an example of a chart-based quadratic question.

---

11 ☐ Mark for Review

Trajectory of a Dolphin's Jump

Horizontal distance (feet)	Vertical height (feet)
0	0
1	2.7
2	4.8
3	6.3
4	7.2
5	7.5
6	7.2
7	6.3
8	4.8
9	2.7
10	0

The table above shows the horizontal distance and vertical height, both in feet, of a typical dolphin jumping out of the water (a height of 0 represents the surface of the water). If d represents the horizontal distance and h represents the vertical height, which of the following equations would best represent the trajectory of the dolphin's jump?

Ⓐ $h = -0.3d^2 + 3d$

Ⓑ $h = -0.4d^2 + 4d$

Ⓒ $h = -0.5d^2 + 5d$

Ⓓ $h = -0.6d^2 + 6d$

Here's How to Crack It

The question asks for an equation to model the trajectory of a dolphin's jump based on a table of values. This is a similar task to "building a function" that we discussed earlier in this chapter. You should plug values from the table into the equations in the answer choices to see which equation works. According to the table, when $d = 1$, $h = 2.7$. Plug these values into (A) to get $2.7 = -0.3(1^2) + 3(1)$. Solve the right side of the equation to get $2.7 = -0.3 + 3$ or $2.7 = 2.7$.

Keep (A) but check the remaining answers just in case. Choice (B) becomes $2.7 = -0.4(1^2) + 4(1)$. Solve the right side of the equation to get $2.7 = -0.4 + 4$ or $2.7 = 3.6$. This is not true, so eliminate (B). Choice (C) becomes $2.7 = -0.5(1^2) + 5(1)$. Solve the right side of the equation to get $2.7 = -0.5 + 5$ or $2.7 = 4.5$. Eliminate (C). Choice (D) becomes $2.7 = -0.6(1^2) + 6(1)$. Solve the right side of the equation to get $2.7 = -0.6 + 6$ or $2.7 = 5.4$. Eliminate (D). The correct answer is (A).

Forms of Quadratics

When graphed in the xy-plane, quadratics form a parabola. The PSAT will ask questions using three different forms of the equation for a parabola.

> The **standard form** of a parabola equation is as follows:
>
> $$y = ax^2 + bx + c$$

In the standard form of a parabola, the value of a tells whether a parabola opens upward or downward (if a is positive, the parabola opens upward, and if a is negative, the parabola opens downward).

> The **factored form** of a parabola equation is as follows:
>
> $$y = a(x - s)(x - t)$$
>
> In the factored form, s and t are the x-intercepts.

We discussed factoring quadratics a few pages back. The result of factoring a parabolic equation is the factored form.

> The **vertex form** of a parabola equation is as follows:
>
> $$y = a(x - h)^2 + k$$
>
> In the vertex form, the point (h, k) is the vertex of the parabola.

Simply knowing what the vertex form looks like may help you answer a question, like the following example.

---

12 ☐ Mark for Review

Which of the following equations has its vertex at (–4, 3)?

Ⓐ $y = (x - 4)^2 + 3$

Ⓑ $y = (x + 4)^2 + 3$

Ⓒ $y = (x - 3)^2 + 4$

Ⓓ $y = (x + 3)^2 - 4$

Here's How to Crack It

The question asks for a quadratic equation that has a given vertex. If you know the vertex form, you can create the correct equation for the parabola. Be careful with the signs, though, as the signs are all changing in the answer choices. In the vertex (–4, 3), –4 is h and 3 is k. The correct answer should end in + 3, so eliminate (C) and (D). For the $(x - h)^2$ part of the equation, it becomes $(x - (-4))^2$, or $(x + 4)^2$, so the correct answer is (B).

Knowing the form makes Process of Elimination a quick way to answer these, but if you forget the form, you can always use the built-in graphing calculator to graph the equations in the answer choices and see which one has the correct vertex.

The vertex form is great for answering questions about the minimum or maximum value a parabolic function will reach or the x-value that results in that minimum or maximum y-value. So, another good thing to know is the method for turning a quadratic in the standard form into the vertex form. One way is to complete the square, but it is often simpler to use the formula

$$h = -\frac{b}{2a}$$

This solves for h, the x-coordinate of the vertex, using the values of a and b in standard form. Then plug the value of h into the standard form equation to find k, the y-coordinate of the vertex.

Say you were given the equation $x^2 - 4x - 12$. The equation for the x-coordinate of the vertex becomes $h = -\dfrac{-4}{2(1)}$, or $h = 2$. Plug that into the standard form quadratic to get $2^2 - 4(2) - 12$, which becomes $4 - 8 - 12 = -16$. The vertex is $(2, -16)$, and vertex form of the equation is $y = (x - 2)^2 - 16$.

You can also find the vertex quickly by using the built-in graphing calculator. Carefully enter the equation of the line. The graph will be in red with the vertex and intercepts shown as gray dots. Hover over or click on the dot at the vertex and it will show the coordinates. Your screen will look like this:

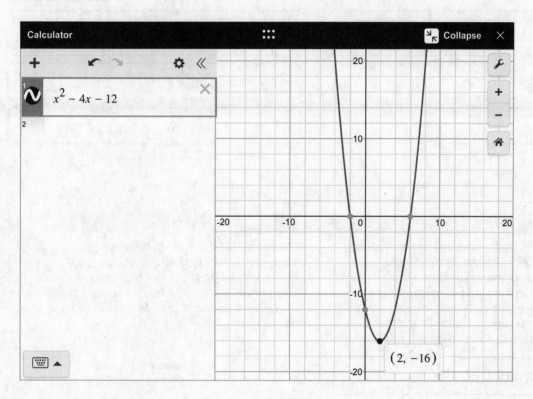

Drill 2

Answers can be found in Part IV.

1 ☐ Mark for Review

If $12 - (t + 2)^2 = 3$, which of the following could be the value of t?

- Ⓐ −9
- Ⓑ −5
- Ⓒ 5
- Ⓓ 7

2 ☐ Mark for Review

Aubri determines that her score in a particular video game can be calculated using the formula $x^4 - y^4$, where x represents the number of treasures she discovers, and y represents the number of hidden traps she falls into. Which of the following expressions would be a suitable equivalent for Aubri's score calculation formula?

- Ⓐ $(x + y)(x - y)(x^2 + y^2)$
- Ⓑ $(x + y)^2(x^2 + y^2)$
- Ⓒ $(x - y)^2(x^2 + y^2)$
- Ⓓ $(x + y)(x - y)(x^2 - y^2)$

3 ☐ Mark for Review

Which of the following equations has a vertex of $(-5, 2)$?

- Ⓐ $y = (x + 5)^2 - 2$
- Ⓑ $y = (x - 5)^2 - 2$
- Ⓒ $y = 2(x + 5)^2 + 2$
- Ⓓ $y = 2(x - 5)^2 + 2$

4 ☐ Mark for Review

The profit that a donut shop makes can be expressed by the equation $P = -4(x - 3)^2 + 2,000$, where x is the price per donut sold (in dollars). What price, in dollars, should the donut shop charge its customers in order to maximize its profit?

☐

5 ☐ Mark for Review

In his physics class, Yigit determined that the height in feet (h) of a projectile t seconds after being launched can be expressed using the function $h(t) = -5t^2 + 20t + 45$. Which of the following represents the initial height of the projectile?

Ⓐ $h(0)$

Ⓑ $h(1)$

Ⓒ $h(2)$

Ⓓ $h(3)$

6 ☐ Mark for Review

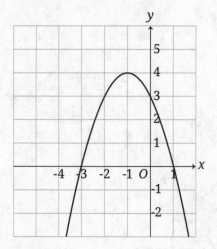

Which of the following equations is shown in the graph above?

Ⓐ $y = -(x - 3)(x + 1)$

Ⓑ $y = -(x + 3)(x - 1)$

Ⓒ $y = -(x + 3)(x + 4)$

Ⓓ $y = -(x - 1)(x + 4)$

7 ☐ Mark for Review

If $f(x) = x^2 - x + 4$, a is non-negative, and $f(a) = 10$, what is the value of a?

8 ☐ Mark for Review

In the equation $x^2 + 24x + c = (x + 9)(x + p)$, c and p are constants. If the equation is true for all values of x, what is the value of c?

Ⓐ 33

Ⓑ 135

Ⓒ 144

Ⓓ 216

9 ☐ Mark for Review

The stream of water that shoots out of a certain fountain takes the form of a parabola. The water shoots from a spout that is 8 feet above the ground and reaches a maximum height of 39.25 feet. If y represents the height of the water, in feet, and x represents the time, in seconds, which of the following equations could describe the trajectory of the stream of water?

Ⓐ $y = -x^2 + 15$

Ⓑ $y = -5x^2 + 25x + 8$

Ⓒ $y = 2x^2 + 32x + 8$

Ⓓ $y = 8x + 39.25$

10 ☐ Mark for Review

If $\dfrac{7}{x+4} = \dfrac{x+3}{y}$, then which of the following represents an equivalent equation for y, in terms of x?

Ⓐ $y = \dfrac{7(x+3)}{x+4}$

Ⓑ $y = \dfrac{x^2+7x+12}{7}$

Ⓒ $y = \dfrac{x+3}{7(x+4)}$

Ⓓ $y = \dfrac{7}{x^2+7x+12}$

11 ☐ Mark for Review

$$\frac{2(p-2) + 2(3-p)}{p-2} = \frac{2(3p-6) + 3(6-2p)}{p-2}$$

Which of the following is a true statement about the equation above?

Ⓐ There are no solutions to the equation.

Ⓑ The only solution is $p = 2$.

Ⓒ The only solution is $p = 3$.

Ⓓ There are infinitely many solutions to the equation.

MATH STORY TIME

If some of the questions you've seen so far are reminding you of science class, you're not crazy. Approximately 30% of the Math questions on the PSAT are word problems. The test-writers like to use scientific topics and other "real world" contexts to make things look more complicated.

Many of the strategies we've already discussed will help you to answer these questions regardless of the context.

Here's an example.

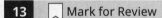

---

13 🔖 Mark for Review

The electric potential of a point charge Q is given by the equation $V = \frac{kQ}{r}$, where V is the charge in volts or Joules per Coulomb, Q is the charge in Coulombs, r is the distance from the charge in meters, and k is a constant. What is the charge in Coulombs in terms of the other variables and constants?

- (A) $Q = Vrk$

- (B) $Q = \frac{Vk}{r}$

- (C) $Q = \frac{k}{Vr}$

- (D) $Q = \frac{Vr}{k}$

Here's How to Crack It

The question asks for a variable in terms of other variables and constants. Plugging in on this question would be difficult with four letters to substitute for. Instead, read the question carefully to see that the charge in Coulombs is represented by Q, and solve for Q. To begin to isolate Q, multiply both sides of the equation by r to get $Vr = kQ$. Divide both sides of the equation by k to get $\frac{Vr}{k} = Q$. The correct answer is (D).

Sometimes, you will be asked questions based on a chart or graph. In those cases, carefully look up the numbers in question, do the required calculations, and eliminate answers that aren't true.

Let's look at one.

---

14 ☐ Mark for Review

Marble Ramp Rolling Times

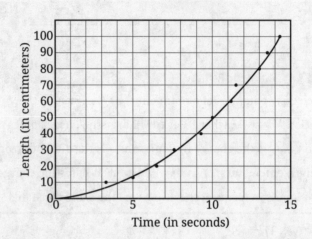

A student is rolling a marble down ramps of varying lengths. The scatterplot above shows the time, in seconds, it takes the marble to roll down each ramp. Based on the curve of best fit to the data represented, which of the following is the closest to the expected length of a ramp if a marble takes 12 seconds to roll down?

Ⓐ 61

Ⓑ 71

Ⓒ 79

Ⓓ 84

Here's How to Crack It

The question asks for the expected length of a ramp given a certain roll time based on the graph. Roll time is shown on the horizontal axis of the graph, given in seconds. Look for the mark indicating 12 seconds on this axis; then use the mouse or the edge of your scratch paper to go from that mark to the curve of best fit. Once you hit it, use the mouse or scratch paper again to move over to the vertical axis. It should hit between 60 and 80 centimeters, right around 70. This makes (B) the credited response, since it is slightly closer to the mark for 70.

You may also be asked to graph the data presented in a table. Your knowledge of graphing in the xy-plane should help you with most of those questions. If anything gets too tricky, consider skipping it and spending your time on something else.

Some word problems don't involve charts, graphs, or equations. In fact, these don't even look much like math questions at all. They will have a lot of words to describe a situation and ask about the conclusion that can be drawn. Just use a lot of Process of Elimination and a little knowledge of what makes a good experiment, and you should be fine.

Try this one.

---

15 ☐ Mark for Review

A psychologist wants to know whether there is a relationship between increased water consumption and exam scores. He obtains survey responses from a random sample of 3,500 20-year-old college students in the United States and finds a strong positive correlation between increased water consumption and test scores. Which of the following conclusions is well-supported by the data?

(A) There is a positive association between increased water consumption and test scores for 20-year-olds in the United States.

(B) There is a positive association between increased water consumption and test scores for adults in the United States.

(C) High test scores are caused by increased water consumption for 20-year-olds in the United States.

(D) High test scores are caused by increased water consumption for adults in the United States.

Here's How to Crack It

The question asks for the conclusion that is well-supported by the data of a survey. Consider each answer choice one at a time and use Process of Elimination. Choice (A) merely restates what the evidence says, which makes it a safe conclusion, so keep it. Choice (B) is similar but shifts from "20-year-old college students" to "adults." This is a less safe conclusion than (A), because it generalizes from a more particular group, so eliminate (B). Choices (C) and (D) both introduce the idea of causation. This is a problem—no information was given about cause. Maybe people who tend to score higher on tests are also smart enough to drink more water, or maybe there is another factor causing both high test scores and increased water consumption. Eliminate (C) and (D) and choose (A).

MEANING IN CONTEXT

Some questions, instead of asking you to come up with an equation, just want you to recognize what a part of the equation stands for. It sounds like a simple enough task, but when you look at the equation, they have made it really hard to see what is going on. For this reason, Meaning in Context questions are a great opportunity to plug in real numbers and start to see how the equation really works!

First things first, though, you want to think about your POOD. Does this question fit into your pacing goals? It might take a bit of legwork to get an answer, and you may need that time to go collect points on easier, quicker questions.

If this question does fit into your pacing plan, you should read carefully, label everything you can in the equation, and POE to get rid of any answer choices that are clearly on the wrong track. Then, it's time to plug some of your own numbers in to see what is going on in there.

Here's an example.

---

16 🔖 Mark for Review

Two groups spend the morning cleaning windows, and each person takes the same amount of time per window cleaned. Group A cleans p windows per person, and group B cleans q windows per person. At the end of the morning, the two groups have cleaned a total of 122 windows. If the situation can be represented by the equation $5p + 11q = 122$, what is the best interpretation of the number 11 in this context?

(A) Group A cleans 11 windows per person.

(B) Group B cleans 11 windows per person.

(C) Group A has 11 people in it.

(D) Group B has 11 people in it.

Here's How to Crack It

The question asks for the meaning of a number in context. Start by reading the final question, which asks for the meaning of the number 11. Then label the parts of the equation with the information given. The question states that *Group A cleans p windows per person, and group B cleans q windows per person*. There's no way for two parts of the equation to represent the same thing, so 11 cannot be the number of windows cleaned by one of the groups. Eliminate (A) and (B).

Since *q* represents the number of windows washed by each person in group B, the number multiplied by *q* must have something to do with group B. Eliminate (C). If 5 and 11 represent the number of people in group A and group B, respectively, that would mean that 5 times the number of windows washed per person in group A plus 11 times the number of windows washed per person in group B equals the total number of windows washed, so the equation makes sense. You didn't really need to figure that out, though, because labeling and using Process of Elimination got you the right answer, which is (D).

Let's look at a slightly different one now.

---

17   🔖 Mark for Review

$$n = 1{,}273 - 4p$$

The equation above was used by the cafeteria in a large public high school to model the relationship between the number of slices of pizza, *n*, sold daily and the price of a slice of pizza, *p*, in dollars. What does the number 4 represent in this equation?

(A) For every \$4 the price of pizza decreases, the cafeteria sells 1 more slice of pizza.

(B) For every dollar the price of pizza decreases, the cafeteria sells 4 more slices of pizza.

(C) For every \$4 the price of pizza increases, the cafeteria sells 1 more slice of pizza.

(D) For every dollar the price of pizza increases, the cafeteria sells 4 more slices of pizza.

Here's How to Crack It

The question asks what the number 4 represents in an equation modeling a certain situation. Rewrite the equation on your scratch paper, read the question very carefully, and label the variables in the equation. You know that *p* is the price of pizza, and *n* is the number of slices, so you can add that information to the equation. If you can, eliminate answer choices that don't make sense. But what if you can't eliminate anything, or you can eliminate only an answer choice or two?

Even with everything labeled, this equation is difficult to decode, so it's time to plug in! Try a few of your own numbers in the equation, and you will get a much better understanding of what is happening.

Let's try it out with $p = 2$. When you put 2 in for p, $n = 1{,}273 - 4(2)$ or 1,265.

So, when $p = 2$, $n = 1{,}265$. In other words, at \$2 a slice, the cafeteria sells 1,265 slices.

When $p = 3$, $n = 1{,}261$, so at \$3 a slice, the cafeteria sells 1,261 slices.

When $p = 6$, $n = 1{,}249$, so at \$6 a slice, the cafeteria sells 1,249 slices.

So now, let's use POE. First of all, is the cafeteria selling more pizza as the price goes up? No, as the price of pizza goes up, the cafeteria sells fewer slices of pizza. That means you can eliminate (C) and (D).

Choice (A) says that for every \$4 the price goes down, the cafeteria sells 1 more slice of pizza. Does your Plugging In back that up? No. When the price drops from \$6 to \$2, the cafeteria sells 16 more slices, not 1 more slice, so (A) is no good.

Now, let's take a look at (B). Does the cafeteria sell 4 more slices of pizza for every dollar the price drops? Yes! Choice (B) is the correct answer.

Here are the steps for using Plugging In to solve Meaning in Context questions:

Meaning In Context

1. Read the question carefully. Make sure you know which part of the equation you are being asked to identify.

2. Use your pencil to rewrite the equation and label the parts of it.

3. Eliminate any answer choices that clearly describe the wrong part of the equation, or go against what you have labeled.

4. Plug in! Use your own numbers to start seeing what is happening in the equation.

5. Use POE again, using the information you learned from plugging in real numbers, until you can get it down to one answer choice. Or, get it down to as few choices as you can, and guess.

Drill 3

Answers can be found in Part IV.

1 ☐ Mark for Review

A shipping company pays a driver a fixed fee for each delivery and deducts a separate fee daily for the use of the company's delivery truck. The driver's net pay in dollars, P, for one day is given by the equation $P = 8d - 40$, where d is the number of deliveries made in one day. What does the number 40 most likely represent?

Ⓐ The amount, in dollars, that the company deducts for use of the delivery truck

Ⓑ The amount, in dollars, that the driver is paid for each delivery

Ⓒ The average number of deliveries per hour made by the driver

Ⓓ The total number of deliveries made per day by the driver

2 ☐ Mark for Review

A group of students decided to have a car wash to raise funds for the school. The students charged the same rate to wash each car, and they paid for cleaning supplies out of the proceeds. If the net amount, $N(c)$, in dollars, raised from washing c cars is given by the function $N(c) = 8c - 0.40c$, which of the following can be deduced from the function?

Ⓐ The students paid a total of $8 for cleaning supplies.

Ⓑ The students paid a total of $40 for cleaning supplies.

Ⓒ The students paid $0.40 per car for cleaning supplies.

Ⓓ The students paid $8 per car for cleaning supplies.

3 ☐ Mark for Review

An oceanographer is trying to determine the concentration profile of dissolved oxygen in the ocean at depths lower than 10 meters. He determines that the dissolved oxygen concentration is 0.0022 g/L at a depth of 15 meters, and it is 0.00125 g/L at a depth of 20 meters. If $C(d)$ is the concentration of dissolved oxygen at d meters, which of the following equations best describes the concentration profile below 10 meters?

(A) $C(d) = \frac{1}{2} - \frac{1}{d^2}$

(B) $C(d) = \frac{1}{100d}$

(C) $C(d) = \frac{1}{d}$

(D) $C(d) = \frac{1}{2d^2}$

4 ☐ Mark for Review

At a buffet restaurant, students pay \$5 per meal and non-students pay \$7. The total revenue, R, in dollars, earned per day by the restaurant is given by the equation $R = 5s + 7n$. Which of the following could represent the total number of customers on a given day?

(A) $s - n$

(B) $s + n$

(C) sn

(D) $\frac{s}{n}$

5 ☐ Mark for Review

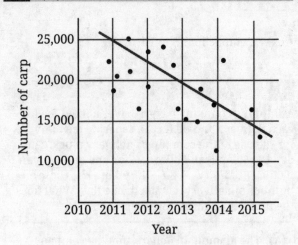

Between 2010 and 2015, researchers tracked populations of Crucian carp in the Ohio River. The graph above displays population sizes as counted by the researchers. According to the line of best fit, what is the approximate average yearly decrease in the number of Crucian carp?

(A) 1

(B) 2.5

(C) 1,200

(D) 2,500

6 ☐ Mark for Review

Delphine is studying the growth of bacteria in a petri dish. She grows 100 colonies of bacteria in dishes at varying temperatures to find the optimal temperature for bacteria growth. The temperature of the 10 colonies with the most rapid growth is used to determine the optimal temperature range, which Delphine finds to be from 30° to 37°C, inclusive. Which of the following inequalities represents the optimal temperature range, t, for bacteria growth?

(A) $|t + 7| \leq 37$

(B) $|t - 3.5| \leq 33.5$

(C) $|t - 30| \leq 7$

(D) $|t - 33.5| \leq 3.5$

7 ☐ Mark for Review

$$B = 250\left(1 + \frac{0.05}{12}\right)^{12t}$$

If interest deposits are made monthly into an account with a beginning balance of $250, supposing no withdrawals are made from the account, the balance B of an account with an annual interest rate of 5% after t years can be computed using the equation above. Which of the following describes what the quantity $\frac{0.05}{12}$ represents in the equation?

(A) The amount of money deposited into an account with balance B during a given month

(B) The amount of money in an account with balance B after a monthly interest deposit is made

(C) The percentage of the starting balance B added during a monthly interest deposit

(D) The number of months over which interest payments will be made in a year

Summary

o   Given a function, you put an *x*-value in and get an *f*(*x*) or *y*-value out.

o   Look for ways to use Plugging In and PITA on function questions.

o   For questions about the graphs of functions, remember that *f*(*x*) = *y*.

o   If the graph contains a labeled point or the question gives you a point, plug it into the equations in the answers and eliminate any that aren't true.

o   To find a point of intersection, set the equations equal, plug a given point into both equations to see if it works, or graph the equations on your calculator or the built-in calculator.

o   When solving quadratic equations, you may need to FOIL or factor to get the equation into the easiest form for the question task.

o   The standard form of a quadratic equation is $ax^2 + bx + c = 0$. The factored form is $y = a(x - s)(x - t)$, where *s* and *t* are the *x*-intercepts.

o   To solve for the roots of a quadratic equation, set it equal to zero by moving all the terms to the left side of the equation, or use the quadratic formula:

$$x = \frac{-b \pm \sqrt{b^2 - 4ac}}{2a}$$

o   When solving radical and rational equations, be on the lookout for extraneous solutions. They are answers you get that don't work when plugged back into the original equation.

o   The vertex form of a parabola equation is $y = a(x - h)^2 + k$, where (*h*, *k*) is the vertex. To get a parabola in the standard form into vertex form, use the equation $h = -\dfrac{b}{2a}$. To find the vertex, use the on-screen graphing calculator.

o   Plugging In can also be used on Meaning In Context questions. If a question asks you to identify a part of an equation, plug your own amounts into the equation so you can start to see what is going on.

o   Some word problems with a scientific context may seem weird, but they can usually be handled with the same strategies as those used for other math questions. Plug in or translate, read the chart or text carefully, and always use Process of Elimination to get rid of answers that don't match the data or don't make sense.

o   If you come across a hard Meaning in Context question or word problem, see if you can eliminate anything and make a guess. If not, find another question to do!

Chapter 14
Geometry and Trigonometry

Approximately 15% of the questions on the PSAT Math section will be about geometry and trigonometry. While there are many topics in these categories that could be tested, each one will only appear once or twice on the test. Everything you've learned so far, such as Plugging In and POE, will often work on geometry and trig questions. Spend time on this chapter only after you have mastered the topics and techniques in the previous three chapters.

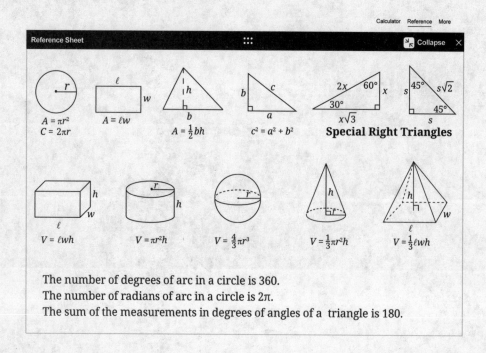

The number of degrees of arc in a circle is 360.
The number of radians of arc in a circle is 2π.
The sum of the measurements in degrees of angles of a triangle is 180.

You can access the reference sheet above at any point during the Math section by clicking **Reference** in the upper right corner of the screen. Once you look up the information you need, click the **X** to return to the question. You can also click **Collapse** to shrink the reference window in order to see the formulas and the question at the same time or **Expand** to make it full size.

GEOMETRY

Lines and Angles

Common sense might tell you what a line is, but for this test you are going to have to learn the particulars of a line, a ray, and a line segment.

A **line** continues on in each direction forever. You need only two points to form a line, but that line does not end at those points. A straight line has 180 degrees on each side.

A **ray** is a line with one distinct endpoint. Again, you need only two points to designate a ray, but one of those points is where it stops—it continues on forever in the other direction. A ray has 180 degrees as well.

A **line segment** is a line with two distinct endpoints. It requires two points, and it is the length from one point to the other. A line segment has 180 degrees.

Whenever you have angles on a line, remember *the rule of 180*: The angles on any line must add up to 180. These angles are called *supplementary angles*. In the figure below, what is the value of *x*? We know that $2x + x$ must add up to 180, so we know that $3x = 180$. This makes $x = 60$.

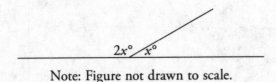

Note: Figure not drawn to scale.

If two lines cross each other, they make *vertical angles*—that is, angles opposite each other when two lines intersect. These angles will always have the same measure. In the figure below, *z* and *x* are vertical angles, and *y* and the 130° angle are vertical angles. Also, we know that *z* must equal 50, since $130 + z$ must equal 180. We know that *y* is 130, since it is across from the 130° angle. We also know that *x* is 50, since it is across from *z*.

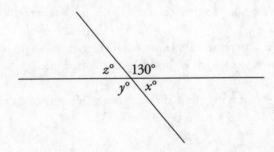

Any time you have two parallel lines and a line that crosses them, you have two kinds of angles: big angles and small angles. All of the big angles have the same measure, and all of the small angles have the same measure. In the following figure, angles *a*, *d*, *e*, and *h* all have the same measure; angles *b*, *c*, *f*, and *g* also all have the same measure. The sum of the measure of any big angle plus any small angle equals 180 degrees.

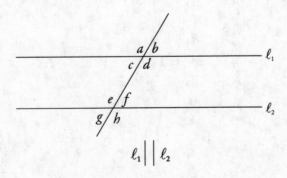

Four-Sided Figures

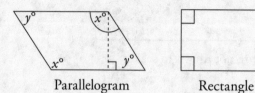

Parallelogram

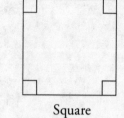

Rectangle   Square

A figure with two sets of parallel sides is a **parallelogram**. In a parallelogram, the opposite angles are equal, and any adjacent angles add up to 180 degrees. (In the left-hand figure above, $x + y = 180$ degrees.) Opposite sides are also equal. The sum of all angles of a parallelogram is 360 degrees.

If all of the angles are also right angles, then the figure is a **rectangle**. And if all of the sides are the same length, then the figure is a **square**.

The *area* of a square, rectangle, or parallelogram is *length* × *width*. (In the parallelogram above, the length is shown by the dotted line.)

The *perimeter* of any figure is the sum of the lengths of its sides. A trapezoid with sides of 6, 8, 10, and 8 has a perimeter of 32.

Drill 1

Answers can be found in Part IV.

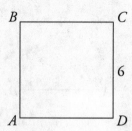

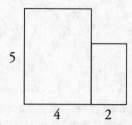

a. What is the area of square *ABCD* above? _____

e. If the above figure is composed of two rectangles, what is the perimeter of the figure? _____

b. What is the perimeter of square *ABCD* above? _____

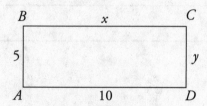

c. If *ABCD* is a rectangle, *x* = _____
y = _____

d. What is the perimeter of rectangle *ABCD* above? _____

1 ☐ Mark for Review

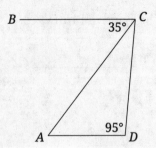

In the figure above, lines *a* and *b* are parallel. Which of the following pairs of angles must have equal degree measures?

I. 1 and 5
II. 2 and 7
III. 3 and 9

Ⓐ I only

Ⓑ II only

Ⓒ III only

Ⓓ II and III only

2 ☐ Mark for Review

In the figure above, $\overline{BC}$ is parallel to $\overline{AD}$. What is the measure of angle *ACD*?

Ⓐ 35°

Ⓑ 40°

Ⓒ 50°

Ⓓ 55°

3 ☐ Mark for Review

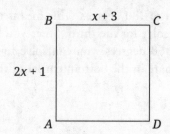

If $ABCD$ is a square, what is the area of the square?

(A) 2

(B) 4

(C) 20

(D) 25

4 ☐ Mark for Review

The diagonal of rectangle $ABCD$ is 13 inches long. What is the area of rectangle $ABCD$?

☐

TRIANGLES

The sum of the angles inside a triangle must be equal to 180 degrees. This means that if you know two of the angles in a triangle, you can always solve for the third. Since you know that two of the angles in the following figure are 90 and 60 degrees, you can solve for the third angle, which must be 30 degrees. (Note: The little square in the bottom corner of the triangle indicates a right angle, which is 90°.)

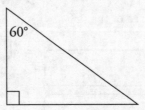

An **isosceles triangle** has two sides that are equal. Angles that are opposite equal sides must be equal. The figure below is an isosceles triangle. Since $AB = BC$, you know that angles x and y are equal. And since their sum must be 150 degrees (to make a total of 180 degrees when you add the last angle), they each must be 75 degrees.

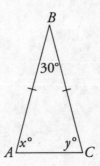

The **area** of a triangle is $\frac{1}{2}$ *base × height*. Note that the height is always perpendicular to the base.

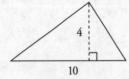

$$\text{Area} = \frac{1}{2} \times 10 \times 4 = 20 \qquad \text{Area} = \frac{1}{2} \times 6 \times 4 = 12$$

An **equilateral triangle** has all three sides equal and all of its angles equal to 60 degrees.

Here's a typical example of a PSAT question on triangles.

───────────○───────────

| 1 | 🔖 Mark for Review |

In triangle *ABC* above, what is the value of *x*?

(A) 30

(B) 40

(C) 50

(D) 60

Here's How to Crack It

The question asks for the value of *x*, which is an angle measure in a triangle. Redraw the figure on your scratch paper. We know that the angle adjacent to the 100° angle must equal 80° since we know that a straight line is 180°. Fill it in on your diagram. Now, since we know that the sum of the angles contained in a triangle must equal 180°, we know that 80 + 60 + *x* = 180, so *x* = 40. That's (B).

───────────○───────────

Being Aggressive on Geometry Questions

The most important problem-solving technique for tackling PSAT geometry is to learn to be aggressive. This means, whenever you have a diagram, ask yourself, *What else do I know?* Write everything you can think of on your scratch paper. You may not see right away why it's important but write it down anyway. Chances are good that you will be making progress toward the answer, without even knowing it.

The PSAT is also fond of disguising familiar figures within more complex shapes by extending lines, overlapping figures, or combining several basic shapes. So be on the lookout for the basic figures hidden in complicated shapes.

The Pythagorean Theorem

Whenever you have a right triangle, you can use the Pythagorean Theorem. The theorem says that the sum of the squares of the legs of the triangle (the sides that form the right angle) will equal the square of the hypotenuse (the side opposite the right angle).

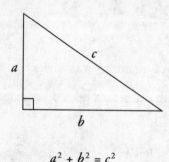

$$a^2 + b^2 = c^2$$

Two of the most common ratios of sides that fit the Pythagorean Theorem are 3-4-5 and 5-12-13. Since these are ratios, any multiples of these numbers will also work, such as 6-8-10 and 30-40-50.

Try the following example.

---

2 ☐ Mark for Review

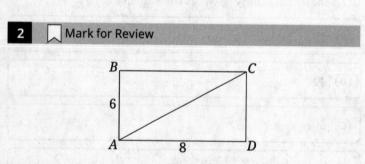

If *ABCD* is a rectangle, what is the perimeter of triangle *ABC*?

Here's How to Crack It

The question asks for the perimeter of triangle *ABC* based on the figure. Redraw the figure on your scratch paper. We can use the Pythagorean Theorem to figure out the length of the diagonal of the rectangle—since it has sides 6 and 8, its diagonal must be 10. (If you remembered that this is one of those well-known Pythagorean triples, you didn't actually have to do the calculations.) Therefore, the perimeter of the triangle is 6 + 8 + 10, or 24.

Special Right Triangles

There are two specific right triangles, the properties of which may play a role in some harder PSAT math questions. They are the right triangles with angles 45°-45°-90° and 30°-60°-90°. These triangles are on the reference sheet that you can click open at any time, so you don't have to memorize them.

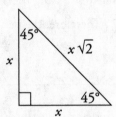

An isosceles right triangle has angles that measure 45, 45, and 90 degrees. Whenever you have a 45°-45°-90° triangle with sides of x, the hypotenuse will always be $x\sqrt{2}$. This means that if one of the legs of the triangle measures 3, then the hypotenuse will be $3\sqrt{2}$.

This right triangle is important because it is half of a square. Understanding the 45°-45°-90° triangle will allow you to easily find the diagonal of a square from its side or find the side of a square from its diagonal.

Here's an example.

---

 3   🔖 **Mark for Review**

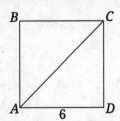

In square $ABCD$ above, what is the perimeter of triangle ABC?

Ⓐ $6\sqrt{2}$

Ⓑ 8

Ⓒ $12 + \sqrt{2}$

Ⓓ $12 + 6\sqrt{2}$

Here's How to Crack It

The question asks for the perimeter of triangle *ABC* based on the figure. This question looks like a question about a square, and it certainly is in part, but it's really more about the two triangles formed by the diagonal. Redraw the figure on your scratch paper to get started.

In this square, we know that each of the triangles formed by the diagonal $\overline{AC}$ is a 45°-45°-90° right triangle. Since the square has a side of 6, using the 45°-45°-90° right triangle rule, each of the sides is 6 and the diagonal is $6\sqrt{2}$. Therefore, the perimeter of the triangle is $6 + 6 + 6\sqrt{2}$, or $12 + 6\sqrt{2}$ and the answer is (D).

The other important right triangle to understand is the 30°-60°-90° right triangle.

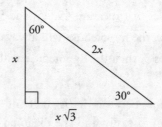

A 30°-60°-90° triangle with a short side of *x* will have a hypotenuse of 2*x* and a middle side of $x\sqrt{3}$. If the smallest side (the *x* side) of the triangle is 5, then the sides measure 5, $5\sqrt{3}$, and 10. This triangle is important because it is half of an equilateral triangle, and it allows us to find the height of an equilateral triangle, which is what we'll need in order to find the area of an equilateral triangle.

Try the following.

---

4 🔖 Mark for Review

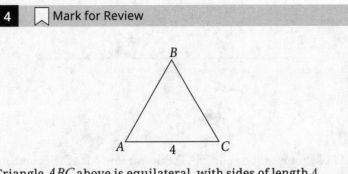

Triangle *ABC* above is equilateral, with sides of length 4.
What is its area?

Ⓐ 3

Ⓑ $4\sqrt{2}$

Ⓒ $4\sqrt{3}$

Ⓓ 8

Triangle Tip
An easy way to figure out the height of an equilateral triangle is to take half of its side and multiply it by the square root of 3.

Here's How to Crack It

The question asks for the area of an equilateral triangle with a given side length. First, redraw the figure on your scratch paper. To find the area of the triangle, we need to know the base and the height. The question tells you that the base $\overline{AC}$ is 4; now we need to find the height, which is *perpendicular* to the base. You can create the height by drawing a line from angle *B* straight down to the base. Now you have two 30°-60°-90° triangles, and you can use the rules of 30°-60°-90° triangles to figure out the height. Half of the base would be 2, and that's the side across from the 30° angle, so you would multiply it by $\sqrt{3}$ to get the height.

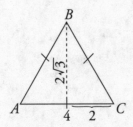

Now we know that the base is 4 and the height is $2\sqrt{3}$, so when we plug those numbers into the formula for area of a triangle, we get $A = \dfrac{1}{2} \times 4 \times 2\sqrt{3}$, which equals $4\sqrt{3}$. Thus, (C) is the correct answer.

SOHCAHTOA

Trigonometry will likely appear on your PSAT. But fear not! Many trigonometry questions you will see mostly require you to know the basic definitions of the three main trigonometric functions. SOHCAHTOA is a way to remember the three functions:

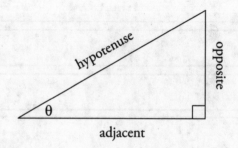

$$\text{sine } \theta = \frac{\text{opposite}}{\text{hypotenuse}} \qquad \text{cosine } \theta = \frac{\text{adjacent}}{\text{hypotenuse}} \qquad \text{tangent } \theta = \frac{\text{opposite}}{\text{adjacent}}$$

Let's see an example.

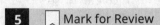

5 🔖 Mark for Review

In triangle DEF shown above, $\cos(E) = \dfrac{\sqrt{33}}{7}$. What is the value of $\tan(F)$?

(A) $\dfrac{4}{7}$

(B) $\dfrac{\sqrt{33}}{7}$

(C) $\dfrac{7\sqrt{33}}{33}$

(D) $\dfrac{\sqrt{33}}{4}$

Here's How to Crack It

The question asks for the value of the tangent in a right triangle. Start by redrawing the triangle on your scratch paper so you can mark it up. Next, write out SOHCAHTOA since the question is all about the trig functions. The CAH part of SOHCAHTOA defines the cosine as $\dfrac{\text{adjacent}}{\text{hypotenuse}}$, and the question states that the cosine of angle E is $\dfrac{\sqrt{33}}{7}$. Label the side adjacent to angle E as $\sqrt{33}$ and the hypotenuse as 7.

The TOA part of SOHCAHTOA defines the tangent as $\dfrac{\text{opposite}}{\text{adjacent}}$. The side opposite angle F is already labeled as $\sqrt{33}$. Use the Pythagorean Theorem to solve for the third side: $a^2 + \left(\sqrt{33}\right)^2 = 7^2$. This becomes $a^2 + 33 = 49$. Subtract 33 from both sides of the equation to get $a^2 = 16$. Take the square root of both sides of the equation to get $a = 4$. Label the side adjacent to angle F as 4.

Now that all three sides are labeled, plug in the correct sides to find the tangent of angle F, which is $\dfrac{\sqrt{33}}{4}$. The correct answer is (D).

Use Your Tools!

The online tools won't be very useful on this question because you can't mark the figure. But your scratch paper is enormously helpful on geometry and trig questions. Use it to redraw figures, label figures, write out formulas, and perform calculations. Your scratch paper should look something like this after finishing the previous question.

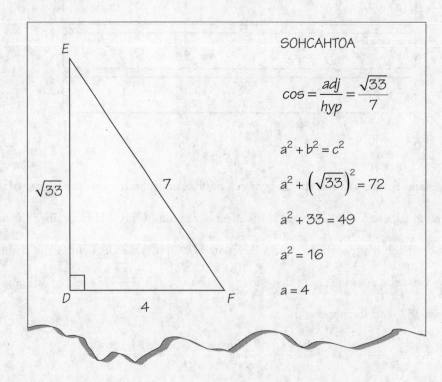

Similar Triangles

Similar triangles have the same shape, but they are not necessarily the same size. Having the same shape means that the angles of the triangles are identical and that the corresponding sides have the same ratio. Look at the following two similar triangles:

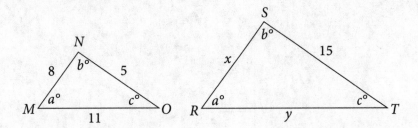

These two triangles both have the same set of angles, but they aren't the same size. Whenever this is true, the sides of one triangle are proportional to those of the other. Notice that sides $\overline{NO}$ and $\overline{ST}$ are both opposite the angle that is $a°$. These are called corresponding sides, because they correspond to the same angle. So, the lengths of $\overline{NO}$ and $\overline{ST}$ are proportional to each other. In order to figure out the lengths of the other sides, set up a proportion: $\dfrac{MN}{RS} = \dfrac{NO}{ST}$.

Now fill in the information that you know: $\dfrac{8}{x} = \dfrac{5}{15}$. Cross-multiply and you find that $x = 24$. You could also figure out the length of y: $\dfrac{NO}{ST} = \dfrac{MO}{RT}$. So, $\dfrac{5}{15} = \dfrac{11}{y}$, and $y = 33$. Whenever you have to deal with sides of similar triangles, just set up a proportion.

Give it a try.

○

---

6   🔖 Mark for Review

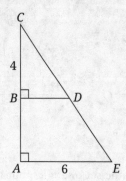

Note: Figure not drawn to scale.

If the area of triangle *ACE* is 18, what is the area of triangle *BCD*?

┌─────────┐
│   │
│ ───── │
└─────────┘

Here's How to Crack It

The question asks for the area of triangle *BCD*. Start by redrawing the figure on your scratch paper. It might help to draw the two triangles separately. The formula to find the area of a triangle is $A = \frac{1}{2}bh$. Plugging in the area and base of triangle *ACE* as given in the question and the figure gives you the equation $18 = \frac{1}{2}(6)h$. Simplify the fraction and you will get $18 = 3h$. Divide both sides by 3 and you can see that the height of triangle *ACE* is 6. Label this on your scratch paper. Because triangle *ACE* and triangle *BCD* have the same angle measures, they are similar. Therefore, create a proportion to find the length of $\overline{BD}$. The proportion should look like this: $\frac{4}{x} = \frac{6}{6}$, if *x* represents the length of $\overline{BD}$. Simplify your fractions and cross-multiply to see that *x* = 4. Plug the base and height of triangle *BCD* into the area formula: $A = \frac{1}{2}(4)(4)$. Simplify the equation and you will see that the area of triangle *BCD* is 8.

○

Drill 2

Answers can be found in Part IV.

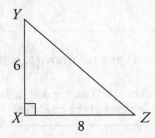

a.   What is the area of triangle *XYZ* above?

_____

b.   What is the length of *YZ*? _____

c.   What is the sine of ∠*Z*? _____

d.   If the area of the triangle above is 400, what is the length of *AC*? _____

e.   What is the length of *BC*? _____

f.   What is the cosine of ∠*C*? _____

1 ◻ Mark for Review

In similar triangles LMN and PQR, angles L and P are both 90°, and angles N and R have the same measure. If $\cos(Q) = \frac{24}{145}$, which of the following is the value of $\sin(N)$?

Ⓐ $\frac{24}{145}$

Ⓑ $\frac{143}{145}$

Ⓒ $\frac{143}{24}$

Ⓓ $\frac{145}{24}$

2 ◻ Mark for Review

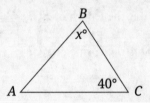

Note: Figure not drawn to scale.

In triangle ABC above, if $AB = BC$, what is the value of x?

3 ◻ Mark for Review

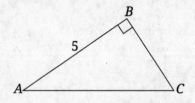

Note: Figure not drawn to scale.

In the figure above, if triangle ABC is isosceles, what is the perimeter of the triangle?

Ⓐ 12.5

Ⓑ $10\sqrt{2}$

Ⓒ $10 + 5\sqrt{2}$

Ⓓ $15\sqrt{2}$

4 ☐ Mark for Review

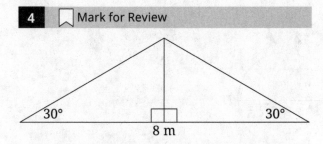

8 m

The owner of a barn needs to paint the front of the barn's roof. As shown in the figure above, the roof measures 8 m along the bottom, and the sides of the roof meet the bottom at a 30° angle. If one bucket of paint can cover 5 m², what is the minimum number of buckets the owner needs to purchase?

Ⓐ 1

Ⓑ 2

Ⓒ 3

Ⓓ 4

5 ☐ Mark for Review

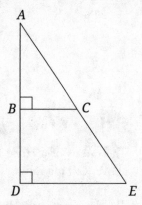

Note: Figure not drawn to scale.

In the figure above, if $AB = 5$, $AC = 13$, and $DE = 24$, what is the value of BD?

Ⓐ 5

Ⓑ 8

Ⓒ 10

Ⓓ 12

6 ☐ Mark for Review

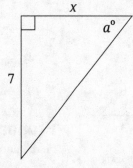

In the triangle above, $\tan a° = \frac{14}{15}$. What is the value of x?

CIRCLES

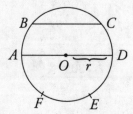

The **radius** of a circle is the distance from the center to the edge of the circle. In the figure above, $\overline{OD}$ is a radius, and so is $\overline{OA}$.

The **diameter** is the distance from one edge, through the center, to the other edge of the circle. The diameter will always be twice the measure of the radius and will always be the longest line you can draw through a circle. In the figure above, $\overline{AD}$ is a diameter.

A **chord** is any line drawn from one point on the edge of the circle to the other. In the figure above, $\overline{BC}$ is a chord. The diameter is the longest chord in a circle.

An **arc** is any section of the circumference (the edge) of the circle. $\overset{\frown}{EF}$ is an arc in the figure above.

The **circumference** is the distance around the outside edge of the circle. The circumference of a circle with radius r is $2\pi r$. A circle with radius of 5 has a circumference of 10π.

The **area** of a circle with radius r is πr^2. A circle with a radius of 5 has an area of 25π.

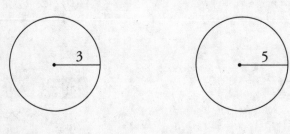

Area = 9π

Circumference = 6π

Area = 25π

Circumference = 10π

Proportionality in a Circle

Here's another rule that plays a role in more advanced circle questions.

> Arc measure is proportional to interior angle measure, which is proportional to sector area.

This means that whatever fraction of the total degree measure is made up by the interior angle, the arc described by that angle is the same fraction of the circumference, and the pie piece created has the same fraction of the area.

Take a look at the figure below.

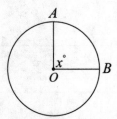

If angle x is equal to 90 degrees, which is one-quarter of 360 degrees, then arc $\overset{\frown}{AB}$ is equal to one-quarter of the circumference of the circle and the area of the sector of the circle enclosed by radii $\overline{OA}$ and $\overline{OB}$ is equal to one-quarter of the area of the circle.

To see how this works, try the following question.

---

7 🔖 Mark for Review

The circle above with center O has a radius of 4. If $x = 30$, what is the length of minor arc AB?

(A) $\dfrac{\pi}{6}$

(B) $\dfrac{2\pi}{3}$

(C) 3

(D) $\dfrac{3\pi}{2}$

Here's How to Crack It

The question asks for the length of minor arc AB. Since the interior angle x is equal to 30°, which is $\frac{1}{12}$ of 360°, we know that minor arc AB will be equal to $\frac{1}{12}$ of the circumference of the circle. Since the circle has radius 4, its circumference will be 8π. Therefore, arc AB will measure $\frac{1}{12} \times 8\pi$, or $\frac{2\pi}{3}$, (B).

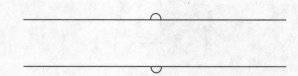

---

8 🔖 Mark for Review

Points A and B lie on a circle with center O such that the measure of angle OAB is 45°. If the area of the circle is 64π, what is the perimeter of triangle AOB?

(A) $8 + 8\sqrt{2}$

(B) $16 + 8\sqrt{2}$

(C) $16 + 16\sqrt{2}$

(D) $32 + 16\sqrt{2}$

Here's How to Crack It

The question asks for the perimeter of triangle AOB. This time a diagram isn't given, so drawing the circle on your scratch paper should be your first step. Since points A and B lie on the circle, $\overline{OA}$ and $\overline{OB}$ are both radii and equal in length, making $\triangle AOB$ isosceles. The question indicates that $\angle OAB$ is 45°, which means that $\angle OBA$ is also 45°, which makes $\triangle AOB$ a 45°-45°-90° triangle (remember those special right triangles?).

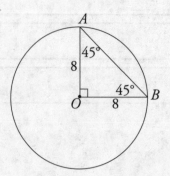

Given the circle's area of 64π, the radii of the circle (which are the legs of the isosceles right triangle) are 8 and the hypotenuse is $8\sqrt{2}$, making the perimeter $8 + 8 + 8\sqrt{2}$, or $16 + 8\sqrt{2}$, which is (B).

───────────○───────────

Tangents to a Circle

A tangent is a line that touches the edge of a circle at exactly one point. A radius drawn to the point of tangency forms a 90-degree angle with the tangent line. This comes up occasionally on hard questions, so take a look at the example below. As you work through this question, if you're thinking that you'd never know how to do it yourself, there's still a valuable lesson here, and it's that this question is not in your POOD, so you should look instead for a plug-in or something you're more familiar with.

───────────○───────────

9 ☐ Mark for Review

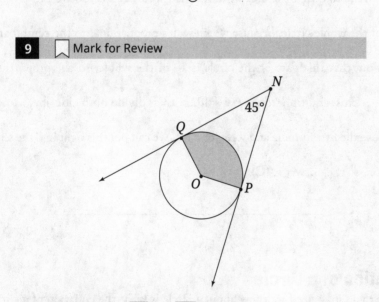

In the figure above, $\overline{NP}$ and $\overline{NQ}$ are tangent to the circle with center O at points P and Q, respectively. If the area of the shaded region is 24π, what is the circumference of the circle?

Ⓐ 8π

Ⓑ 12π

Ⓒ 16π

Ⓓ 40π

Here's How to Crack It

The question asks for the circumference of the circle. The key is remembering that any line or line segment drawn tangent to a circle is perpendicular to a radius drawn from the center of the circle to that tangent point; this means both $\angle OQN$ and $\angle OPN$ equal 90°. With $\angle QNP$ given as 45°, that leaves the central $\angle QOP$ of quadrilateral $QNPO$. Since all quadrilaterals contain 360° and the three angles mentioned so far account for $90 + 90 + 45 = 225°$, that remaining angle must be $360 - 225 = 135°$. As all circles contain 360° of arc, this means the shaded area represents $\dfrac{135}{360}$, or $\dfrac{3}{8}$, of the area of the entire circle.

Remember, we want to write down the formulas for quantities the question talks about, so that's $A = \pi r^2$ and $C = 2\pi r$. So far, we don't have anything we can put directly into a formula, so what do we know? We're told that the area of the shaded sector is 24π, so we can use that to figure out the area of the whole circle, because we know it's proportional to the central angle. In fact, we've figured out that this part of the circle is $\dfrac{3}{8}$ of the whole, so the proportion looks like this: $\dfrac{3}{8} = \dfrac{24\pi}{x}$. Cross-multiply to get $3x = 192\pi$, then divide both sides by 3 to get $x = 64\pi$. Now we can use the first formula and solve for $r = 8$. We can put this right into the second formula and get $C = 16\pi$, so the answer is (C).

The Equation of a Circle

One last thing you may need to know about a circle is what the equation of a circle in the xy-plane looks like.

The equation of a circle is as follows:

$$(x - h)^2 + (y - k)^2 = r^2$$

In the circle equation, the center of the circle is the point (h, k), and the radius of the circle is r.

Let's look at one.

---

10 ☐ Mark for Review

What is the equation of a circle with center (2, 4) that passes through the point (–6, –2)?

Ⓐ $(x + 2)^2 + (y + 4)^2 = 100$

Ⓑ $(x + 2)^2 + (y + 4)^2 = \sqrt{20}$

Ⓒ $(x - 2)^2 + (y - 4)^2 = 100$

Ⓓ $(x - 2)^2 + (y - 4)^2 = \sqrt{20}$

Here's How to Crack It

The question asks for the equation of a circle with a given center and containing a certain point. Take the given center and put it into the circle equation above. Plugging in $h = 2$ and $k = 4$, you get $(x - 2)^2 + (y - 4)^2 = r^2$. Eliminate (A) and (B) because they show the left side of the equation with incorrect signs. In the circle equation, x and y are the coordinates of a point on the circle. Plugging in the point (–6, –2), you get $(-6 - 2)^2 + (-2 - 4)^2 = r^2$, which simplifies to $(-8)^2 + (-6)^2 = r^2$, or $64 + 36 = r^2$. This means $r^2 = 100$, so the equation is $(x - 2)^2 + (y - 4)^2 = 100$. The correct answer is (C).

There is a chance that you might see a circle equation that is not in the form shown above. If this happens, you will need to complete the square to get the given equation into the proper form. The steps below show you how to do that. You may decide, however, that such a question is not worth your time. In that case, move on to something else!

To convert a circle equation to standard form, complete the square.

1. Move any constants over to the right side of the equation.
2. Factor out the coefficients on the squared terms if there are any.
3. Take half the coefficient on the x-term, square it, and add it to both sides of the equation.
4. Convert the x-terms and the number on the left to square form: $(x - h)^2$.
5. Do the same thing with the y-terms to get $(y - k)^2$.

Drill 3

Answers can be found in Part IV.

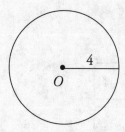

a. What is the area of the circle above with center O? _____

b. What is its circumference? _____

What is the center of a circle with equation $x^2 + y^2 - 2x + 8y + 8 = 0$?

Ⓐ $(-1, 4)$

Ⓑ $(1, -4)$

Ⓒ $(-2, 8)$

Ⓓ $(2, -8)$

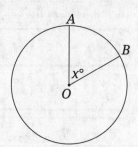

The circle shown above has its center at O. If $x = 60$ and the length of minor arc AB is 2π, what is the area of circle O?

Ⓐ 6

Ⓑ 6π

Ⓒ 12π

Ⓓ 36π

3 🔖 Mark for Review

A circle with center O has diameter $\overline{AB}$. Segment $\overline{AC}$ is tangent to the circle at point A and has a length of 5. If the area of the circle is 36π, what is the perimeter of triangle ABC?

Ⓐ 15

Ⓑ 25

Ⓒ 30

Ⓓ 60

4 🔖 Mark for Review

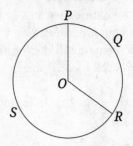

Note: Figure not drawn to scale.

Arc PSR is $\frac{4}{3}$ the length of arc PQR. The length of major arc PSR is 6π units. What is the radius of the circle?

VOLUME

Volume questions on the PSAT can seem intimidating at times. The PSAT sometimes gives you questions featuring unusual shapes such as pyramids and spheres. Luckily, the reference sheet contains all the formulas you will ever need for volume questions on the PSAT. Remember to click it open whenever you need a geometry formula that you don't have memorized.

Let's look at an example.

---

11 🔖 Mark for Review

A sphere has a volume of 36π. What is the surface area of the sphere? (The surface area of a sphere is given by the formula $A = 4\pi r^2$.)

Ⓐ 3π

Ⓑ 9π

Ⓒ 27π

Ⓓ 36π

Here's How to Crack It

The question asks for the surface area of a sphere with a given volume. Start by writing down the formula for the volume of a sphere from the reference sheet: $V = \dfrac{4}{3}\pi r^3$. Put what you know into the equation: $36\pi = \dfrac{4}{3}\pi r^3$. From this you can solve for r. Divide both sides by π to get $36 = \dfrac{4}{3}r^3$. Multiply both sides by 3 to clear the fraction: $36(3) = 4r^3$. Note that we left 36 as 36 because the next step is to divide both sides by 4, and 36 divided by 4 is 9, so $9(3) = r^3$ or $27 = r^3$. Take the cube root of both sides to get $r = 3$. Now that you have the radius, use the formula provided to find the surface area: $A = 4\pi(3)^2$, which comes out to 36π, (D).

PLUGGING IN ON GEOMETRY

You can also use Plugging In on geometry questions, just as you can for algebra. Any time that you have variables in the answer choices or hidden variables, use Plugging In! As long as you follow all the rules of geometry while you solve, you'll get the answer.

Take a look at this question.

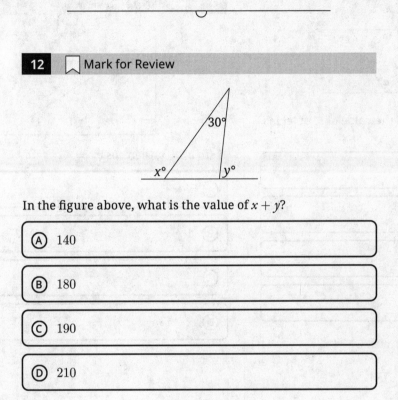

12 ☐ Mark for Review

In the figure above, what is the value of $x + y$?

Ⓐ 140

Ⓑ 180

Ⓒ 190

Ⓓ 210

Here's How to Crack It

The question asks for the value of $x + y$, which are two angle measures on a figure. You could answer this question using algebra, but why? You can plug in whatever numbers you want for the other angles inside the triangle—as long as you make sure that all the angles in the triangle add up to 180°. So, plug in 60 and 90 for the other angles inside that triangle. Now you can solve for x and y: if the angle next to x is 60°, then x will be equal to 120. If the angle next to y is equal to 90°, then y will be equal to 90. This makes the sum $x + y$ equal to 120 + 90, or 210. No matter what numbers we pick for the angles inside the triangle, we'll always get the same answer, (D).

Drill 4

Try to use Plugging In on the following questions. Answers can be found in Part IV.

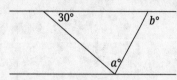

In the figure above, what is the value of b, in terms of a?

(A) $30 - a$

(B) $30 + a$

(C) $60 + a$

(D) $80 - a$

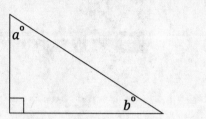

If $\sin a° = x$, then $\cos b° =$

(A) x

(B) $1 - x$

(C) $\dfrac{1}{x}$

(D) $x - 1$

3 ☐ Mark for Review

Cone A and Cone B are both right circular cones of the same height. If the radius of Cone A is $\frac{3}{4}$ of the radius of Cone B, which of the following is the ratio of the volume of Cone A to the volume of Cone B?

Ⓐ 27:64

Ⓑ 9:16

Ⓒ 3:4

Ⓓ 4:3

4 ☐ Mark for Review

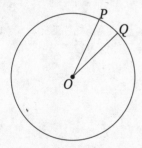

In the figure above, O is the center of the circle, the radius of the circle is x, and the length of minor arc PQ is $\frac{\pi x}{18}$. What is the area of sector POQ?

Ⓐ $\frac{\pi x^2}{36}$

Ⓑ $\frac{\pi x^2}{18}$

Ⓒ $\frac{\pi x^2}{9}$

Ⓓ $\frac{\pi x^2}{3}$

5 ☐ Mark for Review

Three spherical balls with radius r are contained in a rectangular box. Two of the balls are each touching 5 sides of the rectangular box and the middle ball. The middle ball also touches four sides of the rectangular box. What is the volume of the space between the balls and the rectangular box, in terms of r?

Ⓐ $r^3(3 - 4\pi)$

Ⓑ $4r^2(14 - \pi)$

Ⓒ $4r^3(6 - \pi)$

Ⓓ $12r^2(r - \pi)$

6 ☐ Mark for Review

A rectangular box is half as long as it is wide and one-third as wide as it is tall. If the volume of the box is 96, then what is its surface area? (Note: The formula for the volume of a rectangular solid is $V = lwh$.)

☐

Summary

o Be sure to review your basic geometry rules before the test; often, questions hinge on knowing that vertical angles are equal or that the sum of the angles in a quadrilateral is 360°.

o On all geometry questions, draw figures on your scratch paper and aggressively fill in everything you know.

o When two parallel lines are cut by a third line, the small angles are equal, the big angles are equal, and the sum of a big angle and a small angle is 180°.

o The perimeter of a rectangle is the sum of the lengths of its sides. The area of a rectangle is *length × width*.

o The perimeter of a triangle is the sum of the lengths of its sides. The area of a triangle is $\frac{1}{2}$ *base × height*.

o Knowing the Pythagorean Theorem, common Pythagorean triples (such as 3-4-5 and 5-12-13), and special right triangles (45°-45°-90° and 30°-60°-90°) will help you figure out angles and lengths in a right triangle.

o For trigonometry questions, remember SOHCAHTOA:

- sine $= \dfrac{opposite}{hypotenuse}$

- cosine $= \dfrac{adjacent}{hypotenuse}$

- tangent $= \dfrac{opposite}{adjacent}$

o   Similar triangles have the same angles, and their side lengths are proportional.

o   The circumference of a circle is $2\pi r$. The area of a circle is πr^2.

o   Circles that show an interior angle (an angle that extends from the center of the circle) have proportionality. The interior angle over the whole degree measure (360°) equals the same fraction as the arc enclosed by that angle over the circumference. Likewise, both of these fractions are equal to the area of the segment over the entire area of the circle.

o   When you see a line that is "tangent to" a circle, remember two things:
- The line touches the circle at exactly one point.
- The radius of the circle that intersects the tangent line is perpendicular (90°) to that tangent line.

o   The formulas to compute the volumes of many three-dimensional figures are supplied in the reference sheet that can be clicked open at any time during the Math section.

o   When plugging in on geometry questions, remember to use your knowledge of basic geometry rules; e.g., there are still 180° in a triangle when you're using Plugging In.

Part IV
Drill Answers
and Explanations

CHAPTER 7

Reading Drill (page 168)

1. **C**   The question asks for a word that *completes the text with the most logical word or phrase*, so this is a Vocabulary question. Read the text and highlight what can help you fill in the blank. In the dog-human relationship, the *dog grants the elderly person a true companion,* and the human is described as *providing the dog with shelter, food, medical care, and affection.* The human here is responding to the dog's positive contributions with some of his or her own, so write "gives back" or "returns the favor" in your annotation box. Choice (A), *diverges,* is the opposite of what we wrote—the human returns what the dog did in kind, rather than diverge from it. Eliminate (A). Choice (B), *exaggerates,* is extreme. The text doesn't support that the human is going too far, rather the human gives the appropriate positive reply to what the dog gave. Choice (C), *reciprocates,* is a good synonym for "gives back," so keep (C). Choice (D), *counters,* suggests a negative interaction between dog and human, which is the opposite of what is stated in the text. Eliminate (D). The correct answer is (C).

2. **B**   The question asks for the *overall structure of the text,* so this is a Purpose question. Read the text and highlight what can help understand the overall structure. The author states that *the war... was then at an end,* that the *vanquished... concluded they might wear their chains in peace,* and that they had *signed a bond of submission... purchasing life at the price of all that makes life estimable.* Write down in your annotation box that the Scots had "lost the war and hoped to keep their lives." Choice (A) mentions *one group's strategy for winning a war,* but no war strategy is ever discussed in the text. Eliminate (A). Choice (B) states that *it details the outcome of a war, and then explains a group's reasoning for accepting that outcome.* This is consistent with the annotation, so keep (B). Choice (C) is Half-Right: the group mentioned does seem distraught, but there is no mention of allies or speculation as to why allies haven't assisted the group. Eliminate (C). Choice (D) is also Half-Right: the passage does express concerns about foreign leadership, but no specifics of that government are mentioned in the text. Eliminate (D). The correct answer is (B).

3. **A**   The question asks *how would the author of Text 2 most likely respond to the underlined claim in Text 1,* so follow the Dual Texts Approach. The underlined claim in Text 1 states that *domesticated felines... did not respond when called by their owners.* Highlight this claim and see what should be highlighted in Text 2 regarding the same idea. Text 2 states that *cats increased their behavior intensity when directly addressed by the voice on their owners' audio* but did not show the same increase when listening to the audio from strangers. So, note in the annotation box that "Text 2 would disagree." Choice (A) is consistent with the author of Text 2 showing disagreement with Text 1's claim, so keep (A). Choice (B) is the opposite of what was annotated—Text 2 would not *strongly concur* with the claim from Text 1. Eliminate (B). Choice (C) is a Could Be True trap—as likely as it is that domesticated cats inherited their instincts from feral, or wild, ancestors, that doesn't mean the author of Text 2 would praise the claim. In fact, the annotation said that the author disagrees with the claim. Eliminate (C). Choice (D) is Half-Right

because the author of Text 2 probably would criticize the claim, but Text 1 never assumes that cats responded to the human voice before being domesticated. Eliminate (D). The correct answer is (A).

4. **C**   The question asks *why was the Cornish language declared extinct*, so this is a Retrieval question. Read the text and aim to highlight the exact reason given for the extinction. The text states directly that *the language experienced a sharp decline in users from 1300 to 1800, after which no living user of the language was recorded.* Choice (A) mentions that the language had *complex syntax*, but the text doesn't mention any features of language's construction. Eliminate (A). Choice (B) is Recycled Language: it misuses the word *linguists* from the text. Eliminate (B). Choice (C) is consistent with the highlighting, so keep (C). Choice (D) says that *it stopped spreading into new regions because it was surpassed by other languages*, but no other languages are mentioned in the text. Eliminate (D). The correct answer is (C).

5. **B**   The question asks *which choice best states the main idea of the text*, so this is a Main Idea question. Read the text and highlight the main phrases or lines that all of the other sentences seem to support. The author first states *A little while, a year agone, I knew her for a romping child* but then later states *And turning with a quick surprise, I wondered at her stateliness, I wondered at her altered eyes.* The lines indicate that the speaker is registering his surprise at how different the woman looks from before. Choice (A) Could Be True: we don't know from the text whether the speaker and the woman ever had a romantic relationship. Eliminate (A). Choice (B) is consistent with what was highlighted, so keep (B). Choice (C) states that *the speaker is an expert in observing subtle changes in others*, but this is the fact that he noticed big changes in one person does not make him an expert at noticing *subtle changes* in all people. Eliminate (C). Choice (D) states that *the speaker uses intricate and complex thought processes to impress those around him*, but while we get the speaker's thoughts, it would be an Extreme statement to say his thoughts are intricate and complex or that anyone is impressed by them. Eliminate (D). The correct answer is (B).

6. **D**   The question asks *which finding, if true, would most directly undermine the team's hypothesis*, so this is a Claims question that wants to find the hypothesis and then weaken it by selecting an answer as contradictory to the claim as possible. Read the text and highlight the claim, which is that *the team theorized that zebra stripes must confuse the biting flies' landing and biting patterns* which *reduces the number of bites each cow receives.* Choice (A) mentions *the number of bites caused by insects other than biting flies*, which are not referenced by the claim, so eliminate (A). Choice (B) is the Opposite of what is asked for as it would strengthen the claim, not undermine it. Eliminate (B). Choice (C) is an Opposite trap answer for the same reason: it strengthens the link between zebra stripes and reducing bites from biting flies. Eliminate (C). Choice (D) directly contradicts the team's hypothesis that zebra stripes lower bites caused by biting flies. Keep (D). The correct answer is (D).

7. **D**   The question asks *which choice most effectively uses date from the graph to illustrate the claim*, so this is a Charts question. The graph charts audio performance, video performance, and general performance satisfaction from 2018–2022. Read the text and highlight the claim or statement referencing as many of these ideas as possible. The last sentence states that a *notable aspect* of the study *is that consumer satisfaction with general performance does not always correlate with satisfaction with specific performance areas,*

so an answer that is as consistent with this claim as possible is needed. Choice (A) is the Opposite of what is asked for as it says that general performance satisfaction *correlated* with video performance satisfaction in 2018, but the claim says that they do not necessarily correlate, so eliminate (A). Choice (B) states that general performance satisfaction was consistently higher than video performance satisfaction for all five years, but this isn't consistent with the graph, so eliminate (B). Choice (C) is similarly inconsistent, as when general performance satisfaction hit its lows in 2019, that year is neither the highest for audio performance nor video performance. Eliminate (C). Choice (D) is consistent with the claim, as it shows that general performance satisfaction does not show any type of set relationship with video performance. Keep (D). The correct answer is (D).

8. **C** The question asks *which choices most logically completes the text*, so this is a Conclusions question: the right answer should reference the main ideas presented in the other sentences. Read the text and highlight the main ideas. The text states that tunnel hobbyists *simply continued digging once the initial job was completed* and that many of them *stated that the effort required to make their tunnels seemed disproportionate to the stated purpose*. Therefore, hobby tunneling must go beyond simply completing a goal or construction project. Choice (A) states that many tunnel hobbyists are uncertain of why they started their tunnels, but this is the Opposite of the examples given in the passage where the reasons are clearly stated. Eliminate (A). Choice (B) is Extreme as it says tunnel hobbyists should *only* build tunnels on their own properties, and as logical as such a restriction may seem, it's not discussed in the text. Choice (C) is consistent with the main ideas that were highlighted, so keep (C). Choice (D) states that *hobby tunneling can improve mental condition more than physical condition,* but this is Recycled Language as the passage never states which is bolstered more by hobby tunneling. Eliminate (D). The correct answer is (C).

CHAPTER 8

Punctuation Drill (page 195)

1. **B** In this Rules question, periods and question marks are changing in the answer choices, so it's testing questions versus statements. The sentence after the blank indicates that the team wants to *find out* something. Thus, the previous sentence must be asking a question that this is responding to. Eliminate (C) and (D). Next, compare (A) and (B). For a question, the verb must come before the subject. Choice (A) is phrased as a statement, so it's not correctly written. Eliminate (A). The correct answer is (B).

2. **D** In this Rules question, verb forms are changing in the answer choices, so it's testing sentence structure. Eliminate any answer that does not produce a complete sentence. Choices (A) and (C) contain *–ing* verbs, which in this case produce an incomplete sentence. Eliminate (A) and (C). The verb *to explore* also does not produce a complete sentence, so eliminate (B). With (D), the sentence states that the novel *explores the inner life and complexities of the main character*, which does make the sentence complete. The correct answer is (D).

3. **D** In this Rules question, pronouns and apostrophes are changing in the answer choices, so it's testing punctuation and consistency. Choice (A) means "they are," and it wouldn't be correct to say, "they are was," so eliminate (A). The pronoun *it* in (B) is not clear, so eliminate (B). Choice (C) uses the possessive pronoun *their*, but for this to be correct it would need to be followed by a noun that is being possessed. That isn't the case here, so eliminate (C). Choice (D) uses the correct form, *there*. The correct answer is (D).

4. **D** In this Rules question, punctuation is changing in the answer choices. One answer contains STOP punctuation, so use the Vertical Line Test. Write the words *Ball* and *for* on scratch paper with a vertical line in between. The first part of the sentence, *Cristina Ibarra's documentary Las Marthas follows two girls who are preparing to participate in the Colonial Ball*, is a complete idea, so mark it with a C. The second part of the sentence, *for over 100 years the ball in Laredo, Texas, has been part of the celebration of George Washington's birthday*, is also a complete idea, so mark it with a C. Since the sentence contains two complete ideas, it must have STOP or HALF-STOP punctuation. Eliminate (A), (B), and (C) because they can't connect two complete ideas. Only (D) uses STOP punctuation. The correct answer is (D).

5. **A** In this Rules question, punctuation is changing in the answer choices. Some answers contain STOP punctuation, so use the Vertical Line Test. Write the words *categories* and *though* on scratch paper with a vertical line in between. The first part of the sentence, *These winners share an average age (64) and geographical diversity with those in other categories*, is a complete idea, so mark it with a C. The second part of the sentence, *though they have not attended the same schools—not by a long shot*, is an incomplete idea, so mark it with an I. In this case, GO punctuation is needed, so eliminate (B) and (D), which are both STOP. Choices (A) and (C) both have a comma after *categories*, but (C) has an additional comma after *though*. There isn't a reason to put a comma after *though*, so eliminate (C). The correct answer is (A).

6. **C** In this Rules question, apostrophes with nouns are changing in the answer choices. Start with the first word and consider whether it is possessing anything. The posts belong to the company or companies, so eliminate (A), which doesn't have an apostrophe. Next, consider whether the second word is possessing anything. Nothing belongs to *posts*; it is plural but not possessive. Eliminate (D) because it has an apostrophe on *post*. Compare (B) and (C). Choice (B) is plural, while (C) is singular. The word *a* precedes the blank, which indicates that it refers to a single company. Eliminate (B). The correct answer is (C).

7. **B** In this Rules question, punctuation is changing in the answer choices. Some answers contain STOP or HALF-STOP punctuation, so use the Vertical Line Test. Write the words *pets* and *from* on scratch paper with a vertical line in between. The first part of the sentence, *For many years, veterinarians have provided a series of basic services for household pets*, is a complete idea, so mark it with a C. The second part of the sentence, *from basic check-ups and shots to neutering and defanging*, is an incomplete idea, so mark it with an I. To link a complete idea to an incomplete idea, HALF-STOP or GO punctuation is needed. Eliminate (A) and (C), as they are both STOP punctuation. While either a dash or no punctuation could potentially work, (D) has an extra comma after *from* that should not be there. Eliminate (D). The correct answer is (B).

8. **A** In this Rules question, punctuation is changing in the answer choices. Note that some answers have two dashes, suggesting unnecessary versus necessary information. There's also an option with a colon, so examine (B). This choice puts a colon after *Kevlar, a high-strength material used in*, which isn't a complete idea, so eliminate (B). Next, look for an unnecessary phrase. The phrase *a high-strength material used in personal armor, sports equipment, and musical instruments* describes Kevlar. Without it, the sentence still works, so this phrase is unnecessary and therefore should be surrounded by commas, dashes, or parentheses. Keep (A) because it puts dashes before and after the phrase. Eliminate (C) because the second dash is in the wrong spot, and the sentence does not work if the phrase *a high strength material* is removed. Eliminate (D) because it does not put a second comma after the phrase. The correct answer is (A).

9. **B** In this Rules question, punctuation changes in the answer choices. Only commas are changing, so decide whether each comma has a reason to exist. The first potential comma is in (C), after *tremendous*. The word *tremendous* describes *unemployment*, so there shouldn't be a comma in between. Eliminate (C). Next, (A) puts a comma before and after *among World War I veterans*. Removing this phrase from the sentence alters the meaning, as the first sentence sets up this sentence to relate to *veterans*. Thus, the phrase is necessary and should not be set off with punctuation. Eliminate (A). Choice (D) puts a comma after *veterans*, but there is no reason to put a comma here; in fact, a single comma should never separate a subject (in this case *unemployment*) and a verb (in this case *was seen*). Eliminate (D). The correct answer is (B).

10. **B** In this Rules question, punctuation changes in the answer choices. Notice that semicolons and commas are the only marks changing, which suggests that this could involve a list. Check the rest of the sentence to see whether there is a list of three or more things. The sentence does contain a list of three works in the same format: type of work, comma, title, comma, year. The first item contains the type of work, comma, and title, so the next thing is a comma. Eliminate (C) and (D) because they put a semicolon instead of a comma after the title. Compare (A) and (B). They both have the year next, but after that should be a semicolon because that is the end of the first item. Eliminate (A) because it doesn't have a semicolon after *in 2016*. The correct answer is (B).

CHAPTER 9

Grammar Drill (page 209)

1. **D** In this Rules question, verbs are changing in the answer choices, so it's testing consistency with verbs. Find and highlight the subject for the verb: *co-writers*. This subject is plural, so a plural verb is needed in order to be consistent. Eliminate (A), (B), and (C) because they are singular. Keep (D) because it is plural. The correct answer is (D).

2. **A**   In this Rules question, verbs are changing in the answer choices, so it's testing consistency with verbs. In this case, the verb is part of a list of two things, the first of which is *she studied*. Therefore, this verb should be consistent with *studied*, and you can highlight that word. Keep (A) because *obtained* is consistent with *studied*. Eliminate (B), (C), and (D) because they aren't consistent with *studied*. The correct answer is (A).

3. **B**   In this Rules question, pronouns are changing in the answer choices, so it's testing consistency with pronouns. Identify and highlight the noun or pronoun that the blank needs to refer back to. In this case, it's *A hikaye*, which is singular, so the pronoun needs to be singular in order to be consistent. Eliminate (A) because *they* is plural. Keep (B) because *it* is singular. Eliminate (C) because while *one* is singular, it's not appropriate to refer back to the work. Eliminate (D) because *you* doesn't refer back to the work. The correct answer is (B).

4. **A**   In this Rules question, verbs are changing in the answer choices, so it's testing consistency with verbs. All of the answers are consistent with the subject, *He,* so consider tense. The sentence uses the phrase *since 1976*, a phrase that you can highlight, so the answer must be in the right tense to describe something that has happened over time. Keep (A). Eliminate (B) because it describes an action that has ended, but there is no indication in the sentence that his teaching has ended, considering that the first verb is *is*. Eliminate (C) because the sentence is in a type of present tense, as indicated by *is* in the beginning of the sentence, and (C) is past tense. Eliminate (D) because *teaches* is not the right tense to describe something that started in the past and continues. The correct answer is (A).

5. **B**   In this Rules question, verbs are changing in the answer choices, so it's testing consistency with verbs. In this case, the verb is part of a list of two things, the first of which is *could grow*. Highlight that verb. Therefore, this verb should be consistent with *grow*. Eliminate (A) because *fertilizing* isn't consistent with *grow*. Keep (B) because *fertilize* and *grow* are in the same form. Eliminate (C) and (D) because *fertilized* and *fertilizes* aren't consistent with *grow*. The correct answer is (B).

6. **C**   In this Rules question, verbs are changing in the answer choices, so it's testing consistency with verbs. All of the answers are consistent with the subject, *Her interest*, so consider tense. The sentence describes an *experience* from Wauneka's past, so the verb should be in past tense. Eliminate (A), (B), and (D) because they are not past tense. Keep (C) because *was* is past tense. The correct answer is (C).

7. **D**   In this Rules question, pronouns are changing in the answer choices, so it's testing consistency with pronouns. Identify and highlight the noun or pronoun that the blank needs to refer back to. In this case, it's *birds*—the birds are presenting "themselves" *as potential mates*. Eliminate (A), which suggests that they present the feathers *as potential mates*, which isn't correct. Eliminate (B) and (C), which are singular and can't refer back to *birds*. The correct answer is (D).

8. **A**   In this Rules question, pronouns are changing in the answer choices, so it's testing consistency with pronouns. Identify and highlight the noun or pronoun that the blank needs to refer back to. In this case, it's *the beaver*, which is singular. The answer must be singular in order to be consistent. Eliminate (C) because *they* is plural. Keep (A) because *it* is singular. Eliminate (B) because it's not clear what *this* refers to. Eliminate (D) because it's not clear that *one* refers to the beaver population in general. The correct answer is (A).

9. **A**   In this Rules question, verbs are changing in the answer choices, so it's testing consistency with verbs. Find and highlight the subject for the verb: *Work*, which is singular. To be consistent, the verb in the answer choices must also be singular. Eliminate (B), (C), and (D) because they are plural. Keep (A) because it is singular. The correct answer is (A).

10. **C**   In this Rules question, the subjects of the answers are changing, which suggests it may be testing modifiers. Look for and highlight a modifying phrase: *Analyzing the genomes of existing populations and fossil DNA*. Whoever is *analyzing* needs to come immediately after the comma. Eliminate (A) because *donkeys* can't analyze anything. Eliminate (B) because *the research* itself can't analyze something. Keep (C) because *the scientists* did the analysis. Eliminate (D) because *the genetic information* didn't analyze anything. The correct answer is (C).

CHAPTER 10

Rhetoric Questions Drill (page 222)

1. **C**   This is a transition question, so follow the basic approach. Highlight ideas that relate to each other. The first sentence says that *Monopoly rewards players who compete*. The second sentence says that the original version *has a much different objective*. Therefore, the ideas disagree, and a contrasting transition is needed. Eliminate (A) and (D), which are same-direction transitions. *Regardless* is used to dismiss the previous idea, which isn't the correct relationship here, so eliminate (B). Choice (C), *By contrast*, is appropriate for the relationship between ideas here. The correct answer is (C).

2. **A**   This is a transition question, so follow the basic approach. Highlight ideas that relate to each other. The sentence before the blank says that the play *has been updated with each production*. This sentence states what the current version *added*, so it's an example of an update. Keep (A) because *For instance* is appropriate to introduce an example. Eliminate (B), (C), and (D) because they aren't used for examples. The correct answer is (A).

3. **C**   This is a transition question, so follow the basic approach. Highlight ideas that relate to each other. The sentence before the blank states that researchers *found nanoplastics* in *the larvae*. This sentence states that *they also found nanoplastics* in *the fish*. These ideas agree, so eliminate (D), which is a contrasting transition. Next, use POE. Eliminate (A) because *To that end* means "with that goal in mind," and there's no goal in the previous sentence. Eliminate (B) because this sentence is not providing specifics from the sentence before. Keep (C) because this sentence describes a similar finding in a different species. The correct answer is (C).

4. **B**   This is a transition question, so follow the basic approach. Highlight ideas that relate to each other. The sentence before states that *it may be too late* to save the dugong from extinction. This sentence states that *hope is not lost*, so these ideas contrast with each other. Eliminate (A) and (D), which are same-direction transitions. Keep (B) because it contrasts with the previous idea. Eliminate (C) because *Instead* suggests a substitute, which isn't the case here. The correct answer is (B).

5. **B**   This is a transition question, so follow the basic approach. Highlight ideas that relate to each other. The previous sentence states that the sculpture looks *like a large, silver bean*. This sentence states that it *has been nicknamed "The Bean."* These ideas agree, so eliminate (A) and (D), which are contrasting transitions. Keep (B) because *Indeed* is used to support the previous idea. Eliminate (C) because this sentence is not a conclusion based on evidence; it is simply reinforcing the appearance of the sculpture. The correct answer is (B).

6. **B**   This is a Rhetorical Synthesis question, so follow the basic approach. Highlight the goal(s) stated in the question: *present a possible explanation for the chimpanzees not "saying goodbye."* Then, go to POE. Eliminate (A) because it doesn't provide an *explanation*. Keep (B) because it states that the chimps *may not "say goodbye"* and follows that statement with *because*, indicating an explanation. Eliminate (C) because it doesn't explain why they don't "say goodbye." Eliminate (D) because it doesn't mention "saying goodbye" at all. The correct answer is (B).

7. **C**   This is a Rhetorical Synthesis question, so follow the basic approach. Highlight the goal(s) stated in the question: *various literary accolades*. Then, go to POE. Choice (A) mentions one *accolade* (award), but the question implies that the answer should reference multiple awards. Eliminate (A). Eliminate (B) because it says nothing about *accolades*. Keep (C) because it mentions two different awards. Eliminate (D) because it only mentions one *accolade*, not various ones. The correct answer is (C).

8. **B**   This is a Rhetorical Synthesis question, so follow the basic approach. Highlight the goal(s) stated in the question: *introduce crème brûlée* and *audience familiar with caramelization*. The answer should introduce crème brûlée but should not explain caramelization, as the audience is already familiar. Go to POE. Eliminate (A) because it explains caramelization unnecessarily. Keep (B) because it introduces crème brûlée and mentions caramelization without explaining it. Eliminate (C) because it doesn't actually *introduce* crème brûlée—it never says what it is. Eliminate (D) because it doesn't introduce crème brûlée, as it isn't mentioned at all. The correct answer is (B).

9. **B** This is a Rhetorical Synthesis question, so follow the basic approach. Highlight the goal(s) stated in the question: *introduce the main point* and *audience unfamiliar with US city and state names*. The answer should summarize the notes and explain the US location names, as the audience is unfamiliar. In this case, read the notes first, since the question is asking for a summary. The main point is provided in the first bullet: *Many place names in the US have French origins*. Then it gives examples of city and state names that come from French. Go to POE. Eliminate (A) because it doesn't explain what *Little Rock* and *Wisconsin* are, and the audience is unfamiliar according to the question. Keep (B) because it gives the main point and specifies which of the names are *cities* and which are *states*. Eliminate (C) and (D) because they don't summarize the main point, which is about both cities and states. The correct answer is (B).

10. **D** This is a Rhetorical Synthesis question, so follow the basic approach. Highlight the goal(s) stated in the question: *emphasize the two results of the study*. The correct answer must state *two results*. In this case, it may be necessary to read the notes to find out what the study did. The last two bullet points reveal the results: *reduced mowing was connected to an increase in the abundance of arthropods* and *reduced mowing was connected to an increase in the taxa richness (or diversity) of arthropods*. Go to POE. Eliminate (A) because it doesn't mention *two results* of the study—the first point is a general claim, not a result of the study. Eliminate (B) because it only mentions one result. Eliminate (C) because it doesn't give the *results*. Keep (D) because both results from the last two bullet points are given. The correct answer is (D).

CHAPTER 11

Drill 1 (page 231)

1. **c** Examples: –7, 0, 1, 8

2. **d** Examples: 0.5, 2, 118

3. **g** Examples: –0.5, –2, –118

4. **f** Examples: –4, 0, 10

5. **b** Examples: –5, 1, 17

6. **a** Examples: *Factors* of 12 are 1, 2, 3, 4, 6, and 12. Factors of 10 are 1, 2, 5, and 10.

7. **i** Examples: *Multiples* of 12 include –24, –12, 0, 12, 24, and so on. Multiples of 10 include –20, –10, 0, 10, 20, 30, and so on.

8. **h** Examples: 2, 3, 5, 7, 11, and so on. There are no negative *prime numbers*, and 1 is not prime.

9. **e** Examples: 3 and 4 are *distinct* numbers. –2 and 2 are also distinct.

10. **j** Examples: In the number 274, 2 is the *digit* in the hundreds place, 7 is the digit in the tens place, and 4 is the digit in the ones place.

11. **p** Examples: –1, 0, 1, and 2 are *consecutive* numbers. Be careful—sometimes you will be asked for *consecutive even* or *consecutive odd* numbers, in which case you would use just the odds or evens in a consecutive list of numbers.

12. **n** Examples: 6 is *divisible* by 2 and 3, but not by 4 or 5.

13. **l** Examples: When you divide 26 by 8, you get 3 with a *remainder* of 2 (2 is left over). When you divide 14 by 5, you get 2 with a remainder of 4 (4 is left over).

14. **k** Examples: When you add 2 and 3, you get a *sum* of 5. When you add –4 and 1, you get a sum of –3.

15. **r** Examples: When you multiply 2 and 3, you get a *product* of 6. When you multiply –4 and 1, you get a product of –4.

16. **m** Examples: When you subtract 2 from 3, you get a *difference* of 1. When you subtract –4 from 1, you get a difference of 5.

17. **q** Examples: When you divide 2 by 3, you get a quotient of $\frac{2}{3}$. When you divide –4 by 1, you get a quotient of –4.

18. **o** Examples: The absolute value of –3 is 3. The absolute value of 41 is 41.

Drill 2 (page 235)

a. 3^5 g. $2\sqrt{2}$
b. 3^1 h. -4
c. 3^6 i. $7\sqrt{3}$
d. x^8 j. $y\sqrt{y}$
e. x^4 k. $-y$
f. x^{12} l. $6x\sqrt{y}$

1. **A** The question asks for the value of a variable in an equation involving exponents. When given equivalent exponents with different bases, rewrite the exponent terms using the same base. Rewrite 3^4 as $3 \times 3 \times 3 \times 3 = 9 \times 9$. Therefore, $3^4 = 9^2$ and $x = 2$. An alternative solution is to calculate $3^4 = 81$. If $3^4 = 9^x$, then $81 = 9^x$, and $x = 2$. The correct answer is (A).

2. **B** The question asks for the value of a variable in an equation involving exponents. When dealing with questions about exponents, remember the MADSPM rules. The PM part of the acronym indicates that raising a base with an exponent to another Power means to Multiply the exponents. By the MADSPM rules, $(3^x)^3 = 3^{3x}$. If $3^{3x} = 3^{15}$, then $3x = 15$. Divide both sides by 3 to get $x = 5$. The correct answer is (B).

3. **D** The question asks for a possible value of a variable. Solve for s. To begin to isolate s, add 3 to both sides to get $\sqrt{s}$ = 12. Square both sides of the equation to get s = 144. The correct answer is (D).

4. **D** The question asks for an equivalent form of an expression. When dealing with a question about negative and fractional exponents, remember the exponent rules. Since x^6 doesn't change form, eliminate (C). A negative exponent means to take the reciprocal of what would be the result if the negative weren't there. Therefore, y^{-3} can be rewritten as $\dfrac{1}{y^3}$, so eliminate (A). In a fractional exponent, the numerator is the power the base is raised to and the denominator is the root of the base. Therefore, $z^{\frac{1}{2}}$ can be rewritten as $\sqrt{z}$, so eliminate (B). The correct answer is (D).

5. **A** The question asks for the value of a constant and refers to two functions that are equal to each other. Solve for B. Since the question states that the two functions are equivalent, set them equal to one another. Since $k^{0.3x} = k^{\frac{Bx}{9}}$, $0.3x = \dfrac{Bx}{9}$. To begin to isolate B, multiply both sides by 9 to get $2.7x = Bx$. Divide both sides by x to get $2.7 = B$. The correct answer is (A).

6. **C** The question asks for the value of a variable. Solve for m. To begin to isolate m, square both sides of the equation to get $m^2 + 39 = 64$. Subtract 39 from both sides of the equation to get $m^2 = 25$. Take the square root of both sides to get $m = 5$. Therefore, one possible value for m is 5. The correct answer is (C).

7. **D** The question asks for the value of an expression based on two equations involving exponents. When dealing with questions about exponents, remember the MADSPM rules. Take the two equations separately. The MA part of the MADSPM acronym indicates that multiplying matching bases means to add the exponents. If $x^y \times x^6 = x^{54}$, then $x^{y+6} = x^{54}$. Therefore, $y + 6 = 54$. Subtract 6 from both sides to get $y = 48$. The PM part of the MADSPM acronym indicates that raising a base with an exponent to another Power means to Multiply the exponents. If $(x^3)^z = x^9$, then $x^{3z} = x^9$. Therefore, $3z = 9$. Divide both sides by 3 to get $z = 3$. Now you know that $y = 48$ and $z = 3$, so $y + z = 51$. The correct answer is (D).

8. **A** The question asks for an equivalent form of an expression. Notice the fractional exponents in the answer choices; when dealing with a question about fractional exponents, remember the exponent rules. Start with applying the root to coefficient 81. Use a calculator to find $\sqrt[4]{81} = 3$. Eliminate (C) and (D) because these answer choices include the wrong coefficient. Next, apply the root to the b^3 term. In a fractional exponent, the numerator is the power the base is raised to and the denominator is the root of the base. Therefore, $\sqrt[4]{b^3} = b^{\frac{3}{4}}$. Eliminate (B) because this answer choice includes b^3 instead. Similarly, $\sqrt[4]{c} = c^{\frac{1}{4}}$, and (B) can be eliminated because it includes c instead. The correct answer is (A).

9. **B** The question asks for the value of a variable in an equation involving a fractional exponent. When dealing with a question about fractional exponents, remember the exponent rules: in a fractional exponent, the numerator is the power the base is raised to and the denominator is the root of the base. Therefore, $x^{\frac{5}{2}}$ can be written as $\sqrt[2]{x^5}$, so $\sqrt[2]{x^5} = 8x$. Solve for x. To begin to isolate x, square both sides of the equation to get $x^5 = 64x^2$. Divide by x^2 on each side. Remember the MADSPM rules: the DS part of

the MADSPM acronym indicates that Dividing matching bases means to Subtract the exponents. So, $\frac{x^5}{x^2} = x^3$, and $x^3 = 64$. Take the cube root of both sides to get $x = 4$. The correct answer is (B).

10. **B** The question asks for an equivalent form of an expression. When dealing with a question about fractional exponents, remember the exponent rules. In a fractional exponent, the numerator is the power the base is raised to and the denominator is the root of the base. Start with applying the fractional exponent to the coefficient of 3. Therefore, $3^{\frac{2}{3}} = \sqrt[3]{3^2}$, or $\sqrt[3]{9}$. Eliminate (A), (C), and (D) because they do not include the correct coefficient. Simplifying the m and n terms confirms this. Remember the MADSPM rules: the PM part of the MADSPM acronym indicates that raising a base with an exponent to a power means to multiply the exponents. Therefore, $(m^2)^{\frac{2}{3}} = m^{\frac{4}{3}}$. Similarly, $(n^{-3})^{\frac{2}{3}} = n^{-2}$. The correct answer is (B).

Drill 3 (page 248)

1. **B** The question asks for the relationship between two variables. Translate one piece of information at a time in order to build the equation. Translate *is* as equals, translate *2 more than* as + 2, and translate *one-fourth of the number b* as $\frac{1}{4}b$. The translated equation is $a = 2 + \frac{1}{4}b$. Rearrange the terms on the right side of the equation to get $a = \frac{1}{4}b + 2$. The correct answer is (B).

2. **C** The question asks for what is equivalent to bc. To solve, isolate bc on one side of the equation. Start by cross-multiplying to get $18ad = 20bc$. Divide both sides by 20 to get $bc = \frac{18ad}{20}$. Reduce the fraction to get $\frac{9ad}{10}$. The correct answer is (C).

3. **C** The question asks for a system of equations that can be solved to find the number of skis and the number of snowboards rented over the three-day weekend. Use Bite-Sized Pieces and translate the given information into equations. Start with the number of skis and snowboards. The number of skis and snowboards rented on Friday was 40, on Saturday was 55, and on Sunday was 85. The total number of skis and snowboards rented for the weekend is 180. In equation form, $s + b = 180$. Eliminate (A) and (D), which both contain the incorrect equation for the number of skis and snowboards rented. Next write an equation for the amount of money collected in rental fees. Skis are rented for $30 and snowboards are rented for $20. The rental fees collected were $1,100 on Friday, $1,400 on Saturday, and $2,100 on Sunday. The total amount of fees collected was $4,600. In equation form, $30s + 20b = 4,600$. Eliminate (B), which contains the incorrect equation for rental fees collected. The correct answer is (C).

4. **B** The question asks for the value of h. Isolate h on one side of the equation. Start by distributing the numbers in front of the parentheses to get $-4h - 20 = -6 + 3h + 14$. Combine like terms on the right side to get $-4h - 20 = 3h + 8$. Add $4h$ to both sides to get $-20 = 7h + 8$. Subtract 8 from both sides to get $-28 = 7h$. Divide both sides by 7 to get $h = -4$. The correct answer is (B).

5. **D** The question asks for the value of a. Since the equation has infinitely many solutions for x, any value of x can be used to find the value of a. Try out an easy number for x. If $x = 1$, the equation becomes $10(3(1) + a) - a(4(1) + 2) = 2a(1 + 4)$. Distribute the numbers before the parentheses to get $30 + 10a - 4a - 2a = 2a + 8a$. Combine like terms to get $30 + 4a = 10a$. Subtract $4a$ from both sides to get $30 = 6a$. Divide both sides by 6 to get $a = 5$. The correct answer is (D).

6. **C** The question asks for a certain number that works for the given information. Translate the English into math in order to write an equation. In math terms, "is" means equals, "more" is addition, and "times" is multiplication. The equation becomes $x = 3 + 7x$. Solve the equation for x. Subtract $7x$ from both sides to get $-6x = 3$. Divide both sides by -6 to get $x = \dfrac{3}{-6}$. Reduce to get $-\dfrac{1}{2}$. The correct answer is (C).

7. **D** The question asks for an inequality that represents all values of r. Translate the question in Bite-Sized Pieces and use Process of Elimination. The total number of recipes Ann will include in her book is the sum of 32 main dish recipes, 18 dessert recipes, and r additional recipes. The book will include up to 98 recipes, meaning the greatest possible number of recipes in the book is 98. This information can be written as the inequality $32 + 18 + r \le 98$. Subtract 32 and 18 from both sides to get $r \le 48$. Isolate r in the answer choices to find the one that matches $r \le 48$. For (A), add 50 to both sides to get $r \ge 148$. Eliminate (A). For (B), add 50 to both sides to get $r \le 148$. Eliminate (B). For (C), add r to both sides to get $98 - (32 + 18) \le r$, which becomes $48 \le r$. Eliminate (C). For (D), add r to both sides to get $98 - (32 + 18) \ge r$, which becomes $48 \ge r$. The correct answer is (D).

8. **B** The question asks for the value of m. Isolate m on one side of the equation. To start, multiply the whole equation by 21 to eliminate the fractions. $21\left(\dfrac{m + 9}{3} + 2\right) = 21\left(\dfrac{m - 2}{7} + 3\right)$ becomes $7(m + 9) + 42 = 3(m - 2) + 63$. Distribute to get $7m + 63 + 42 = 3m - 6 + 63$. Combine like terms to get $7m + 105 = 3m + 57$. Subtract $3m$ and 105 from both sides to get $4m = -48$. Divide both sides by 4 to get $m = -12$. The correct answer is (B).

9. **C** The question asks which equation represents a sale the students could make during the fundraiser. Translate the English into math to create a system of equations, and then solve the equations to find the prices for snickerdoodle and cinnamon cookies. The first sale described can be written as $2s + 7c = 14.00$. The second sale described can be written as $8s + 3c = 17.50$. Multiply the first equation by -4 to get $-8s - 28c = -56.00$, stack the equations, and add.

$$
\begin{aligned}
-8s - 28c &= -56.00 \\
+8s + 3c &= 17.50 \\
\hline
-25c &= -38.50
\end{aligned}
$$

Divide both sides by -25 to get $c = 1.54$. Plug in the value for c into the original first equation to get $2s + 7(1.54) = 14.00$. Subtract $7(1.54)$ from both sides and divide by 2 to get $s = 1.61$. Plug the values for s and c into the answer choices to find an equation that works. $2(1.61) + 3(1.54)$ does not equal 8, so eliminate (A). $4(1.61) + 6(1.54)$ does not equal 16.25, so eliminate (B). $6(1.61) + 5(1.54)$ does equal 17.36. The correct answer is (C).

10. **A** The question asks for the cost of ten eggs. Translate the English into math to create a system of equations and then solve the equations to find the price of eggs. The first purchase can be written as $5e + 4f = 5.50$. The second purchase can be written as $9e + 8f = 10.50$. Multiply the first equation by -2 to get $-10e - 8f = -11.00$, stack the equations, and add.

$$
\begin{array}{r}
-10e - 8f = -11.00 \\
\underline{9e + 8f = 10.50} \\
-e = -0.50
\end{array}
$$

Therefore, $e = 0.50$. Multiply 0.50 by 10 to find the price of 10 eggs, which is $5.00. The correct answer is (A).

Drill 4 (page 258)

a. 6

b. 6

c. −1

d. −1

e. 1

f. $6\sqrt{2}$

g. (0, 1)

1. **B** The question asks for the value of a constant in one of the two given equations. The slope-intercept form of the equation of a line is $y = mx + b$, where m is the slope and b is the y-intercept. So, the slope of the line given by the first equation is 6. The question states that the two equations are of perpendicular lines. The slopes of perpendicular lines are negative reciprocals, so the slope of the second line is $-\frac{1}{6}$. The second equation is also in slope-intercept form with a slope of c, so $c = -\frac{1}{6}$. The correct answer is (B).

2. **D** The question asks for the y-intercept of a line with a given equation. The slope-intercept form of the equation of a line is $y = mx + b$, where m is the slope and b is the y-intercept. Manipulate this equation to solve for y. Subtract $2x$ from both sides of the equation to get $3y = -2x + 12$, and then divide both sides by 3 to get $y = -\frac{2}{3}x + 4$. Therefore, the y-intercept is 4. The correct answer is (D).

3. **D** The question asks for an equation that represents a graph. To find the best equation, compare features of the graph to the answer choices. In the line shown, the point at which the line crosses the y-axis is 1, so the y-intercept is 1. Use the two points on the line, (0, 1) and (8, 0), to calculate the slope: $\frac{y_2 - y_1}{x_2 - x_1} = \frac{(0 - 1)}{(8 - 0)} = -\frac{1}{8}$. The correct answer must be the equation of a line with a slope of $-\frac{1}{8}$ and a y-intercept of 1. Rewrite the answers in the slope-intercept form of the equation, $y = mx + b$, where m is the slope of the line and b is the y-intercept. In (A), the equation becomes $2y = x - 8$, or $y = \frac{1}{2}x - 4$. The slope of this line is $\frac{1}{2}$, and the y-intercept is -4, so eliminate (A). In (B), the equation becomes

$4y = -x - 8$, or $y = -\frac{1}{4}x - 2$. The slope of this line is $-\frac{1}{4}$, and the y-intercept is -2, so eliminate (B). In (C), the equation becomes $8y = 3x + 8$, or $y = \frac{3}{8}x + 1$. The slope of this line is $\frac{3}{8}$, and the y-intercept is 1, so eliminate (C). In (D), the equation becomes $8y = -x + 8$, or $y = -\frac{1}{8}x + 1$. The slope of this line is $-\frac{1}{8}$, and the y-intercept is 1, which is the same as the slope and y-intercept of the line shown in the graph. The correct answer is (D).

4. **2**   The question asks for the sum of the x-coordinates of the two points of intersection of a system of equations. Since both equations are set equal to the same value, set the right sides of the two equations equal to each other and solve for x. This gives $4x^2 - 6x + 4 = 2x + 4$. Subtract $2x$ and 4 from both sides to set the equation equal to 0, so the equation becomes $4x^2 - 8x = 0$. Divide both sides of the equation by 4 to get $x^2 - 2x = 0$. Factor x out of the equation to get $x(x - 2) = 0$. Therefore, the two possible values for x are $x = 0$ and $x = 2$. Add these two values of x to find the sum: $0 + 2 = 2$. The correct answer is 2.

5. **B**   The question asks for the equation of a line that is parallel to a line shown in a graph. Parallel lines have equal slopes. Therefore, because the line in the graph has a negative slope, the correct answer will also have a negative slope. Eliminate (C) and (D) right away because they have positive slopes. Now find the exact slope of the line shown, and compare it with the remaining answers to see which line equation has the same slope. The slope of a line is determined by the equation $\frac{y_2 - y_1}{x_2 - x_1}$. Calculate the slope of the line shown to get $\frac{-1 - 0}{0 - (-3)} = -\frac{1}{3}$. The answers are all in the slope-intercept form of an equation, $y = mx + b$, where m = slope. Only (B) has a slope of $-\frac{1}{3}$. The correct answer is (B).

6. **D**   The question asks for the x-intercept of the line shown in the graph. The x-intercept of a line is the point where the line crosses the x-axis. The line in the graph has a positive x-intercept, so eliminate (A) and (B). To find the x-intercept, first find the slope of the line and then use one of the points given to determine the value of x. The slope of a line is determined by the equation $\frac{y_2 - y_1}{x_2 - x_1}$. The slope of the line shown is $\frac{-4 - (-2)}{-6 - (-2)} = \frac{-2}{-4}$. Continue to simplify the expression to find a slope of $\frac{1}{2}$. At the x-intercept, $y = 0$, so the coordinates for the x-intercept are $(x, 0)$. To find x, plug points $(x, 0)$ and $(-2, -2)$ into the slope equation and solve for x: $\frac{-2 - 0}{-2 - x} = \frac{1}{2}$; so, $\frac{-2}{-2 - x} = \frac{1}{2}$. Cross-multiply to get $-2 - x = -4$, or $-x = -2$. Therefore, $x = 2$. The correct answer is (D).

7. **B**   The question asks for the slope of a line shown in a graph. Use the two points on the line, $\left(-\dfrac{7}{2}, \dfrac{16}{3}\right)$ and $\left(\dfrac{11}{2}, -\dfrac{17}{3}\right)$, to calculate the slope: $\dfrac{y_2 - y_1}{x_2 - x_1} = \dfrac{-\dfrac{17}{3} - \dfrac{16}{3}}{\dfrac{11}{2} - \left(-\dfrac{7}{2}\right)} = \dfrac{-\dfrac{33}{3}}{\dfrac{18}{2}}$. Continue simplifying to get $-\dfrac{33}{3} \times \dfrac{2}{18} = -\dfrac{66}{54} = -\dfrac{11}{9}$. The correct answer is (B).

8. **A**   The question asks for an equation that represents a graph. To find the best equation, compare features of the graph to the answer choices. In the line shown, the point at which the line crosses the y-axis is -2, so the y-intercept is -2. The answers are all in the slope-intercept form, $y = mx + b$, where m is the slope and b is the y-intercept. Eliminate (B), which has a y-intercept of 2. Next, calculate the slope of the line with two points on the line. The given points are all in terms of a, so that variable will cancel out when the points are put into the slope formula: $\dfrac{y_2 - y_1}{x_2 - x_1}$. The slope becomes $\dfrac{2a - a}{\dfrac{9}{2}a - 3a} = \dfrac{a}{\dfrac{9}{2}a - \dfrac{6}{2}a} = \dfrac{a}{\dfrac{3}{2}a}$. Cancel the a in the numerator with the a in the denominator, then multiply the numerator and denominator by 2 to get rid of the fraction in the denominator. The resulting slope is $\dfrac{2}{\dfrac{3}{2}(2)} = \dfrac{2}{3}$. Eliminate (C) and (D) because they do not have this slope. The correct answer is (A).

Drill 5 (page 268)

1. **−625**   The question asks for the value of an expression. Use the given equation $5x^2 = 125$ to find the value of x. Divide both sides of the equation by 5 to get $x^2 = 25$. Squaring a negative number makes the result positive, so x could be 5 or −5. The question states that $x < 0$, so in this case $x = -5$. Plug $x = -5$ into $5x^3$ to get $5(-5)^3$. This equals $5(-125)$, or −625. The correct answer is −625.

2. **15/36**   The question asks for the value of z. Isolate z on one side of the equation. Follow order of operations, and start with the innermost parentheses. Distribute the number in front of the parentheses to get $z = 5 - 5[5z - 2 + 2z]$. Combine like terms in the brackets to get $z = 5 - 5[7z - 2]$. Distribute the number in front of the brackets to get $z = 5 - 35z + 10$. Combine like terms to get $z = 15 - 35z$. Add $35z$ to both sides to get $36z = 15$. Divide both sides by 36 to get $z = \dfrac{15}{36}$. This fits in the fill-in box, so there is no reason to reduce the fraction. The correct answer is 15/36.

3. **2** The question asks for the value of a variable in a system of equations. Solve the system of equations to find the value of b. Multiply the first equation by -2 to get $-6a - 4b = -74$, stack the equations, and add:

$$7a + 4b = 85$$
$$\underline{-6a - 4b = -74}$$
$$a = 11$$

Plug in 11 for a in the original first equation to get $3(11) + 2b = 37$ and then $33 + 2b = 37$. Subtract 33 from both sides to get $2b = 4$. Divide both sides by 2 to get $b = 2$. The correct answer is 2.

4. **100** The question asks for the number of ounces of Solution 2 used to make Solution 3. Use Bite-Sized Pieces to write an equation. Solution 3 is composed of 50 ounces of Solution 1 and x ounces of Solution 2. Solution 1 has a sugar content of 25%, and Solution 2 has a sugar content of 10%. Apply those sugar contents to the amounts of Solution 1 and Solution 2 in Solution 3 to get $0.25(50) + 0.10x$. Solution 3 has a sugar content of 15%; since Solution 3 is made up of 50 ounces of Solution 1 and x ounces of Solution 2, the expression $0.15(50 + x)$ represents Solution 3. Set the two expressions equal to each other to solve for x. $0.25(50) + 0.10x = 0.15(50 + x)$. Distribute the numbers in front of the parentheses to get $12.5 + 0.10x = 7.5 + 0.15x$. Subtract 7.5 from both sides to get $5 + 0.10x = 0.15x$. Subtract $0.10x$ from both sides to get $5 = 0.05x$. Divide both sides by 0.05 to get $x = 100$. The correct answer is 100.

5. **9** The question asks for the value of z. Isolate z on one side of the equation. Start by squaring both sides of the equation to get $(5 - \sqrt{z})(5 - \sqrt{z}) = z - 5$. Use FOIL on the left side to get $25 - 5\sqrt{z} - 5\sqrt{z} + z = z - 5$. Combine like terms to get $25 - 10\sqrt{z} + z = z - 5$. Subtract z and 25 from both sides to get $-10\sqrt{z} = -30$. Divide both sides by -10 to get $\sqrt{z} = 3$. Square both sides to get $z = 9$. The correct answer is 9.

6. **5** The question asks for the difference in temperature between the first and second day in Celsius. Start by converting the temperatures from Fahrenheit into Celsius. To convert to Celsius, subtract 32 and then multiply by $\frac{5}{9}$. The first temperature is $(95 - 32)\frac{5}{9} = 35$. The second temperature is $(86 - 32)\frac{5}{9} = 30$. The difference in temperature is $35 - 30 = 5$. The correct answer is 5.

7. **350** The question asks how much Moriah paid. Translate English into math to find how much Moriah paid. Moriah, m_1, and Mathew, m_2, paid a total of \$540. In equation form, $m_1 + m_2 = 540$. The amount Moriah paid was \$30 less than twice the amount Mathew paid. In equation form, $m_1 = 2m_2 - 30$. Plug the second equation into the first to get $2m_2 - 30 + m_2 = 540$. Combine like terms to get $3m_2 - 30 = 540$. Add 30 to both sides to get $3m_2 = 570$. Divide both sides by 3 to get $m_2 = 190$. \$190 is the amount Mathew paid. Moriah paid \$540 − \$190 = \$350. Do not include the dollar sign in your answer. The correct answer is 350.

CHAPTER 12

Drill 1 (page 280)

1. **C** The question asks for an equivalent expression. There are variables in the answers, so plug in. Make $x = 2$ and plug it into the expression. The expression becomes $-2(2) - [3(2) - 8(2)]$. Simplify the expression to get $-4 - (6 - 16)$, which becomes $-4 - (-10)$. Subtracting a negative is the same thing as adding, so the result is $-4 + 10 = 6$. This is the target value; circle it. Now plug $x = 2$ into the answer choices and eliminate any that do not match the target value of 6. Choice (A) becomes $-13(2) = -26$. This does not match the target, so eliminate (A). Choice (B) becomes $-7(2) = -14$; eliminate (B). Choice (C) becomes $3(2) = 6$. This matches the target, so keep (C), but check (D) just in case. Choice (D) becomes $9(2) = 18$; eliminate (D). The correct answer is (C).

2. **D** The question asks for the value of an expression. There are variables in the answer choices, so plug in. Pick numbers for a, b, and c such that $a = \dfrac{b}{c^2}$; $1 = \dfrac{4}{2^2}$, so make $a = 1$, $b = 4$, and $c = 2$. Now, $\dfrac{1}{b^2} = \dfrac{1}{4^2} = \dfrac{1}{16}$. This is the target value; circle it. Now plug $a = 1$ and $c = 2$ into the answer choices to see which one matches the target value. Choice (A) becomes $(1)(2)^2 = (1)(4)$. This becomes 4, which does not match the target, so eliminate (A). Choice (B) becomes $(1)^2(2)^4 = (1)(16)$. This becomes 16, so eliminate (B). Choice (C) becomes $\dfrac{1}{(1)(2)^2} = \dfrac{1}{(1)(4)}$. This becomes $\dfrac{1}{4}$, so eliminate (C). Choice (D) becomes $\dfrac{1}{(1)^2(2)^4} = \dfrac{1}{(1)(16)}$. This becomes $\dfrac{1}{16}$, which matches the target. The correct answer is (D).

3. **A** The question asks for the value of an expression. There are variables in the answer choices, so plug in. Make $p = 2$. The expression becomes $\dfrac{\frac{1}{8}}{2(2)} = \dfrac{\frac{1}{8}}{4}$. Continue simplifying to get $\dfrac{1}{8} \times \dfrac{1}{4} = \dfrac{1}{32}$. This is the target value; circle it. Now plug $p = 2$ into the answer choices to see which one matches the target value. Choice (A) becomes $\dfrac{1}{16(2)} = \dfrac{1}{32}$. This matches the target value, so keep (A), but check the remaining answers just in case. Choice (B) becomes $\dfrac{2}{4} = \dfrac{1}{2}$. This does not match the target, so eliminate (B). Choice (C) becomes $\dfrac{4}{2} = 2$. Eliminate (C). Choice (D) becomes $4(2) = 8$. Eliminate (D). The correct answer is (A).

4. **C** The question asks for an equation that models a specific situation. There are variables in the answer choices, so plug in. The variable c appears on the more complicated side of the equations in the answers, so plug in a value for c, which is the number of correct answers. The total number of questions is 50, so c must be less than 50. Make $c = 46$. Now work the question in Bite-Sized Pieces. The student got 46 questions correct and 4 questions wrong. The student earned 1 point for each of the 46 correct answers and lost $\frac{1}{4}$ point for each of the 4 incorrect answers. The student's score would be $(1)(46) - \frac{1}{4}(4) = 46 - 1$. Subtract $46 - 1 = 45$. This is the target answer; circle it. Now plug $c = 46$ into the answer choices to see which one matches the target value. Choice (A) becomes $S = 50 - 0.25(46) = 50 - 11.5$. This becomes 38.5, which does not match the target, so eliminate (A). Choice (B) becomes $S = 50 - 0.75(46) = 50 - 34.5$. This becomes 15.5, so eliminate (B). Choice (C) becomes $S = 46 - 0.25(50 - 46) = 46 - 0.25(4)$. Continue simplifying to get $46 - 1 = 45$. This matches the target. Keep (C), but check (D) just in case. Choice (D) becomes $S = 46 - 0.75(50 - 46) = 46 - 0.75(4)$. Continue simplifying to get $46 - 3 = 43$. Eliminate (D). The correct answer is (C).

5. **B** The question asks for an expression that models a specific situation. There are variables in the answer choices, so plug in. Make $m = 10$. If David goes over his limit by 10 megabytes, then David pays $25 + \$0.05(10) = \$25.50$. This is the target value; circle it. Now plug $m = 10$ into the answer choices to see which one matches the target value. Choice (A) becomes $25 + 1.05(10) = \$35.50$. This does not match the target, so eliminate (A). Choice (B) becomes $25 + 0.05(10) = \$25.50$. Keep (B) but check the remaining answers just in case. Choice (C) becomes $0.05(25 + 10) = \$1.75$. Eliminate (C). Choice (D) becomes $1.05(25 + 10) = \$36.75$. Eliminate (D). The correct answer is (B).

6. **D** The question asks for the value of a constant in the equivalent form of an expression. Although there are numbers in the answer choices, a question with a variable that asks for an equivalent expression is still a good chance to plug in. Make $x = 2$ and plug it into the expression. The expression becomes $2^2 + 4(2) - 4$, which becomes $4 + 8 - 4$, or 8. Plug $x = 2$ into the equivalent form of the expression to get $(2 + 2)^2 - a$, which becomes $(4)^2 - a$ and then $16 - a$. Since the two expressions are equivalent, set them equal to each other to get $8 = 16 - a$. Add a to both sides of the equation to get $a + 8 = 16$, then subtract 8 from both sides of the equation to get $a = 8$. The correct answer is (D).

7. **D** The question asks for a value in terms of a variable. There are variables in the answer choices, and the question includes the phrase *in terms of*, so plug in. The problem involves taking $\frac{1}{6}$ of the amount in the account, so choose a number for x that is divisible by 6. Make $x = 18$. Now work the question in Bite-Sized Pieces. $\frac{1}{6}$ of the $18 in the account is $18 \times \frac{1}{6} = 3$. That means Jodi withdraws $3 and has $18 - \$3 = \$15$

remaining. Then she withdraws another \$3 and has \$15 − \$3 = \$12 remaining. Next, Jodi deposits y dollars into her account. Make y = \$8. Jodi has \$12 + \$8 = \$20. Last, Jodi withdraws half the money in her account, so she withdraws \$10 and has \$20 − \$10 = \$10 left in her account. This is the target, circle it.

Plug x = 18 and y = 8 into the answer choices to see which one matches the target value. Choice (A) becomes $\frac{4(18) - 3(8)}{6} = \frac{72 - 24}{6}$. Continue simplifying the expression to get $\frac{48}{6}$ = 8. This does not match the target, so eliminate (A). Choice (B) becomes $\frac{3(18) - 5(8)}{6} = \frac{54 - 40}{6}$. Continue simplifying to get $\frac{14}{6} = \frac{7}{3}$. Eliminate (B). Choice (C) becomes $\frac{3(18) - 8}{6} = \frac{54 - 8}{6}$. Continue simplifying to get $\frac{46}{6} = \frac{23}{3}$. Eliminate (C). Choice (D) becomes $\frac{2(18) + 3(8)}{6} = \frac{36 + 24}{6}$. Continue simplifying to get $\frac{60}{6}$ = 10. This matches the target. The correct answer is (D).

Drill 2 (page 286)

1. **D** The question asks for the value of the variable n in the given equation. Since the question asks for a specific value and the answers contain numbers in increasing order, plug in the answers. Begin by labeling the answers as n and starting with (B), 3. Plug n = 3 into the equation and work the steps of the question. The equation becomes 2(3 + 5) = 3(3 − 2) + 8, or 2(8) = 3(1) + 8. This simplifies to 16 = 11, which is false. Eliminate (B). Next, try (C). Plug n = 4 into the equation to get 2(4 + 5) = 3(4 − 2) + 8, or 2(9) = 3(2) + 8. This simplifies to 18 = 14, which is false. Eliminate (C). Next, try (D). Plug n = 8 into the equation to get 2(8 + 5) = 3(8 − 2) + 8, or 2(13) = 3(6) + 8. This simplifies to 26 = 26, which is true. Since (D) works, stop here. The correct answer is (D).

2. **C** The question asks for the point that satisfies a system of inequalities. There are specific points in the answers, so plug in the answers. Test the ordered pairs in each inequality from the question and look for a pair that makes both inequalities true. Start by plugging (A) into the first inequality to get 2(−4) − (−1) > −3. This becomes −8 − (−1) > −3, or −7 > −3. Since this is not true, eliminate (A). Now plug the point in (B) into the first inequality to get 2(−3) − (−2) > −3. This becomes −6 − (−2) > −3, or −4 > −3. Since this is not true, eliminate (B). Now plug the point in (C) into the first inequality to get 2(−1) − (−1) > −3. This becomes −2 − (−1) > −3, or −1 > −3. This is true, but the point must work in both inequalities. Plugging the point in (C) into the second inequality gives 4(−1) + (−1) < 5. This becomes −4 + (−1) < 5, or −5 < 5. This is also true. The point in (C) satisfies both inequalities in the system. The correct answer is (C).

3. **D** The question asks for one possible value of the variable x in the given equation. Since the question asks

for a specific value and the answers contain numbers in increasing order, plug in the answers. Begin by

labeling the answers as x and starting with (C). Plug $x = \dfrac{1}{4}$ into the equation and work the steps of the ques-

tion. The equation becomes: $\dfrac{24\left(\dfrac{1}{4}\right)}{4} + \dfrac{1}{\frac{1}{4}} = 5$. This simplifies to $\dfrac{6}{4} + 4 = 5$. Since $\dfrac{6}{4}$ will not simplify to

a whole number, the left side of the equation cannot add up to a whole number and will not equal 5.

Eliminate (C). Next, try (D). Plug $x = \dfrac{1}{2}$ into the equation to get $\dfrac{24\left(\dfrac{1}{2}\right)}{4} + \dfrac{1}{\frac{1}{2}} = 5$. This simplifies to $\dfrac{12}{4}$

$+ 2 = 5$, or $3 + 2 = 5$. This is true. Since (D) works, stop here. The correct answer is (D).

4. **C** The question asks for the value of the variable x in the given equation. Since the question asks for a specific value and the answers contain numbers in increasing order, plug in the answers. Begin by labeling
the answers as x and working with (C). Plug $x = 3$ into the equation and work the steps of the question.
The equation becomes $3^{3+2} = 243$, or $3^5 = 243$. This simplifies to $243 = 243$, which is true. Since (C)
works, stop here. The correct answer is (C).

5. **A** The question asks for the value of the variable x in the given equation. Since the question asks for a specific value and the answers contain numbers in increasing order, plug in the answers. Begin by labeling
the answers as v and working with (C). Plug $v = -3$ into one of the equations and work the steps of the
question to solve for u. Plug $v = -3$ into the second equation because it does not contain fractions and
will be quicker to solve than the first equation. The equation becomes $2(-3) = 7 + 5u$, or $-6 = 7 + 5u$.
Solve for u to get $u = -\dfrac{13}{5}$. Next, plug the values for u and v into the first equation to see if the equation
holds true. The equation becomes $-\dfrac{5}{7} - \dfrac{11}{7}\left(-\dfrac{13}{5}\right) = -(-3)$. This simplifies to $-\dfrac{5}{7} + \dfrac{143}{35} = 3$, or $\dfrac{118}{35} = 3$.
This is not true, so eliminate (B). If it is not clear if a larger or smaller value is needed, just pick a direc-
tion to go in. Try (A) next. Plug $v = -4$ into the second equation to get $2(-4) = 7 + 5u$, or $-8 = 7 + 5u$.
Solve for u to get $u = -3$. Next, plug the values for u and v into the first equation to see if the equation
holds true. The equation becomes $-\dfrac{5}{7} - \dfrac{11}{7}(-3) = -(-4)$. This simplifies to $-\dfrac{5}{7} + \dfrac{33}{7} = 4$, or $\dfrac{28}{7} = 4$.
This is true. Since (A) works, stop here. The correct answer is (A).

6. **A** The question asks for a possible value of a variable in a system of inequalities. Since the question asks for a specific value and the answers contain numbers in increasing order, plug in the answers. Begin by labeling the answers as *y* and start with (B), 5. The point that is in the graph of the system becomes (8, 5). Plug both values into the second inequality to get 8 − 7(5) ≥ −12. Multiply on the left side of the inequality to get 8 − 35 ≥ −12, and then −27 ≥ −12. This is not true, so eliminate (B). It may be difficult to tell whether a larger or smaller number is needed, so pick a direction and try (C), 12. Plug the point (8, 12) into the second inequality to get 8 − 7(12) ≥ −12. Multiply on the left side of the inequality to get 8 − 84 ≥ −12, and then −76 ≥ −12. This is also not true, so eliminate (C). That was the wrong direction, so the answer must be (A). To check, plug the point (8, 2) into the second inequality to get 8 − 7(2) ≥ −12. Multiply on the left side of the inequality to get 8 − 14 ≥ −12, and then −6 ≥ −12. This is true, so stop here. The correct answer is (A).

7. **D** The question asks for the number of a certain type of item. Since the question asks for a specific value and the answers contain numbers in increasing order, plug in the answers. Begin by labeling the answers as "enchanted items" and start with (B), 4. The question states that *enchanted items are worth 15 points each*, so the player has 4 × 15 = 60 points from enchanted items. The question also states that the player *has 9 items*, which means the player has 9 − 4 = 5 normal items. Since *normal items are worth 4 points each*, the player has 5 × 4 = 20 points from normal items. The player thus has 60 + 20 = 80 total points. This does not match the information in the question that the player has 102 points, so eliminate (B). The result was too small by 22 points, so try a larger number and plug in (D), 6. The player has 6 × 15 = 90 points from enchanted items. The player has 9 − 6 = 3 normal items and 3 × 4 = 12 points from normal items. The player thus has 90 + 12 = 102 total points. This matches the information in the question, so stop here. The correct answer is (D).

Drill 3 (page 305)

a. 90
b. 320
c. 6
d. $x = 8$
e. 5
f. 3
g. 10
h. 120%
i. 108
j. 10%

k. $\dfrac{2,600}{18,600}$ = approximately 14%

The amount of money in a savings account after *m* months is modeled by the function $f(m) = 1,000(1.01)^m$.

l. $1,000
m. 1%
n. 40
o. 1.5
p. 5 kPa

1. **D** The question asks for an unknown value in relation to three known values. This relationship is a proportion, or direct variation, so set up two equal fractions, being sure to match the units. $\frac{10 \text{ pecks}}{2.5 \text{ bushels}} = \frac{x \text{ pecks}}{4 \text{ bushels}}$. Solve for x by cross-multiplying: $(4)(10) = (2.5)(x)$. Divide both sides of the equation by 2.5 to get $x = 16$. The correct answer is (D).

2. **B** The question asks for an expression that represents a specific situation. Use Bite-Sized Pieces to eliminate answer choices. The air squad is decreasing the size of the fire by a certain percent over time, so this question is about exponential decay. When the decay rate is a percent of the total, the decay formula is *final amount* = (*original amount*)$(1 - rate)^{number\ of\ changes}$. In this case, $F(t)$ is the final amount, and the question asks for the right side of the formula. The original amount is 10, so eliminate (D) because it does not include 10. The original amount must be multiplied by $(1 - rate)$, so eliminate (A) and (C), which use subtraction instead of multiplication. The only remaining answer is (B), and it matches the decay formula: the rate of 7%, or 0.07, is subtracted from 1, and this amount is raised to a power of $\frac{t}{12}$. In this case, t is the number of hours the fire has been burning, and the change happens every 12 hours. To see this, plug in $t = 24$. In 24 hours, there should be 2 changes, and indeed $\frac{24}{12} = 2$. The correct answer is (B).

3. **84** The question asks for an average based on two other averages. For averages, use the formula $T = AN$, in which T is the total, A is the average, and N is the number of things. For the first three tests, 80 is the average and 3 is the number of things. The formula becomes $T = (3)(80) = 240$. Use the formula again for the last two tests, with 90 as the average and 2 as the number of things to get $T = (2)(90) = 180$. Now, use the formula one more time to find the average for all five tests. The total for all 5 tests is $240 + 180 = 420$, so the formula becomes $420 = A(5)$. Divide both sides by 5 to get $84 = A$. The correct answer is 84.

4. **C** The question asks for an amount after a period of time. The amount remaining to pay on the student loans is decreasing by one-half every 5 years, so use the formula for growth or decay by a multiplier. That formula is *final amount* = (*original amount*)$(multiplier)^{number\ of\ changes}$. In this case, $20,000 is the *original amount*. If the amount decreases by $\frac{1}{2}$, there is $1 - \frac{1}{2} = \frac{1}{2}$ left after every decrease, so $\frac{1}{2}$ is the *multiplier*. Read carefully to find the *number of changes*. The question states that the amount is reduced *every 5 years* and asks about *after 20 years*. The number of changes is thus $\frac{20}{5} = 4$. The formula becomes *final amount* = $(20,000)\left(\frac{1}{2}\right)^4$ Use a calculator or solve by hand to get *final amount* = $(20,000)\left(\frac{1}{16}\right)$, and then *final amount* = $1,250. The correct answer is (C).

5. **C** The question asks for a percent difference between two values. To find the percent change between numbers, use the formula $\frac{difference}{original} \times 100$. Read the table carefully to find the values. The question asks about *the number of registered Republicans who plan to vote for Candidate B*, which is 70, and *the number of registered Democrats who plan to vote for Candidate B*, which is 56. The question asks *what percent greater*, which means the *original* amount will be the smaller number. Put these numbers into the percent change formula to get $\frac{70-56}{56} \times 100 = 25$. The correct answer is (C).

6. **C** The question asks for the percent difference between two times. The question gives information about averages, so use the formula $T = AN$, in which T is the total, A is the average, and N is the number of things. For Everett's drive, the total is 594 miles, and the average is 66 miles per hour. The formula becomes $594 = (66)(N)$. Divide both sides of the equation by 66 to get $N = 9$ hours. For the parents' drive, the total is 594 miles, and the average is 54 miles per hour. The equation becomes $594 = (54)(N)$. Divide both sides of the equation by 54 to get $N = 11$ hours. To find the percent difference between the two travel times, use the formula $percent\ change = \frac{difference}{original} \times 100$. The question asks for the *percent less*, which means the original is the larger number. The formula becomes $percent\ change = \frac{11-9}{11} \times 100$. Solve to get $percent\ change = \frac{2}{11} \times 100$, and then percent change = $18.\overline{18}$. The correct answer is (C).

7. $\frac{5}{6}$ The question asks for a probability, which is defined as $probability = \frac{number\ of\ outcomes\ you\ want}{number\ of\ possible\ outcomes}$. Read the table carefully to find the right numbers. The question asks for the probability that a cell phone user in 2022 is a contracted user, so look at the row labeled 2022. In 2022, there were 225 contracted users, so that is the *number of outcomes you want*. There were 270 total cell phone users in 2022, so that is the *number of possible outcomes*. Therefore, the probability is $\frac{225}{270}$. Reduce the fraction to get $\frac{5}{6}$, or express it as a decimal, which is $0.8\overline{33}$. Fill in either the fraction or the decimal. To fill in a repeating decimal, include as many places as will fit or round at the end, so fill in .8333 or .8334. The correct answer is $\frac{5}{6}$, .8333 or .8334.

8. **45** The question asks for the time it takes to do a certain amount of work at a certain rate, so use the rate formula and pay close attention to the units. The formula is $W = RT$, in which W is the amount of work done, R is the rate or speed, and T is the time. The question says that Marcia and David *work together*, so start by finding their combined rate. If Marcia types 18 pages per hour and David types 14 pages per hour, then together they will be able to type $18 + 14 = 32$ pages per hour. The total number of pages

they need to type is 24. Use the rate formula with 32 as the rate and 24 as the work to get 24 = (32)T. To find the time in hours that it takes Marcia and David to type 24 pages, divide both sides by 32 to get 0.75 hours = T. The question asks *how many minutes* the work will take, so multiply 0.75 × 60 = 45 minutes. The correct answer is 45.

CHAPTER 13

Drill 1 (page 317)

1. **C** The question asks for a certain form of the equation. There are many forms in which a quadratic can be written. To see x-intercepts or solutions, a quadratic must be in factored form, since factoring is used to find solutions. The factored form is $y = a(x - m)(x - n)$, where m and n are the x-intercepts. Only (C) is in this form. The correct answer is (C).

2. **C** The question asks for the equation of a function. Notice that there are variables in the question and in the answer choices, so try to plug in. Since m represents months, plug in a number that works easily with the question. The number must be within the range $0 \le m \le 36$, so choose $m = 10$. After 10 months, the total amount paid will be: \$3,200 (the down payment) + \$380 × 10 months, or 3,200 + (380)(10) = \$7,000. This is the target value; circle it. Now plug $m = 10$ into each answer choice to see which one matches the target value. Choice (A) becomes $f(10) = 380 + 3,200(10)$. $3,200(10)$ is much larger than the target value, so eliminate (A). Choice (B) becomes $f(10) = 3,200 + 36(10)$, or 3,560. This does not match the target value, so eliminate (B). Choice (C) becomes $f(10) = 3,200 + 380(10)$. This matches the target value, so keep (C), but check (D) just in case. Choice (D) becomes $f(10) = 10,480 - 380(10)$, or 6,680. This does not match the target value, so eliminate (D). The correct answer is (C).

3. **C** The question asks for the value of the constant a. The question states that the number of bonus points increases by 25 when the number of purchases (p) increases by 4. To avoid working with multiple variables, pick a starting number for p. If $p = 0$, then the number of bonus points is: $B(p) = a(0) + 7$, or 7. When the number of purchases is increased by 4, the number of bonus points increases by 25. So, if $p = 0 + 4 = 4$, then $B(p) = 7 + 25 = 32$. To find the value of a, plug $B(p) = 32$ and $p = 4$ into the equation and solve for a. The equation becomes $32 = a(4) + 7$, or $32 = 4a + 7$. This simplifies to $25 = 4a$, or $a = 6.25$. The correct answer is (C).

4. **B** The question asks for the value of a variable in the table. Since the values in the table are part of a *linear function*, they must all lie on the same line. Recall that, in function notation, the number inside the parentheses is the x-value that goes into the function, and the value that comes out of the function is the y-value. Plug the x- and y-values into the slope formula to find the value of j. The slope

formula is $slope = \dfrac{y_2 - y_1}{x_2 - x_1}$. Plug the two known points, (–1, 2) and (5, –6), into the equation. The equation becomes $slope = \dfrac{-6 - 2}{5 - (-1)} = \dfrac{-8}{6} = \dfrac{-4}{3}$. Now use the slope of the line and one of the known points to solve for j. Plug (j, j) and (–1, 2) into the slope equation. The equation becomes $\dfrac{-4}{3} = \dfrac{2 - j}{-1 - j}$. Cross-multiply to get $-4(-1 - j) = 3(2 - j)$, or $4 + 4j = 6 - 3j$. Add $3j$ to both sides and subtract 4 from both sides to get $7j = 2$. Divide both sides by 7 to get $j = \dfrac{2}{7}$. The correct answer is (B).

5. **D** The question asks for the value of an expression made of two functions. To solve, first evaluate each function. In function notation, the number inside the parentheses is the x-value that goes into the function, and the value that comes out of the function is the y-value. Start with the top function. Plug $x = 8$ into the $f(x)$ function to get $f(8) = 8^{-\frac{2}{3}}$. Remember the rules of exponents: when a value is raised to a negative exponent, take the reciprocal and make the exponent positive. So, $8^{-\frac{2}{3}} = \dfrac{1}{8^{\frac{2}{3}}}$. When dealing with fractional exponents, remember that the numerator raises the base to a power and the denominator takes a root of the base. So, $\dfrac{1}{8^{\frac{2}{3}}} = \dfrac{1}{\sqrt[3]{8^2}} = \dfrac{1}{\sqrt[3]{64}} = \dfrac{1}{4}$. Next, find $f(3)$. Plug $x = 3$ into the $f(x)$ function to get $f(3) = 3^{-\frac{2}{3}}$. This is equivalent to $\dfrac{1}{3^{\frac{2}{3}}} = \dfrac{1}{\sqrt[3]{3^2}} = \dfrac{1}{\sqrt[3]{9}}$. Simplifying this expression any further will give a complex decimal, so it is easier to leave it as a fraction. $\dfrac{f(8)}{f(3)} = \dfrac{\frac{1}{4}}{\frac{1}{\sqrt[3]{9}}} = \dfrac{1}{4} \times \dfrac{\sqrt[3]{9}}{1} = \dfrac{\sqrt[3]{9}}{4}$. The correct answer is (D).

6. **B** The question asks for the equation of a function. In function notation, the number inside the parentheses is the x-value that goes into the function, and the value that comes out of the function is the y-value. The question gives two values for each, and the correct function must work for both. Start by plugging $x = 2$ and $f(x) = -5$ into each answer choice and eliminate any that don't work. Choice (A) becomes $-5 = 5(2) - 25$, then $-5 = 10 - 25$, then $-5 = -15$. This is not true, so eliminate (A). Choice (B) becomes $-5 = 10(2) - 25$, then $-5 = 20 - 25$, then $-5 = -5$. This is true, so keep (B), but check the remaining answers. Choice (C) becomes $-5 = 10(2) - 5$, then $-5 = 20 - 5$, then $-5 = 15$. This is not true; eliminate (C). Choice (D) becomes $-5 = 10(2)$, then $-5 = 20$. This is not true; eliminate (D). Choice (B) also works when $x = 4$ and $f(x) = 15$ since $15 = 10(4) - 25$. The correct answer is (B).

7. **148** The question asks for a comparison between the values of two different functions. In function nota-tion, the number inside the parentheses is the x-value that goes into the function, and the value that comes out of the function is the y-value. Since the question asks for the values of each function when $x = 12$, it asks for the y-values of each function at this point. First, plug $x = 12$ into the f function to get $f(12) = 12^2 - 4 = 144 - 4 = 140$. Now plug $x = 12$ into the g function to get $g(12) = -\frac{1}{3}(12) - 4 = -4 - 4 = -8$. At $x = 12$, $f(x)$ is $140 - (-8) = 148$ greater than $g(x)$. The correct answer is 148.

Drill 2 (page 330)

1. **B** The question asks for the value of t. Since the question asks for a specific value and the answers contain numbers in increasing order, plug in the answers. Begin by labeling the answers as t and starting with (B), –5. The equation becomes $12 - (-5 + 2)^2 = 3$ or $12 - (-3)^2 = 3$. This becomes $12 - 9 = 3$, which is true, so stop here. The correct answer is (B).

2. **A** The question asks for an equivalent form of an expression. There are variables in the answer choices, so plug in. Make $x = 3$ and $y = 2$. The expression becomes $3^4 - 2^4 = 81 - 16 = 65$. This is the target value; circle it. Now plug $x = 3$ and $y = 2$ into the answer choices to see which one matches the target value. Choice (A) becomes $(3 + 2)(3 - 2)(3^2 + 2^2) = (5)(1)(9 + 4) = (5)(1)(13) = 65$. This matches the target value, so keep (A), but check the remaining answers just in case. Choice (B) becomes $(3 + 2)^2(3^2 + 2^2) = (5^2)(9 + 4) = (25)(13) = 325$. Eliminate (B). Choice (C) becomes $(3 - 2)^2(3^2 + 2^2) = (1)^2(9 + 4) = (1)(13) = 13$. Eliminate (C). Choice (D) becomes $(3 + 2)(3 - 2)(3^2 - 2^2) = (5)(1)(9 - 4) = (5)(1)(5) = 25$. Eliminate (D). The correct answer is (A).

3. **C** The question asks for an equation with a vertex of (–5, 2). There are variables in the answer choices, so plug in. Use the given point to make $x = -5$ and $y = 2$. Now plug $x = -5$ and $y = 2$ into the answer choices to see which one is true. Choice (A) becomes $2 = (-5 + 5)^2 - 2 = (0)^2 - 2 = -2$. Since $2 = -2$ is not true, eliminate (A). Choice (B) becomes $2 = (-5 - 5)^2 - 2 = (-10)^2 - 2 = 100 - 2 = 98$, which is not true. Eliminate (B). Choice (C) becomes $2 = (2)(-5 + 5)^2 + 2 = 2(0)^2 + 2 = 0 + 2 = 2$. Keep (C), but check (D) just in case. Choice (D) becomes $2 = 2(-5 - 5)^2 + 2 = 2(-10)^2 + 2 = 2(100) + 2 = 200 + 2 = 202$. Eliminate (D). The correct answer is (C).

4. **3** The question asks for the price per donut, x, that a donut shop should charge to maximize its profit, P. To see the maximum, the quadratic must be in vertex form since the vertex is that value. The vertex form is $y = a(x - h)^2 + k$, in which (h, k) is the vertex. The equation given in the question is $P = -4(x - 3)^2 + 2{,}000$, which is already in vertex form, so the vertex is (3, 2,000). The x-coordinate is the price, so the shop should charge $3. The correct answer is 3.

5. **A** The question asks what represents the initial height of a projectile. The initial height of the projectile corresponds to the moment that it is launched before it ever moves, with t equal to the seconds since its launch. The function $h(t)$ represents the height h at time t, so $h(0)$ represents the height when $t = 0$. The correct answer is (A).

6. **B** The question asks for an equation that matches the graph. The answer choices are quadratic equations that have already been factored, so use the roots from the graph to eliminate wrong answers. The roots, or solutions, of a graph are where it crosses the x-axis: look at the graph to see that the correct solutions will be –3 and 1. Eliminate (C) and (D), which have a 4 in one of the factors instead of 1 and 3. To decide between (A) and (B), plug in a point from the graph. The vertex appears to be at $(-1, 4)$. Plug $x = -1$ and $y = 4$ into (A) to get $4 = -(-1 - 3)(-1 + 1)$. This becomes $4 = -(-4)(0)$ or $4 = 0$. This is not true, so eliminate (A), but check (B) just in case. Choice (B) becomes $4 = -(-1 + 3)(-1 - 1)$ or $4 = -(2)(-2)$. This simplifies to $4 = 4$. The correct answer is (B).

7. **3** The question asks for the value of a function. In function notation, the number inside the parentheses is the x-value that goes into the function, and the value that comes out of the function is the y-value. Therefore, $x = a$ and $f(x) = f(a) = 10$. Plug $x = a$ into the function to get $f(a) = a^2 - a + 4$. Since $f(a) = 10$, replace $f(a)$ with 10 to get $10 = a^2 - a + 4$. To solve for a, subtract 10 from both sides of the equation and factor. The equation becomes $0 = a^2 - a - 6$, which can be factored into $0 = (a - 3)(a + 2)$. Set both factors equal to 0 to get $a = 3$ or $a = -2$. There are two possible solutions to this equation, but the question states that a is *non-negative*, so –2 cannot be a solution. The correct answer is 3.

8. **B** The question asks for a value of the constant c in the given quadratic equation. Since the question asks for a specific value and the answers contain numbers in increasing order, plug in the answers. Begin by labeling the answers as c and starting with (B), 135. The equation becomes $x^2 + 24x + 135 = (x + 9)(x + p)$. The left side of the equation is a quadratic in standard form, and the right side is a factored quadratic; this means that 135 from the left side of the equation would equal $9p$ once the right side was expanded to standard form. Divide 135 by 9 to get $x^2 + 24x + 135 = (x + 9)(x + 15)$. Test whether this is the right answer by using FOIL to expand $(x + 9)(x + 15)$ into $x^2 + 15x + 9x + 135 = x^2 + 24x + 135$. The middle term is $24x$, which matches the value given on the left side, so stop here. The correct answer is (B).

9. **B** The question asks for an equation that models a specific situation. Translate the question in Bite-Sized Pieces and eliminate after each piece. One piece of information says that the correct equation should be a parabola. The standard form of a parabola equation is $y = ax^2 + bx + c$. The equation should include an x^2 term, so eliminate (D), which is a linear equation. The value of a tells whether a parabola opens upward (positive a) or downward (negative a). Since the water from the fountain shoots up and down, the parabola should open downward and have a negative value for a. Eliminate (C), which has a positive value for a. Compare the remaining answers. The important difference between (A) and (B) is the c term. The question states that the fountain's spout is 8 feet above the ground. Since y is the height of the water and x is the time from the spout, $y = 8$ when $x = 0$. Plug $x = 0$ into (A) to see whether it becomes $y = 8$. Choice (A) becomes $y = -0^2 + 15 = 15$. This means $y = 8$ does not appear in (A), so eliminate (A). The correct answer is (B).

10. **B** The question asks for an equivalent equation for y. To find the equivalent equation, isolate y on one side of the equation. Start by cross-multiplying to get $7y = (x + 3)(x + 4)$. Use FOIL on the right side to get $7y = x^2 + 7x + 12$. Divide both sides by 7 to get $y = \dfrac{x^2 + 7x + 12}{7}$. The correct answer is (B).

11. **A** The question asks for a true statement about the equation. Solve the equation to find the true statement. Since the denominator of both equations is $p - 2$, set both numerators equal to each other to get $2(p - 2) + 2(3 - p) = 2(3p - 6) + 3(6 - 2p)$. Distribute the numbers in front of the parentheses to get $2p - 4 + 6 - 2p = 6p - 12 + 18 - 6p$. Combine like terms to get $2 = 6$. Since this statement is false and the variables were eliminated, the equation has no solution. The correct answer is (A).

Drill 3 (page 339)

1. **A** The question asks for the meaning of a number in context. Start by reading the full question, which asks for the meaning of the number 40. Then label the parts of the equation with the information given. The question states that P is the driver's net pay and d is the number of deliveries. Notice that the 40 is being subtracted from the rest of the equation, which means that there is a $40 reduction in the driver's net pay. Look for other information in the question that suggests some type of reduction. The only information on any type of reduction is that the shipping company *deducts a separate fee daily for the use of the company's delivery truck*. Therefore, it is reasonable to assume that the 40 represents this fee. Choice (A) matches this description. The correct answer is (A).

2. **C** The question asks what can be deduced from the given function. Label the parts of the equation to determine what they represent. In this question, $N(c)$ is the net amount the students raised, and c is the number of cars washed. The question also says that the students paid for cleaning supplies. The number 0.40 is multiplied by the number of cars and subtracted, so it must have something to do with the cost of the cleaning supplies. Next, use Process of Elimination to get rid of answer choices that are not consistent with the labels. Choices (A) and (D) associate the number 8 with the cleaning supplies, so eliminate (A) and (D). Choice (B) says that the students paid a total of $40 for the cleaning supplies, but the number in the equation is 0.40, not 40, and it is multiplied by the number of cars, so it is not a total. Eliminate (B). Choice (C) matches the given function. The correct answer is (C).

3. **D** The question asks for an equation that best models a specific situation. The question says that at a depth of 15 meters, the dissolved oxygen concentration is 0.0022. Plug $d = 15$ into the answers to see which one equals the corresponding oxygen concentration of 0.0022. Choice (A) becomes $\frac{1}{2} - \frac{1}{15^2} = \frac{1}{2} - \frac{1}{225}$. In decimal form, the expression is $0.5 - 0.00\overline{4} \approx 0.496$. This does not match the target number, so eliminate (A). Choice (B) becomes $\frac{1}{100(15)} = \frac{1}{1,500}$. In decimal form, this is equal to $0.000\overline{6}$. Eliminate (B). Choice (C) becomes $\frac{1}{15} = 0.0\overline{6}$. Eliminate (C). Choice (D) becomes $\frac{1}{2(15)^2} = \frac{1}{2(225)}$. Continue simplifying to get $\frac{1}{450} = 0.00\overline{22}$. This is a very close match for the target. The correct answer is (D).

4. **B** The question asks for an expression that could represent a certain piece of information in the context of an equation. Start by reading the full question, which asks for an expression that represents *the total number of customers on a given day*. Then label the parts of the equation with the information given. The question states that R is the *total revenue* earned by the restaurant in one day, so the right side of the

equation adds up to the total revenue. The question also states that *students pay $5 per meal and non-students pay $7.* The variables being multiplied by 5 and 7 must represent the number of people paying those amounts. If *s* customers pay $5 each and *n* customers pay $7, there are *s* + *n* total customers. The correct answer is (B).

5. **D** The question asks for the approximate *average yearly decrease in the number of Crucian carp* based on the line of best fit shown in the graph. In this graph, the slope of the line of best fit represents the average yearly change. The formula for slope is $\frac{y_2 - y_1}{x_2 - x_1}$. Choose two points from the graph to plug into the slope formula. On the graph, the number of carp in 2011 was 25,000 and in 2012, the number of carp was 22,500. Using these *x*- and *y*-values, the expression becomes $\frac{25,000 - 22,500}{2010 - 2011}$. Simplify the expression to get $\frac{2,500}{-1}$, or –2,500. Since the result is negative, it represents a decrease of 2,500 carp per year. The correct answer is (D).

6. **D** The question asks for an inequality that represents a given situation. There are variables in the answer choices, so plug in. Plug in a value for *t* from the optimal temperature range (30–37) and use Process of Elimination. If *t* = 37, the correct answer will provide a statement that is true. Plug *t* = 37 into the answers and eliminate any answers that are not true. Choice (A) becomes |37 + 7| ≤ 37 or |44| ≤ 37. Since this statement is false, eliminate (A). Choice (B) becomes |37 – 3.5| ≤ 33.5 or |33.5| ≤ 33.5. Since this statement is true, keep (B). Choice (C) becomes |37 – 30| ≤ 7, or |7| ≤ 7. Since this statement is true, keep (C). Choice (D) becomes |37 – 33.5| ≤ 3.5, or |3.5| ≤ 3.5. Since this statement is true, keep (D). Next, plug in a value that is *not* in the optimal temperature range, such as *t* = 29, and eliminate any answers that provide a true statement. Choice (B) becomes |29 – 3.5| ≤ 33.5 or |25.5| ≤ 33.5. Since this statement is true, eliminate (B). Choice (C) becomes |29 – 30| ≤ 7 or |–1| ≤ 7. Since this statement is true, eliminate (C). The correct answer is (D).

7. **C** The question asks for the meaning of an expression in context. Start by reading the full question, which asks for the meaning of the expression $\frac{0.05}{12}$. Then label the parts of the equation with the information given. The question states that *B* is the balance of the account, and that *t* is the time in years. It also says that 250 is the beginning balance, that the account has an annual interest rate of 5%, and that interest deposits are made to the account monthly. The 0.05 must have something to do with the 5% interest rate, and the 12 must have something to do with the 12 months in a year. Next, use Process of Elimination to get rid of answer choices that are not consistent with the labels. Eliminate (A) because 0.05 is the interest rate; it represents a percentage and cannot be the actual *amount of money* that is deposited. Eliminate (B) because $\frac{0.05}{12} \approx 0.004$; this is less than 1 cent. The beginning balance was $250, and it doesn't make sense that there would be less money in the account after a deposit was made. Choice (C) refers to the *percentage* of the balance added during a *monthly interest deposit*, so keep (C). Eliminate (D) because 0.004 is too small to be a number of months. The correct answer is (C).

CHAPTER 14

Drill 1 (page 349)

a. 36
b. 24
c. $x = 10, y = 5$
d. 30
e. 22

1. **D** The question asks for the pairs of angles that must have equal degree measures on a figure. Start by redrawing the figure on the scratch paper. Then label the figure with the given information. Mark lines *a* and *b* as parallel. In Statement (I), angles 1 and 5 do not have to be equal because a side of angle 1 is line *c*, which only intersects one parallel line in the figure; there is not enough information to determine whether any angle formed by line *c* is equal to one formed by line *b*. Thus, the angles in Statement (I) do not have to be equal; eliminate (A). Angles 2 and 7 are vertical angles (angles opposite each other when two lines intersect), and vertical angles must be equal. Therefore, the angles in Statement (II) have to be equal, so eliminate (C). Any time a line crosses two parallel lines, all of the small angles have the same measure, and all of the big angles have the same measure. Angles 3 and 9 are both small angles formed where the same line (line *d*) crosses one of the parallel lines. Since the angles in Statement (III) must be equal, eliminate (B). Only Statements (II) and (III) are true. The correct answer is (D).

2. **C** The question asks for the value of an angle on a figure. Start by redrawing the figure on the scratch paper. Then label the figure with the given information. Mark $\overline{BC}$ and $\overline{AD}$ as parallel. It may not be immediately obvious how to get the value of angle *ACD*, so see what else can be determined. Any time a line crosses two parallel lines, all of the small angles have the same measure, and all of the big angles have the same measure. The big and small angles are *supplementary angles*: the sum of the measure of any big angle plus any small angle equals 180°. In this figure, angle *BCD* and angle *ADC* are supplementary big and small angles. Because angle *ADC* has a measure given of 95°, subtract 95 from 180 to see that angle *BCD* must have a measure of 85°. Subtract 35 from 85 to see that angle *ACD* must have a measure of 50°. The correct answer is (C).

3. **D** The question asks for the area of square *ABCD*. The lengths of the sides are given as variable expressions instead of numbers, so solve for *x* first. In a square, all sides are equal, so $2x + 1 = x + 3$. First, subtract 1 from each side so that $2x = x + 2$. Then subtract *x* from each side so that $x = 2$. Plug that value of *x* into the expression $x + 3$ to get $2 + 3 = 5$, which is the length of each side. The formula for the area of a square is $A = (length)(width)$, so the area is $(5)(5) = 25$. The correct answer is (D).

4. **60**   The question asks for the area of rectangle *ABCD*. Start by redrawing the figure on the scratch paper. Then label the figure with the given information. The length of one side is 5, and the question states that the length of the diagonal, *BD* (or *AC*), is 13. The formula for the area of a rectangle is $A = (length)(width)$, so find the width first. Since the corner of the rectangle is a right angle, use the Pythagorean Theorem: $a^2 + b^2 = c^2$. Plug in *AB* for *a* and *BD* for *c* so that $5^2 + b^2 = 13^2$. Then solve for *b*, which will be *AD*, the length of the other side of the right triangle, and thus the width of the rectangle. First, simplify: $25 + b^2 = 169$. Then subtract 25 from both sides and take the square root: $\sqrt{b^2} = \sqrt{144}$. Then, *b* = 12. Since *AD* = 12, plug the length and width into the formula for the area of a rectangle to get $A = (5)(12) = 60$. The correct answer is 60.

Drill 2 (page 363)

a. 24

b. 10

c. $\dfrac{6}{10}$, $\dfrac{3}{5}$, or 0.6

d. 20

e. $20\sqrt{5}$

f. $\dfrac{20}{20\sqrt{5}}$, $\dfrac{1}{\sqrt{5}}$, or $\dfrac{\sqrt{5}}{5}$

1. **A**   The question asks for the value of a trigonometry function given similar triangles. Start by drawing two triangles on the scratch paper, being careful to match up the vertices. Since the triangles are similar, and two pairs of angles have already been identified as having the same measure, the third pair of angles also has the same measure. Next, write down SOHCAHTOA. The CAH part of the acronym defines the cosine as $\dfrac{\text{adjacent}}{\text{hypotenuse}}$, and the question states that the cosine of angle *Q* is $\dfrac{24}{145}$. Label the side adjacent to *Q* as 24, and label the hypotenuse as 145. Label the equivalent sides in the second triangle, keeping in mind that these are proportions, not the actual side lengths. The scratch paper should look something like this.

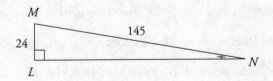 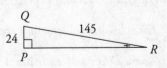

Next, find the value of sin(*N*). The SOH part of the acronym defines the sine as $\frac{opposite}{hypotenuse}$. The side opposite angle *N* is 24, and the hypotenuse is 145, so the sine of angle *N* is $\frac{24}{145}$. It will always be the case that the two sides in a right triangle that are not the right angle add up to 90°, and that the sign of one equals the cosine of the other. The correct answer is (A).

2. **100** The question asks for the value of an angle on a figure. Start by redrawing the figure on the scratch paper. Then label the figure with the given information. Because *AB* = *BC*, *ABC* is an *isosceles triangle*, which has two sides that are equal. In an isosceles triangle, angles that are opposite equal sides must be equal. Therefore, angle *A* and angle *C* have the same measure, so angle *A* is also 40°. Angle *A* and angle *C* have a combined measure of 80°. The sum of the angles inside a triangle must equal 180°. Subtract 80 from 180, and *x* must measure 100°. The correct answer is 100.

3. **C** The question asks for the perimeter of an isosceles triangle. Start by redrawing the figure on the scratch paper. Then label the figure with the given information. The question says that the triangle is isosceles, and there is a right angle present in the figure. An isosceles right triangle has angles that measure 45°, 45°, and 90°. Since *AB* = 5, that means *BC* = 5 as well. Using the 45°-45°-90° right triangle rule, $AC = 5\sqrt{2}$. Therefore, the perimeter of the triangle is $5 + 5 + 5\sqrt{2}$ or $10 + 5\sqrt{2}$. The correct answer is (C).

4. **B** The question asks for the minimum number of buckets of paint needed to cover the front of a barn's roof. Start by redrawing the figure on the scratch paper. To find the answer, solve for the total area. The formula for the area of a triangle is $A = \frac{bh}{2}$. The figure provides that the base, *b*, is 8 m. The two smaller right triangles both have angles of 30° and 90°, so the other angle must be 60° in both. Since they share a side (the height), the two triangles are the same size, and the 8 m base is equally split to be 4 m for each right triangle. To find the height, use the 30°-60°-90° right triangle rule: if the short side (opposite 30°) is *h*, the middle side (opposite 60°) is $h\sqrt{3}$. Make $4 = h\sqrt{3}$ and divide both sides by $\sqrt{3}$ to get $h \approx 2.4$. Then set $A = \frac{(8)(2.4)}{2} = (4)(2.4) = 9.6$. To cover 9.6 m^2, the owner will need $\frac{9.6}{5}$ buckets, which is 1.92. Since 1 bucket is not enough, round up to 2. The correct answer is (B).

5. **A** The question asks for the length of a line segment in a figure containing triangles. Start by redrawing the figure on the scratch paper. Then label the figure with the given information. When given two or more triangles and information about the lengths of the sides, look for similar triangles. Both triangles share angle *DAE,* and each has a right angle. Since all triangles have 180°, the third angles in each triangle must also be equal. The two triangles must have the same set of angles, but they aren't the same size; they are *similar triangles*, so the sides of one triangle are proportional to those of the other.

$BD = AD - AB$, and AB is given; find AD to get the answer. In the small right triangle, two sides are given, so use the Pythagorean Theorem to find the third: $a^2 + b^2 = c^2$. Plug in AB for a and AC for c so that $5^2 + b^2 = 13^2$. Then solve for b, which will be BC, the length of the other side of the right triangle. First, simplify: $25 + b^2 = 169$. Then subtract 25 from both sides and take the square root: $\sqrt{b^2} = \sqrt{144}$. Therefore, $b = 12$. Another way to solve for b would be to recognize the Pythagorean triple: 5-12-13. Since $BC = 12$, set up a proportion with corresponding sides: $\dfrac{AB}{AD} = \dfrac{BC}{DE}$ or $\dfrac{5}{AD} = \dfrac{12}{24}$. Cross-multiply: $(AD)(12) = 120$. Divide both sides by 12 to get $AD = 10$. Now solve $BD = AD - AB = 10 - 5 = 5$. The correct answer is (A).

6. **7.5** The question asks for the value of x, the length of a side of a right triangle. The value of $\tan a°$ is given, and the length of the side opposite to that angle is 7. SOHCAHTOA says that tangent $\theta = \dfrac{opposite}{adjacent}$. The needed side is adjacent to that angle, so set up a proportion: $\dfrac{14}{15} = \dfrac{7}{x}$. Cross-multiply to get $14x = 105$. Divide both sides by 14, so $x = 7.5$. The correct answer is 7.5.

Drill 3 (page 372)

a. 16π

b. 8π

1. **B** The question asks for the center of the circle with the provided circle equation. The equation of a circle in standard form is $(x - h)^2 + (y - k)^2 = r^2$, where (h, k) are the coordinates of the circle's center and r is the radius. Start by grouping terms with the same variable together to rewrite the equation as $x^2 - 2x + y^2 + 8y = -8$. In order to rewrite the given equation in standard form, you must complete the square. Take the coefficient of the first linear term, $-2x$, and divide the coefficient by 2 to get -1. Then, square this result to get 1. Add 1 to both sides of the equation to get $(x^2 - 2x + 1) + y^2 + 8y = -8 + 1$. Then, do the same with the coefficient of the other linear term, $8y$. Divide 8 by 2, which is 4, and then square that, which is 16. Add 16 to both sides to get $(x^2 - 2x + 1) + (y^2 + 8y + 16) = -8 + 1 + 16$. Finally, factor the groups of terms in parentheses on the left side and do the arithmetic on the right side to get $(x - 1)^2 + (y + 4)^2 = 9$. The coordinates of the center of the circle are given by (h, k) in the standard form, so, for this circle, the center is located at $(1, -4)$. The correct answer is (B).

2. **D**   The question asks for the area of the circle. The parts of a circle are directly proportional to one another. In this circle, the fraction of the central angle of 360° is the same as the fraction of the arc length of the total circumference. Set up the proportion $\frac{central\ angle}{360°} = \frac{arc\ length}{circumference}$, then plug in the given information to get $\frac{60°}{360°} = \frac{2\pi}{circumference}$. Cross-multiply to get $60(circumference) = 360(2\pi)$. Divide both sides by 60 to get $circumference = 12\pi$. Since the formula for circumference is $2\pi r$, the radius of the circle is 6. Then, find the area using the formula πr^2. If $r = 6$, then the circle has an area of $\pi(6)^2 = 36\pi$. The correct answer is (D).

3. **C**   The question asks for the perimeter of triangle ABC. Start by drawing the figure according to the description in the question. The figure should look like the following:

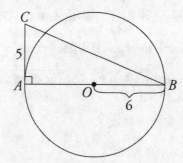

Next, write down the equations needed to answer the question. Since the area of the circle is 36π, and the formula is $A = \pi r^2$, the radius of the circle is 6. Therefore, the diameter of the circle is 12. Since a line that is tangent to a circle forms a 90° angle with the radius at the point of tangency, the side lengths of this right triangle are a 5-12-13 Pythagorean triple. To find the perimeter of the triangle, add the side lengths to get $5 + 12 + 13 = 30$. The correct answer is (C).

4. **5.25**   The question asks for the radius of the circle. Start by translating English to math. *Arc PSR is* $\frac{4}{3}$ *the length of arc PQR* means $\overarc{PSR} = \frac{4}{3}\overarc{PQR}$. Since $\overarc{PSR}$ is 6π, substitute for $\overarc{PSR}$ to get $6\pi = \frac{4}{3}\overarc{PQR}$. Multiply both sides by 3 to cancel out the fraction to get $18\pi = 4\overarc{PQR}$. Divide both sides by 4 to get $\frac{18\pi}{4} = \overarc{PQR}$, or $\overarc{PQR} = 4.5\pi$. The two arcs, $\overarc{PSR}$ and $\overarc{PQR}$, add up to the circumference of the circle, so $C = 6\pi + 4.5\pi = 10.5\pi$. Since $C = 2\pi r$, the radius of the circle is 5.25. The correct answer is 5.25.

Drill 4 (page 376)

1. **B** The question asks for the value of an angle in the figure. There are variables in the answer choices, so plug in. Make $a = 90$. The third angle will be 60°. Since the 60° angle and b° are supplementary angles, $60 + b = 180$. Subtract 60 from both sides to get $b = 180 - 60 = 120$. This is the target value; circle it. Now plug $a = 90$ into the answer choices to see which one matches the target value. Choice (A) becomes $30 - 90 = -60$. This does not match the target, so eliminate (A). Choice (B) becomes $30 + 90 = 120$. Keep (B), but check (C) and (D) just in case. Choice (C) becomes $60 + 90 = 150$. Eliminate (C). Choice (D) becomes $80 - 90 = -10$. Eliminate (D). The correct answer is (B).

2. **A** The question asks for the value of a trigonometric function. There are variables in the answer choices, so plug in. You are given a right triangle, so plug in for the sides of the triangle. Use the Pythagorean triple 3-4-5 to make the math easy. Add these side lengths to the figure as follows:

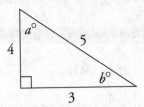

$sin\,\theta = \dfrac{opposite}{hypotenuse}$, so calculate $sin\,a° = \dfrac{3}{5}$. Let $x = \dfrac{3}{5}$. $cos\,\theta = \dfrac{adjacent}{hypotenuse}$, so calculate $cos\,b° = \dfrac{3}{5}$. This is

the target value; circle it. Now plug $x = \dfrac{3}{5}$ into the answer choices to see which one matches the target

value. Choice (A) becomes $\dfrac{3}{5}$. Keep (A), but check (B), (C), and (D) just in case. Choice (B) becomes

$1 - \dfrac{3}{5} = \dfrac{2}{5}$. This does not match the target, so eliminate (B). Choice (C) becomes $\dfrac{1}{\frac{3}{5}} = \dfrac{5}{3}$. Eliminate

(C). Choice (D) becomes $\dfrac{3}{5} - 1 = -\dfrac{2}{5}$. Eliminate (D). The correct answer is (A).

3. **B** The question asks about the ratio of the volumes of two cones with different radii. The question also describes a relationship between unknown numbers, so plug in. The relationship between the radii of the cones is provided, so plug in numbers that fit this relationship. Plug in $r = 6$ for Cone A and $r = 8$ for Cone B. Let $h = 3$. The formula for the volume of a cone is $V = \dfrac{1}{3}\pi r^2 h$, so plug in the values for r and h to determine the volume of each cone. The volume of Cone A is $\dfrac{1}{3}\pi(6)^2(3) = 36\pi$, and the volume of Cone B is $\dfrac{1}{3}\pi(8)^2(3) = 64\pi$. Therefore, the ratio of volume A to volume B is $36\pi:64\pi$, which reduces to 9:16. The correct answer is (B).

4. **A** The question asks for the area of a sector of the circle. There are variables in the answer choices, so plug in. Plug in $x = 3$. Write down the equations needed to answer the question. The equation for area of a circle is $A = \pi r^2$, so the area of the circle is $\pi(3)^2 = 9\pi$. The equation for circumference is $C = 2\pi r$, so the circumference of the circle is $2\pi(3) = 6\pi$. The length of arc PQ is $\dfrac{\pi(3)}{18} = \dfrac{\pi}{6}$. The parts of a circle have a proportional relationship. In this circle, the fraction of the arc length out of the total circumference is the same as the fraction of the sector area out of the total area. Set up the proportion $\dfrac{arc\ length}{circumference} = \dfrac{sector\ area}{total\ area}$, then plug in the given information to get $\dfrac{\frac{\pi}{6}}{6\pi} = \dfrac{sector\ POQ}{9\pi}$. Divide the fraction on the left side of the equation to get $\dfrac{1}{36} = \dfrac{sector\ POQ}{9\pi}$. Cross-multiply to get $9\pi = 36(sector\ POQ)$, then divide both sides by 36 to get $sector\ POQ = \dfrac{\pi}{4}$. This is the target value; circle it. Now plug $x = 3$ into the answer choices to see which one matches the target value. Choice (A) becomes $\dfrac{\pi(3)^2}{36} = \dfrac{\pi}{4}$. Keep (A), but check (B), (C), and (D) just in case. Choice (B) becomes $\dfrac{\pi(3)^2}{18} = \dfrac{\pi}{2}$. This does not match the target, so eliminate (B). Choice (C) becomes $\dfrac{\pi(3)^2}{9} = \pi$. Eliminate (C). Choice (D) becomes $\dfrac{\pi(3)^2}{3} = 3\pi$. Eliminate (D). The correct answer is (A).

5. **C** The question asks for the volume of the space between the spheres and the rectangular box. Since no figure is provided, start by drawing the figure according to the description in the question. The figure should look like the following:

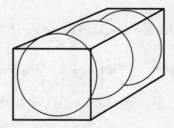

There are variables in the answer choices, so plug in. Make $r = 2$. Therefore, the diameter of the sphere is 4, which is also the width and height of the box. There are 3 spheres in a row, so the length of the box is $3(4) = 12$. The formula for volume of a rectangular solid is $V = lwh$, so plug in the values for the length, width, and height to get $(12)(4)(4) = 192$. The formula for volume of a sphere is $V = \dfrac{4}{3}\pi r^3$. So, the volume of each sphere is $\dfrac{4}{3}\pi(2)^3 = \dfrac{32\pi}{3}$. There are 3 spheres, so multiply this result by 3 to get a total volume of 32π. Therefore, the volume of the spaces between the balls and the box is $192 - 32\pi$. This is the target value; circle it. Now plug $r = 2$ into the answer choices to see which one matches the target value.

Choice (A) becomes $(2)^3(3 - 4\pi) = 8(3 - 4\pi)$. Distribute the 8 to get $24 - 32\pi$. This does not match the target, so eliminate (A). Choice (B) becomes $4(2)^2(14 - \pi) = 16(14 - \pi)$. Distribute the 16 to get $224 - 16\pi$. Eliminate (B). Choice (C) becomes $4(2)^3 (6 - \pi) = 32(6 - \pi)$. Distribute the 32 to get $192 - 32\pi$. Keep (C), but check (D) just in case. Choice (D) becomes $12(2)^2 (2 - \pi) = 48(2 - \pi)$. Distribute the 48 to get $96 - 48\pi$. Eliminate (D). The correct answer is (C).

6. **160** The question asks for the surface area of a rectangular solid. The values of the side lengths are relative to each other, so write the side lengths using a single variable. Translate English to math to find that $l = \frac{1}{2}w$ and $w = \frac{1}{3}h$, or $h = 3w$. Since $V = lwh$, substitute the values for l, w, and h into the equation to get $96 = \left(\frac{1}{2}w\right)(w)(3w)$. Simplify the right side to get $96 = \frac{3}{2}w^3$. Multiply both sides by $\frac{2}{3}$ to get $w^3 = 64$, then take the cube root of both sides to get $w = 4$. Use this value for w to find the values of l and h. The length becomes $\frac{1}{2}(4) = 2$ and the height becomes $3(4) = 12$. The surface area is the sum of the areas of all the faces of the rectangular box, or $2lw + 2lh + 2wh$. Substitute the values for l, w, and h to get $2(2)(4) + 2(2)(12) + 2(4)(12) = 16 + 48 + 96$. Add these values to find that the surface area is 160. The correct answer is 160.

NOTES

NOTES

NOTES

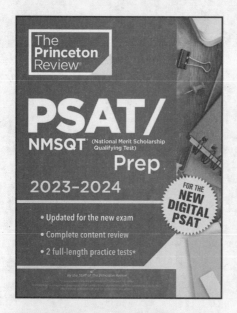